CAMBRIDGE GREEK AI

VERGIL

ECLOGUES

EDITED BY

ROBERT COLEMAN

Fellow of Emmanuel College,
Cambridge

CAMBRIDGE
UNIVERSITY PRESS

PUBLISHED BY THE PRESS SYNDICATE OF THE
UNIVERSITY OF CAMBRIDGE
The Pitt Building, Trumpington Street, Cambridge CB2 1RP,
United Kingdom

CAMBRIDGE UNIVERSITY PRESS
The Edinburgh Building, Cambridge CB2 2RU, UK
40 West 20th Street, New York, NY 10011-4211, USA
10 Stamford Road, Oakleigh, VIC 3166, Australia
http://www.cambridge.org

Library of Congress catalogue card number: 76–16917

First published 1977
Reprinted 1981, 1986, 1989, 1991, 1994, 1998, 2001

ISBN 0 521 29107 0 paperback

Transferred to digital printing 2003

CONTENTS

[v]

PREFACE

Although the Eclogues have received a good deal of scholarly and critical attention in recent years, no English commentary has been produced in this century nor – more surprisingly – does there exist in any language an edition as extensive as the present one. There is thus a real need, and I hope that I have been able to meet it.

In the introduction I have confined my attention to general questions concerning the poems and their place in the history of the genre, the chronology and arrangement of the collection and the establishment of the text. The commentary is intended to cover everything that seemed to me relevant to the understanding and appreciation of the poet's words. Hence I have in many places preferred to summarize and adapt, sometimes tacitly correcting, information provided in standard lexicons and handbooks, rather than to cite the appropriate pages of such works and, with suitable caveats, leave the reader to hunt out for himself what he requires. The notes on each Eclogue include a brief final discussion of the poem as a whole. Autolycus is the patron of commentators, and I have seldom acknowledged explicitly my obligations to the writings of others, even when I have remembered what they are; nor have I indicated precisely whose opinions were being refuted in any given place. The reading list at the end of the volume does, however, include all the books and articles on Vergil and the pastoral to which I am aware of being most indebted. It also contains a representative sample of recent work on the subject, not all of which, I am bound to confess, is sympathetic to my own approach to the poems.

Among personal debts my first is to the generations of students who have attended my lectures and classes on the Eclogues and on classical pastoral during the last seventeen years. Most of what is to be found in the following pages will be familiar to them in one form or another; much of it has benefited from their challenging questions, enthusiasm and sympathetic suggestions. Cambridge is an enviable place for the student of Vergil to do his work and I have learned much over the years from conversations with Mr L. P. Wilkinson and Mr A. G. Lee not only about Vergil but about Latin poetry in general. My wife Dr Dorothy G. Coleman has encouraged me in periods of despondency and helped me by criticizing the introduction and by sharing the burden of proof-reading. Only those who have contributed to this series can appreciate how much I owe to the general editors, Professor E. J. Kenney and Mrs P. E. Easterling. Between them they have removed many infelicities of presentation, pruned much of my verbiage and corrected more factual errors than they ought ever to have been exposed to. Some defects are bound to have escaped even their scholarly vigilance – a commentator can hardly expect others to do *all* his work for him – and I shall, no doubt, come to regret my stubbornness in not accepting their advice far more often than in fact I have done.

Writing a commentary is both a chastening and an instructive experience. Once the work is finished, one feels very nearly equipped to begin the task properly. If the things that I have got right can assist others to a more complete reading of these great poems, and what I have got wrong can stimulate them to progress further than I have been able to, then the labour and the doubts that have gone with it will not have been in vain.

Emmanuel College   R.G.G.C.
15 October 1976

INTRODUCTION

1. THE PASTORAL BEFORE VERGIL

The pastoral myth is the creation of a highly civilized urban sensibility. It is a reaction against certain aspects of the culture and material environment of the city: *Musa illa rustica et pastoralis non forum modo uerum ipsam etiam urbem reformidat* (Quint. 10.1.55). In his longing for a simple innocence and carefree spontaneity that he has lost urban man looks to the country and its way of life, which he knows only as an outsider and from a distance, and creates out of it a myth embodying the ideals that he seeks. This idealization of the rustic life is well portrayed by Shakespeare in the Duke's speech in *As You Like It* 2.1 and the King's soliloquy in *Henry the Sixth, pt 3* 2.5. The tendency of the upper classes to idealize certain aspects of urban proletarian life, which in modern times has occasionally taken over a similar role, was not unknown even in antiquity (see Athenaeus 12.536e).

The pastoral conception, like the romantic 'return to nature' with which it is often contrasted, is informed throughout by the sophisticated sensibility that produced it. Its illusion consists 'in exposing only the best side of a shepherd's life and in concealing its miseries'.[1] It conjures up a pretty, fictional world into which one may escape from the real world now and then in imagination; it is not a programme for the reform or conversion of that world. There is thus little room for the realistic portrayal of country life. For this we must look not to the pastorals of Theocritus or Pope but to the poetry of true countrymen like Hesiod or George Crabbe, whose *Village* in fact contains an explicit protest against the pastoral tradition.

Although there are references to shepherds' music-making as early as Homer (*Iliad* 18.525–6), the earliest pastoral poetry in Greek literature is the work of the third-century Syracusan Theocritus. The only predecessors mentioned by ancient authors are the mythical Sicilians Diomus and Daphnis.[2] The Theocritean scholiasts' accounts of the origins of the genre in popular cult hymns to Artemis – com-

---

[1] Alexander Pope *Discourse on pastoral poetry* (1709) §5, reproducing the view of Fontenelle and other continental theorists.
[2] Athen. 14.619a–b and Diod. 4.84, Aelian *V.H.* 10.18.

[1]

plete with aetiological fables[1] – are highly implausible when one considers the predominantly secular character of much of the earliest pastoral and the very minor part played by the chaste goddess of the hunt in the devotional life of Arcady[2] in comparison with Pan, Apollo, Hermes and Priapus, the patrons of country life and music, and the nymphs and muses, who inspire country song. Some modern scholars have detected in the epigrams of Theocritus' contemporary Anyte of Tegea hints of an earlier Peloponnesian school of pastoral writing. But such pastoral motifs as appear occasionally in her poetry (e.g. *A.P.* 9.313, *Plan.* 228) are a common feature of Hellenistic epigram (e.g. *A.P.* 9.823, *Plan.* 12).

While Theocritus may be credited with inventing the pastoral, it is only in the work of his successors Moschus and Bion that it emerges as a distinctive genre, to become established in Latin in the work of Vergil, Calpurnius, the anonymous author of the two Einsiedeln Eclogues and Nemesianus. The pastorals of Theocritus in fact form a loosely knit group within the collection of thirty Idylls[3] that have been traditionally attributed to him. Nevertheless they established definitively much of the formal and thematic character of the later pastoral tradition.

The short dramatic form – sometimes a dialogue, complete in itself (4) or combined with a singing display (5, 10, also 7, where it is given a narrative framework), sometimes a reported monologue (3, 11) – is also found in the urban idylls (2, 15). It clearly owes much to that other specifically Sicilian invention, the mime, which is represented for us by the meagre fragments of the fifth-century Epicharmus and Sophron and by the *Mimiamboi* of Theocritus' contemporary Herodas. The ancient references to the mime however give no hint of pastoral

---

[1] See *Scholia in Theocritum Vetera* (Wendel) 1–13 and for the corresponding Latin accounts 13–22.

[2] 'Arcady' is used for the setting of the pastoral myth throughout this introduction, though it is not found in this sense before Vergil. See *Ecl.* 7.4n.

[3] The Greek word *eidúllion* 'a little scene' 'a miniature form (of poetry)' – the precise meaning is obscure – does not occur before Pliny (*Ep.* 4.14.9). Of the twelve pastoral Idylls (1, 3–11, 20, 27) only the first ten were included in the Pastoral canon known to Servius (*Buc. prooem.* 3.21). Two of the ten (8, 9) together with 20 and 27 are nowadays generally acknowledged to be post-Theocritean.

motifs. The only attested parallels are with Theocritus' urban idylls: the magic rites of *Id.* 2 and a fragment of Sophron (Page *Greek literary papyri* 1.328ff.), the Syracusan women at the Adonis-festival in *Id.* 15 and Herodas *Mim.* 4.

The singing competition, which is one of the recurrent forms in the genre, seems to be a stylized derivative of actual country music-making. The test of wits involved in the amoebaean contest (*Idd.* 5, 6, 8, 9), with its requirement that the second singer must match the themes or figures employed by the first, is widely paralleled in folk culture. The use of refrains (*Idd.* 1, 2), a familiar device in folk song, is probably also popular in origin.

The language of the herdsmen's conversation, though vivid and animated, is on the whole refined, reflecting the urbanity of their creator. They even show, occasionally, some surprising pieces of literary erudition; e.g. *Id.* 3.40–51, where the goatherd is admittedly showing off, and 5.150, where Morson clearly is not. There are colloquial touches, it is true, notably in *Idd.* 4, 5 and 10, though not on the scale of the urban mime *Id.* 14 or of the *Mimiamboi* of Herodas, where the sustained colloquialism brings a coarse verisimilitude to the low urban world that he patronizingly depicts. Even so the coarse language of *Id.* 4 was explicitly condemned by the seventeenth-century critics, Rapin and Fontenelle.[1]

The Doric dialect, which Theocritus established for Greek pastoral, is often praised for its naturalness and simplicity. Dryden in his *Dedication to the Pastorals* (*Works* ed. Scott–Saintsbury 12, 323–4) even declares that 'the boorish dialect of Theocritus has a secret charm in it which the Roman language cannot imitate'. But that dialect is in fact a highly artificial synthesis of Doric forms belonging to different districts and periods with occasional Ionic and even Aeolic usages. In this respect it is like all Greek literary dialects, including Herodas' Ionic. Its affinities are not primarily with any spoken dialect but with literary Doric, as exemplified in choral lyric poetry from Alcman and Stesichorus onwards.[2] To the stylized evocation of Sicilian or Coan

---

[1] Cf. Boileau's censure of the pastoral idiom of Ronsard who 'abject en son langage | fait parler ses bergers comme on parle au village' (*L'Art poétique* 2.17–18) – a judgement which Theocritus would not perhaps have been much inclined to dissent from.

[2] Elsewhere in the Idylls it is used for the mime of *The fishermen* (21), urban mimes (2, 14, 15), heroic and mythological pieces (18, 19, 26) and

rusticity is thus added a lyric dimension appropriate to the dream-like world of the pastoral. The association of literary genres with distinct dialects of the language – usually those of their earliest exponents – was a notable, perhaps unique, feature of classical Greek literature.[1] Attempts to recapture something of the effect of the Doric of Greek pastoral in other languages – whether by translators or imitators – have for the most part proved disastrous. Samuel Johnson's censure (*Rambler* no. 37, 1750) on Spenser's *Shepheardes calendar* for its medley of 'obsolete terms and rustic words', 'a mangled dialect which no human being could have spoken', could equally well be applied to Theocritus. Indeed Dryden (*op. cit.* 325) believed Spenser to have 'exactly imitated the Doric of Theocritus'. Johnson's comment illustrates the great difference between the linguistic conventions that were acceptable within the two literary traditions.

More surprisingly, Theocritus adopted for both his pastoral and other Idylls[2] not the iambic metre traditionally associated with dialogue in the drama and the mime but the dactylic hexameter, which was long established in the higher literary genres of epic, cult-hymn and didactic poetry, as represented among Theocritus' contemporaries by Apollonius' *Argonautica*, Callimachus' *Hymns* and Aratus' *Phaenomena* respectively. Indeed *Id.* 22 is in the form of a cult-hymn and 13, 24, 25 are short occasional narrative poems on subjects from heroic mythology of the kind favoured by Callimachus and his associates. That Theocritus belonged to this circle is indicated by *Id.* 7, where Lycidas after praising Philitas and 'Sicelidas' expresses some very Callimachean sentiments on poetry (39–48), and the songs of both Lycidas and Simichidas (52–89, 96–127) have more in common with

erotic narrative (23). Of these 19, 21, 23 are post-Theocritean. The use of Doric in 18 and 26 may be intended to relate these poems to the treatment of such themes in choral lyric. Both Moschus (*Europa*) and Bion (*Adonis*) employed Doric in mythological poems.
[1] Hence the choice of dialects in the non-pastoral Idylls is not whimsical. The Ionic of the two heroic poems (22, 25) relates them to the tradition of epic narrative and the 'Homeric' hymn. In *Id.* 12 the same dialect places the theme in the tradition of Ionian elegy and epigram. In *Id.* 13 the Doricized Ionic may be intended to give pastoral colour to the myth; in *Id.* 24 and the two patronage poems (16, 17) it contributes an appropriate Pindaric colour to the 'epic' contexts. The Aeolic of *Idd.* 28–30 evokes the personal and especially erotic character of Aeolian lyric.
[2] Except 8, which is partly in elegiacs, and 28–30, in Aeolic metres.

Hellenistic erotic poetry than with pastoral. The poem is in fact a literary manifesto. Indeed the Idylls as a whole can be seen as another manifestation of the development of literary forms *katà leptón* 'on a small scale' – to use Callimachus' own phrase (*Aet.* fr. 1.11Pf.) – in conscious reaction against full-scale epic writing. The pastoral was always *katà leptón*: Theocritus' longest pastoral (*Id.* 7) has 157 lines, Vergil's (*Ecl.* 3) 111 lines, Calpurnius' (*Ecl.* 4) 169 lines. The hexameter became the regular metre of Greek and Latin pastoral,[1] and in the anonymous *Lament for Bion* (71–84) not only is Bion accorded a status equal to Homer but the themes of pastoral are extolled in rivalry to those of traditional epic:

> 'Both poets were the favourites of fountains; one drank from the spring of Pegasus, the other took his drink from Arethusa. The former sang of Tyndareus' fair daughter and the mighty son of Thetis and Menelaus son of Atreus; but the theme of this poet's music was not wars and tears but Pan. With the clear voice of the herdsman he sang as he pastured his herds, he fashioned pipes and milked the placid cows; he taught the delights of boys' kisses, nursed Eros in his arms and roused Aphrodite herself.'

The attractions of the countryside to disillusioned urban man were of course recognized in earlier Greek literature, e.g. Eur. *Hipp.* 73–87, Plato *Phdr.* 230d, where Socrates expressly rejects them. The Bacchants' cult represented a temporary periodic revolt against the constraints of civilization, but its orgiastic flights were to wild nature, not to the inhabited countryside. Nevertheless their *thíasos* did confer upon initiates a sense of belonging for a time to a community set apart and – when the rites were over – a serene and joyous feeling of being in sympathetic communion with nature, which have much in common with the mood of the herdsmen in Arcady. But in the classical city-state town and country were closely in contact, and it is not till the growth of the large metropolitan complexes of the Hellenistic period that they were sufficiently dissociated to admit the idealization of

---

[1] Quintilian, while noting the distinctively pastoral mood of Theocritus' verses, places him among the Hellenistic epic and didactic poets (10.1.55; cf. 'Longinus' *Sublim.* 33). Servius however assigns the pastoral to the *humile genus* (*Buc. prooem.* 1.16–2.5; cf. Hermog. *Id.* 2.3), clearly distinguishing the Eclogues from the *grandiloquus character* of the *Aeneid*.

rustic life that characterizes the pastoral. In the generations immediately preceding Theocritus the longing for a lost simplicity and
naturalness had found expression in the Cynic philosophy. Although
Cynicism has at first sight little in common with pastoral, they both
share a rejection of civilized constraints on natural behaviour and an
acceptance of anarchy in human society. An even closer affinity with
pastoral can be found in the philosophy of Theocritus' older contemporary Epicurus, who preached 'tranquillity' and *ataraxía*, 'freedom
from disturbance', and with his disciples withdrew from the world
into the idyllic seclusion and frugal simplicity of 'the garden'. In
Seneca's definition of Epicurean *uoluptas* (*Ben.* 4.13.1) the phrases
sub densa umbra latitare and *intra hortorum latebram* recall the secluded
otium of the pastoral 'green shade'. It may not be coincidental that
when Vergil forsook philosophy for literature, he passed from
the idyllic world of Siro's Epicurean *hortus* to that of pastoral
poetry.

The literary tradition provides evidence for the survival of an older,
mythological concept that is important in the formation of the
pastoral. In Euripides' description of the Maenads in repose (*Ba.* 704–
11) and in Lucretius' setting for the Epicurean life of primitive man
(5.1379–96) there are details that belong to traditional accounts of
the Golden Age. Many mythological traditions preserve a belief that
in the remote past, before the invention of agriculture, the use of
metals and the building of cities and ships, men lived in an age of
peaceful anarchy and innocent ease, sustained by the spontaneous
fruits of the earth. The Golden Age first appears in Greek literature in
Hesiod's *Works and days* 109–19. Most of its characteristic features are
familiar to English readers from Gonzalo's commonwealth in Shakespeare *Tempest* 2.1. Varro *R.* 2.1.4–5 cites Dicaearchus for the view
that the Golden Age was succeeded by a pastoral culture, when men
first tamed animals but had not yet learnt the corrupting habits of
commerce and city life.[1] Hence the idealized picture of the herdsman's
life in the pastoral easily incorporated features of the Golden Age
myth, and Donatus could justly assert that *illud erit probabilissimum*

---

[1] In Hebrew mythology similarly the pastoral stage intervenes between
the expulsion from the Garden and the building of cities: Abel 'the feeder of
sheep' is murdered by his brother Cain 'the tiller of the ground', who subsequently builds the first city (Genesis 2 and 4.2, 8, 17).

bucolicum carmen originem ducere a priscis temporibus, quibus uita pastoralis exercita est et ideo uelut aurei saeculi speciem in huiusmodi personarum simplicitate cognosci (*Vit. Verg.* 240–4).[1]

But the myth of the pastoral is brought close to the present day. For although the poems are often set in the past, it always seems a recent past, so that we have the persistent illusion of a world that is permanently 'there', timeless and unchanging. Moreover, it is often given a geographical location – Sicily, South Italy, or Cos in Greek pastoral, Arcadia in Vergil's later pastorals and in much of the subsequent history of the genre. In this way it is related to the real world but in a way that is so vague in its specification and so remote from the environment of the reading public as to be immune to the intrusion of grimmer realities from the more accessible countryside. In more recent times Utopias have generally been situated *in* the world but at a safe distance: the Indies or Ceylon in sixteenth- and seventeenth-century European literature, the South Sea Islands in the eighteenth and nineteenth. Sicily and South Italy were often disrupted by war in Theocritus' own time (cf. *Id.* 16.76–97), but they were a long way from readers in Cos or Alexandria.

The pastoral landscape is always idyllic. The herdsmen may sometimes speak of the excesses of summer heat and winter cold but the prevailing season seems always to be early summer or spring 'the fairest season of the year' (*Ecl.* 3.57), and the immediate setting always a *locus amoenus* with shady rocks and leafy trees rustling in the breeze, the sound of cicadas and bees among the shrubs, a cool spring and a stream flowing through lush flowery meadows. The delights of shade in summer heat were familiar enough to ordinary countrymen; *circiter meridianos aestus*, says Varro (*R.* 2.2.11) in his account of the herdsman's day, *dum deferuescant, sub umbriferas rupes et arbores patulas subigunt* [sc. *greges*] *quoad refrigeratur*. The *locus amoenus* itself as a literary theme has a long history from Homer onwards. It is always an inhabited landscape,[2] a setting for the activity or repose of gods and

[1] Cf. Pope's definition of the pastoral (*Discourse* §5), 'an image of what they call the Golden Age; so that we are not to describe our shepherds as shepherds at this day really are, but as they may be conceived then to have been; when the best of men follow'd the employment'.

[2] Praise of the countryside ultimately became a poetic common-place (cf. Persius *Sat.* 1.70–1) and its ingredients codified in the rhetorical schools (see Libanius 1.517, §200). However the description of natural beauty as an

men, but one which like the Golden Age has a dream-like quality that
sets it apart from the ordinary world of experience. Three instances
will suffice to illustrate its functional range. Homer's idyllic account
of Calypso's island (*Od.* 5.63–84) is contrasted with the picture of the
homesick Odysseus alone on the shore, weeping as he gazes out over
the sea. In *O.C.* 668–92 the Sophoclean chorus extol the serene beauty
of Colonus, where the wandering Oedipus is destined at last to find
peace and a refuge from the world. Ovid's exquisite account of
Diana's bathing-place (*M.* 3.155–64) serves to heighten the subsequent pathos of Actaeon's unwitting intrusion.[1]

In the pastoral there are few passages of extended landscape des-
scription: the picture is built up gradually from details scattered
incidentally in the course of the poem. But the evocation of the *locus
amoenus* here too is never gratuitous. It provides the appropriate
setting for making music, e.g. *Idd.* 1.12–14, 5.31–4. Even the most
elaborate Theocritean landscape (*Id.* 7.135–46), though it forms the
setting for a harvest celebration, comes at the end of a singing contest.[2] We are often made aware – at the beginning or end of a poem,
in the incidental dialogue, even (as in *Id.* 5) within the formal songs
themselves – of the workaday world of the herdsmen apart from their
music-making. Nevertheless music occupies a central place in
Arcadian life; it is the social activity to which the herdsmen instinc-
tively turn whenever they gather together with their flocks in the cool
shade; it is their chief, almost their only, artistic pursuit. For the
carved cup in *Id.* 1 is an import (56–8), the cups in *Ecl.* 3 the work of
Alcimedon (37, 44), whose name is otherwise unknown to pastoral.
The pastoral herdsman in his ideal landscape is *ex officio* a poet and the
traditional image of the poet as shepherd (Hes. *Th.* 22–3) is now
reversed. It is very un-Arcadian of Meliboeus in Calpurnius *Ecl.*
4.19–28 to reprimand Corydon for neglecting his rustic tasks in order
to make music.

The formal songs of the herdsmen are dominated by three themes –

independent self-contained poetic subject is perhaps not found before
Tiberianus' *Amnis* and Asmenius' *Adeste Musae*.

[1] To these may be added Plato *Phdr.* 229–30 and Lucr. 5.1379–96
referred to earlier.

[2] Music-making in the country is a common theme in Hellenistic epigram;
e.g. Plato *App. Plan.* 13, Nicaenetus *ap.* Athen. 15.673b, Meleager *A.P.*
9.363.

the beauties and comforts of the countryside, the pleasures of music and the joys and sorrows of love. All three are brought together in various combinations in the singing contest of *Id.* 8.

The representation of a sympathetic correspondence between external nature and the events for which it provides the setting is of course widespread in ancient literature; e.g. the opening scene of [Aesch.] *P.V.*, Soph. *Phil.* 1453–68, and Vergil *A.* 4.160–72. The sympathetic bond that links the Arcadian landscape, its inhabitants and their music is often noted:

'Pleasant is the whisper of the pine tree over there beside the spring, friend goatherd, and pleasant too is your piping' (*Id.* 1.1–3).

It gives added point to a characteristic pastoral figure, the *rustic analogy*:

'Cicada is dear to cicada, ant to ant and hawk to hawk, but to me it is the Muse and Song' (*Id.* 9.31–2).

Nature-comparisons are of course common in Greek literature from Homer onwards; but the accumulation of parallels and the homeliness of some of the detail – both illustrated in this example – suggest that the figure may have affiliations with popular poetry. Much more important: the Arcadian symbiosis provides an appropriate context for the *sympathy figure*, in which surrounding nature is portrayed as reflecting the emotions and moods of its human inhabitants:

'Everywhere that Nais roams there is spring and pastures, everywhere milk flows forth from the udders and the young are nourished. But if ever she departs, the cattle and the cattle-herd alike waste away' (*Id.* 8.45–8).

The 'fallacy' of the figure, which is explicitly remarked in Nemesianus' *Ecl.* 2 (44–52, after 27–36), may be intended to show the naivety of the herdsmen. But it is found in other poetic genres. In erotic poetry a complex version of it appears as early as Ibycus (fr. 286P *ap.* Athen. 13.601b). The 'Where'er you walk' variant of it, illustrated just now, recalls a motif traditionally associated with the blessings conferred by a god or goddess (e.g. Callim. *H.* 3.129–35). In the pastoral itself it becomes so stylized as to rule out any suggestion of the singers' naivety.

The concept of love in the pastoral seems at times crude and superficial: a relationship that is almost wholly sensual, casually entered
into with partners of both sexes (for like the lyric and elegiac traditions
of erotic poetry the pastoral accepted bisexuality as normal and
natural) and no less casually terminated. In *Id.* 4.38–44 Battus is easily
consoled for the death of his Amaryllis, and the easy promiscuity dis-
played in the coarse exchanges of *Id.* 5 recurs even in the charming
Id. 27, whose form and mood, if not its outcome, has much in common
incidentally with the mediaeval *pastourelle*. Where a lover's constancy
is depicted, it is usually in terms of the pain and sorrow that it causes:
a discordant note in the idyllic world of Arcady.

The rejected goatherd of *Id.* 3 is a ludicrous and comic figure, as he
sings his futile serenade outside Amaryllis' cave. The poem is a parody
of the *paraklausíthuron* 'the address to the closed door', which belongs
to the comic and elegiac tradition (e.g. Aristoph. *Eccl.* 952ff., Plaut.
Curc. 147ff., Callim. *A.P.* 5.23, Tib. 1.2.5–14), and exposes the
essential absurdity of the slighted suitor's predicament. In *Id.* 20 by
contrast the rejected goatherd is vaunting and vindictive. In *Id.* 7
Lycidas' address to Ageanax is in the form of a *propemptikón* or 'farewell poem' familiar from the elegiac and lyric genres; e.g. Callim. fr.
400 Pf., Prop. 1.8, Hor. *C.* 1.3. It is lightened by thoughts of the boy's
joyous home-coming but the good wishes are strictly conditional. The
competing song from Simichidas is about Aratus' unrequited love for
the boy Philinus.

The most famous of Theocritus' love-poems is *Id.* 11, an exquisite
blend of the comic and pathetic. Polyphemus' playful affair with
Galatea was the subject of the singing competition in *Id.* 6, but now
the Cyclops' emotions are far more deeply engaged; the monster
shepherd is mellowed, his grosser physical and mental characteristics
purged away; he has become an Arcadian and love has inspired him
to undreamt-of powers of Arcadian song. His serenade to the sea-
nymph is offered by Theocritus to his physician-friend as a model of
the 'medicine of the Muses', by which the disappointed lover can
soothe his sorrow. Theocritus' finest study of rejected love, *Id.* 2, is not
in the pastoral genre. So it is the singing Cyclops, already portrayed
in a dithyramb of Philoxenus (Plut. *Mor.* 622c), who now becomes the
pastoral exemplar of the rejected lover; as in Bion fr. 16, [Bion] 2.1–3
(cf. Callim. *A.P.* 12.150).

The consolations of music in Arcady were to become a permanent theme of later pastoral. So too was the alienation of the lover, which is the antithesis of the sympathetic relation between man and idyllic nature in Arcady. It is hinted at here in the Cyclops' neglect of the flocks in which he takes such pride, and more fully elaborated in the preceding Idyll. For in *Id.* 10 Bucaeus' alienation is two-fold: his 'starveling love' (57) for Bombyca has distracted him from the work of the harvest, and the love-song that he sings to cure the affliction is, as his friend points out, a high-flown piece quite unfitted for his station. The homely edifying verses that Milon offers as a model, reminiscent of the closing pages of Hesiod's *Works and Days*, come dangerously close, like old Canthus' song in Calp. *Ecl.* 5, to exploding the fragile illusion of Arcady. It may however be no accident that the context here is agricultural, not pastoral, and Bucaeus' status as 'a working man who toils in the sun', stressed at the beginning and end, mark him off from the Arcadian herdsmen. The lover's dissociation from the normal pattern of life and the inspiration to music that his passion brings him certainly provide a link with the elegiac tradition; cf. Prop. 1.1.6, 2.1.4.

Erotic themes are even more prominent in the fragments of Theocritus' successors, and Bion proclaims explicitly (fr. 9)

'if ever a man sings who has not love in his soul, the Muses slink away and refuse to instruct him; but if anyone whose mind is stirred by Eros makes sweet music, then they all come thronging to him in a great rush'.

This is the voice of Hellenistic epigram rather than pastoral, and a number of the fragments find their closest parallels in the Anthology: the poet's encounter with Eros (Bion fr. 3 and 10) and the character-sketches of the malicious young god (Mosch. *Id.* 1, and his epigram, *Plan.* 200, Bion fr. 13 and 14), though they have their precedent in the fable of Cupid and the Bees, [Th.] *Id.* 19, have much more in common with the sequence of epigrams in *A.P.* 5 beginning with Meleager's 176 and 177.[1] The address to Hesperus in Bion fr. 11 belongs with the 'nocturnal serenade'- or *kômos*-epigrams, in particular Meleager

---

[1] The relative chronology of the examples here, as elsewhere, is less important for our purpose than the occurrence of the theme in the two separate genres.

A.P. 5.191. Unless the surviving extracts are wholly untypical, it seems that both Moschus and Bion intensified the Theocritean bias towards the exploration of the pains and sorrows of love, a universal literary theme to be sure but one that finds an especially poignant context in the idyllic world of Arcady.

The other melancholy note in the pastoral is that of untimely death. The extinction of youthful promise like the sorrows of love is a perennial motif of folk-literature. In the traditional mythology it is linked symbolically with the cycle of nature's brief season of fertile beauty through such figures as Attis, Linus and Adonis. The link is already implicit in Homer's comparison of the dying Gorgythion to a poppy bent by the spring winds (*Il.* 8.306–7). But in the pastoral this theme finds an appropriately pathetic setting. The pastoral landscape is depicted at its fairest season and peopled by herdsmen and women in the flower of their youth. In fact older characters rarely intrude and are never in the foreground: e.g. the absent Aegon (*Id.* 4.4), the old fisherman on the cup (*Id.* 1.39). Moreover traditional mythology had filled the countryside with monuments to the pathos of love and the extinction of youth in the metamorphoses of Daphne, Syrinx, Hyacinthus, Adonis... These are seldom explicitly alluded to in pastoral; e.g. Mosch. fr. 3 (Alpheus and Arethusa), Bion fr. 1, *Lament for Bion* 37–43; but they provided for the reader brought up in the mythological tradition of literature resonances that the pastoral poet could tacitly exploit.

The two themes of the sorrows of love and untimely death come together in one of Theocritus' finest poems, *Id.* 1, where Thyrsis sings a dirge for the master poet and herdsman Daphnis. The precise circumstances of Daphnis' suffering are not made explicit. (In *Id.* 7.72–7 it is the love of Xenea that causes his death.) But his status as a pastoral *hero*[1] is underlined by his Promethean silence at the advent of the three deities, the Hippolytan defiance of his final taunts to Aphrodite and the fact that all nature mourns for him.

In Bion's *Lament for Adonis* the pastoral colour and some of its characteristic figures are employed, as in Theocritus' *Hylas* (*Id.* 13), on

---

[1] For his prowess as musician and cattleherd see *Idd.* 5.80, 8.81–7 and *A.P.* 9.433. In *Idd.* 6, 8, 9, 27 he appears as a typical Arcadian. Both Diodorus and Aelian (see p. 1 n. 2) make him the inventor of pastoral. See *Ecl.* 5.20n.

a subject from traditional mythology; but, characteristically, attention is concentrated less on the image of the dead shepherd, pathetically drawn though it is, than on the grief of the love-stricken goddess. Bion fr. 1 suggests that the death of Hyacinthus may have been treated similarly in that poem. In the anonymous *Lament for Bion* the theme finds yet a further dimension, applied as it is to the death of a real person. A long tradition was thus initiated, which lasted into the nineteenth century, with Shelley's *Adonais* and Arnold's *Thyrsis*; but in the Hellenistic exemplar the fact that the dead poet is a pastoralist enables the pastoral colour and the imagery of nature in mourning, elaborated superbly from hints in *Id.* 1, to be sustained with a homogeneity that is uniquely appropriate. The analogy between the brevity of nature's beauty and the fragility of human life is here broken, once and for all:

'Alas, when the mallows die away in our gardens and the green parsley and exuberant dill with its curly leaves, they live and grow again for another year; but we men, tall and strong as we are and wise too, once we are dead, lie there in the hollowed earth unhearing, in a long sleep that has no end and no awakening' (99–104).

Pastoral consolation is thus darkened by a note of sombre pessimism that was to have its definitive utterance in Horace's spring Odes (*C.* 1.4, 4.7).

With Theocritus the range of pure pastoral had been defined in its form, figures and subject matter. The melancholy vein that has characterized the whole European tradition is already there in the sorrows of love – most finely depicted in *Idd.* 10 and 11 – and of untimely death – in *Id.* 1. In *Id.* 10 the setting is already subtly widened beyond the strictly pastoral way of life in a manner that Vergil was to exploit far more boldly. In *Id.* 7 the genre is brought into relation with other modes of poetic creation and the literary controversies in which Theocritus and his friends were involved, but in a manner that risks turning the pastoral setting into a mere framework for other forms of poetry – as it has already become in the fragment of 'Myrson and Lycidas' ([Bion] 2: *The Epithalamium of Achilles and Deidameia*). The extension of the genre to traditional mythological subjects, as in Bion's *Adonis* and Moschus' *Europa*, whose opening is rich in pastoral colour, can be recognized as a specifically Hellenistic development, without significant influences in later pastoral literature. But the *Lament for Bion* and the prevalence of erotic themes in the post-Theocritean pastoral both provide integral features of the tradition. It is against this background that we must attempt to place the Eclogues of Vergil.

2. THE CHRONOLOGY AND ARRANGEMENT OF THE ECLOGUES

Greek pastoral poetry was known to Vergil and contemporary Latin poets chiefly from the collected edition published in the first half of the first century B.C. by Artemidorus, who was probably the authority for the Theocritean canon of ten bucolic idylls.[1] There is, however, no evidence for any Latin pastoral poetry before Vergil. If Valerius Messalla wrote pastorals, [V.] *Catal.* 9.13–20 indicates that they must have been in Greek; Pliny's reference to a Catullan *incantamentorum amatoria imitatio* (*Nat.* 28.19) gives no indication of genre; the bucolic ingredients in other genres, e.g. Porcius' epigram cited by Aulus Gellius (*N.A.* 19.9) and certain poems of the *Appendix Vergiliana*, have adequate precedents in Hellenistic elegiac poetry.

The natural inference from the words addressed to Pollio in *Ecl.* 8 *a te principium, tibi desinam*, can be set beside the explicit statement in the Servian *Vita* 24–5 *tunc ei proposuit Pollio ut carmen bucolicum scriberet, quod eum constat triennio scripsisse et emendasse*, which in its context is unlikely to refer to just one *carmen*, e.g. *Ecl.* 2 or 8. It was Pollio who suggested to Vergil that he try his hand at pastoral, having been impressed no doubt by the promise of his earlier poetry.[2]

The ancient *testimonia* concerning the date of the Eclogues are somewhat ambiguous and inconsistent. Thus besides *Vit.* 24–5 (cited above) Serv. *Buc. prooem.* 3.26–7 *sane sciendum Vergilium XXVIII annorum scripsisse bucolica*, Don. *Vit.* 89–90 *Bucolica triennio, Georgica VII, Aeneida XI perfecit annis*; and from the commentary attributed to Probus *scripsit Bucolica annos natus VIII et XX Theocritum secutus, Georgica Hesiodum et Varronem* (323.13–14) and *eum, ut Asconius Pedianus dicit, XXVIII annos natum Bucolica edidisse* (329.6–7). Relevant too is

[1] Cf. *A.P.* 9.205, 434 with Serv. *Buc. Prooem.* 3.21.
[2] Some of which is probably preserved in the *Appendix Vergiliana*, e.g. *Catal.* 5 and 7.

Servius' remark *quae* [sc. *eclogae*] *licet decem sint, incertum tamen est quo ordine scriptae sint* (*Buc. prooem.* 3.15-16). Two clues can however be salvaged from all this: the importance of the poet's twenty-ninth year, viz. the year beginning 15 October 42 B.C., and the period of three years that is mentioned by both Servius and Donatus. As at least three of the poems, 6, 8, and 10, are in their present form manifestly later than 42–41 B.C., we may infer that in this year Vergil either began writing the Eclogues or more likely published the first of them. For it is reasonable to suppose that the poems were first published individually or in pairs, each with a title and a dedication. Neither the titles given by Donatus (*Vit.* 306ff.: *Tityrus, Alexis, Palaemon, Pollio, Daphnis, Varus* or *Silenus, Corydon, Damon* or *pharmaceutria, Moeris, Gallus*) nor those recorded in the manuscript tradition and noted in the apparatus to each poem can be authenticated; but the dedications of some at least are certain: 4 and 8 to Pollio, 6 to Varus, 10 to Gallus. This piecemeal publication of the *Bucolica* accounts perhaps for the alternative name *Eclogae*: each poem was an *eklogé* 'excerpt, extract' from a projected whole. Part of the confusion in the *testimonia* may be due to the use of *Bucolica* in two different senses: individual 'pastoral poems' and 'the pastoral poems' as a collected group. The latter meaning is certain in the Donatus and first 'Probus' passages. The three year period takes us to October 39 B.C. The significance of this date will appear shortly.

Apart from the *testimonia* we have three criteria for dating.

The first is by references in the poems to external events. Thus the occasion of *Ecl.* 4 is Pollio's consulship. The miraculous sequence of events that is to begin in his year of office is spoken of in the future tense, but this does not guarantee a date before 40 B.C.; ancient poets like modern ones were not averse from producing their occasional verses after the occasions that they purport to herald. A publication date in late 41 or 40 B.C. is therefore equally possible. Similarly the dedication of *Ecl.* 8 looks forward to Pollio's triumphal return from his Macedonian proconsulate and so provides a notional date in the late summer of 39 B.C. But again the actual date may be later. The allusion to Varus' campaigning in *Ecl.* 6 must be to his proconsular service in 38 (he was consul in the preceding year); and that takes us beyond the *triennium* mentioned by the ancient authorities.

Some of the external allusions are disputable. Thus the publication of *Ecl.* 5 must be placed after July 42 B.C. only if (as is maintained on pp. 28–9 and in the commentary) it was connected with the first celebration of Julius Caesar's birthday with full divine honours. Other allusions are now irrecoverable: for instance the date of Pollio's *noua carmina* (3.86), of Gallus' aetiological poem (6.72–3) or his love affair with Cytheris (10 passim). Even *Ecl.* 1 and 9, concerned with the aftermath of the land-confiscations, cannot be accurately placed; for although the resettlement of veterans that necessitated the evictions was begun by the triumvirs late in 42 B.C. after the battle of Philippi, it continued right through the thirties. The reference to Varus and Mantua in 9 point to a notional date in 42–40 B.C., but there is no such clue in the other poem.

The first criterion enables us at best to place Eclogues 5, 4, 8 and 6, in that order, within the period 42 B.C. to 38 or a little later.

Cross-references and echoes between Eclogues provide a second dating criterion. Thus 5.85–7 reveals that 2 and 3 were already published, otherwise the allusion to them would be not only pointless but unintelligible. The oblique reference to the theme of 5 at 9.46–50 likewise presupposes the reader's familiarity with the former poem. Indeed Menalcas' fragments in 9.23–5 etc. would lose much of their impact if most of the other Eclogues had not already been published. Again the probable connection between 8.97–9 and 9.54 is the more effective if the former passage was the earlier. By contrast the much-discussed links between 3.89 and 4.25, 30 and between 1.74 and 9.50 cannot by themselves be used to establish priority one way or the other, and the echoes in 10 from 2 and 8 add nothing to our knowledge of the relative chronology of these two poems.

The second criterion, combined with the first, suggests an order 2, 3, 5, 4, 8, 9, 6, 10 (with the possibility that 9 preceded 8).

Lastly there is the stylistic criterion. Inevitably subjective impressions enter at this point and the time-span of the whole collection is too short for the application of objective statistical checks. Moreover such distinctive features as can be plotted – like the relatively high incidence of spondaic rhythm in *Ecl.* 4 or of fourth-foot homodynes and contracted perfect forms of the verb in *Ecl.* 6 – are more likely to be connected with the thematic individuality of the poems in which they occur than with their chronological location.

Of more importance is Vergil's changing relationship to Greek pastoral. Here too caution is needed; for so little survives of post-Theocritean Greek pastoral that apparent innovations by the Latin poet may have had more precedent than we are aware. So far as Theocritus is concerned a 'spectrum' of *imitatio* can be observed both at the level of whole poems and in terms of local detail. 2, 3, 7 and 8 stand formally or thematically within the Theocritean tradition; 5, 10 and 9 employ settings and motifs from Theocritus, but in new contexts or in association with new material; 1, 4 and 6 are original compositions with few essential traces of Theocritean influence. As for local detail: many lines of *Ecl.* 3 are little more than paraphrases of Theocritus; but a freer more original mode of adaptation is revealed for instance in the description of the cups in 3.35–48, the recollection of the first falling in love in 8.37–41 and the visitation of the gods in 10.21–30; and a distinctively Vergilian handling of conventional figures is to be found in the rustic analogies of 5.16–18, 45–7, 82–4, the sympathy figure in 7.53–60 and the *locus amoenus* of 1.51–8. Lastly we find in all the poems details that are entirely without Theocritean precedent.

The pattern of Vergilian *imitatio* is in fact very complex and cannot be neatly reconciled with the chronology suggested by the other criteria; there is far more of Theocritus for example in 8 than in 4, and we may have to reckon here with the reworking of earlier compositions. Nevertheless it is broadly true that poems which can be shown on other evidence to be late exhibit a bolder, more independent treatment of such Theocritean material as they employ. Taking Eclogues that are comparable in form or subject matter, we can detect in 1, 7 and 8 signs of greater maturity both of conception and composition than in their partners 9, 3 and 2 respectively.

The third criterion gives no ground for revising the order proposed earlier; but it does support the location of 7 in the latter half of the series and 1 in the latest group, along with 6 and 10.

Taking together the phrase *a te principium* in 8.11, the tribute to Pollio in 3.84–7 and the ancient tradition concerning the motivation of *Ecl.* 2, which is discussed in the final note on this poem, we may conclude that certainly the second Eclogue and probably also the third were dedicated explicitly to Pollio. From 45 B.C. Pollio was in Hispania Ulterior, whence he returned in 42 or 41 to take charge of Gallia Cisalpina on Antony's behalf. His return from Spain would have provided an appropriate occasion for Vergil to present him with the first-fruits of his patronage. So the publication of *Ecl.* 2 and 3 can be assigned to 42–41 B.C., when the poet was *XXVIII annos natus*. The words *tibi desinam* also in 8.11 suggest that this poem, dedicated again to Pollio on the occasion of his triumphal return in 39 B.C., was intended to complete Vergil's Pastoral *œuvre*. To date this would have comprised a pair of Eclogues on the pains and perils of love, both homosexual (2) and heterosexual (8), a pair on political themes, 5 and 4, and the contest-poem 3. To these we can surely add 7, the other contest-poem, on the assumption that 7 and 8 were intended to form a complementary pair to 3 and 2 and published close to each other in 39 B.C. The *Bucolica* that Vergil *triennio perfecit* were thus 2, 3, 5, 4, 7 and 8. With minor revisions to the earlier ones (Servius' *emendasse*) these could all have been published in a collected edition towards the end of 39 B.C. and dedicated to Pollio. They form a nicely varied set of pastorals and the chronological order also provides a neat chiastic arrangement of forms and themes for the whole group.

If a Theocritean Bucolic corpus of ten idylls was already accepted, it is likely that Vergil had the idea of a decad of Eclogues in mind from the start. However, even if the Pollio group were not actually published as a collection, the implication of 8.11 is that he had put aside any such idea, at any rate until new sources of inspiration for pastoral invention could be found. In the event some of his most novel and important work in the genre was to come; for it is probable that 9 and 1, certain that 6 and 10 belong to the years after 39 B.C.

It is not known at what date all ten Eclogues were republished as a single book; but the early years of the Principate seem the most likely period. There is no reason to doubt that the order of the poems in that edition was the one that is observed consistently in the manuscript tradition, or that Vergil himself intended it to have some significance. What that significance was seems already to have eluded the ancient commentators: *naturalem consertumque ordinem nullum esse certissimum est* (Don. *Vit.* 322–3). In recent years the question has been much discussed. Arithmetical explanations have been especially in favour, ranging from fantastic structural analogues with 'Bucolic chapels' and Neo-Pythagorean number-symbolism, through the calculation of 'Golden sections', to more sober ingenuities concerning 'Symmetry and sense'. There is little agreement among the scholars who choose this kind of approach, and the firm numerical facts are hardly sensational, e.g. that 2 and 8 together have almost the same number of lines (182 or 183) as 3 and 7 (181), which may be deliberate, or that 4 and 6 together have almost the same number (149) as 1 and 9 (150), which is probably coincidental. The discussion that follows is on altogether different lines.

Clearly the Pollio group forms the core of the book: 2, 3, 5, 4, 7, 8. The four poems published subsequently form two pairs: 9 and 1 on the effects of the land confiscations, 6 and 10 on Gallus and poetry. *Ecl.* 10 is explicitly the end-piece of the collection. A straight chronological arrangement would probably have given 2, 3, 5, 4, 7, 8, 9, 1, 6, 10, or something very similar. But if the Pollio group was kept intact and its chiastic arrangement of complementary pairs continued, with the earlier poem preceding in each instance, the order would have been 6, 9, 2, 3, 5, 4, 7, 8, 1, 10, with the two pairs of conventional pastorals, 2 and 3, 7, and 8 alternating with the three pairs of more original poems, 6 and 9, 5 and 4, 10 and 1, and the political Eclogues 5 and 4 in central position. The prominent position of 6 and 10 would reflect both the influence of Gallus on Vergil's literary ideas at the time when these two Eclogues were published and the personal esteem in which Vergil held him. The opinion reported by Servius, *alii primam illam uolunt 'prima Syracosio'* (*Buc. prooem.* 3.19–20; cf. Don. *Vit.* 324–5), which is usually taken as a silly inference from the first word of the sixth Eclogue, may ultimately reflect Vergil's intention for the first decad edition.

It seems clear that Ovid (*A.* 1.15.25) and Calpurnius (4.62–3) knew *Tityrus* as the first poem of the *Bucolica*. But the implications of *G.* 4.565–6, *carmina qui lusi pastorum audaxque iuuenta,* | *Tityre, te patulae cecini sub tegmine fagi,* are much less certain. We do not know the date of this coda to the Georgics, and in any case the reference may be not to the Eclogues as a whole but specifically to *Ecl.* 1. It is not difficult however to see why *Ecl.* 6 was not retained in first position. It would have been aesthetically somewhat disconcerting to begin the collection with its least pastoral member. The Eclogue is dedicated to a minor patron who on the evidence of 9.27 had in the event done little to earn the poet's gratitude. Moreover, if the final edition came out in the early Augustan period, it would not have seemed inappropriate to promote to a prominent position the one Eclogue in which the

Princeps himself appears; *deus nobis haec otia fecit* would now have a significance far beyond its immediate context in the poem. If that edition postdated Gallus' public disgrace and suicide in 26 B.C., then the political motive would have acquired a more sinister urgency.

The demotion of 6 and the concomitant transposition of 1 and 9 (if indeed they were not already in this order) entailed adjustments to the pattern of the book. With 10 now taking on the status of an epilogue to the chiastically ordered group 1, 2, 3, 5, 4, 7, 8, 9, the obvious place for 6 was in the centre of 1–9, between 5 and 4. Instead Vergil chose, somewhat surprisingly, to place it before 7 and to reverse the order of 5 and 4 (assuming that they were not already in this order). Now to have left 5, 4, 6 in that order would have spoiled the chiastic symmetry, since 5 and 6 cannot on any interpretation be paired together like 3 and 7, 2 and 8; but it would have left the Messianic Eclogue in central position, a fine Augustan gesture from the poet who was to write, if he had not already written, of *Augustus Caesar* as founder of the new *aurea...saecula* (*A.* 6.792–3). The arrangement finally adopted detaches 4 from its original thematic counterpart 5 and sets it in a new relationship with 6 – Sibyl's prophecy balanced by Silenus' song – leaving 5 centrally placed within the chiastic group, and incidentally in a new relationship with the concluding 10, comparable to that of 4 with 6. The effect of placing 5 centrally and after 4 rather than before it is to place the emphasis on the vaguer, less extravagant, statement of political optimisim, which may reflect the poet's feelings towards the Augustan Golden Age after the persecution of his friend Gallus.

Something of the pattern discernible in the Pollio group of six has indeed survived into the final edition of ten. The impressively ranging sequence of themes – poetic manifestos, the dispossessions, the pains and perils of love, the conventional topics of pastoral singing contests, political tributes and aspirations, and then back again – has been truncated, to be sure, but at least the pattern of formal variation remains. First the odd-numbered poems: 1 and 9 are conversation-pieces, 3 and 7 singing competitions introduced by conversation, 5 a conversation enclosing a pair of balanced songs. Among the even poems: in 8 a brief scene-setting leads to a competition in the form of two balanced songs, in 2 it is followed by a monologue, 6 and 10 have a narrative scene leading to a monologue, 4 has a brief proem followed by a monologue in the poet's own person. While the even-numbered poems are thus more varied in form, the general distinction holds throughout: in contrast to the other five they are all non-conversational. Indeed this formal criterion, which was clearly important in the general arrangement, may have determined the final order of 4, 5, 6 after 6 had been demoted.

Much of this discussion has of necessity been speculative. Many readers of the Eclogues would no doubt prefer, given the impossibility of definitive answers, to leave questions of both chronology and arrangement unexplored. Yet arguments about the order in which the poems were written are closely bound up with our views of what Vergil was attempting to do with the pastoral genre and how his conception of it developed as he wrote. Furthermore a poet's decisions about the arrangement of his book are an integral part of the creative process itself, even if only a minor one. Hence in grappling with both questions we are continually brought back to various aspects of the poems and their interrelationships, some of which will be taken up in the concluding section. This is perhaps the chief justification of the enquiry.

3. VERGIL'S ACHIEVEMENT AS A PASTORAL POET

The reader who comes to the Eclogues direct from Theocritus immediately recognizes much that is familiar, and we have already noticed some of the modes of Vergilian *imitatio* (p. 17). Yet the conventional figures and motifs are often treated with an originality of detail and a care for their integration into the new contexts that is both striking and effective. Thus, for instance, the rustic analogy (p. 9), which in 2.63–5 still retains much of its Theocritean naivety, becomes in its recurrent variations at 5.16–18, 45–7, 82–4 a vehicle for asserting the pastoral integrity of the poem. Similarly with the sympathy figure (p. 9). In 1.38–9 the image of Tityrus' farm mourning his departure grows naturally out of the preceding lines, in which the signs of neglect resulting from his absence are realistically depicted. Again at 7.53–60 the 'Where'er you walk' variant of the figure has been transformed by Vergil into a subtle and evocative conceit, reminiscent – like much else in the poem – of Hellenistic epigram at its best.

The conventional singing competition appears in two of the poems. The first of them, *Ecl.* 3, is in many places little more than a pastiche of Theocritean reminiscences. The original details, though significant for the direction that Vergil's concept of the genre was already taking, are either obscure – like the symbolic figures on the cups and the related pair of riddles at the end – or else clumsy – like the abrupt intrusion of Pollio and contemporary literary controversy into the songs of the two herdsmen. By contrast Vergil reverts in *Ecl.* 7 to a purer, more homogeneous pastoral conception. The range of themes – rustic piety, delight in the countryside and its music, the pleasures and sorrows of country love – is entirely conventional. But the detail is almost all original, the technique is mature and the choice of quatrains rather than couplets enables each theme to be elaborated more fully. Moreover Vergil manages subtly to characterize the two singers through the songs that he assigns to them. In fact this highly wrought poem stands as one of the finest essays in pure pastoral ever written.

An important innovation in *Ecl.* 7 is the description of the two singers as *Arcades*. The mythical character of their Arcady is indicated by its setting here (7.13) beside the Mantuan river Mincio: it represents a synthesis of the conventional pastoral myth, certain traditions about Arcadia (see 7.4n.), and Vergil's own view of the Italian countryside and its way of life, coloured by the memories of his own boyhood home in Cisalpine Gaul. The definitive presentment of this Arcady occurs only in the last pastoral that he wrote, *Ecl.* 10, whence it was mediated by way of Sannazaro's *Arcadia* (1504) to the Renaissance exponents of the genre.

As in Theocritus, the very full picture that we get of the idealized landscape is built up gradually by descriptive details scattered through each poem. At first sight it is remarkably consistent in the two poets. In the foreground meadows grazed by goats, sheep or cattle, with flowers and shrubs humming with bees, nearby springs and rivers lined with willows and marsh-reeds, hollow rocks and shady trees to provide shelter from the heat, in the branches above the rustle of the breeze and the throaty cooing of pigeons and doves; not far off are orchards, vines and ploughed fields – here Vergil widens the Golden Age landscape of the pastoral to incorporate more of the real countryside – and in the near distance wooded hills, sometimes a tract of open water – specifically the sea in 2.26 – and further away a market town. That the poet of the *Georgics*, born and brought up in the farming region of Mantua, depended for any of this on the writings of his distinguished Syracusan predecessor passes all belief. The details of the scene right down to the flowers and trees that are named belong not to exotic places evoking magical landscapes but to the familiar Italian countryside. In Vergil's *locus amoenus* as in so much else the Theocritean convention has been revitalized and enriched by personal experience and observation of the world about him.

The few passages of detailed description are all contextually significant, but in ways that go far beyond Theocritus. Meliboeus' description of Tityrus' farm (1.51–8) as a *locus amoenus* is contrasted emphatically with his brutally realistic account of the place a few lines earlier (1.47–8). But the intervening couplet, recalling the hazards that await him in exile, reveals the significance of the contrast. To one deprived even the familiar scene of the humblest farm takes on the aura of Arcady.

The same contrast is to be found as early as *Ecl.* 2, where Corydon describes in detail (46–55) the gift of flowers and fruits that the Nymphs will bring to Alexis, if by some chance he deigns to descend to the *sordida rura* (28). It is a rich complex of sensuous imagery: colour, scent and texture. But it is entirely the product of his imagination – for the ingredients could never be in season together – and its significance lies, like Meliboeus' *locus amoenus*, in its revelation of the power of the humble countryside to inspire in its inhabitants a truly Arcadian vision, one which in the end no alien townsman can fully share.

Intimations of the real countryside and its routines occur in Theocritus of course, especially before and after the interludes of song. But they are more numerous and wide-ranging in Vergil. Thus, in addition to Theocritean details like the dangers to the flocks (3.94–9) and the basketwork (2.72), there are references to ploughing and sowing (2.66, 5.36) and pruning (9.61), swineherding (10.19), marketing (1.34–5) and even the technicalities of animal husbandry (1.45). Hunting too figures more prominently in the Eclogues than in the Idylls (2.29, 3.75, 5.60–1, 7.29–30). References to Italian religion, e.g. the *Ambarualia* in 3.76, Pales and Ceres in 5.35, 79, Fauni in 6.27,

Silvanus in 10.24, are less remarkable, as are the riddles in 3.104–7, a rustic detail without precedent nevertheless in extant pastoral. Calpurnius adds to the Italian colour by including for instance the finger-game and the deities Flora and Pomona in his *Ecl.* 2.25–33. Even socio-legal concepts, which are distinctly foreign to pure pastoral, are introduced in the Eclogues – citizen and slave status (1.32, 71), formal marriage (8.29–30), the rights of *possessio* (9.3). Some of these details, to be sure, have a particular contextual rele-vance, but this in itself indicates the widening of the range of the genre. We can certainly reconstruct far more of the conditions of ordinary life in the country from the Eclogues than we ever could from the Idylls.

The herdsmen, as in most subsequent pastoral, still have Greek names. To Vergil's contemporaries, familiar with the *latifundia* of the Italian countryside, which were heavily dependent upon slave-labour from the Greek-speaking world, this would not have seemed remote from reality. Yet Meliboeus in *Ecl.* 1 and Menalcas in *Ecl.* 9 seem to be Roman citizens, and the retention of the Greek names here is a device for integrating them fully into the pastoral fiction. Indeed the retention of the Greek case forms *Alexi, Daphnin, Amaryllida* etc. throughout the Eclogues intensifies the Greek colour. As in Theocritus, it is not easy to determine the precise status of individual herdsmen: some may be slaves, others hired farm-hands, others again small-holders. However where social status is relevant to the dramatic situation of the poem it is usually clarified, as with Tityrus and Meliboeus in *Ecl.* 1, Corydon and Alexis in *Ecl.* 2. Donatus' observa-tion (*Vit.* 215–18) that cattleherds take precedence over shepherds, shepherds over goatherds – swineherds do not even merit a mention – certainly applies to the real countryside, where the type of stock grazed reflects the quality of the land. However apart from the fact that, as in Theocritus, the prestigious Daphnis is always a cattleherd and Tityrus generally in a position of subservience to the other characters, there seems to be no particular hierarchy among the herds-men. Some of Vergil's herdsmen graze a variety of animals, for instance Tityrus (1), Meliboeus (7); and even when they are ex-plicitly associated with one kind – Mopsus (5) and Corydon (7) have goats, Menalcas (3) and Thyrsis (7) sheep, Damoetas (3) cattle – this hardly ever excludes the possibility of diversification, nor is it implied that one kind of herdsman is superior to another. Indeed goats and sheep, not cattle, appear in the Golden Age imagery of *Ecl.* 4 and Vergil's choice of the goatherd's role for himself in *Ecl.* 10, though it may be a suggestion of humility (as Servius believed), is more likely to mark the difference between the poet and Gallus in their commitment to Arcardian life.

The fact that Corydon is a Mantuan goatherd in *Ecl.* 7 and a Sicilian herdsman grazing principally sheep in *Ecl.* 2 raises specifically a more general question: how far can we expect to see connections between characters in different poems who bear the same name? Certainly the two gentle Corydons have much in common and 7.37–40 seems a deliberate, if oblique, invitation to associate them. Amaryllis too is consistently portrayed throughout, and it is possible, as with some of the other characters, to compose a biographical sketch of her. She is pretty (1.5), quick-tempered (2.14, 3.81), an efficient housewife (1.30), not unfamiliar with the occult (8.77), fancied by Corydon (2.52), Damoetas (3.81), Lycidas and Menalcas (or Moeris, 9.22), but she settled for security with old Tityrus (1.5, 30). Again the subservient role assigned to Tityrus elsewhere is clearly relevant to his situation in *Ecl.* 1; and the possibility that in Moeris' words at 9.54 we are meant to recall the Moeris of 8.97–8 adds to the pathos of the former context. On the other hand the Meliboei of 3.1 and 7.9 seem irrelevant to the Meliboeus of *Ecl.* 1, and Daphnis can hardly be the same person in 5.56–7 as in 9.46. On the whole it seems that with the exception of Menalcas (see pp. 29, 31) there is, as in Theocritus, nothing much to be gained (or for that matter lost) from a general assumption that the recurrence of the same name is significant.

Latin had of course no literary dialects. So in an effort to reproduce something of the effect of Theocritus' Doric Vergil puts into the mouths of his herdsmen colloquial and archaic forms and idioms redolent of rural dialects. Whether he went as far as introducing rustic spellings like *hedus* for *haedus* is very doubtful; for although such forms are often attested in our manuscripts of the poems, they may reflect late Latin pronunciation rather than the rusticity of the classical period. The colloquialisms that do occur come chiefly in conversations or in those parts of the formal songs that concern practical husbandry. It is likely that ancient purists objected, as Boileau and Pope did later, to such linguistic realism as being beneath the dignity of the genre; and it can hardly be coincidental that colloquialism is prominent in all three parodies of the Eclogues cited in Donatus' *Vita* (174–7) and Servius (on 5.36). However such details do not seem to have affected Horace's assessment of the general tone of the Eclogues as being *molle atque facetum* 'delicate and witty' (*S.* 1.10.44). The two epithets probably refer to style rather than matter, and are notoriously difficult to translate.[1] They clearly imply a register far removed from that of epic (cf. Prop. 2.1.2, 41); which is indeed the point of the phrase in Horace's own context. The combination of Latin rusticity with Greek colour, produced by the frequency of Greek proper names complete with Greek case forms, is the linguistic counterpart of the blend of Greek myth and Latin reality that is the distinctive characteristic of the Eclogues.

molle atque facetum would serve as a description of the personal poetry of Catullus or the Hellenistic epigrammatists. Indeed the affinities between the Greek pastoral and elegiac treatment of erotic themes were taken up and explored further by Vergil in the Eclogues. As in Theocritus and his successors, the emphasis is again on the sorrows of constant love, set against a background of more carefree bisexual promiscuity.

Ecl. 2, the lament of Corydon, has many echoes of Greek pastoral – the comic serenader of *Id.* 3, the angry goatherd of *Id.* 20, the alienated reaper of *Id.* 10 and above all the love-sick Polyphemus of *Id.* 11. The formative influence of Meleager's Alexis epigram (*A.P.* 12.127) is seen in the homosexuality of the poem and the conceit that it exploits in the contrast between the transient heat of the midday sun and the unabating fires of frustrated passion. Moreover Vergil has added to the situation a successful rival, Iollas, the *diues amator* familiar from Augustan elegy. Out of this material he is able to create a more complex human character, whose abrupt changes of mood – between longing and brutal self-awareness – bring a dramatic movement to the shepherd's monologue. Like the lovers of Roman elegy Corydon is more preoccupied with the pains of his love than with the praises of the beloved, and is at once a comic and a pathetic figure. In fact here

---

[1] *mollis* is associated with *perlucens* 'translucent', *tener* and *flexibilis* 'supple' (e.g. Cic. *Brut.* 274) and contrasted with *durus, fortis; facetus* associated with *elegans* (ib. 292) and *urbanus* (Cic. *de Or.* 1.159), contrasted with *grauis, seuerus,*

in this elegiac pastoral we have the true prototype of the Passionate Shepherd of the later pastoral tradition.

In *Ecl.* 8 we are presented with a study in the contrasting reactions of lovers to infidelity, real or imagined. Formally the carefully balanced songs of Damon and Alphesiboeus represent a *contaminatio* of motifs taken from the first two idylls of Theocritus. Damon's goatherd, who has been jilted by Nysa, reveals all the passivity of Corydon in *Ecl.* 2, but with none of the turbulent fluctuations of mood; and his grief, intensified by the memory of their first meeting – a brilliant adaptation of a scene from *Id.* 11 – leads not to the day-dreaming resignation that we saw in *Ecl.* 2 or to the defiant martyrdom of Theocritus' Daphnis but to suicidal despair. In Alphesiboeus' song, a pastoral adaptation of one of Theocritus' urban idylls, the girl, suspecting her absent lover's infidelity, resorts to the *carmina* of magic to bring him back. Unlike the goatherd she is positive and determined, and in a passage inspired by Lucretius, which subtly exposes her own vulnerability, she looks forward to the triumphal conclusion of her arts. There is here perhaps an implied *praeceptum amoris*: to the forsaken lover resourceful boldness may accomplish more than the application of the 'Muses' medicine'.

Finally in *Ecl.* 10 the theme of *sollicitus amor* appears in relation to an historical person; Vergil's friend and fellow-poet Cornelius Gallus is depicted languishing in Arcady. The opening scene recalls the setting of Daphnis' death in *Id.* 1, but Gallus' address to the Arcadians is wholly new to pastoral. Gallus longs to have escaped from his troubles by becoming an Arcadian; yet his commitment is half-hearted. His conception of Arcady is dominated by the image of its abundant and varied love-life and the pleasures of hunting. No suggestion here of tending the flocks and pastures. Indeed some of the details of his monologue (10.44–9, 53–4) recall non-pastoral motifs from elegy. Like Corydon in *Ecl.* 2 – and the comparison is reinforced by several echoes of that poem – he experiences abrupt changes of mood; his yearning to escape to Arcady leads to a desire to share its delights with the faithless Lycoris. His conclusion, *omnia uincit Amor, et nos cedamus Amori*, takes us back in this the latest of all the Eclogues to the resignation of the rejected lover, which was the theme of the earliest of them.

The Vergilian treatment of love in these three poems is more complex, its melancholy more distinctively elegiac than in Theocritus, and it is not surprising that Propertius and Ovid recognized in the Eclogues a kindred voice (*Eleg.* 2.34.67ff., *Tr.* 2.537–8). Nevertheless, if we apply Johnson's criterion of true pastoral as a 'poem in which any action or passion is represented by its effects on a country life' it must be admitted that in Vergil, as in Theocritus and even more in later pastoral, the rustic setting is but a masque for the presentment of a generalized study of the *chagrins d'amour*. Only in *Ecl.* 2 is the rustic voice essential to the conception of the lover's suffering.

The presence of Gallus in *Ecl.* 10 brings us to another feature of Vergilian pastoral: the concern to relate the mythical world directly and explicitly to contemporary reality. The precedents were there in *Id.* 7 and the *Lament for Bion*. As early as *Ecl.* 3 we can see an attempt to extend it in the explicit reference to Pollio, Bavius and Mevius. Apart from the dedication of *Ecl.* 6 (Varus), historical characters are introduced in their own names also in *Ecl.* 4 (Pollio), 6 and 10 (Gallus) and 9 (Varus, Varius and Cinna); and *iuuenem* in 1.42 clearly alludes to Octavian. So Vergil did not scruple to break the pastoral illusion when it suited his purpose. But it must be admitted that, apart from Pollio in *Ecl.* 4 and Gallus in *Ecl.* 10, who are portrayed in a way that is not inorganic to the mythical context, these unassimilated intrusions of real persons are awkward and disconcerting. Johnson's comment on *Ecl.* 6 is very much to the point: after conceding that it 'rises to the dignity of philosophic sentiment and heroic poetry' he concludes that 'since the compliment paid to Gallus fixes the transaction to his own time, the fiction of Silenus seems injudicious' (*The Adventurer* no. 92, 22 Sept. 1753).

A different mode of allusion appears as early as *Ecl.* 5. Like *Ecl.* 8 it contains a pair of equally balanced and thematically complementary songs: on the death and deification of Daphnis. In contrast to the other *retractationes* of the Daphnis-motif in 8.17–61 and 10.9–30 the erotic context of Daphnis' death in *Id.* 1 has been removed and the apotheosis of Daphnis added. Vergil has in fact gone back beyond Theocritus to the original Daphnis, the Sicilian rustic hero, and used the myth of his death and deification to allude to recent history, paying a poetic tribute to Julius Caesar and proclaiming in pastoral imagery his own political sympathies. In *Ecl.* 8 he was to bring together the treatment of erotic themes from urban and pastoral idylls of Theocritus. In *Ecl.*5 he introduced the political themes of *Idd.* 16 and 17 into the pastoral genre. The image of the ruler as shepherd of his people is as old as Homer (*Iliad* 2.243). Pastoral precedent for panegyric on the death of an historical person existed in the *Lament for Bion*. The further step that Vergil has taken is a small one, but it was decisive. For it opened the way to the employment of pastoral in the praise of princes, which appears already in the eulogies of Nero in *Einsiedeln Ecl.* 1 and Calpurnius *Ecl.* 1 and 4, and in the Renaissance provided a precedent for converting the genre into elaborate allegory, to the eventual impoverishment of its distinctive character. In *Ecl.* 5 the technique is allusive rather than allegorical. All the detail is organic to the pastoral myth; it is only in the poem taken as a whole and read in its historical context that we can see that it is more than a variation on the traditional pastoral theme. The representation of Vergil and Caesar through the pastoral figures of Menalcas and Daphnis assimilates them to the Arcadian world[1] in a way that Pollio, Varus and the rest never are; the retention of their historical names marks them off as outsiders, not necessarily hostile but intruders nonetheless from the historical world beyond the myth.

Menalcas' song reflects the optimism inspired by the Julian comet, which had appeared in the heavens in the summer of 44 B.C. These hopes for a new era of peace and prosperity, reiterated in 9.46–50, also inspired a far more original pastoral. *Ecl.* 4 is based upon the contrapuntal elaboration of two powerful apocalyptic images, the miraculous birth of a Wonder-Child and the return of nature's Golden Age.

As we have already observed, the Golden Age had close links with the pastoral myth; but Vergil seems to have been the first poet to conceive the *Saturnia regna* not as belonging exclusively to the irrecoverable past but as something destined to return to the earth in the future. Here we can detect the influence of cyclic conceptions of history like the *magnus annus*, which is in fact alluded to in the opening thematic exposition. The image of the Child, easily associated with the primaeval innocence of the Golden Age and the pastoral, seems to have had a prominent role in many myth–ritual patterns relating to

---

[1] Mopsus too must represent in pastoral terms, if not a specific fellow-poet, then at least a type of those whose Caesarian sympathies caused them to mourn the dictator's death.

the annual rebirth of the seasons. As an apocalyptic figure it belongs to Near Eastern culture and is most familiar to us from the prophetic verses of the Book of Isaiah, which Christians have always interpreted as foretelling the birth of Jesus. St Augustine likewise identified Vergil's Child here, and *Ecl.* 4, combining with the pastoralism of the Gospels, as represented in Luk. 2.8, 15.4, Joh. 10.11 (cf. Heb. 13.20), 21.16, established Messianism as a theme for Christian pastoral. Vergil himself probably took the image of the Child from Sibylline oracle, to which allusion is made explicitly in the opening exposition of the poem, and saw the imaginative possibilities of combining it with ingredients of the Hesiodic Golden Age to form a new kind of pastoral poem. The hopes for peace in time of crisis that had been expressed by Theocritus in the non-pastoral context of *Id.* 16.88ff. are thus incorporated into the thematic range of this most pacific of all poetic genres.

Fifteen years or so later, in *A.* 6.791–7, Vergil purported to see the fulfilment of the prophesied Golden Age in the principate of Augustus. But when the Eclogue was published, few could have dreamt that the struggle for power between the triumvirs would end as it did. In 40 B.C. the immediate future looked dark indeed, and it is not surprising that the optimism of the poem is qualified, at its centre, by the prediction of heroic wars still to come.

One of the legacies of continuing civil war was the upheavals throughout Italy caused by the confiscation of land for the resettlement of veterans from the victorious armies. The dispossessions began late in 42 B.C., after Philippi, and continued until after Actium. Their effects on the Italian countryside are the subject of the next two poems.

Both are conversation-pieces. In *Ecl.* 9 Lycidas and Moeris meet on the way to town – the situation vaguely recalls *Id.* 7. Moeris' former master, the poet Menalcas, has lost his land and gone away, leaving him in reluctant service – perhaps as a hired farm-hand – to the new absentee landlord. On their way the two men sing snatches of Menalcas' poetry, and the contrast between Lycidas' eagerness to sing and Moeris' growing reluctance brings out the more intimate relationship of the latter to the departed poet. The fragments – on themes of Theocritean pastoral, on Varus and Mantua and on Daphnis and the Julian comet – clearly allude to the range of styles and subject matter found in the Eclogues themselves. So we may conclude that, as in *Ecl.* 5, Menalcas represents Vergil.[1] There is perhaps a touch of presumption in the tribute that he thus obliquely pays to himself; but it is set in the context of the impotence of poetry in times of civil strife, the protest against which becomes explicit in lines 11–13. By adopting the pastoral mask of Menalcas he is able not only to identify himself with the pastoral scene that he has created but also to generalize his own misfortunes. In the same way the pastoral figures of Lycidas and Moeris serve to typify the harsh effects of the dispossessions in breaking up old friendships and associations. The sadness of the two herdsmen must have been repeated many times up and down Italy.

The first Eclogue, one of the finest poems in the language, is a study of the contrasting fortunes and temperaments of two typical Italian countrymen. The ageing slave Tityrus, threatened by the evictions with the loss of his one hope of gaining freedom, has secured both his land and his freedom by joining in the protest march to Rome. Octavian, the *iuuenis* of line 42, has conceded the demonstrators' requests and is rewarded by the promise of divine honours. Meliboeus, apparently a Roman citizen, has been evicted but has done nothing to help himself. As in *Ecl.* 8 there is the same contrast between the gentle, passive sufferer and the more resourceful and determined character. Meliboeus, who has all the finest poetry of the Eclogue, is wistful as he goes off into exile, and his envy, not marred by any bitterness towards his friend, gives way to anger only at the thought of the barbarian usurper on his land. Tityrus' success has made him complacent and hard, insensitive to others' plight, and it is only at the end – with his offer of a night's hospitality – that the Arcadian values of sympathy and friendship are reasserted.

From *Ecl.* 9 it is clear that Vergil like Meliboeus had known the pain of eviction. But although the loss of his ancestral land at Mantua must have affected him deeply, he could at least rely on powerful friends to secure material compensation. In these two poems, then, he is less concerned with his own personal troubles than with the plight of his fellow-countrymen in rural Italy, the recent disruption of that peace

---

[1] The identification in both Eclogues poses in a particularly acute form the question raised on p. 25. Can we avoid associating this Menalcas with the Menalcas of *Ecl.* 3, of 2.15 and 10.20, even though Vergil has there given us no comparable clues to identification? Ought we to?

on which the prosperity of farmers and of the arts alike depends, and the grim reminder that such things were at the mercy of dynasts and generals. Through the refined verses of the two Eclogues we catch the authentic voice of the countryman, modulated with a sympathetic understanding that is far removed from the patronizing urbanity of most pastoral poets before or since.

Vergil saw in the myth of Arcady not just a pretty *divertissement* for those disaffected citizens who were refined enough to appreciate it but an embodiment of certain moral ideals that he could himself identify closely with the real countryside: a simple way of life, contentment with little, delight in natural beauty, homely piety, friendship and hospitality, devotion to poetry and to peace. If the longing for a lost organic culture is, as some modern theorists have claimed, implicit in the pastoral concept, it was Vergil who developed and exploited this potentiality, to make the genre a vehicle for positive moral criticism of the urban society of his own day. Hence the truth of the Renaissance view, as represented for instance by George Puttenham in *The Arte of English poesie* (1589), 1.18: 'These Eglogues came after to containe and enforme morall discipline for the Amendment of man's behauiour...'

Throughout the Eclogues the city represents a constant threat to Arcadian values: in *Ecl.* 2 the urban Alexis despises Corydon's humble passion and simple rustic life, in *Ecl.* 8 it is the city that threatens to deprive the girl of her lover, in *Ecl.* 9 the city is the goal of Moeris' distasteful journey, in *Ecl.* 1 the *ingrata urbs* preys on farmers in peace and has them at its mercy in time of war. The antithesis of rural and urban life provides a further link with the Golden Age myth, and the walled cities are symptoms of *priscae uestigia fraudis* in 4.31–3. Within the pastoral itself the countryman's hostility towards the city, taken from the real world, is the ideological counterpart to the idealized view of the country that is urbanely exhibited in the orthodox genre itself. In earlier pastoral the very existence of towns seems to have been ignored nor is antagonism to towns an explicit theme of later classical pastoral. On the contrary in Calp. *Ecl.* 7 the countryman Lycotas is reprimanded for neglecting the delights that the city has to offer. But the antithesis of town and country, which was important in Horace's moralizing (e.g. *C.* 3.29, *Ep.* 1.10), became an important ingredient in the Renaissance tradition of the pastoral, where it was enriched by the mediaeval *pastourelle* and by the '*Nature* v. *Nurture*' topos.

The moral criticism borne by the antithesis was elaborated and deepened by Vergil himself in the Georgics (especially 2.467ff.). The Arcadian *otium* of the Theocritean tradition is there counterpoised by the Hesiodic doctrine of *labor*. Hard and soft primitivism are thus brought together and the idea of a sympathetic bond between man and his natural environment is underpinned not by the Epicurean *securitas* of the pastoral but by a more distinctly Stoic creed. It is carried through even into the idyllic homeliness of Evander's Arcadian settlement in *Aeneid* 8, which is exhibited as a model to the contemporary Augustan metropolis.

The notion that pastoral *otium* and rustic *labor* are complementary, that the ideals of Arcady are attainable only to those who accept the humble round of work in the country, is already there in the Eclogues. Corydon's eulogy of the music of Pan and his imaginative rhapsody on the fruits of his land go with his acceptance of the *sordida...rura* and *humilis...casas*. The disconsolateness of Gallus who seeks only *otium* in Arcady is set against the homely picture of the Arcadian herdsmen themselves (10.19–20) and the concluding image of the Arcadian poet plaiting baskets even while he sings. Within this synthesis of myth and reality the linguistic blend of exoticism and realism mentioned earlier (pp. 24–6) finds its appropriate context.

Yet the fine balance of myth and reality on which Vergilian pastoral depends was too delicate to remain for long undisturbed. The introduction of allusions to contemporary history opened the way to the presentment of situations that have little to do with the country. The identification of Menalcas with Vergil in *Ecl.* 5 and 9 became the cue for commentators to hunt for politicians and poets in all the characters of the Eclogues. Servius is representative: *aliquibus locis per allegoriam agit gratias Augusto uel aliis nobilibus, quorum fauore amissum agrum recepit. in qua re tantum dissentit a Theocrito; ille enim ubique simplex est, hic necessitate compulsus aliquibus locis miscet figuras quas perite plerumque etiam ex Theocriti uersibus facit, quos ab illo dictos constat esse simpliciter (Buc. prooem. 2.17ff. cf. Don. Vit. 294ff.).* It is significant that there are no such allegorizing speculations in the *scholia* to Theocritus. This tradition of Vergilian exegesis, which is illustrated in Servius' note on *Ecl.* 1.39, was reinforced by mediaeval and Hermetic traditions of allegorizing, in which special importance was assigned to the *arcana significatio* of shepherd names and the obscure symbolism of every detail in the setting and landscape. From Petrarch and Boccaccio onwards pastoral became a recognized vehicle for social, political and ecclesiastical controversy. The shepherds' cloak conceals not a countryman but a prelate or courtier or even some allegorical abstraction. The descriptive details of the rustic setting, the conversations and songs of its inhabitants have become an elaborate code to be cracked by the ingenious reader. The range of themes of course was greatly extended in other ways. New settings appeared in the piscatory and venatory Eclogues, new subjects included autobiographical fragments and the deaths of friends and relatives, state occasions such as royal birthdays and funerals, invasions and armistices, religious devotions to Christ and the Mother of God, and especially ecclesiastical and theological controversy with moral allegorizing. Johnson's strictures on Milton in this respect (*Lives of the English poets*, ed. Hill, 1.163–5) are well known. There was some fine poetry still, both in Latin and in vernacular pastoral, not least by Milton himself; but the fragile integrity of the genre had been almost totally surrendered. Only perhaps in the treatment of the lover's misfortunes, equally elaborated with allegory and symbolism in the hands of Sannazaro or Sidney, can we see anything essential to the original Theocritean genre surviving. For much of Renaissance pastoral the rustic setting often seems merely a pretty frame for alien material.

Here too Vergil provided something of a precedent with one of his latest pastorals, the enigmatic *Ecl.* 6. The charming bucolic mime in the first part of the poem is the setting for the decidedly un-Arcadian song that the monster Silenus sings to the shepherd boys. After a cosmogony the recital passes, like Ovid's *Metamorphoses*, to a series of myths concerned in the main with disastrous love-affairs and sensational transformations. It is true that we can interpret the lusty satyr's recital as the portrayal of love in both its creative and destructive aspects; for there is an erotic undertone to the whole poem, from the opening reference to the reader *captus amore* to the closing image of the singing Phoebus. But this is a tenuous link indeed with the pastoral eroticism of *Ecl.* 2, 8 and 10.

In fact the style of the recital, like its content, recalls the tradition not of pastoral but of neoteric narrative: elliptical, allusive, picturesque and subjective. It is therefore no surprise to find already in the opening dedication to Varus an echo from the prologue to Callimachus' *Aetia*. The Eclogue is Vergil's counterpart to *Id*. 7: a manifesto of poetic principles expounded obliquely in an appropriate poetic form. Silenus' song asserts the universality of poetry: science and mythology alike are its province, 'things that are true' and 'fictions that are just like fact', to quote the Muses' commission to Hesiod. For Vergil himself this conception was associated specifically with the neoteric movement and Gallus, whose Hesiodic initiation makes an abrupt intrusion into the mythological sequence of Silenus' song.

This view of the universality of poetry recalls the symbolic figures of Orpheus and the astronomers in *Ecl*. 3. It points forward to the exquisite blend of science and mythology that Vergil was to achieve in that most Alexandrian and yet most Italian of didactic poems, the Georgics. *Ecl*. 6 reveals the direction in which his thoughts were turning even before his pastoral œuvre was complete and so stands somewhat apart from the rest of the collection, even more than 4 and 10, which Donatus (*Vita* 302–3) also excludes from those that are *proprie bucolica*. But like 4 it is surely not unrelated to the particular synthesis of myth and reality that characterizes Vergil's conception of pastoral. The bucolic frame to Silenus' song is after all more significant than it is in the anonymous *Achilles and Deidameia* ([Bion] 2) of Greek pastoral or in Calpurnius' first Eclogue in praise of Nero.

In the Eclogues Vergil had explored ways of extending the pastoral that nevertheless preserved and even deepened its essential character. He had developed the theme of *solliciti amores* in directions that brought out the affinities of the genre with the elegiac tradition; he had brought the Arcadian myth into closer relation with the realities of country life and used it as a model by which to criticize the moral values of the world in which he lived, while at the same time enriching the vision of pure pastoral itself. In making the impersonal myth of Arcady the vehicle for an intense, if oblique, form of personal poetry he – far more than Theocritus – can be deemed the father of European pastoral. He might well have disowned much of his progeny, in particular those works that claimed to find their precedent in the Eclogues but for all their undoubted poetic qualities emptied the genre of its essential character and lacked his own passionate commit-

ment to country life. But he could justly take pride in what he himself
had achieved in the genre. Moreover the popular success of the poems
was instantaneous: *Bucolica eo successu edidit ut in scaena quoque per
cantores crebro pronuntiarentur* (Don. *Vit.* 90f.; cf. Tac. *Dial.* 13.2, Serv. *ad
Ecl.* 6.11), and they became a classic text for study in the schools. At
the end of the Georgics Vergil contrasts Octavian's achievements in
politics and war with his own cloistered devotion to the Muses:

> ...illo Vergilium me tempore dulcis alebat
> Parthenope studiis florentem ignobilis oti,
> carmina qui lusi pastorum audaxque iuuenta,
> Tityre, te patulae cecini sub tegmine fagi.

The modest humility of the contrast is ironical, coming from the poet
who had so eloquently championed Arcadian peace against the discord of *tela Martia*; and the irony is underlined by the allusion to *Ecl.* 1.
Octavian is dead; he has gone the way of Ozymandias, King of Kings.
But Vergil lives, and a precious part of that life is this little book
written 'in the boldness of youth', which contains some of the finest
and most original pastoral poetry ever written.

4. THE TEXT

The manuscripts of Vergil that include the Eclogues fall broadly into
two groups. The following list comprises those cited in the apparatus
to the text:

(i) *Early*

M   *codex Mediceus* (5th century), containing 6.48–10.77.
P   *codex Palatinus* (4th–5th century), complete but for 3.72–4.51.
R   *codex Romanus* (5th century), lacking 7.1–10.9.
V   *fragmenta Veronensia* (5th century), containing 3.27–52, 5.86–6.20,
     7.12–37, 8.19–44.

Apart from 3.72–4.51, where only *R* is available, we are thus in the
unusually fortunate position of having the testimony of at least two
fifth-century manuscripts for any given passage.

(ii) *Late*

γ   *codex Gudianus* (9th century), complete.

a b d e   codd. *Bernenses* (9th century), complete, save that *a* lacks 1.1–48.
f   codex *Oxoniensis* (9th century), lacking only 1.1–55.
r   codex *Parisinus* (9th century), complete.
α   codex *Mediolanensis* (13th–14th century), complete.

Detailed descriptions of *MPRV*γ are given in the editions of Ribbeck and of Sabbadini, who also collated α. All the variants attested in these manuscripts are recorded in Sabbadini's apparatus. Descriptions of *a b d e f r* and other ninth-century manuscripts are given by Mynors, whose apparatus records their more important readings. The apparatus to the present text is wholly dependent on the reports of these three scholars, so far as the manuscript evidence is concerned. The superscript numerals 1 and 2 indicate respectively the original reading in a manuscript and a correction thereto by a subsequent hand; ω signifies a consensus or near consensus of *a b d e f r*.

Other evidence for Vergil's text is provided by the ancient commentators, especially Servius, and by citations in the works of grammarians and rhetoricians. Where these are recorded in the apparatus, a distinction is made between what is actually certified by the author's argument and what only appears in his manuscript tradition. The distinction between the shorter Servian commentary and the so-called *Seruius auctus*, first published in 1600 by Pierre Daniel, is indicated throughout by the respective abbreviations Serv. and D.Serv.

The apparatus records the most important manuscript variants and such emendations as are adopted into the text. A few conjectures not so listed are mentioned in the commentary. Variants that are of importance only for determining the history of the textual tradition and the affinities of the manuscripts to one another are omitted. So too are ungrammatical and unmetrical variants and, for the most part, purely orthographic ones. The most notable of the latter are discussed in the following note.

NOTE ON ORTHOGRAPHY

A poet's orthography is part of his creative use of the words in his language. Vergil's practice can be reconstructed, very imperfectly to be sure, from three sources: variants recorded in the manuscripts, the conventions of formal inscriptions dating from the middle and late first century B.C. and the testimony of ancient grammarians and commentators concerning the relevant literary and especially Vergilian usage.

In heteroclite nouns like *fagus* and *laurus* the manuscripts present an inconsistent picture, though the second declension forms are the more frequently indicated: gen. sg. *fagi* (1.1 PR) but abl. sg. *pinu* (7.24 MPV); nom. pl. *cupressi* (1.25 PR), *lauri* (2.54 PR, certified by the metre, 10.13 MPR, where the form produces hiatus) but *pinus* (1.38 P²R. P¹ has *nobis*); acc. pl. *fagos* (2.3 PR, 9.9 MP), *lauros* (6.83 PR), *myrtos* (7.6 MP). At 8.13 MP have *lauros*, Charisius 1.172 B *laurus*; at 8.22 P¹ has *pinus*, MV *pinos*; at 8.82 P has *lauros*, M *laurus*. Euphonic considerations no doubt affected the poet's usage in particular instances, but we cannot be sure of having chosen correctly.

The replacement of *-īs* by *-ēs* in the acc. pl. of *i*-stem words begins in inscriptions before 100 B.C. but is not frequent until the Augustan period. Again Vergil's choice was no doubt partly motivated by euphonic considerations (cf. Gell. *N.A.* 13.21.1–8) and no attempt has been made to normalize the inconsistencies of the MSS. Thus *finis* (1.3 P¹R) but *similes* (1.22 PR), *uiridis* (7.12 MV) but *loquentes* (8.22 MV), etc.

Although the replacement of *u* by *i* in *optumus*, *decumus* etc. is sporadically found in inscriptions much earlier than Julius Caesar, with whom Quintilian (1.7.21) associates the change, *i*-spellings do not predominate before the first century A.D. The inconsistencies in the MSS of the Eclogues reflect a period of transition; thus M has originally *pluruma* (8.96) but *plurimus* (7.49), P has *proxumus* (2.54) but *proxima* (7.22). The only instance of normalization in the present text is *possumus* (see below).

The change of disyllabic *ŭŏ* to *ŭŭ* begins in inscriptions of the midfirst century B.C., e.g. *suum* on *CIL* 1.593.32, but monosyllabic *u̯u* for *u̯o* is not attested till the Augustan period, e.g. *uiu̯us* on *R.G.* 20.3. Disyllabic *ŭŭ* is therefore consistently adopted from the MSS except for *carduos* (5.39), restored from *cardos* (P¹). Monosyllabic *u̯ŏ* however is written throughout whether it has good manuscript authority, as in *curuos* (3.42 P¹), *nouom* (2.22: *nuom* P¹), *paruos* (7.29 M¹), *riuom* (8.87 P¹), *uolgo* (4.25 R), *uoltis* (6.25 P¹R), *uoltus* (1.63 P¹R²), or none at all, as in *diuom* (3.73), *nouom* (5.71), *saeuos* (8.47), *saluos* (7.9), *uolpes* (3.91).

The imperial spelling *quu* is anachronistic for the Eclogues. Both *quo* and *cu*, which are well attested in Augustan epigraphy, are adopted here, though with an inconsistency appropriate to a period of transition. Thus *cum* (3.77 etc.) is preferred to *quom* for the conjunction, *cur* (5.1) to *quor*, *aecum* (5.4 P), *locuntur* (5.28 R) for *aequom*, *loquontur*, but not *adlocur* (8.20: *adlocuor* P). *quoi* is written for *cui* (1.43, cf. 1.20n.) and *quoium* for *cuium* (3.1). As for *hirquis* (3.8) the imperial variation between *c* and *qu* suggests an earlier *hirquos -qui*, whence Augustan *hircus -qui*, later *hircus -ci*.

The choice between *formonsus* and *formosus* is notoriously difficult. The only remotely plausible etymology for *-ōsus* (< *-onsus* < **-o-ụṇt-tos*) favours *-onsus*. The spelling with *n* has some MS support at every one of its frequent occurrences in the Eclogues, and the testimony is especially strong at 3.57 (PR), 4.57 (P¹R), 5.86 (P¹RV²), 5.90 (P¹RV).

Quintilian (1.7.20) reports as Vergilian the spellings *caussae*, *cassus*, *diuissiones*. Hence *caussa* (1.26), *diuissus* (1.66), *inmissi* (2.59), *caussando* (9.56) have been restored in the text.

Macrobius (*Sat.* 5.17.19) testifies to Vergil's fondness for the Greek inflection of Greek names. Some of these have been protected in the tradition by their metrical position. A representative sample is: nom. sg. *Corydon* (2.1) and *Conon* (3.40), voc. sg. *Alexi* (2.6) and *Lycida* (7.67), acc. sg. *Amaryllida* (1.5) and *Daphnin* (5.52), nom. pl. *grypĕs* (8.27) and *Naiadĕs* (10.10), acc. pl. *heroas* (4.16) and *Aonas* (6.65). Other Greek forms have good manuscript authority: *Mnasyllos* (6.13 P¹ cf. *-ylos* V), *Hesperos* (8.30 P), *Tmaros* (8.44 MP), *Alexin* (2.1 R), *Menalcan* (2.15, 9.10 P), *Daphnin* (2.26 P), *Thetin* (4.32 R), *Oetan* (8.30 V), *Moerin* (9.54 P), *Amaryllidos* (2.14 P² *-us* P¹), *Orphei* (dat. 4.57 P), *Dryadas* (5.59 P), *Phaethontiadas* (6.62 MPR). In addition *Phyllidos* (5.10) underlies *-es* in R, and *Daphnidos* (3.12) is supported by the reference in anon. *Ult. Syllab.* (*G.L.* 4.228). All these together seem adequate to justify the normalization of Greek forms elsewhere – *Amaryllidos* (3.81), *Ismaros* (6.30) etc. – even where the MSS preserve no trace of them.

In the transliteration of Greek *-eia* the MSS of the Eclogues strongly favour *-ēa* rather than *-īa*: thus *Calliopea* (4.57 PR), *Galatea* (1.30 PR, 7.37 MP), *Thalea* (6.2 PRV). At 10.59 *Cydonĕa* (M¹P²) rather than *Cydonia* (P¹) is less certain. Although *y* was regularly used at this period to represent Greek *u* (phonetically *ü*) in Greek proper names, common nouns borrowed from Greek at an earlier date usually retained the *u*-spelling and, as Romance reflexes show, the normal Latin *u*-pronunciation, e.g. *tumba, gubernare*. Hence *cutisus* has been preferred (1.78 etc., cf. *cutisum* at 2.64 R) for Greek *kútisos, murtus* (2.54 etc.) for Greek *múrtos*. In other Greek words *y* has been retained. In the two native Latin words, *corulus* (1.14 etc.) and *serpullum* (2.11), the late Hellenizing spellings with *y* have been rejected.

Whether in addition to colloquialism in lexicon, morphology and syntax (see pp. 25–6 and index: *colloquialism*) Vergil also introduced popular and rustic spellings here and there in his text is difficult to determine, especially as some of these forms would coincide with common variants in post-classical orthography generally. Thus *(h)edos* for *haedos* (1.22 P, 3.34 V, 9.62 M) is inconclusive when *que* for *quae* (1.10 P), *ipse* for *ipsae* (1.38 P¹R¹) are also well attested in MSS of the other Vergilian works. *quodannis* is attested by PR¹ at 1.42, P²R at 5.67, V at 7.33, but does not occur epigraphically before the Empire (cf. *quot annis* at *CIL* 1.583.16, 124–3 B.C.) and so has not been admitted into the text. Velius Longus (*G.L.* 7.69–70) attests the 'correctness' of *at* (conjunction) but *ad* (preposition), *quit* (verb) but *quid* (pronoun), *quot* (numeral pronoun) but *quod* (relative), *apud* not *aput, sed* before voiced but *set* before unvoiced initials. The familiar spellings have been retained throughout, though it is at least possible that the colloquial phrase *si quit habes* (3.52 PR, 9.32 MP¹) was indeed thus written by Vergil himself. Similarly *possimus*, which is recorded as a variant of *possumus* in the Augustan period (Suet. *Aug.* 87.2, Mar. Vict. *G.L.* 6.9.5) may well be authentic in the proverbial phrase at 7.23 (M¹P¹Vr) and 8.63 (r). But it seemed expedient to retain the more familiar form.

THE ECLOGUES

SIGLA CODICVM

M (Mediceus) = Florentinus Laur. xxxix.1, saec. v
P (Palatinus) = Vaticanus Palatinus lat. 1631, saec. iv/v
R (Romanus) = Vaticanus lat. 3867, saec. v
V = fragmenta Veronensia, saec. v
M²P²R² corrector aliquis antiquus

Codices saeculi noni
  γ = Guelferbytanus Gudianus lat. 2°. 70
  a = Bernensis 172
  b = Bernensis 165
  d = Bernensis 255
  e = Bernensis 167
  f = Oxoniensis Bodl. Auct. F.2.8
  r = Parisinus lat. 7926
    ω = *consensus horum uel omnium uel quotquot non separatim nominantur*

α = codex Mediolanensis, saec. xiii–xiv

P. VERGILI MARONIS
BVCOLICA

ECLOGA I

MELIBOEVS   TITYRVS

M. Tityre, tu patulae recubans sub tegmine fagi
siluestrem tenui Musam meditaris auena;
nos patriae finis et dulcia linquimus arua.
nos patriam fugimus; tu, Tityre, lentus in umbra
formonsam resonare doces Amaryllida siluas.   5
T. O Meliboee, deus nobis haec otia fecit.
namque erit ille mihi semper deus, illius aram
saepe tener nostris ab ouilibus imbuet agnus.
ille meas errare boues, ut cernis, et ipsum
ludere quae uellem calamo permisit agresti.   10
M. Non equidem inuideo, miror magis; undique totis
usque adeo turbatur agris. en ipse capellas
protenus aeger ago; hanc etiam uix, Tityre, duco.
hic inter densas corulos modo namque gemellos,
spem gregis, a, silice in nuda conixa reliquit.   15
saepe malum hoc nobis, si mens non laeua fuisset,
de caelo tactas memini praedicere quercus.
sed tamen iste deus qui sit da, Tityre, nobis.
T. Vrbem quam dicunt Romam, Meliboee, putaui
stultus ego huic nostrae similem, quoi saepe solemus 20
pastores ouium teneros depellere fetus.
sic canibus catulos similes, sic matribus haedos

1.1–83 *PR*   bucolicon meliboeus tityrus *P*   2 agrestem *Quint.* 9.4.86
(*cf. Ecl.* 6.8)   12 turbatur α *Seru. Quint.* 1.4.28, *Consent. G.L.* 5.372.35:
turbamur *PR*γω *Philarg., reicit Seru.*   13 protenus γbα *Seru., Non.* 377:
protinus *PR*   20 quoi saepe *Burman*: quo saepe *P²R*: quaepe *P¹*

[43]

noram, sic paruis componere magna solebam.
uerum haec tantum alias inter caput extulit urbes
quantum lenta solent inter uiburna cupressi.   25
M. Et quae tanta fuit Romam tibi caussa uidendi?
 T. Libertas, quae sera tamen respexit inertem,
candidior postquam tondenti barba cadebat,
respexit tamen et longo post tempore uenit,
postquam nos Amaryllis habet, Galatea reliquit.   30
namque – fatebor enim – dum me Galatea tenebat,
nec spes libertatis erat nec cura peculi.
quamuis multa meis exiret uictima saeptis
pinguis et ingratae premeretur caseus urbi,
non umquam grauis aere domum mihi dextra redibat. 35
M. Mirabar quid maesta deos, Amarylli, uocares,
quoi pendere sua patereris in arbore poma.
Tityrus hinc aberat. ipsae te, Tityre, pinus,
ipsi te fontes, ipsa haec arbusta uocabant.
 T. Quid facerem? neque seruitio me exire licebat   40
nec tam praesentis alibi cognoscere diuos.
hic illum uidi iuuenem, Meliboee, quot annis
bis senos quoi nostra dies altaria fumant,
hic mihi responsum primus dedit ille petenti:
‘pascite ut ante boues, pueri, submittite tauros.’   45
M. Fortunate senex, ergo tua rura manebunt
et tibi magna satis, quamuis lapis omnia nudus
limosoque palus obducat pascua iunco.
non insueta grauis temptabunt pabula fetas
nec mala uicini pecoris contagia laedent.   50
fortunate senex, hic inter flumina nota
et fontis sacros frigus captabis opacum;
hinc tibi, quae semper, uicino ab limite saepes
Hyblaeis apibus florem depasta salicti
saepe leui somnum suadebit inire susurro;   55
hinc alta sub rupe canet frondator ad auras,

nec tamen interea raucae, tua cura, palumbes
nec gemere aeria cessabit turtur ab ulmo.

T. Ante leues ergo pascentur in aethere cerui
et freta destituent nudos in litore pisces,   60
ante pererratis amborum finibus exsul
aut Ararim Parthus bibet aut Germania Tigrim,
quam nostro illius labatur pectore uoltus.

M. At nos hinc alii sitientis ibimus Afros,
pars Scythiam et rapidum cretae ueniemus Oaxen   65
et penitus toto diuissos orbe Britannos.
en umquam patrios longo post tempore finis
pauperis et tuguri congestum caespite culmen,
post aliquot, mea regna, uidens mirabor aristas?
impius haec tam culta noualia miles habebit,   70
barbarus has segetes. en quo discordia ciuis
produxit miseros; his nos conseuimus agros!
insere nunc, Meliboee, piros, pone ordine uites.
ite meae, felix quondam pecus, ite capellae.
non ego uos posthac uiridi proiectus in antro   75
dumosa pendere procul de rupe uidebo;
carmina nulla canam; non me pascente, capellae,
florentem cutisum et salices carpetis amaras.

T. Hic tamen hanc mecum poteras requiescere noctem
fronde super uiridi. sunt nobis mitia poma,   80
castaneae molles et pressi copia lactis,
et iam summa procul uillarum culmina fumant
maioresque cadunt altis de montibus umbrae.

59 pascuntur *P*   62 ararem *P*   63 labantur *P¹*   65 cretae *nomen proprium accipit Seru. ad Ecl. 2.24, reicit Philarg.*   72 perduxit γ*bd*α his nos *PR*: en quis γα: en quos *d*   consueuimus agris *R¹*   74 quondam felix *P*   75 protectus *P¹*   78 calices *P¹*   79 hac...nocte *P²* poteris α *codd. Arus. G.L.* 7.505.25   83 a montibus *P¹*

ECLOGA II

Formonsum pastor Corydon ardebat Alexin,
delicias domini, nec quid speraret habebat.
tantum inter densas, umbrosa cacumina, fagos
adsidue ueniebat. ibi haec incondita solus
montibus et siluis studio iactabat inani: 5
    'O crudelis Alexi, nihil mea carmina curas?
nil nostri miserere? mori me denique cogis?
nunc etiam pecudes umbras et frigora captant,
nunc uirides etiam occultant spineta lacertos,
Thestylis et rapido fessis messoribus aestu   10
alia serpullumque herbas contundit olentis.
at mecum raucis, tua dum uestigia lustro,
sole sub ardenti resonant arbusta cicadis.
nonne fuit satius tristis Amaryllidos iras
atque superba pati fastidia? nonne Menalcan,   15
quamuis ille niger, quamuis tu candidus esses?
o formonse puer, nimium ne crede colori;
alba ligustra cadunt, uaccinia nigra leguntur.
    Despectus tibi sum nec qui sim quaeris, Alexi,
quam diues pecoris, niuei quam lactis abundans.   20
mille meae Siculis errant in montibus agnae;
lac mihi non aestate nouom, non frigore defit.
canto quae solitus, si quando armenta uocabat,
Amphion Dircaeus in Actaeo Aracyntho.
nec sum adeo informis; nuper me in litore uidi,   25
cum placidum uentis staret mare. non ego Daphnin
iudice te metuam, si numquam fallit imago.
    O tantum libeat mecum tibi sordida rura
atque humilis habitare casas et figere ceruos
haedorumque gregem uiridi compellere hibisco!   30

2.1–73 *PR*   poeta corydon *PR*   1 corydon pastor *R*   7 coges *R*
9 lacertas *P*¹   12 at γω *Seru.*: ad *P*: ac *R*: ad me cum *agnoscit Seru.*
tua nunc *P*¹   24 arctaeo *P*   27 fallat *P*¹*R* · fallet *hf*

mecum una in siluis imitabere Pana canendo.
Pan primum calamos cera coniungere pluris
instituit, Pan curat ouis ouiumque magistros;
nec te paeniteat calamo triuisse labellum.
haec eadem ut sciret, quid non faciebat Amyntas?   35
est mihi disparibus septem compacta cicutis
fistula, Damoetas dono mihi quam dedit olim
et dixit moriens: 'te nunc habet ista secundum';
dixit Damoetas, inuidit stultus Amyntas.
praeterea duo – nec tuta mihi ualle reperti –   40
capreoli sparsis etiam nunc pellibus albo,
bina die siccant ouis ubera; quos tibi seruo.
iam pridem a me illos abducere Thestylis orat;
et faciet, quoniam sordent tibi munera nostra.

Huc ades, o formonse puer. tibi lilia plenis   45
ecce ferunt Nymphae calathis; tibi candida Nais,
pallentis uiolas et summa papauera carpens,
narcissum et florem iungit bene olentis anethi;
tum casia atque aliis intexens suauibus herbis
mollia luteola pingit uaccinia caltha.   50
ipse ego cana legam tenera lanugine mala
castaneasque nuces, mea quas Amaryllis amabat;
addam cerea pruna – honos erit huic quoque pomo –
et uos, o lauri, carpam et te, proxuma murte,
sic positae quoniam suauis miscetis odores.   55
Rusticus es, Corydon; nec munera curat Alexis
nec, si muneribus certes, concedat Iollas.
heu heu, quid uolui misero mihi? floribus Austrum
perditus et liquidis inmissi fontibus apros.

Quem fugis, a, demens? habitarunt di quoque siluas   60
Dardaniusque Paris. Pallas quas condidit arces
ipsa colat; nobis placeant ante omnia siluae.

32 primus ωα codd. Seru. (ad Ecl. 3.25) et Philarg.   41 ambo R   42 quod R
47 papauere P   56 est P¹R   57 certet R   58 heheu P: eheu γabα
61 quase P¹: quae R

torua leaena lupum sequitur, lupus ipse capellam,
florentem cutisum sequitur lasciua capella,
te Corydon, o Alexi; trahit sua quemque uoluptas.   65
    Aspice, aratra iugo referunt suspensa iuuenci
et sol crescentis decedens duplicat umbras.
me tamen urit amor; quis enim modus adsit amori?
a, Corydon, Corydon, quae te dementia cepit!
semiputata tibi frondosà uitis in ulmo.   70
quin tu aliquid saltem potius, quorum indiget usus,
uiminibus mollique paras detexere iunco?
inuenies alium, si te hic fastidit, Alexin.'

ECLOGA III

MENALCAS DAMOETAS PALAEMON

M. Dic mihi, Damoeta, quoium pecus? an Meliboei?
D. Non, uerum Aegonos; nuper mihi tradidit Aegon.
M. Infelix o semper, oues, pecus! ipse Neaeram
  dum fouet ac ne me sibi praeferat illa ueretur,
  hic alienus ouis custos bis mulget in hora,   5
  et sucus pecori et lac subducitur agnis.
D. Parcius ista uiris tamen obicienda memento.
  nouimus et qui te transuersa tuentibus hirquis
  et quo – sed faciles Nymphae risere – sacello.
M. Tum, credo, cum me arbustum uidere Miconos   10
  atque mala uitis incidere falce nouellas.
D Aut hic ad ueteres fagos cum Daphnidos arcum
  fregisti et calamos, quae tu, peruerse Menalca,
  et, cum uidisti puero donata, dolebas
  et, si non aliqua nocuisses, mortuus esses.   15
M. Quid domini faciant, audent cum talia fures?
  non ego te uidi Damonos, pessime, caprum

70 ulmo est *R Seru.*   73 alexis *P¹*   3.1–26 *PR*   menalcas damoetas
palaemon *PR*   3 ouis *P*   4 ille *R*   16 facient γ¹α

excipere insidiis multum latrante Lycisca?
et cum clamarem 'quo nunc se proripit ille?
Tityre, coge pecus', tu post carecta latebas.   20
D. An mihi cantando uictus non redderet ille,
quem mea carminibus meruisset fistula caprum?
si nescis, meus ille caper fuit; et mihi Damon
ipse fatebatur sed reddere posse negabat.
M. Cantando tu illum? aut umquam tibi fistula cera   25
iuncta fuit? non tu in triuiis, indocte, solebas
stridenti miserum stipula disperdere carmen?
D. Vis ergo inter nos quid possit uterque uicissim
experiamur? ego hanc uitulam – ne forte recuses,
bis uenit ad mulctram, binos alit ubere fetus –   30
depono; tu dic mecum quo pignore certes.
M. De grege non ausim quicquam deponere tecum.
est mihi namque domi pater, est iniusta nouerca,
bisque die numerant ambo pecus, alter et haedos.
uerum, id quod multo tute ipse fatebere maius,   35
insanire libet quoniam tibi, pocula ponam
fagina, caelatum diuini opus Alcimedontos,
lenta quibus torno facili superaddita uitis
diffusos hedera uestit pallente corymbos.
in medio duo signa, Conon et – quis fuit alter,   40
descripsit radio totum qui gentibus orbem,
tempora quae messor, quae curuos arator haberet?
necdum illis labra admoui, sed condita seruo.
D. Et nobis idem Alcimedon duo pocula fecit
et molli circum est ansas amplexus acantho   45
Orpheaque in medio posuit siluasque sequentis;
necdum illis labra admoui sed condita seruo.
si ad uitulam spectas, nihil est quod pocula laudes.
M. Numquam hodie effugies; ueniam quocumque uocaris.

25 haut *ex Philarg.*: haud *d*   26 uincta *R*   27–52 *PRV*   27 stipula
miserum *V¹*   38 facili *Seru.*: facilis *V Don. ap. Seru.*: factis *P²*: faciis *P¹*:
fragilis *R*   41 toto *V¹*

audiat haec tantum uel qui uenit, ecce Palaemon.　50
efficiam posthac ne quemquam uoce lacessas.

D. Quin age, si quid habes; in me mora non erit ulla
nec quemquam fugio. tantum, uicine Palaemon,
sensibus haec imis – res est non parua – reponas.

P. Dicite, quandoquidem in molli consedimus herba.　55
et nunc omnis ager, nunc omnis parturit arbos,
nunc frondent siluae, nunc formonsissumus annus.
incipe, Damoeta; tu deinde sequere, Menalca.
alternis dicetis; amant alterna Camenae.

D. Ab Ioue principium Musae, Iouis omnia plena;　60
ille colit terras, illi mea carmina curae.

M. Et me Phoebus amat; Phoebo sua semper apud me
munera sunt, lauri et suaue rubens hyacinthus.

D. Malo me Galatea petit, lasciua puella,
et fugit ad salices et se cupit ante uideri.　65

M. At mihi sese offert ultro meus ignis, Amyntas,
notior ut iam sit canibus non Delia nostris.

D. Parta meae Veneri sunt munera; namque notaui
ipse locum aeriae quo congessere palumbes.

M. Quod potui, puero siluestri ex arbore lecta　70
aurea mala decem misi; cras altera mittam.

D. O quotiens et quae nobis Galatea locuta est!
partem aliquam, uenti, diuom referatis ad auris.

M. Quid prodest quod me ipse animo non spernis, Amynta,
si, dum tu sectaris apros, ego retia seruo?　75

D. Phyllida mitte mihi; meus est natalis, Iolla,
cum faciam uitula pro frugibus, ipse uenito.

M. Phyllida amo ante alias; nam me discedere fleuit
et longum 'formonse, uale, uale,' inquit, Iolla.

D. Triste lupus stabulis, maturis frugibus imbres,　80
arboribus uenti, nobis Amaryllidos irae.

M. Dulce satis umor, depulsis arbutus haedis,

53–71 PR　70 tecta P¹　72–111 R　77 uitula α Seru., Macrob. 3.2.15:
uitulam Rγ

lenta salix feto pecori, mihi solus Amyntas.
D. Pollio amat nostram, quamuis est rustica, Musam;
   Pierides, uitulam lectori pascite uestro.   85
M. Pollio et ipse facit noua carmina; pascite taurum,
   iam cornu petat et pedibus qui spargat harenam.
D. Qui te, Pollio, amat, ueniat quo te quoque gaudet;
   mella fluant illi, ferat et rubus asper amomum.
M. Qui Bauium non odit, amet tua carmina, Meui,   90
   atque idem iungat uolpes et mulgeat hirquos.
D. Qui legitis flores et humi nascentia fraga,
   frigidus – o pueri, fugite hinc – latet anguis in herba.
M. Parcite, oues, nimium procedere; non bene ripae
   creditur; ipse aries etiam nunc uellera siccat.   95
D. Tityre, pascentis a flumine reice capellas;
   ipse, ubi tempus erit, omnis in fonte lauabo.
M. Cogite oues, pueri; si lac praeceperit aestus,
   ut nuper, frustra pressabimus ubera palmis.   99
D. Heu heu, quam pingui macer est mihi taurus in eruo!
   idem amor exitium pecori pecorisque magistro.
M. His certe – neque amor caussa est – uix ossibus haerent;
   nescio quis teneros oculus mihi fascinat agnos.
D. Dic quibus in terris – et eris mihi magnus Apollo –
   tris pateat caeli spatium non amplius ulnas.   105
M. Dic quibus in terris inscripti nomina regum
   nascantur flores, et Phyllida solus habeto.
P. Non nostrum inter uos tantas componere lites:
   et uitula tu dignus et hic et quisquis amores
   aut metuet dulcis aut experietur amaros.   110
   claudite iam riuos, pueri; sat prata biberunt.

---

84 sit *bdα codd. Seru.*   91 mulceat *R*   97 fronte *R*   98 aestas *R*
100 eheu *b Seru. ad A.* 2.69, *codd. Philarg., Schol. Bern.*   eruo *γf codd. Seru.*
loc. cit.: aruo *R*   101 exitium est *Rγ²*   pecori est *γ¹b*   magistro est *r*
107 nascuntur *bdfα codd. Philarg. et Prob. G.L.* 4.213.20   110 amores *r*

ECLOGA IV

Sicelides Musae, paulo maiora canamus.
non omnis arbusta iuuant humilesque myricae;
si canimus siluas, siluae sint consule dignae.
    Vltima Cumaei uenit iam carminis aetas;
magnus ab integro saeclorum nascitur ordo.   5
iam redit et Virgo, redeunt Saturnia regna,
iam noua progenies caelo demittitur alto.
tu modo nascenti puero, quo ferrea primum
desinet ac toto surget gens aurea mundo,
casta faue Lucina; tuus iam regnat Apollo.   10
    Teque adeo decus hoc aeui, te consule, inibit,
Pollio, et incipient magni procedere menses;
te duce, si qua manent sceleris uestigia nostri,
inrita perpetua soluent formidine terras.
ille deum uitam accipiet diuisque uidebit   15
permixtos heroas et ipse uidebitur illis
pacatumque reget patriis uirtutibus orbem.
    At tibi prima, puer, nullo munuscula cultu
errantis hederas passim cum baccare tellus
mixtaque ridenti colocasia fundet acantho.   20
ipsae lacte domum referent distenta capellae
ubera nec magnos metuent armenta leones;
ipsa tibi blandos fundent cunabula flores.
occidet et serpens et fallax herba ueneni
occidet; Assyrium uolgo nascetur amomum.   25
    At simul heroum laudes et facta parentis
iam legere et quae sit poteris cognoscere uirtus,
molli paulatim flauescet campus arista
incultisque rubens pendebit sentibus uua

    4. 1–51 R   saeculi noui interpraetatio R   7 demittitur γ*er*: dimittitur
R   17 patris R¹   18 ac tibi nulla pater primo R   20 fundit γ¹ *codd.*
Macrob. 6.6.18   21 referant γ¹   26 ac R   parentis γ¹ω *Seru., codd.*
Philarg.: parentum R   28 flauescet γ²*der*: flauescit R

et durae quercus sudabunt roscida mella.   30
   Pauca tamen suberunt priscae uestigia fraudis,
quae temptare Thetin ratibus, quae cingere muris
oppida, quae iubeant telluri infindere sulcos.
alter erit tum Tiphys et altera quae uehat Argo
delectos heroas; erunt etiam altera bella   35
atque iterum ad Troiam magnus mittetur Achilles.
   Hinc, ubi iam firmata uirum te fecerit aetas,
cedet et ipse mari uector nec nautica pinus
mutabit merces; omnis feret omnia tellus.
non rastros patietur humus, non uinea falcem,   40
robustus quoque iam tauris iuga soluet arator;
nec uarios discet mentiri lana colores,
ipse sed in pratis aries iam suaue rubenti
murice, iam croceo mutabit uellera luto,
sponte sua sandyx pascentis uestiet agnos.   45
   'Talia saecla' suis dixerunt 'currite' fusis
concordes stabili fatorum numine Parcae.
   Adgredere o magnos – aderit iam tempus – honores,
cara deum suboles, magnum Iouis incrementum.
aspice conuexo nutantem pondere mundum,   50
terrasque tractusque maris caelumque profundum;
aspice, uenturo laetantur ut omnia saeclo.
   O mihi tum longae maneat pars ultima uitae,
spiritus et quantum sat erit tua dicere facta:
non me carminibus uincat nec Thracius Orpheus   55
nec Linus, huic mater quamuis atque huic pater adsit,
Orphei Calliopea, Lino formonsus Apollo.
Pan etiam, Arcadia mecum si iudice certet,
Pan etiam Arcadia dicat se iudice uictum.
   Incipe, parue puer, risu cognoscere matrem;   60

---

33 tellurem...sulco *R*   48 magnus *R*   52–63 *PR*   52 laetentur *P*
53 longe *P*   55 uincet *P²R*   teracius (< traecius?) *P¹*   56 adste
(< adstet?) *P¹* 58 arcadiedicacat (*cf. uers. seq.*) *P¹*   59 arcadiaedicat
R: arcadiedicacat *P¹*: arcadiadicet *P²* *codd. Macrob.* 5.14.6

matri longa decem tulerunt fastidia menses.
incipe, parue puer. qui non risere parenti,
nec deus hunc mensa dea nec dignata cubili est.

ECLOGA V

MENALCAS   MOPSVS

Me. Cur non, Mopse, boni quoniam conuenimus ambo,
tu calamos inflare leuis, ego dicere uersus,
hic corulis mixtas inter consedimus ulmos?
Mo. Tu maior; tibi me est aecum parere, Menalca,
siue sub incertas Zephyris motantibus umbras   5
siue antro potius succedimus. aspice ut antrum
siluestris raris sparsit labrusca racemis.
Me. Montibus in nostris solus tibi certat Amyntas.
Mo. Quid, si idem certet Phoebum superare canendo?
Me. Incipe, Mopse, prior, si quos aut Phyllidos ignes   10
aut Alconos habes laudes aut iurgia Codri.
incipe; pascentis seruabit Tityrus haedos.
Mo. Immo haec, in uiridi nuper quae cortice fagi
carmina descripsi et modulans alterna notaui,
experiar. tu deinde iubeto certet Amyntas.   15
Me. Lenta salix quantum pallenti cedit oliuae,
puniceis humilis quantum saliunca rosetis,
iudicio nostro tantum tibi cedit Amyntas.
sed tu desine plura, puer; successimus antro.
Mo. Exstinctum Nymphae crudeli funere Daphnin   20
flebant – uos coruli testes et flumina Nymphis –
cum complexa sui corpus miserabile nati
atque deos atque astra uocat crudelia mater.

61 matris *P²*   tulerant *de*α: tulerint *l·*: abstulerint 'alii' ap. Seru.   62
qui *Quint.* 9.3.8 corr. *Politianus*: cui *PR Seru., codd. Quint.* parenti *Quint.*
corr. *Schrader*: parentes *PR Seru., codd. Quint.*   63 cubile est *P²*: cubilest *R*
5.1–85 *PR*   menalcas mopsus *PR*   3 considimus γ²*de*   8 certet *P*
15 iubeto ut certet *R*

non ulli pastos illis egere diebus
frigida, Daphni, boues ad flumina, nulla neque amnem 25
libauit quadrupes nec graminis attigit herbam.
Daphni, tuum Poenos etiam ingemuisse leones
interitum montesque feri siluaeque locuntur.
Daphnis et Armenias curru subiungere tigris
instituit, Daphnis thiasos inducere Bacchi 30
et foliis lentas intexere mollibus hastas.
uitis ut arboribus decori est, ut uitibus uuae,
ut gregibus tauri, segetes ut pinguibus aruis,
tu decus omne tuis. postquam te fata tulerunt,
ipsa Pales agros atque ipse reliquit Apollo. 35
grandia saepe quibus mandauimus hordea sulcis,
infelix lolium et steriles nascuntur auenae;
pro molli uiola, pro purpureo narcisso
carduos et spinis surgit paliurus acutis.
spargite humum foliis, inducite fontibus umbras, 40
pastores – mandat fieri sibi talia Daphnis –
et tumulum facite et tumulo superaddite carmen:
'Daphnis ego in siluis, hinc usque ad sidera notus,
formonsi pecoris custos, formonsior ipse.'
Me. Tale tuum carmen nobis, diuine poeta, 45
quale sopor fessis in gramine, quale per aestum
dulcis aquae saliente sitim restinguere riuo.
nec calamis solum aequiperas sed uoce magistrum:
fortunate puer, tu nunc eris alter ab illo.
nos tamen haec quocumque modo tibi nostra uicissim 50
dicemus, Daphninque tuum tollemus ad astra,
Daphnin ad astra feremus; amauit nos quoque Daphnis.
Mo. An quicquam nobis tali sit munere maius?
et puer ipse fuit cantari dignus et ista
iam pridem Stimichon laudauit carmina nobis. 55

27 gemuisse *R*   28 ferunt *P* siluaesque *P*¹   38 uiolae *P*¹: uiola
et *R*   purpurea *Diom. G.L.* 1.453.36   40 aras *R*   46 lassis *R*
49 apollo *R*   50–1 *ordinem turbauit P*¹

Me. Candidus insuetum miratur limen Olympi
    sub pedibusque uidet nubes et sidera Daphnis.
    ergo alacris siluas et cetera rura uoluptas
    Panaque pastoresque tenet Dryadasque puellas.
    nec lupus insidias pecori nec retia ceruis   60
    ulla dolum meditantur; amat bonus otia Daphnis.
    ipsi laetitia uoces ad sidera iactant
    intonsi montes, ipsae iam carmina rupes,
    ipsa sonant arbusta: 'deus, deus ille, Menalca.'
    sis bonus o felixque tuis. en quattuor aras;   65
    ecce duas tibi, Daphni, duas altaria Phoebo.
    pocula bina nouo spumantia lacte quot annis
    craterasque duo statuam tibi pinguis oliui
    et multo in primis hilarans conuiuia Baccho
    ante focum, si frigus erit, si messis, in umbra   70
    uina nouom fundam calathis Ariusia nectar.
    cantabunt mihi Damoetas et Lyctius Aegon;
    saltantis Satyros imitabitur Alphesiboeus.
    haec tibi semper erunt, et cum sollemnia uota
    reddemus Nymphis et cum lustrabimus agros.   75
    dum iuga montis aper, fluuios dum piscis amabit,
    dumque thymo pascentur apes, dum rore cicadae,
    semper honos nomenque tuum laudesque manebunt.
    ut Baccho Cererique, tibi sic uota quot annis
    agricolae facient; damnabis tu quoque uotis.   80
Mo. Quae tibi, quae tali reddam pro carmine dona?
    nam neque me tantum uenientis sibilus Austri
    nec percussa iuuant fluctu tam litora nec quae
    saxosas inter decurrunt flumina ualles.
Me. Hac te nos fragili donabimus ante cicuta;   85
    haec nos 'formonsum Corydon ardebat Alexin',
    haec eadem docuit 'quoium pecus? an Meliboei?'

61 modum *R*[1]   63 ipsa etiam *R*   66 duoque altaria α *codd.*
D.Seru. ad A. 3.305   68 duos *fr*   80 uoti *R*[1]   85 donauimus *R*[2]
86–90 *PRV*

Mo. At tu sume pedum quod, me cum saepe rogaret,
  non tulit Antigenes – et erat tunc dignus amari –
  formonsum paribus nodis atque aere, Menalca.   90

ECLOGA VI

Prima Syracosio dignata est ludere uersu
nostra nec erubuit siluas habitare Thalea.
cum canerem reges et proelia, Cynthius aurem
uellit et admonuit: 'pastorem, Tityre, pinguis
pascere oportet ouis, deductum dicere carmen.'   5
nunc ego – namque super tibi erunt qui dicere laudes,
Vare, tuas cupiant et tristia condere bella –
agrestem tenui meditabor harundine Musam.
non iniussa cano. si quis tamen haec quoque, si quis
captus amore leget, te nostrae, Vare, myricae,   10
te nemus omne canet; nec Phoebo gratior ulla est
quam sibi quae Vari praescripsit pagina nomen.
  Pergite, Pierides. Chromis et Mnasyllos in antro
Silenum pueri somno uidere iacentem,
inflatum hesterno uenas, ut semper, Iaccho;   15
serta procul tantum capiti delapsa iacebant
et grauis attrita pendebat cantharus ansa.
adgressi – nam saepe senex spe carminis ambo
luserat – iniciunt ipsis ex uincula sertis.
addit se sociam timidisque superuenit Aegle,   20
Aegle Naiadum pulcherrima, iamque uidenti
sanguineis frontem moris et tempora pingit.
ille dolum ridens 'quo uincula nectitis?' inquit;
'soluite me, pueri; satis est potuisse uideri.
carmina quae uoltis cognoscite; carmina uobis,   25

89 nunc *P¹*: tum *RV*   6.1–20 *PRV*   faunorum satyrorum (et *R*) silenorum delectatio (di- *P*) *PR*   2 siluis *R*   5 deductum *R Seru.*: diductum *PV*   10 legat *dα Prisc. G.L.* 3.246.5   12 perscripsit *γf* 16 iacebat *PV?*   21–47 *PR*   21 namque *P¹*   23 inridens *P¹*

huic aliud mercedis erit.' simul incipit ipse.
tum uero in numerum Faunosque ferasque uideres
ludere, tum rigidas motare cacumina quercus;
nec tantum Phoebo gaudet Parnasia rupes
nec tantum Rhodope miratur et Ismaros Orphea.   30
    Namque canebat uti magnum per inane coacta
semina terrarumque animaeque marisque fuissent
et liquidi simul ignis; ut his exordia primis
omnia et ipse tener mundi concreuerit orbis;
tum durare solum et discludere Nerea ponto   35
coeperit et rerum paulatim sumere formas;
iamque nouom terrae stupeant lucescere solem
altius atque cadant submotis nubibus imbres,
incipiant siluae cum primum surgere cumque
rara per ignaros errent animalia montis.   40
    Hinc lapides Pyrrhae iactos, Saturnia regna,
Caucasiasque refert uolucres furtumque Promethei.
his adiungit Hylan nautae quo fonte relictum
clamassent, ut litus 'Hyla, Hyla' omne sonaret;
et fortunatam, si numquam armenta fuissent,   45
Pasiphaen niuei solatur amore iuuenci.
a, uirgo infelix, quae te dementia cepit!
Proetides implerunt falsis mugitibus agros;
at non tam turpis pecudum tamen ulla secuta
concubitus, quamuis collo timuisset aratrum   50
et saepe in leui quaesisset cornua fronte.
a, uirgo infelix, tu nunc in montibus erras;
ille latus niueum molli fultus hyacintho
ilice sub nigra pallentis ruminat herbas
aut aliquam in magno sequitur grege. 'claudite,
                                                    Nymphae,   55

30 mirantur *R*   33 exordia *R codd. Seru. et Macrob.* 6.2.22: ex omnia *P*
34 omnia *R Seru.*: omnisa *P*¹: omnis *Kirsch*   38 utque *R*   signibus (<igni-
bus) *R*   40 ignotos *P*   41 hic *P*   48–86 *MPR*   49 secuta est *R*
50 timuissent *R*   51 quesissent *P*

Dictaeae Nymphae, nemorum iam claudite saltus,
si qua forte ferant oculis sese obuia nostris
errabunda bouis uestigia; forsitan illum
aut herba captum uiridi aut armenta secutum
perducant aliquae stabula ad Gortynia uaccae.'   60
tum canit Hesperidum miratam mala puellam;
tum Phaethontiadas musco circumdat amarae
corticis atque solo proceras erigit alnos.

   Tum canit errantem Permessi ad flumina Gallum
Aonas in montis ut duxerit una sororum   65
utque uiro Phoebi chorus adsurrexerit omnis;
ut Linus haec illi diuino carmine pastor
floribus atque apio crinis ornatus amaro
dixerit: 'hos tibi dant calamos – en accipe – Musae,
Ascraeo quos ante seni, quibus ille solebat   70
cantando rigidas deducere montibus ornos.
his tibi Grynei nemoris dicatur origo,
ne qui sit lucus quo se plus iactet Apollo.'

   Quid loquar aut Scyllam Nisi, quam fama secuta est
candida succinctam latrantibus inguina monstris   75
Dulichias uexasse rates et gurgite in alto,
a, timidos nautas canibus lacerasse marinis;
aut ut mutatos Terei narrauerit artus,
quas illi Philomela dapes, quae dona pararit,
quo cursu deserta petiuerit et quibus ante   80
infelix sua tecta super uolitauerit alis?

   Omnia quae Phoebo quondam meditante beatus
audiit Eurotas iussitque ediscere lauros
ille canit, pulsae referunt ad sidera ualles,
cogere donec ouis stabulis numerumque referre   85
iussit et inuito processit Vesper Olympo.

61 capit *M*¹   62 amaro *R*   73 nec *P*²*R*   74 ut Scyllam *R*   aut quam
agnoscit Seru.   78 narrauerat actus *R*   79 pararet *P*¹   81 supra *R*
ales *M*¹*R*   83 audit (= audit?) *R*   85 referri *M*¹*P*¹

ECLOGA VII

MELIBOEVS CORYDON THYRSIS

M. Forte sub arguta consederat ilice Daphnis,
compulerantque greges Corydon et Thyrsis in unum,
Thyrsis ouis, Corydon distentas lacte capellas,
ambo florentes aetatibus, Arcades ambo,
et cantare pares et respondere parati.   5
huc mihi, dum teneras defendo a frigore murtos,
uir gregis ipse caper deerrauerat atque ego Daphnin
aspicio. ille ubi me contra uidet, 'ocius' inquit
'huc ades, o Meliboee; caper tibi saluos et haedi;
et, si quid cessare potes, requiesce sub umbra.   10
huc ipsi potum uenient per prata iuuenci,
hic uiridis tenera praetexit harundine ripas
Mincius eque sacra resonant examina quercu.'
quid facerem? neque ego Alcippen nec Phyllida habebam
depulsos a lacte domi quae clauderet agnos,   15
et certamen erat, Corydon cum Thyrside, magnum;
posthabui tamen illorum mea seria ludo.
alternis igitur contendere uersibus ambo
coepere; alternos Musae meminisse uolebant.
hos Corydon, illos referebat in ordine Thyrsis.   20
C. Nymphae, noster amor, Libethrides, aut mihi carmen
quale meo Codro concedite – proxima Phoebi
uersibus ille facit – aut, si non possumus omnes,
hic arguta sacra pendebit fistula pinu.
T. Pastores, hedera crescentem ornate poetam,   25
Arcades, inuidia rumpantur ut ilia Codro;
aut, si ultra placitum laudarit, baccare frontem

7.1–11 *MP*   meliboeus corydon thyrsis *MP*   6 hic *P*   11 ueniunt *a*
12–36 *MPV*   13 et quae *M*¹: atque α¹   15 hedos *M*¹   19 uolebam
'*multi*' *ap. Seru.*   22 phoebo *V*   24 pendebis *D.Seru.*   25 crescentem *M*³*P Seru. ad E.* 4.19: nascentem *M*²*V Seru.*: nascente *M*¹   27 laudauit
V?γ¹

cingite, ne uati noceat mala lingua futuro.

C. Saetosi caput hoc apri tibi, Delia, paruos
et ramosa Micon uiuacis cornua cerui. 30
si proprium hoc fuerit, leui de marmore tota
puniceo stabis suras euincta coturno.

T. Sinum lactis et haec te liba, Priape, quot annis
exspectare sat est; custos es pauperis horti.
nunc te marmoreum pro tempore fecimus; at tu, 35
si fetura gregem suppleuerit, aureus esto.

C. Nereine Galatea, thymo mihi dulcior Hyblae,
candidior cycnis, hedera formonsior alba,
cum primum pasti repetent praesaepia tauri,
si qua tui Corydonos habet te cura, uenito. 40

T. Immo ego Sardoniis uidear tibi amarior herbis,
horridior rusco, proiecta uilior alga,
si mihi non haec lux toto iam longior anno est.
ite domum pasti, si quis pudor, ite iuuenci.

C. Muscosi fontes et somno mollior herba, 45
et quae uos rara uiridis tegit arbutus umbra,
solstitium pecori defendite: iam uenit aestas
torrida, iam lento turgent in palmite gemmae.

T. Hic focus et taedae pingues, hic plurimus ignis
semper, et adsidua postes fuligine nigri. 50
hic tantum Boreae curamus frigora quantum
aut numerum lupus aut torrentia flumina ripas.

C. Stant et iuniperi et castaneae hirsutae,
strata iacent passim sua quaeque sub arbore poma,
omnia nunc rident. at si formonsus Alexis 55
montibus his abeat, uideas et flumina sicca.

T. Aret ager, uitio moriens sitit aeris herba,
Liber pampineas inuidit collibus umbras.

29 capri 'multi' ap. D.Seru.   30 mycon *M¹PV*   37–70 *MP*   41 uideor *P¹*   48 tam *P¹*   lento *M²P*: laeto *M¹γω*   51 hinc γ¹ 'nonnulli'
ap. D.Seru.   52 ripa *PM¹?*   54 quaque *b¹*   56 aberit *P²*: aberi-
turt *P¹*

  Phyllidos aduentu nostrae nemus omne uirebit,
  Iuppiter et laeto descendet plurimus imbri.   60
C. Populus Alcidae gratissima, uitis Iaccho,
  formonsae murtus Veneri, sua laurea Phoebo;
  Phyllis amat corulos; illas dum Phyllis amabit,
  nec murtus uincet corulos nec laurea Phoebi.
T. Fraxinus in siluis pulcherrima, pinus in hortis, 65
  populus in fluuiis, abies in montibus altis;
  saepius at si me, Lycida formonse, reuisas,
  fraxinus in siluis cedat tibi, pinus in hortis.
M. Haec memini, et uictum frustra contendere Thyrsin.
  ex illo Corydon, Corydon est tempore nobis.   70

ECLOGA VIII

  Pastorum Musam Damonos et Alphesiboei,
  immemor herbarum quos est mirata iuuenca
  certantis, quorum stupefactae carmine lynces,
  et mutata suos requierunt flumina cursus,
  Damonos Musam dicemus et Alphesiboei.   5
  tu mihi seu magni superas iam saxa Timaui
  siue oram Illyrici legis aequoris, en erit umquam
  ille dies mihi cum liceat tua dicere facta?
  en erit ut liceat totum mihi ferre per orbem
  sola Sophocleo tua carmina digna coturno?   10
  a te principium, tibi desinam. accipe iussis
  carmina coepta tuis atque hanc sine tempora circum
  intra uictrices hederam tibi serpere lauros.
   Frigida uix caelo noctis decesserat umbra,
  cum ros in tenera pecori gratissimus herba.   15
  incumbens tereti Damon sic coepit oliuae.

---

64 uincet ueneris *Hebri exemplar ap. D.Seru.* 67 ac *M*¹ 68 cedet *P*
69 concedere *a* 8.1–18 *MP* damonis et alphesiboei certamen (certa-
tio *M*) *MP* 4 liquerunt γ²: linquerunt γ¹ 6 tum mihi *P*¹ 11 desinet
*M*γ²ωα *D.Seru., Schol. Bern.*: desinit *br*

D.   Nascere praeque diem ueniens age, Lucifer, almum,
coniugis indigno Nysae deceptus amore
dum queror et diuos, quamquam nil testibus illis
profeci, extrema moriens tamen adloquor hora.   20
  incipe Maenalios mecum, mea tibia, uersus.
Maenalus argutumque nemus pinusque loquentis
semper habet, semper pastorum ille audit amores
Panaque, qui primus calamos non passus inertis.
  incipe Maenalios mecum, mea tibia, uersus.   25
Mopso Nysa datur. quid non speremus amantes?
iungentur iam grypes equis aeuoque sequenti
cum canibus timidi uenient ad pocula dammae.
  incipe Maenalios mecum, mea tibia, uersus.   28a
Mopse, nouas incide faces; tibi ducitur uxor.
sparge, marite, nuces; tibi deserit Hesperos Oetan.   30
  incipe Maenalios mecum, mea tibia, uersus.
o digno coniuncta uiro, dum despicis omnis
dumque tibi est odio mea fistula dumque capellae
hirsutumque supercilium promissaque barba,
nec curare deum credis mortalia quemquam.   35
  incipe Maenalios mecum, mea tibia, uersus.
saepibus in nostris paruam te roscida mala
– dux ego uester eram – uidi cum matre legentem.
alter ab undecimo tum me iam acceperat annus,
iam fragilis poteram a terra contingere ramos.   40
ut uidi, ut perii, ut me malus abstulit error!
  incipe Maenalios mecum, mea tibia, uersus.
nunc scio quid sit Amor; duris in cotibus illum
aut Tmaros aut Rhodope aut extremi Garamantes
nec generis nostri puerum nec sanguinis edunt.   45
  incipe Maenalios mecum, mea tibia, uersus.

18 nisae *M*¹   19–44 *MPV*   20 adloquar *M*¹*P*²*V?*   24 primum *M*:
euanuit in V   26 nisa *V*   28 timidae *M Seru. ad A.* 5.122: timide
*P*¹   *inter* 28 *et* 29 *uersum intercalarem habet* γ, *omittunt ceteri*   34 demis-
saque *P*: prolixaque α: *euanuit in V*   43 qui *a* nudis *P*¹   44 maros
MP: tmarus *V*: ismarus *codd. Seru. et Philarg.*   45–109 *MP*

saeuos Amor docuit natorum sanguine matrem
commaculare manus. crudelis tu quoque, mater.
crudelis mater magis, an puer improbus ille?
improbus ille puer; crudelis tu quoque, mater.   50
    incipe Maenalios mecum, mea tibia, uersus.
nunc et ouis ultro fugiat lupus, aurea durae
mala ferant quercus, narcisso floreat alnus,
pinguia corticibus sudent electra myricae,
certent et cycnis ululae, sit Tityrus Orpheus,   55
Orpheus in siluis, inter delphinas Arion.
    incipe Maenalios mecum, mea tibia, uersus.
omnia uel medium fiat mare. uiuite siluae.
praeceps aerii specula de montis in undas
deferar; extremum hoc munus morientis habeto.   60
    desine Maenalios, iam desine, tibia, uersus.
    Haec Damon. uos quae respꝏnderit Alphesiboeus
dicite, Pierides; non omnia possumus omnes.

A.   Effer aquam et molli cinge haec altaria uitta
uerbenasque adole pinguis et mascula tura,   65
coniugis ut magicis sanos auertere sacris
experiar sensus. nihil hic nisi carmina desunt.
    ducite ab urbe domum, mea carmina, ducite Daphnin.
carmina uel caelo possunt deducere lunam,
carminibus Circe socios mutauit Vlixi,   70
frigidus in pratis cantando rumpitur anguis.
    ducite ab urbe domum, mea carmina, ducite Daphnin.
terna tibi haec primum triplici diuersa colore
licia circumdo terque haec altaria circum
effigiem duco. numero deus impare gaudet.   75
    ducite ab urbe domum, mea carmina, ducite Daphnin.
necte tribus nodis ternos, Amarylli, colores;
necte, Amarylli, modo et 'Veneris' dic 'uincula necto.'
    ducite ab urbe domum, mea carmina, ducite Daphnin.

58 fiat *MP D. Seru.*: fiant γ'ωα *codd. Philarg. et Prisc.* (*G.L.* 2.465.29)
70 ulixis γωα *Schol. Bern.*: olyxis *CIL* 4.1982   76 *habent codd. omnes*

limus ut hic durescit et haec ut cera liquescit   80
uno eodemque igni, sic nostro Daphnis amore.
sparge molam et fragilis incende bitumine laurus;
Daphnis me malus urit, ego hanc in Daphnide laurum.
    ducite ab urbe domum, mea carmina, ducite Daphnin.
talis amor Daphnin qualis cum fessa iuuencum   85
per nemora atque altos quaerendo bucula lucos
propter aquae riuom uiridi procumbit in ulua
perdita nec serae meminit decedere nocti,
talis amor teneat nec sit mihi cura mederi.   89
    ducite ab urbe domum, mea carmina, ducite Daphnin.
has olim exuuias mihi perfidus ille reliquit,
pignora cara sui, quae nunc ego limine in ipso,
Terra, tibi mando; debent haec pignora Daphnin.
    ducite ab urbe domum, mea carmina, ducite Daphnin.
has herbas atque haec Ponto mihi lecta uenena   95
ipse dedit Moeris – nascuntur pluruma Ponto.
his ego saepe lupum fieri et se condere siluis
Moerin, saepe animas imis excire sepulcris
atque satas alio uidi traducere messis.   99
    ducite ab urbe domum, mea carmina, ducite Daphnin.
fer cineres, Amarylli, foras riuoque fluenti
transque caput iace, nec respexeris. his ego Daphnin
adgrediar; nihil ille deos, nil carmina curat.
    ducite ab urbe domum, mea carmina, ducite Daphnin.
aspice, corripuit tremulis altaria flammis   105
sponte sua, dum ferre moror, cinis ipse. bonum sit!
nescio quid certe est et Hylax in limine latrat.
credimus? an qui amant ipsi sibi somnia fingunt?
    parcite, ab urbe uenit, iam parcite carmina, Daphnis.

87 concumbit *P*¹   102 ne *P*²   107 certi est *M*² hylax *ed. Ascensiana*
1500: hylas *codd.*   109 iam carmina parcite *M*

ECLOGA IX

LYCIDAS MOERIS

L. Quo te, Moeri, pedes? an, quo uia ducit, in urbem?
M. O Lycida, uiui peruenimus, aduena nostri
    – quod numquam ueriti sumus – ut possessor agelli
    diceret: 'haec mea sunt; ueteres migrate coloni.'
    nunc uicti, tristes, quoniam fors omnia uersat,   5
    hos illi – quod nec bene uertat – mittimus haedos.
L. Certe equidem audieram, qua se subducere colles
    incipiunt mollique iugum demittere cliuo
    usque ad aquam et ueteres, iam fracta cacumina, fagos,
    omnia carminibus uestrum seruasse Menalcan.   10
M. Audieras et fama fuit; sed carmina tantum
    nostra ualent, Lycida, tela inter Martia quantum
    Chaonias dicunt aquila ueniente columbas.
    quod nisi me quacumque nouas incidere lites
    ante sinistra caua monuisset ab ilice cornix,   15
    nec tuus hic Moeris nec uiueret ipse Menalcas.
L. Heu, cadit in quemquam tantum scelus? heu, tua nobis
    paene simul tecum solacia rapta, Menalca!
    quis caneret Nymphas? quis humum florentibus herbis
    spargeret aut uiridi fontes induceret umbra?   20
    uel quae sublegi tacitus tibi carmina nuper,
    cum te ad delicias ferres Amaryllida nostras?
    'Tityre, dum redeo – breuis est uia – pasce capellas
    et potum pastas age, Tityre, et inter agendum
    occursare capro – cornu ferit ille – caueto.'   25
M. Immo haec, quae Varo necdum perfecta canebat:
    'Vare, tuum nomen, superet modo Mantua nobis,

9.1–67 *MP*   lycidas (lycida *M*) moeris *MP*   1 orbem *P*[1]   6 quos
M[2] bene uertat *P*[2]γ[1]*fα Seru.*: uertat bene *MP*[1]γ[2]   8 incipiant *P*[1]
dimittere ωα *codd. D.Seru. et Quint.* 8.6.46   9 ueteris...fagi *P*γ[1]ωα *codd.*
Philarg. et Quint. loc. cit.   11 audierat *M*[1]*P*[1]   14 quocumque *P*   17
cadet *P*   25 feret *M*[1]   27 uare *Seru.*: bare *M*: uere *P*?

Mantua uae miserae nimium uicina Cremonae,
cantantes sublime ferent ad sidera cycni.'

L. Sic tua Cyrneas fugiant examina taxos,   30
   sic cutiso pastae distendant ubera uaccae;
   incipe, si quid habes. et me fecere poetam
   Pierides, sunt et mihi carmina, me quoque dicunt
   uatem pastores, sed non ego credulus illis.
   nam neque adhuc Vario uideor nec dicere Cinna   35
   digna sed argutos inter strepere anser olores.

M. Id quidem ago et tacitus, Lycida, mecum ipse uoluto,
   si ualeam meminisse; neque est ignobile carmen.
   'huc ades, o Galatea; quis est nam ludus in undis?
   hic uer purpureum, uarios hic flumina circum   40
   fundit humus flores, hic candida populus antro
   imminet et lentae texunt umbracula uites.
   huc ades; insani feriant sine litora fluctus.'
   quid quae te pura solum sub nocte canentem
   audieram? numeros memini, si uerba tenerem.   45

L. 'Daphni, quid antiquos signorum suspicis ortus?
   ecce Dionaei processit Caesaris astrum,
   astrum quo segetes gauderent frugibus et quo
   duceret apricis in collibus uua colorem.
   insere, Daphni, piros; carpent tua poma nepotes.'   50

M. Omnia fert aetas, animum quoque. saepe ego longos
   cantando puerum memini me condere soles.
   nunc oblita mihi tot carmina, uox quoque Moerin
   iam fugit ipsa; lupi Moerin uidere priores.
   sed tamen ista satis referet tibi saepe Menalcas.   55

L. Caussando nostros in longum ducis amores.
   et nunc omne tibi stratum silet aequor et omnes,
   aspice, uentosi ceciderunt murmuris aurae.

---

29 ferant P²   30 cyrneas M¹Seru.: cryneas M²: gryneas γ cod. Schol.
Bern.: grynaeas P   35 uaro MP? 'alii' ap. D.Seru.   42 tentae M
44–5 Lycidae continuant codd.   45 tenebam P¹   46–50 tribuunt Lycidae
MP¹γα, Moeridi P²ω D.Seru., Philarg.   51 fert setas (<fers (a)etas?) P¹

hinc adeo media est nobis uia; namque sepulcrum
incipit apparere Bianoris. hic, ubi densas 60
agricolae stringunt frondis, hic, Moeri, canamus;
hic haedos depone, tamen ueniemus in urbem.
aut si nox pluuiam ne colligat ante ueremur,
cantantes licet usque – minus uia laedet – eamus;
cantantes ut eamus, ego hoc te fasce leuabo. 65
M. Desine plura, puer, et quod nunc instat agamus.
carmina tum melius, cum uenerit ipse, canemus.

ECLOGA X

Extremum hunc, Arethusa, mihi concede laborem.
pauca meo Gallo sed quae legat ipsa Lycoris
carmina sunt dicenda. neget quis carmina Gallo?
sic tibi, cum fluctus subterlabere Sicanos,
Doris amara suam non intermisceat undam, 5
incipe. sollicitos Galli dicamus amores,
dum tenera attondent simae uirgulta capellae.
non canimus surdis, respondent omnia siluae.
    Quae nemora aut qui uos saltus habuere, puellae
Naides, indigno cum Gallus amore peribat? 10
nam neque Parnasi uobis iuga, nam neque Pindi
ulla moram fecere neque Aonie Aganippe.
illum etiam lauri, etiam fleuere myricae,
pinifer illum etiam sola sub rupe iacentem
Maenalus et gelidi fleuerunt saxa Lycaei. 15
stant et oues circum; nostri nec paenitet illas
nec te paeniteat pecoris, diuine poeta:
et formonsus ouis ad flumina pauit Adonis.

59 hic *P*   60 bianori *P¹*   64 laedet *P* γ²ωα *Seru.?*: laedit *M*γ¹:
laedat *f*   66 puer et quod *P²*: puer quod *M¹*: puer nunc quod *M²?P¹*
10.1–9 *MP* conquestio cum gallo poeta de agris *M*: conquaesitio de agris
cum gallo cornelio *P*   1 laborum *P¹*   10–77 *MPR*   10 periret *M¹*
12 aonie *af*α *Seru.*: aoinie *Rb*: aoniae *MP*γ*der Vlt. Syll. G.L.* 4.258.10
13 etiam 2°] illum *Ra¹*: illum etiam *a¹*

uenit et upilio, tardi uenere subulci,
uuidus hiberna uenit de glande Menalcas.   20
omnes 'unde amor iste' rogant 'tibi?' uenit Apollo:
'Galle, quid insanis?' inquit. 'tua cura Lycoris
perque niues alium perque horrida castra secuta est.'
uenit et agresti capitis Siluanus honore,
florentes ferulas et grandia lilia quassans.   25
Pan deus Arcadiae uenit, quem uidimus ipsi
sanguineis ebuli bacis minioque rubentem.
'ecquis erit modus?' inquit. 'Amor non talia curat
nec lacrimis crudelis Amor nec gramina riuis
nec cutiso saturantur apes nec fronde capellae.'   30
    Tristis at ille 'tamen cantabitis, Arcades,' inquit
'montibus haec uestris, soli cantare periti
Arcades. o mihi tum quam molliter ossa quiescant,
uestra meos olim si fistula dicat amores!
atque utinam ex uobis unus uestrique fuissem   35
aut custos gregis aut maturae uinitor uuae!
certe siue mihi Phyllis siue esset Amyntas
seu quicumque furor – quid tum, si fuscus Amyntas?
et nigrae uiolae sunt et uaccinia nigra –
mecum inter salices lenta sub uite iaceret;   40
serta mihi Phyllis legeret, cantaret Amyntas.
    Hic gelidi fontes, hic mollia prata, Lycori,
hic nemus; hic ipso tecum consumerer aeuo.
nunc insanus Amor duri me Martis in armis
tela inter media atque aduersos detinet hostis.   45
tu procul a patria – nec sit mihi credere tantum –
Alpinas, a, dura niues et frigora Rheni
me sine sola uides. a, te ne frigora laedant!
a, tibi ne teneras glacies secet aspera plantas!
    Ibo et Chalcidico quae sunt mihi condita uersu   50

19 opilio P^2: ut filio P^1 tarde P 20 umidus R 23 horrida saxa P^1
28 et quis P^2R nec talia R 29 ripis M^1 32 nostris P^1 40 iaceres
MP^1 42 lycoris M^1P^2 44 inermis P^1 46 sic M^1

carmina pastoris Siculi modulabor auena.
certum est in siluis inter spelaea ferarum
malle pati tenerisque meos incidere amores
arboribus. crescent illae, crescetis, amores.
interea mixtis lustrabo Maenala Nymphis   55
aut acris uenabor apros. non me ulla uetabunt
frigora Parthenios canibus circumdare saltus.
iam mihi per rupes uideor lucosque sonantis
ire; libet Partho torquere Cydonea cornu
spicula – tamquam haec sit nostri medicina furoris   60
aut deus ille malis hominum mitescere discat.
    Iam neque Hamadryades rursum nec carmina nobis
ipsa placent; ipsae rursum concedite siluae.
non illum nostri possunt mutare labores,
nec si frigoribus mediis Hebrumque bibamus   65
Sithoniasque niues hiemis subeamus aquosae
nec si, cum moriens alta liber aret in ulmo,
Aethiopum uersemus ouis sub sidere Cancri.
omnia uincit Amor et nos cedamus Amori.'
    Haec sat erit, diuae, uestrum cecinisse poetam,   70
dum sedet et gracili fiscellam texit hibisco,
Pierides. uos haec facietis maxima Gallo,
Gallo, quoius amor tantum mihi crescit in horas
quantum uere nouo uiridis se subicit alnus.
surgamus; solet esse grauis cantantibus umbra,   75
iuniperi grauis umbra; nocent et frugibus umbrae.
ite domum saturae, uenit Hesperos, ite capellae.

55 lymphis *M*: siluis *R*   56 agris *M*¹   59 cydonia *P*¹: rhodonea *M*¹
60 sint *M*   62 drusum *M*¹: rursus *M*²*PR*   63 rursus *PR*   69 uinct
*P*¹: uincet *M*: uicit *R*   73 hora *P*¹

COMMENTARY

ECLOGUE I

1 Tityre: Landscape in the pastoral is always inhabited, and all the Eclogues except 4, 6 and 10 have a herdsman's name in the first line. Servius says (*Buc. prooem.* p. 4) that *Laconum lingua tityrus dicitur aries maior qui gregem anteire consueuit*, Aelian (*V.H.* 3.40) that *títuros* is synonymous with *sáturos* (see 5.73n.). Tityrus seems conventionally a subordinate among the herdsmen. He receives orders from others in Th. *Id.* 3.2–4 and in *Ecl.* 3.20, 96, 5.12, 9.23. Except at Th. *Id.* 7.72 he is excluded from the formal music-making, which is no doubt significant for the interpretation of *Ecl.* 6.4, 8.55. For the suggestion of piping in *Tityre, tu* and *tu, Tityre* (4) cf. the repetition of *i* and *ü* in Th. *Id.* 1.1–9 ἁδύ τι τὸ ψιθύρισμα καὶ ἁ πίτυς, αἰπόλε, τήνα, | ἁ ποτὶ ταῖς παγαῖσι, μελίσδεται, ἁδὺ δὲ καὶ τύ | συρίσδες 'pleasant is the whisper of the pine tree over there beside the spring, friend goatherd, and pleasant too is your piping'; *Id.* 7.88–9 τὺ δ' ὑπὸ δρυσὶν ἢ ὑπὸ πεύκαις | ἁδὺ μελισδόμενος 'beneath the oaks or pines, making sweet music'.

tegmine, used of the shade of 'the spreading beech tree', attracted the attention of ancient parodists: *Tityre, si toga calda tibi est, quo tegmine fagi?* (cited in Don. *Vit.* 174). The word normally refers to clothing or protective covering, but an extended meaning is attested in *lato sub tegmine caeli* (Cic. *Aratea* in *N.D.* 2.112), *eodem sub tegmine caeli* (Lucr. 2.663). It is not clear whether the censure implied by the parody was on the particular application of the word here or on the archaic form (cf. *tegumen, tegumentum*), which Vergil has perhaps employed to suggest the character of rural dialect (see 3.1n.).

fagi: beeches are a recurrent feature of Vergil's bucolic landscape (2.3, 3.12, 5.13). The Greek cognate *phāgós, phēgós* is used of a species of oak also prized for its shade (Th. *Id.* 12.8) and described by Philemon (Athenaeus 2.52e) as 'an ornament of Pan'.

2 siluestrem...Musam: cf. Lucr. 4.589 *fistula siluestrem ne cesset fundere Musam*. The Lucretian passage, in which the belief in music-

[71]

making woodland deities is explained by echo-phenomena, seems to have impressed Vergil; cf. 2.34, 10.25-6. The prominence of *siluae* in the Eclogues, besides evoking the cool shade of the idyllic landscape, recalls the equation of the Italian Silvanus (10.24) with the Greek Pan, patron of rustic music.

meditaris is intentionally ambiguous: either 'you are meditating on the woodland Muse' or, with the common metonymy of *Musa* (8.1) and *meditari* in the sense that it often bears, perhaps under the influence of Greek μελετᾶν, 'you are practising your woodland music'.

auena in its literal sense 'oaten straw', 'stalk' would produce a tenuous note indeed; cf. the contemptuous *stipula* at 3.27 and καλάμα in Th. *Id.* 5.7. However, both words may perhaps be used generically; Pliny, *Nat.* 19.1.5, uses *auena* of a flax stalk. Rustic pipes, whether single or multiple (*fistula* 'pan-pipes'), were made from stalks of hemlock (5.85) or more often marsh-reed *harundo* (6.8; cf. *calamus* in 10). Thanks to Vergil the 'oaten pipe' became part of the pastoral tradition.

tenui, which Servius saw as expressing the *humilitas* of the genre, may have neoteric literary associations (6.5n.).

3-4 patriae finis like *urbem* (19), *miles* (70) and the specific connotations of *libertas* (27), *peculium* (32), *seruitium* (40) and *limes* (53) represent intrusions from the non-pastoral world. Even *arua* here and *noualia* (70) extend the range of the pastoral to include not only the harvesting of crops, as in Th. *Id.* 10, but ploughing and sowing as well. The repetition of *patriae, patriam* and the starkness of the uncompounded forms *linquimus, fugimus* are very expressive. In the latter verb 'we are fleeing' there is the additional meaning, latent at a first reading, 'we are being banished', for which cf. Greek φεύγειν. In the light of 11-12, 71-2 we can see the plural forms here as extending the catastrophe beyond his own personal sufferings. A slave could not technically have a *patria*; but the implication of 71, which is nowhere contradicted, is that Meliboeus was a *ciuis*.

lentus in umbra 'relaxed', 'at ease'; cf. *lenti consedimus aruis* (*A.* 12.237). The adjective is used of things that are neither rigid nor fluid, the supple vine (3.38), tacky pitch (*G.* 4.41) and even the surface of a calm sea (*A.* 7.28). Countrymen naturally seek *umbriferas rupes et* *arbores patulas* in the midday heat (Var. *R.* 2.2.11, cf. Hor. *C.* 3.29.21–2) ; but the image is especially associated with pastoral *otium* (see 6n.) and music-making, e.g. *Epit. Bion.* 21 and Th. *Id.* 7.88–9 (1n.).

5 formonsam: the adjective occurs frequently in the Eclogues. Unlike *pulcher* it denotes exclusively physical beauty and so is often used of animals as well as persons (5.44).

resonare doces: the woods are personified; they not only respond sympathetically to his song (contrast 2.13) but are also instructed by him, as the bays are by Apollo in 6.83. Thus does the pastoral singer transform his surroundings. For the aural image cf. Prop. 1.18.31 *resonent mihi 'Cynthia' siluae*; for the syntax cf. *G.* 3.338 *litoraque alcyonen resonant* and the more usual *resonat...plangoribus aether* (*A.* 4.668).

Amaryllida: the name means 'sparkling one' (Greek *amarússein* 'to sparkle'). It occurs in Th. *Id.* 4.36ff. and is given to the reluctant girl of *Id.* 3, where Tityrus is also named in the opening couplet. In the Eclogues the name recurs at 2.14, 3.81, 9.22 and is given to the witch or her attendant in the magic rites at 8.77 etc. It may not be fanciful to see Amaryllis here as Tityrus' woodland Muse, the beloved being the inspiration of pastoral as of elegiac song: *ingenium nobis ipsa puella facit* (Prop. 2.1.4).

tu (1) **nos** (3) **nos** (4) **tu:** the chiasmus points the antithesis between Tityrus' idyllic situation and Meliboeus' dejection.

6 Meliboee: although the name is Greek – because *mélei autôi tôn boôn* 'he has care of the cattle' (Servius) – it is not found in extant Greek pastoral. Meliboeus reappears as a superior herdsman in 3.1, and as the narrator of *Ecl.* 7.

deus and *diuus* were doublets. Servius' distinction (*A.* 5.45) between *deos perpetuos* and *diuos ex hominibus factos* is consistent with the use of *diuus* for Roman emperors. However he cites Varro and Ateius for the reverse meanings, and it is not clear whether Vergil is following Varro here or representing Tityrus as actually believing that his benefactor was a god incarnate. The promise of divine honours to an outstanding benefactor is as old as Homer, *Od.* 8.467–8. Superficial precedents occur in Latin in Cicero's description of Lentulus as *parens, deus, salus nostrae uitae* (*Red. Pop.* 11) and of Plato as *deus ille noster* (*Att.* 4.16.3), also Lucretius' famous eulogy of Epicurus, *deus ille fuit, deus, inclute Memmi* (5.8). The attribution of divinity by an Italian herdsman to his benefactor, which is all that we are explicitly required to accept here, is no more than the characteristic gesture of gratitude from a simple and superstitious rustic. Nevertheless, the reference is certainly to Octavian (42n.). At the time when the poem first appeared he must still have been very much the junior partner to Antony; and so there may here be evidence of a second edition of the Eclogue, dating from the early years of the principate, when popular versions of the emperor-cult were already becoming established. However, even in the mid-thirties 'the cities joined in placing [Octavian] among their tutelary gods' (Appian *B.C.* 5.132).

haec otia 'these conditions of leisure'. The plural of abstract nouns in Latin as in English usually has a more concrete or specific meaning, e.g. *curae, gaudia, uoluptates* and their English equivalents. However the choice of plural forms in *-ia* in dactylic verse was also helped by metrical considerations. *otium* forms a cretic before a following consonant and the elision of words of this metrical shape with a following short vowel was avoided as being ugly (3.84n.). *otium* is an essential ingredient of the pastoral myth (p. 6). Like the *otia dia* of primitive man in Epicurean thought (Lucr. 5.1387) it connotes that *securitas* which comes from the rejection of the *negotia* of urban life. The concept was particularly associated with the countryside, as in Hor. *C.* 1.1, 3.29 and especially *C.* 2.16, where the more luxurious and sensual overtones of the word, as exemplified in Cat. 51.13-16, Ov. *Am.* 1.9.41-2, are also prominent. A specific antithesis of *otium* and *bellum* is often found; e.g. Cic. *Mur.* 30 *cedat, opinor, Sulpici, forum castris, otium militiae, stilus gladio, umbra soli*, Caes. *B.C.* 2.36 *multitudo insolens belli diuturnitate oti*; and this is certainly relevant here, since the *otium* of the real Italian countryside has been disrupted by the civil wars and their aftermath. Finally there is the association of *otium* with the pursuit of the arts; e.g. Cic. *de Or.* 1.224 *philosophorum autem libros reseruet sibi ad huiusce modi Tusculani requiem atque otium*, Cat. 50.1-2 *hesterno, Licini, die otiosi | multum lusimus in meis tabellis*. This connotation is also relevant to Tityrus' music-making. All the overtones of the word are sounded in the famous epilogue to the Georgics, 4.559-66.

7 ille...illius...ille (9): the repetition is emphatic. The correption in *illius*, for the more normal *illius* (63), recurs e.g. at *G.* 1.49, *A.* 1.16.

mihi, archaic for the more normal *mihi* (35), recurs in 3.76, 9.53,

10.1; see 2.70n. The contrast with *nobis* may be significant. Tityrus
has not been the only one to receive this blessing, but the way of
honouring the benefactor is his own. As yet there is no widespread
cult of the new *deus*.

7–8 aram...imbuet agnus: cf. the sacrifice to Apollo in Th. *Ep.*
1.5: 'the altar will be stained with the blood of this white horned
goat'.

9–10 meas errare boues...et ipsum ludere forms a single
direct object to *permisit*; cf. *neque auelli quidquam neque deminui iam* |
concedit Natura (Lucr. 1.613–14). This is more concise than the normal
construction with indirect object in the dative and direct object
complement formed by an *ut* clause or infinitival phrase (cf. *ut iam*
ipsis iudicibus...coniecturam facere permittam in Cic. *Verr.* 5.22). See
5.41n. *errare* implies security; the cattle could roam unmolested. The
mention of cattle after the lamb in 8 implies that Tityrus has a mixed
farm like Meliboeus in *Ecl.* 7. By contrast Meliboeus here (12, 77) has
only goats.

10 For *ludere* and *ludus* of poetic activity cf. Cat. 50. As with Greek
παίζειν, παίγνιον, the suggestion that music-making is not serious is
often ironical (6.1, *G.* 4.565). The licence to sing as the spirit moves is
as precious as security of tenure in the truly Arcadian way of life,
though only the latter is actually mentioned in the *responsum* of 45.

calamo is for the normal Latin *harundine*. The loan-word from
Greek *kálamos* occurs as early as Cato *Agr.* 105.2 and may not by now
have seemed exotic. However, as Tityrus has been playing on an
oaten pipe, there may be a reference to the fact that *titúrinos* was the
Italian Doric word for the single reed pipe *kaláminos aulós* (Athen.
4.182d).

11 After Tityrus' tactless exultation in his own good fortune Meliboeus responds without bitterness. He depicts his own wretched plight
as part of a wider catastrophe but is eager to hear his friend's story.

magis for *potius*, as in Cat. 68.30 *non est turpe, magis miserum est*, may
be colloquial; cf. its Romance reflexes *ma*, *mais* etc.

12 usque adeo is a Lucretian phrase (e.g. 1.412, 497), which recurs
at *G.* 4.84, *A.* 12.646.

turbatur is impersonal: 'there is a disturbance'; cf. *si in Hispania*
turbatum esset (Cic. *Sul.* 57).

13 protenus: Caper (*G.L.* 7.100) distinguishes *protenus* of place from *protinus* of time. Either 'without delay' or 'onwards' is equally suitable here.

aeger is commonly used of both mental and physical distress. The contrast between *ago* and *duco* is poignant. The succession of short words in the line produces a halting rhythm, unrelieved by any major pause, since the chief caesural point is blurred by the elision of *ago hanc*.

14 The tendency of hazels to throw up numerous suckers – hence *densas* here – made them a useful source for tough withies as well as firewood (*G.* 2.65, 299).

14–15 The birth of the kids, normally a happy event, is here pathetic. For as Servius observed, *conixa* suggests a more painful labour than the usual *enixa*, and the kids that would normally have been carried in the herdsman's arms have been left dead or to die on the hard stony path. There is a stark contrast between the disastrous loss of this replenishment to Meliboeus' tiny herd and the prosperity implied in the sacrificial vow that Tityrus made. The unusually positioned *a* and the distorted word-order of the whole couplet express the herdsman's distraught feelings.

16 laeua 'ill-fated' and so deluded; cf. Hor. *A.P.* 301.

17 de caelo tactas: of a lightning-stroke; cf. Cic. *Diu.* 1.92. The omen may have been the more threatening in that Jupiter's own sacred tree was struck. The reference to popular religion keeps the scene and its inhabitants close to the real world. The high incidence of spondees in 16–17 adds an aptly ominous note.

memini praedicere 'I remember its foretelling', not 'I remember that it foretold' (*praedixisse*). For this emphasis on the imperfective rather than the preterite character of the action cf. 7.69, 9.52, Cic. *Leg.* 1.13 *a primo tempore aetatis iuri studere te memini.* An additional apodosis to *si mens* etc. is implied, 'and would have persuaded me'; cf. 9.45n.

18 qui The choice between interrogative *quis* and *qui* in classical Latin appears to have been motivated chiefly by euphonic considerations. Manuscript testimony for what it is worth strongly supports *qui* here (PR) and in 2.19 (PR), 6.73 (MP²R).

da for *dic* is colloquial (cf. *sed da mihi nunc: satisne probas?* Cic. *Ac.* 1.10), in keeping with the tone of the whole line. The rhythm of *da, Tityre, nobis* pathetically echoes *uix, Tityre, duco*: Meliboeus is more eager to hear of his friend's good fortune than to burden him with his own troubles.

19 Tityrus is so self-centred in his complacency that he ignores the question and goes on to tell his story in his own way. *urbem*, like *deus* (6) and *libertas* (27), focuses attention immediately on the dominant themes of his narrative. The solemn sequence of heavy syllables with which he begins is appropriate to the theme.

20 quoi: Burman's conjecture for *quo* of the manuscripts. See p. 39. The sense is 'for which we are in the habit of weaning the tender lambs'. For this technical sense of *depellere* cf. 3.82, 7.15, *G.* 3.187. With *quo* the sense would be 'to which we are in the habit of driving the tender lambs'. However ancient Italian farmers like their modern counterparts often marketed their lambs before they were weaned (Colum. 7.3.13). The young animals, being too tender to be driven to market, were carried – as they still are – in crates or baskets (9.6, 65).

solemus...solebam (23)...**solent** (25) emphasize by contrast the uniqueness of Rome.

23 noram = *noueram*. Like *habitarunt* (2.60), *uexasse* and *pararit* beside *narrauerit* (6.76, 79, 78) it was created by analogy with forms where the contraction was purely phonetic, e.g. *implerunt* (6.48), *quaesisset* (6.51). In spite of the pedantic objections to the spread of them reported in Cic. *Or.* 157, these contracted forms seem to have been the commoner by the time of Quintilian (1.6.17, 21).

24 extulit may be preterite '(when I saw it) it towered above' or perfect 'it has raised its head' i.e. 'towers above'. The perennial reaction of the rustic on his first visit to the big city is reflected in this search for appropriate rural comparisons.

25 uiburna: either the 'wayfaring tree' or the wild 'guelder rose', to which *lenta* is slightly more appropriate. Both are hedge-shrubs, contrasting with the tall evergreen cypress. Probably imported from the East (*G.* 2.84, Plin. *Nat.* 16.139), the latter had long been a familiar feature of the Italian landscape. Its sombre associations (cf. the epithets *feralis* in *A.* 6.216 and *funebris* at Hor. *Epod.* 5.18) do not seem relevant in the present context.

26 Given the background to their encounter, it is remarkable that Meliboeus cannot guess the reason for Tityrus' journey.

27   sera tamen respexit inertem 'late though it was, nevertheless had regard for a sluggard'. As in *sera tamen tacitis poena uenit pedibus* (Tib. 1.9.4), the adverb is to be construed with the verb rather than with the adjective; hence *respexit tamen* (29). Cf. *sera sed Ausoniis ueniet prouincia uirgis* (Prop. 3.4.5). *tamen* stands first in its clause at 9.62, 10.31, Cic. *Marcell.* 4 *tamen hoc adfirmo*.

28   candidior: the adjective *canus* is more usual of greying hair. Servius, believing that *Tityri sub persona Vergilium debemus accipere, non tamen ubique sed tantum ubi exigit ratio*, refused to take advantage of his escape clause here and proposed to construe the adjective with *libertas*, since the poet was only twenty-eight at the time when the dispossessions began. But *candidior...barba* suits *senex* (46). The latter does not imply that Tityrus was a dotard – he was after all capable of warming to the charms of a new wife – but it certainly could not refer to a man under thirty. Old men are rare in the conventional pastoral world, which seems to be peopled by teenagers.

  cadebat 'now that my beard was already falling (i.e. had begun to fall)'; cf. *postea quam e scaena...explodebatur, sicut in aram confugit in huius domum* (Cic. *Q. Rosc.* 30). Similarly *habet* (30) denotes a state of affairs that has already begun and is still obtaining: 'now that Amaryllis has taken hold of me'. Both tenses thus contrast with *reliquit* (30), which denotes a precise event marking a point in time.

30   Galatea elsewhere in pastoral is a sea-nymph: 7.37, 9.39, Th. *Id.* 6.10–11, 11.13–14.

31–2 Tityrus' emancipation had been delayed not only by his own *inertia* (27) but also by the spendthrift habits of his former wife. As a slave he could not of course contract any legal marriage; his *coniunx* would be technically *contubernalis*. It is clear now that part of Amaryllis' attraction lay in her domestic efficiency. Spendthrift and domineering wives (*habet, tenebat* in 30, 31) belong to comedy and satire rather than pastoral; the detail thus provides one more touch of realism in the poem.

peculi: a far more important piece of realism, pointing to Tityrus' socio-legal status. This very unpoetical word seems originally to have meant that part of a master's *pecu* or material possessions that constituted his own or his wife's savings (cf. *Dig.* 32.79, 23.3.9.3). Its more specialized use was of that portion of the *patrimonium* which a *pater familias* entrusted in his lifetime to a son, daughter or slave for their own use, though it remained legally his property (cf. *Dig.* 15.1.4, 5). The *peculium* of a rural slave often consisted of the *usufructus* of some part of the flock or herd that he tended (Var. *R.* 1.2.17; cf. *peculiarem* [*ouem*] at Pl. *As.* 541). A frugal slave could amass a considerable *peculium* (Pl. *As.* 498), sufficient in some instances to buy his freedom after five or six years (Cic. *Phil.* 8.32). Hence the confiscation of his master's land and stock would have been disastrous to a man in Tityrus' situation.

33 multa...uictima: the noun may be collective singular, but the adjective is clearly attested in the sense 'many a' at Luc. 3.707-8 *multus sua uolnera puppi | adfixit moriens.*

saeptis: the enclosures of the *ouilia* (8).

34 pinguis: if this refers not to *uictima*, as Servius takes it, but to *caseus*, it presumably means cream-cheese, which, though it keeps longer than cheese that *tenui liquore conficitur*, should be sold quickly *dum adhuc uiridis sucum retinet* (Colum. 7.8, where the process of pressing cheese – cf. *premeretur* here – is also described).

ingratae introduces the third hindrance to Tityrus' emancipation, the meanness of urban consumers – a familiar complaint of real farmers but not part of the conventional pastoral myth.

37 poma is used of any stone- or seed-fruit, e.g. plums (2.53), pears (9.50). In her grief Amaryllis' customary efficiency for once deserted her.

38 aberāt is an archaism, the -a- having been long originally in all the imperfect endings. It was a useful variant metrically, since it enabled the word to occur before vowels as well as consonants in dactylic verse. Cf. *amōr* (10.69n.). Archaisms tend to be restricted to the final position of a line or a colon, as here. A less likely interpretation is that the punctuation affects the syllable division: *-be-rat-ip-sae* instead of *-be-ra-tip-sae*, with the vowel remaining short but the syllable becoming heavy. For the syllable in *-at* is light in *ueniebat. ibi* (2.4) but heavy in *amittebat oculosque* (*A.* 5.853), where the punctuation, if any, is very slight.

39 arbusta, though regularly used in dactylic verse for the unmetrical *arbores* (3.10), may have its more precise meaning here 'plantations' of elms, olives, fruit-trees etc. Servius' allegorizing runs riot in this passage: *Tityrus Vergilius, pinus Roma, fontes senatores, arbusta . . . scholastici.*

uocabant: the echo of *uocares* (36) is revealing; a realistic description of the signs of neglect on the farm has been transformed into the sympathy figure (see pp. 9, 21): Amaryllis' grief at her husband's absence is shared by the whole natural environment. Other instances of the figure occur at 7.53–60, 10.13–15.

40 seruitio me exire forms a single complement to *licebat*; cf. *si parua licet componere magnis* with the simple infinitive (*G.* 4.176) and *non licet me isto tanto bono...uti* (Cic. *Verr.* 5.154). For the syntactic analysis cf. 9n.

41 praesens 'a very present help in trouble'; cf. *tu, dea, tu praesens nostro succurre labori* (*A.* 9.404), *Hercules tantus et tam praesens habetur deus* (Cic. *T.D.* 1.28).

42 iuuenem: Octavian, who was born in 63 B.C., is *diuinus adulescens* in Cic. *Phil.* 5.43 and *iuuenis* still in Verg. *G.* 1.500, Hor. *C.* 1.2.41. Although Antony was in his early forties when the dispossessions began and therefore still technically *iuuenis*, he had taken charge of the Eastern empire and left Octavian to supervise the settlement of the veterans from Philippi (Suet. *Aug.* 13). There was trouble throughout 41 B.C. both from the veterans, dissatisfied with the speed of the settlements, and from the threatened occupants, bands of whom marched to Rome to demand compensation and a more equitable spread of the burden (see Appian *B.C.* 5.2.12–13, Dio 48.6–12). Tityrus had clearly been one of the successful petitioners.

43 bis senos like *duodena* in *G.* 1.232 is used for the unmetrical *duŏdĕcim*. The promise of *saepe* (8) is now given definition. It is probably implied that the benefactor will be associated with the worship of the domestic *Lares*, which took place at various times of the month (Cato *Agr.* 143.2) but particularly on the Kalends (cf. Prop. 4.3.53–4). At a later date the *genius Augusti* was certainly honoured with the *Lares*; cf. Hor. *C.* 4.5.34–5. So this like 6 could be a detail added in a revised version of the poem.

altaria: the neut. pl. of an adjective **altaris*, which the ancients connected with (*ad*)*olere* or *altus*, may have referred originally to the offering. At 5.66 D.Servius cites Varro's opinion, *dis superis altaria, terrestribus ara, inferis focos dicari*, a distinction that suits that line well; but he gives a different distinction at *A.* 2.215, so the sense of the two words cannot have been clear-cut. *altaria* here can hardly be different from *aram* (7).

44 responsum is used of legal opinions (Cic. *de Or.* 1.239), official replies to enquiries in the Senate (Liv. 7.31.8) and prophetic responses (*A.* 6.82, Liv. 23.11.1). Here it probably connotes *auctoritas* without any specifically religious colour.

primus is ambiguous. Either 'right at the start' (the adjectival equivalent of *primo*) – without delaying to consult others he gave the verdict as soon as the petition was placed before him – or 'at long last' – after all the previous protests had failed, his was the first favourable reply. For a similar ambiguity cf. *A.* 7.117–18 *ea uox audita laborum | prima tulit finem.*

45 pueri 'slaves'. Although Tityrus egoistically describes the petition as his own (*mihi...petenti*), the form of the reply shows that he was just one of the crowd. As in 12 and 71–2, we are reminded of the typicality of the two herdsmen's situations.

submittite has been variously interpreted. (i) 'rear', 'raise'; cf. Var. *R.* 2.2.18 *quos arietes submittere uolunt potissimum eligunt ex matribus quae geminos parere solent*, 2.3.4 *ex his potissimum mares solent submitti ad admissuras. arietes* in the former passage supports the proleptic interpretation of *tauros*. This is the most probable meaning of the verb here. It is also appropriate in *G.* 3.73, 159, which are often cited as examples of sense (ii). (ii) sc. *iugo*: 'submit your bulls to the yoke' (so Servius). This would imply tillage as well as pasturage in the young ruler's dispensation; cf. *arua* (3). Tibullus has *colla iugo didicit submittere taurus* (4.1.171), but there is no example in classical Latin of the verb used elliptically in this sense. (iii) = *admittite*, the verb regularly used of putting male animals to stud, *admissura* (Var. *R.* 3.10.3). But *submittendae tauris uaccae* (Pallad. 4.13) suggests that *submittere* was the complementary, not the equivalent, term. This is the least likely interpretation. As with *depellere* (21) Vergil has added a technical detail to enhance the realism of his picture of rustic life.

The *responsum* itself is somewhat allusive. Tityrus had gone to secure his *libertas*, which would be achieved only if he could retain his one means of raising the cost of emancipation, namely the animals and their pasture, which were both the legal property of his master. Security of *usufructus* would thus ultimately guarantee Tityrus his *libertas*. The fact that only *pueri* are explicitly mentioned suggests that the previous owners had been dispossessed. The rights of slaves to farm land for their own profit were thus now safeguarded even under the change of ownership. By contrast Meliboeus, a free man (cf. *patriae* (3), *ciuis* (71)), retained his herd but had nowhere to graze it. There is no indication that Tityrus was actually manumitted by the *responsum*.

46 tua is predicative: 'so the lands will remain yours'. The plural *rura* is specific (cf. 6n.): 'particular parts of the *rus*'.

47-8 The picture of Tityrus' farm with its rocky ground and reedy marsh is very unprepossessing, unlikely to have pleased the new owner. Indeed land that was *aut in saxuosis et sterilibus locis... aut in paludibus* was deemed to be *in soluto*, viz. outside the area for which official survey was required (Frontin. *Contr. Agr.* p. 41.20 Lachm.). So maybe Tityrus' farm would not have qualified after all for *assignatio* to veterans (*op. cit.* p. 156.1); hence the young ruler's eagerness to concede the request. Nevertheless to Meliboeus, as he contemplates the grim alternative, this land seems enviable indeed.

49 fetas could be used of the mother either before or after parturition. *grauis* may be either (i) 'ailing', a meaning that is normally defined by an ablative, e.g. *morbo* (*G.* 3.95), but would suit either interpretation of *fetas* and also accord well with *temptabunt* 'will assail', which is commonly used of diseases, e.g. *G.* 3.441; or (ii) 'pregnant', a synonym for *grauidas* that is attested in *A.* 1.274 but would be redundant here if *fetas* is taken in the first sense.

50 Cf. Hor. *Epod.* 16.61 *nulla nocent pecori contagia*, in a description of the Golden Age.

51 fortunate senex: the repetition introduces a wistful transformation of the humble realities of Tityrus' land into an idyllic landscape, reminiscent of Th. *Id.* 5.45–9 and especially 7.133–45 'Joyfully we lay down on deep couches of sweet rushes and fresh-cut vine-leaves. Many a poplar and elm murmured overhead and close by was the splash of hallowed water pouring from a cave of the Nymphs. On the shady boughs the dusky cicadas chattered away at their work and in the distance the tree-frog was croaking among the dense thornbrake. Larks and finches sang, the dove moaned and the bees hummed hovering around the spring. Everything smelled of the rich summer and the season of fruit. Pears in abundance rolled at our feet, apples on either side, and the branches were poured out over the ground, weighed down with damsons.'

52–3 fontis sacros, like Theocritus' 'hallowed water', evokes not only the cool shade of the pastoral scene but also the piety of the pastoral shepherds; cf. Hor. *C.* 1.1.21–2 *nunc uiridi membra sub arbuto | stratus, nunc ad aquae lene caput sacrae.* Even in the real countryside piety bestowed a tutelary deity on every spring and stream; and this gave a specially intimate quality to the local religion. The *f-* alliteration in 51–2, though difficult to evaluate, can hardly be accidental. The slow spondaic rhythms suggest the languor of *lentus in umbra.*

captabis 'you will make for, seek out'. The intensive suffix *-tā-*, often used in a frequentative sense, here denotes persistence.

quae semper 'as ever'; sc. *suasit*. The antecedent is *saepes.*

limite, from the same root as *limen*, was originally used of the path that marked the boundary, e.g. *lutosi limites* (Var. *R.* 2.4.8), thence the boundary or even boundary-stone (*A.* 12.897–8). The presence of the hedge here suggests the meaning 'on the boundary(-path) side'. The very notion of land-ownership entailed by the word belongs to the realities of country life, not to the pastoral myth.

54 Hyblaeis is both evocative and characterizing. Tityrus' bees are such as one would find around Hybla on the southern slopes of Mount Etna, an area as famous for its honey as the Attic Hymettus (7.37). But the evocation of Theocritus' Sicily also recalls the idyllic landscape of earlier pastoral.

apibus florem depasta ... saepes 'the hedge on whose (willow) blossom the bees feed their fill'. The use of an acc. with the perf.

participle is a feature of the Latin poetic register, influenced in part by the parallel Greek idiom. The construction is significantly frequent in the highly neoteric *Ecl.* 6. Here two analyses are possible. (i) The participle is passive in sense and the phrase corresponds to the active *apes saepem depascunt* with *florem* as either acc. of reference or as second object in a Graecizing whole-and-part construction retained in the passive transformation. For *depascere* 'to feed on' cf. *tauros | qui tibi nunc uiridis depascunt summa Lycaei* (*G.* 4.538–9); for the participial use cf. 6.15, 75. (ii) The participle is middle in sense, corresponding to an active *apibus saepes depascit florem*. For *depascere* 'to provide as food' cf. *pabulum...pecudibus...depascere* (Colum. 6, pr. 2); for the participial use cf. 6.53, 68. See also 3.106n., 7.32n.

salicti: a plantation or clump of *salices*. Both the purple and the white willow, which is probably meant in 5.16, were already common in ancient Italy. Willows were used for supporting vines (10.40) and for cattle fodder (3.83) as well as for hedge-plants (*G.* 2.434); see also Plin. *Nat.* 16.68–9.

55 somnum suadebit inire 'will persuade a falling asleep': for the construction cf. *uide ne facinus facias, cum mori suadeas* (Cic. *Fin.* 2.95) and see 9–10n., 40n. The onomatopoeia of the repeated sibilants in 54–5 is striking.

56 frondator: Servius mentions three *frondationes*: the early pruning (9.61), the later trimming of the thick foliage of the vines and of the trees to which they were trained (2.70n.), and the cutting of leaves at the end of the season for use as winter fodder. All three are mentioned in the Georgics, 2.362ff., 397ff., 1.305f. The *frondator* here is presumably resting in the shade. For the image of singing *sub rupe* cf. [Th.] *Id.* 8.55.

57 palumbes: the use of a word meaning 'wild wood-pigeons' for *columbae* 'domestic pigeons or doves' is censured by Servius here (cf. also his note on *A.* 5.213), but he admits that the usage has the authority of Cicero and others, and Varro certainly uses *palumbi* of the latter (*R.* 3.9.21). Pigeon-fancying and the breeding of turtle-doves (*turtur* here) were popular pastimes in rural Italy (Var. *L.* 9.56, *R.* 3.8). For their nesting in the tall vine-carrying elms cf. Hor. *C.* 1.2.9–10.

57–8 raucae...gemere: the throaty call of the nesting pigeons and doves, another detail repeated from the Theocritean scene cited in 51n., completes the aural imagery that began with *susurro* and *canet*.

59 Tityrus, absorbed with his own good fortune, reverts to the *iuuenem* of 42. Meliboeus' *aeria...ulmo* suggests the starting point for an adynaton, the figure by which the impossibility of an event is asserted by assigning it to circumstances that are themselves impossible. This adynaton has a long history; cf. Archil. fr. 74.7–9 DB: 'not even if animals exchange with dolphins the pastures of the sea, and the roar of the ocean waves becomes more dear to them than dry land', Hdt. 5.92a.1, Rufin. *A.P.* 5.18.5–6. It is clearly related to the figure of nature's disruption in 5.36–9, 8.52–6.

leues: either 'fleet of foot' or 'floating lightly'.

60 freta are properly 'straits', whence by synecdoche 'seas', especially rough ones, e.g. Lucr. 6.427–8.

61 pererratis amborum finibus alludes to the nomadic habits of the *Germani* and *Parthi*, both of whom were outside the imperial boundaries at this period. *amborum* may either have its usual sense or mean 'each other's', for which Latin had no concise equivalent.

62 Ararim is the more common acc., though nom. *Arar* is much more frequent than *Araris*. The Saône joins the Rhône at Lyons in the ancient *Gallia Comata*, but it rises in the highlands of the Vosges, which were occupied in Vergil's time by the *Germani*.

63 quam picks up *ante* from 59, 61.

labatur pectore: as in unreal-condition clauses the subjunctive denotes a hypothetical situation, appropriately following an adynaton: 'would fade away'. The ablative is either locatival or separative: 'in' or 'from my heart'. The omission of the preposition is an archaism common in the concise idiom of poetry.

64 The migrations of Tityrus' adynaton are to be a bitter reality for Meliboeus – and for those like him; for *nos*, as in 3, 4, generalizes his plight.

Afros are the Libyans. *sitientis* suggests the inland regions; for the coastal strip from Cyrene to Abyla was both fertile and prosperous. For the omission of the preposition see 63n.

65 rapidum cretae 'snatching up chalk as it goes'. The active sense of the adj., though less frequent than the medio-passive, 'hurrying', 'being hurried', is common in -*dus* derivatives from transitive verbs; cf. 2.10 and Lucr. 1.15–17 *rapidos...amnis...flouiosque rapaces.* For the genitive *cretae* cf. *cupidus auri, auidus cibi* etc. and *rapax uirtutis* (Sen. *Ep.* 95.36). *Cretae* is impossible. It can hardly be a locative 'in Crete', and a possessive genitive here would entail a personification of *Creta* that even the preceding *Germania* cannot justify. There was a town in Crete called *Axos* or *Oaxos* (Hdt. 4.154.1), and a Cretan river *Axos* is reported by the late author Vibius Sequester (*Flum.* 15); but the island, which is called *gaïēs Oiaxídos* in A.R. *Arg.* 1.1131, is not remote enough to stand in this inhospitable catalogue.

Oaxen: Servius' reference to *Oaxes fluuius Mesopotamiae...uel fluuius Scythiae* is unsupported elsewhere and so suspect. A river *Óxos* or *Ôxos*, flowing from the Caucasus to the Caspian Sea and therefore situated somewhere between the Araks (*Araxes*) and the Volga (*Oaros?*) is described by Arrian, *Anab.* 3.29.2, as sandy and swift-flowing. Further east was a more famous *Oxus* (Plin. *Nat.* 6.48, Mela 3.42), the modern Amu, flowing north from the Hindu Kush to the Aral Sea (*Palus Oxiana*). Curtius describes it (7.10.13) as muddy and turbulent. Vergil may have had one or other of these in mind, and Ladewig even emended *Oaxen* to *ad Oxum*. The actual form *Oaxes* could be either a conflation of *Oxus* and *Araxes* or the adaptation of an older *Oaxos, reflected in the variant *ŏ*- spellings in Arrian's text, to the -*es* that is common in Eastern rivers; cf. *Hydaspes, Euphrates.* Whether Vergil chose the form or invented it, the exotic sound of it, enhanced by the Greek accusative, is very expressive of the remote and inaccessible.

66 toto...orbe 'from the whole world'; the Britons were proverbially *ultimi orbis* (Cat. 11.11–12, Hor. *C.* 1.35.29–30); 'by the whole world (sc. from the Oaxes)' is less likely in spite of Ov. *Pont.* 1.9.48 *aque tuis toto diuidor orbe rogis.*

67 en as in 8.7 introduces an impassioned question. The heightened emotional tone is marked by the alliteration in 68 and the disrupted word-order of 68–9.

68 tuguri: although the ancients connected the word with *tegere*, it was probably of foreign origin. It was used of a temporary shelter or crude hut (Var. *R.* 3.1.3) such as slaves occupied (Sall. *Iug.* 12.5). Once more Vergil introduces a word with very realistic associations, reinforced by *aliquot* in the next line, which like *stultus* in 20 has distinctly prosaic connotations.

69   post is probably adverbial, repeating *longo post tempore*, with *finis* ...*et*...*culmen* and *aristas* in asyndeton as direct objects to *uidens*: 'shall I a long time after marvel at the sight of my native territory and the roof...afterwards too at the sight of a few ears of corn...'. Less likely, *post* is a local preposition 'seeing from behind a few ears of corn my native territory...'.

   aristas: strictly the 'beard', *arista* is often used of the whole ear of corn; e.g. 4.28. Servius understood it by metonymy for *messis* (with *post* as temporal preposition 'after a few harvests') *quasi rusticus per aristas numerat*; but this sense, though supported by the Hellenistic use of ποία to mean 'harvest', 'summer', e.g. Leon. *A.P.* 7.731.4, is not certainly attested in Latin before Claudian. Moreover *aliquot* would be flat after *longo post tempore* (67).

   mea regna is in opposition to *aristas* and probably to *culmen* also.

   uidens mirabor, in contrast to *mirans uidebo*, throws the emphasis on the emotional reaction.

70–1   The frequent homodynes, reinforcing the metrical rhythm – *ímpius, haéc, cúlta* etc. – express the vehemence of Meliboeus' emotion. Unlike those who must go into exile after defeat in war (*G.* 2.511–12) he is an innocent victim; *saeuit toto Mars impius orbe* (*G.* 1.511). The new occupant is not a peace-loving farmer but a *miles*; as a foreigner – *barbarus* could refer to either a foreign mercenary or a provincial auxiliary – he would know nothing of the local Italian *pietas* associated e.g. with the *fontis sacros* (52), and his impiety is compounded by his share in the civil strife.

   noualia, contrasted with *segetes* (71), is another of Vergil's technical terms imported into a pastoral context. *nouale* was used both of unbroken grassland and of crop-land left fallow (Var. *L.* 5.39, Plin. *Nat.* 18.176). *tam culta* here indicates the latter.

71   ciuis: see 3n., and for the phrase cf. Prop. 1.22.5 *Romana suos egit discordia ciuis*.

73   nunc is sarcastic with the imperative here; cf. *A.* 7.425, Pollio *ad Cic.* (*Fam.* 10.32.3) *abi nunc, populi fidem implora*.

insere: in its technical sense 'graft' rather than 'plant'; cf. Varro *R.* 1.40.5. For apples grafted on to pears see *G.* 2.33-4.

ordine: for the pattern of planting see *G.* 2.277-87, Cic. *Sen.* 59 *directos in quincuncem ordines.*

75 antro: apparently the earliest example of the Greek loan-word *ántron* in Latin. Like the native words *cauerna* and *specus* it is often used as here of a hollow or crevice as well as of caves. It seems especially associated with idyllic landscapes: 5.19, 9.41. Cf. 10.52n.

76 pendere: i.e. they seem to be attached to the steep slope without any support under their feet.

The successive alliterations – from *piros, pone* (73) to *pascente, capellae* (77) – indicate once more a heightened emotional tone; cf. 68.

77 Lines 75-8 are Meliboeus' farewell to the idyllic life of the countryside that he has depicted in 1-5, 51-8. In departing he will lose the most precious of all the gifts of Arcady, the inspiration to music; cf. 10n.

non goes not with *me pascente* but with *carpetis*; for he is addressing the animals that are accompanying him (12-13): 'I will be your herdsman but you will not graze on...' Instead they will have *insueta...pabula* (49). It is of course probable that he will have to sell his animals before he migrates, and then they will not have him as their herdsman; but this is not the point that concerns him now.

78 cutisum 'shrub trefoil', Medicago Arborea, whose hungry roots were harmful to other trees, was nevertheless cultivated by Italian farmers (Var. *R.* 1.43) because its abundant clover-like leaves provided food for all the farm animals (9.31, *G.* 3.394-5, Colum. 5.12.1) and its yellow flowers attracted bees (10.30, Plin. *Nat.* 13.131).

79 Like *Ecl.* 2, 6, 9, 10 the poem ends with nightfall. Tityrus' callousness finally melts and his belated offer of hospitality brings Meliboeus at least temporary *securitas.* The form of the invitation perhaps recalls Polyphemus' offer to Galatea 'you will pass the night more pleasantly in the cave beside me' (Th. *Id.* 11.44) – an unprecedented symptom of love in the inhospitable monster. The imperfect *poteras* properly implies an unreal condition: 'you could have, had you wished', but it is used to make a somewhat apologetic invitation at Hor. *S.* 2.1.16, Ov. *M.* 1.679.

80–1 The green foliage on the floor brings a final echo of Th. *Id.* 7.133–45, cited above at 50.

mitia is glossed by Servius as *matura*; *molles* is either 'mealy', of roasted chestnuts, or 'soft', as when they are ripe or pickled.

82–3   uillarum, another detail from the real countryside, indicates houses more substantial than the *tuguria* of 68, and the smoke rising from them a population at peace.

de montibus reveals that Vergil is not thinking here of his native Mantuan plain. The tranquil beauty of this closing couplet is enhanced by the sonorities of the *l*, *u* and nasal sounds.

The relevance of the poem to the land-confiscations has already been observed (42n.). But this gives no clue to the date of the poem, since these began late in 42 B.C. after Philippi and continued until well after Actium. The mature style of the Eclogue as well as some of the detail relating to Octavian suggest a relatively late date – 40–39 B.C. seems too early – or even a second version belonging to the early Augustan period (6n.). Attempts have been made since antiquity to relate the poem closely to Vergil's own fortunes, but neither the landscape nor the situations and lives of the two herdsmen can be easily connected with the poet and his native home. That he suffered personally from the confiscations may reasonably be inferred from *Ecl.* 9, but it is doubtful whether the somewhat confused accounts in the ancient commentaries and *Vitae* are based on much more than inference from the two poems concerned and the desire to reconcile them. Tityrus, who is already identified with the poet himself in Calp. 4.61ff., 162–3, is after all an ageing slave who had never been to Rome before his successful journey; Meliboeus, though like Vergil a citizen dispossessed, has never been to Rome at all! It is unlikely that, with powerful friends like Pollio and Gallus, Vergil suffered any economic hardship as a result of the eviction. Indeed Pollio's connection with the Cisalpine land-commission does not appear to have soured his friendship with the poet. Nevertheless the severing of links with his family home was clearly of emotional importance to him, and his own nostalgic idealization accounts in part for the markedly Arcadian picture that Meliboeus paints of his *patria* in the descriptive set-piece at 46–58. The landscape as a whole is consistent with that of the other poems and incorporates features that are alien to Mantua, e.g. the beeches (1) and the hills (83). There is, however, an exceptional amount of technical detail from ordinary rural life and work, which is appropriate to the poem's chief concern.

In fact the poem is not autobiographical, whatever personal experience may lie behind it. What Vergil has done is to depict the contrasting situations and characters of two typical Italian countrymen whose lives have been disrupted by a crisis of which they themselves are wholly innocent. Tityrus, the ageing slave, has taken a bold initiative to meet the threat of eviction and, having made his first journey to the big city, has been rewarded. He now vaunts his success callously and complacently before his less fortunate friend. Meliboeus, a free-born citizen like Vergil himself but one who has apparently never ventured beyond his native heath, has simply bowed before adversity, and now must go into exile. His is the nobler and more sensitive character, and from him most of the finest poetry in the Eclogue comes. There is no jealousy or spitefulness towards Tityrus, and his indignation, when it does break out, is all directed against the alien usurper. Tityrus' final belated gesture of hospitality reconciles the tensions of the dialogue and reasserts the Arcadian values of friendship and hospitality, but it serves also to underline what his friend has lost. In the closing lines we may detect a plea for charity and sympathy towards those whose lives have been ruined – as Vergil's own can never have been – by the discordant effects of civil war.

The themes are effectively organized, recurring in different patterns of antithesis and in both more and less extended forms: *A*: the delights of possession – present; *B*: the pain of exile – present/future; *C*: the cult of the benefactor – present/future; *D*: the journey to Rome – past; *E*: the reconciliation – present. After the *prelude* (1–4) expounding the major themes *A* and *B*, the *second section* (6–45) comprises themes *C*: 6–10, *B*: 11–18, *D*: 19–35, *C*: 36–45. It is clearly dominated by Tityrus and his story. The *third section* (46–78) is dominated by Meliboeus and the contrast of his future with Tityrus'; it comprises *A*: 46–63, *B*: 64–78. The *epilogue E*: 79–83 reconciles the tensions of the poem.

Apart from the apt reminiscence of *Id.* 7 (50n.) there is little of Theocritus in the poem; it is a boldly original and highly wrought piece presenting in dramatic form the confrontation between pastoral myth and contemporary Italian reality. For a quite different poetic treatment of the dispossessions see Hor. *S.* 2.2, where Ofellus who has lost his land stays on as a tenant-farmer *colonus* of the new owner Umbrenus (112ff.).

ECLOGUE II

1 The line illustrates the expressive possibilities of word order in a language where the inflections suffice to determine grammatical relationships. The juxtaposition *formonsum pastor* sets the essential antithesis between the lover who is not handsome and the male beloved who is not a shepherd. Moreover *formonsum...Alexin* encloses the announcement of Corydon's passion as Alexis himself encompasses Corydon's whole world.

Corydon (cf. Greek *korudós* 'crested lark') is a familiar pastoral name; cf. *Ecl.* 7. He appears in *Id.* 4 as one of Theocritus' less attractive characters, in *Id.* 5.6 as a not very proficient musician.

ardebat in this sense normally has an instrumental abl., e.g. Hor. *C.* 2.4.7–8, or *in* + abl., e.g. Ov. *M.* 8.50. For the transitive use cf. Hor. *C.* 4.9.13–14. It is paralleled by other verbs denoting emotional or physical states, e.g. *deperire*, *dolere*, *horrere*. The consuming fire of love was a traditional metaphor; e.g. Sappho fr. 31.10LP.

Alexin: though he reappears in 7.55, Alexis seems to belong to the elegiac not the pastoral tradition; see Plato *A.P.* 7.100 and especially Meleager *A.P.* 12.127, which is also the source for the conceit of the twin fires that plague Corydon in the Eclogue: 'On the road at noon I saw Alexis walking, when summer was just being shorn of her tresses of ripe corn. Twin rays were consuming me with their flames, the rays of Love from the boy's eyes and those from the sun. These night put to sleep again, but the others were kindled still higher in my dreams by the phantom of his beauty; and sleep, which releases others from labour, forged labour for me, fashioning an image of beauty, a living fire for my soul.'

2   domini: presumably Iollas (57). Whether he is the master of Alexis alone or – more likely – of both Corydon and Alexis, the shepherd's plight is equally hopeless.

nec quid speraret habebat 'nor did he have anythng to hope for'. A direct question form *quid sperem*? is implied. The fine distinction between relative *quod* and interrogative *quid* in such constructions was easily blurred; thus *nihil habeo quod ad te scribam* beside *de pueris quid agam non habeo* in Cic. *Att.* 7.19. Cf. *qui* for *quis* (18).

3 tantum 'all he could do was...'.

densas umbrosa cacumina fagos: for the insertion of the appositional phrase, here perhaps expressive of the way the beeches enclose the cool shade, cf. 9.9. For the lover's *querelae* addressed to the lonely woods cf. Prop. 1.18, esp. 19–20.

4 ueniebat like *iactabat* indicates that what follows is an often repeated performance, like Polyphemus' serenade to Galatea, which was also introduced by a verb in the imperfect, ἄειδε 'he used to sing' (Th. *Id.* 11.17–18). *incondita* therefore can hardly be 'unpremeditated'. Servius glosses it as *agrestia*; cf. Quint. 6.3.107 and *agreste atque inconditum carmen* in Sen. *Ben.* 4.6.5. Though not lacking in detailed polish, Corydon's monologue is 'disjointed' and structurally 'incoherent'. For this sense of the word cf. P. Festus 107M *inconditum non ordinate conpositum*, and the contrast that Cicero makes between Isocrates' rhythmic prose and the *inconditam antiquorum dicendi consuetudinem* (*de Or.* 3.173).

5 montibus...siluis: both probably datives rather than local ablatives; they are Corydon's only audience. The combination suggests that these are not the hospitable woods of the pastoral idyll (1.5) but the wild forests remote from habitation (10.52). His passion is *inane* because it wastes itself upon the desert air. For *iactare* of incoherent utterance cf. *A.* 2.588.

6 Polyphemus in *Id.* 11.19–21 begins with a quaintly graceful tribute to Galatea before chiding her for her coyness. The bitterness of Corydon's opening remonstrances recalls rather the rustic serenader of *Id.* 3. Corydon keeps his praise not for Alexis but for his own native countryside and his music-making.

nihil is the internal object (= *nullam curam*) defining the character of the verbal action, *mea carmina* the external object, defining its goal. Like most internal accusatives it is equivalent to an adverb, e.g. *nullo modo*.

7 cogis 'are you in short driving me to my death?' The climax to the three questions protesting his present wretchedness. The authority for *coges* is equally good and the variation easily explicable by the fact that *ē* and *ĭ* were often indistinguishable in Late Latin pronunciation. If the phrase were taken as a statement, not a question, *coges* would perhaps be preferable: 'you will in the end (if you go on like this) drive me to my death'; for the temporal sense of *denique* see *A.* 2.295.

mori is deliberately vague. The rejected lovers in *Idd.* 3.9 and 23.21 both threaten suicide, but Corydon is too gentle a character to contemplate such violence and too guileless to make empty threats. His death will be the result of the *studium inane* that compels him to wander about in the midday heat.

8 umbras et frigora 'shady and cool spots'; cf. Ov. *M.* 7.809. An instance of hendiadys, the figure by which the head and subordinate parts of a complex idea, e.g. *umbras frigidas* or *umbrosa frigora*, are presented as discrete items equal in status. For *captare* in a similar context see 1.52 and for the pastoral cool shade 1.4–5n.

9 lacertos: masculine as in *G.* 4.13; the word is feminine in Hor. *C.* 1.23.6–7. For the detail itself cf. Th. *Id.* 7.22.

10 Thestylis is the name of the servant to the enchantress in the urban *Id.* 2.

rapido 'consuming' as in *G.* 1.92, Lucr. 5.519; cf. 1.65n.

messoribus indicates the season. Unlike Polyphemus' serenade in *Id.* 11 Corydon's is specifically placed in time: it is the harvest season and the monologue continues from lunch-time to sunset (66–7). This enables Vergil to elaborate the conceit of the fires of *sol* and *amor* from Meleager's epigram.

11 alia serpullumque 'cloves of garlic (*alium*) and wild or creeping thyme' are ingredients in Thestylis' *moretum*. This was a porridge of oil, cheese and various herbs pounded in a mortar (cf. *contundit*). It is described in the pseudo-Vergilian *Moretum* 90ff.

12 mecum: either (i) 'as my only company', emphasizing his isolation from the gathering of his friends (10), or (ii) 'in chorus with me', contrasting the normal pattern of human and animal life at this time of day with his own abnormality in joining the tireless cicadas, who are at their shrillest and most oppressive just before *aestus medios* (*G.* 3.327–8). (i) is slightly preferable with *at*, though *ac* has good authority here. To construe *me* with *resonant* and *cum* with *cicadis* is possible but unnecessary. The lines emphasize one of the poem's themes, the alienation of the lover. Corydon like the love-sick Bucaeus in Th. *Id.* 10.1–6 and the lovers of Latin Elegy has been driven to a life *sine ratione, nullo consilio* (Prop. 1.1.6).

raucis 'shrill', 'screeching'; the usual sense of the epithet (contrast 1.57). The more favourable epithet *argutae* in Calp. 5.56 recalls the traditional esteem in which their sound was held; cf. Th. *Idd.* 1.148, 7.138, and for cicadas as favourites of the Muses Plato *Phdr.* 259c.

tua...uestigia lustro implies that he had seen Alexis on one of Iollas' visits to his estate or perhaps (cf. *montibus et siluis* in 5) on a hunting expedition. See 29n. The original meaning of *lustrare* 'to purify ritually' was extended through 'make a ceremonial tour of' to the general sense 'travel purposefully all over'; which it has here and at 10.55 (of hunting). Cf. *uestigia lustrat* (*A.* 11.763).

arbusta 'trees' or plantations e.g. of elms (1.39n.).

13   sole sub ardenti is perhaps putting on the agony a little, since Vergil has already indicated that Corydon was at this particular moment *inter densas umbrosa cacumina fagos*. But Eros after all is not a truthful god (Mosch. 1.11) and suitors have a licence to exaggeration.

14   An abrupt change of tone: Corydon's first explicit awareness of alienation not only from his normal condition of life but from his own folk as well.

fuit is either to be taken literally, as *esses* (16) perhaps suggests, or for *foret*, as in Prop. 2.25.11 *nonne fuit satius duro seruire tyranno?*

14–15   iras...fastidia 'outbursts of anger...disdainful ways'; like the Amaryllis of *Id.* 3. For the plural see 1.6n. It appears that Corydon was no more happy in his normal love-life than he is now in his passion for Alexis.

15   nonne Menalcan is emphasized by its isolation after the major pause at the bucolic diaeresis. The name occurs in various tales of unhappy love (see Ath. 14.619c, *schol. ad Id.* 9 *argum.*) and in pastoral, associated with *Daphnis* (12n.), in [Th.] *Idd.* 8 and 9. *Menalcas* reappears in *Ecl.* 3, 5, 9, 10.20. See p. 31. The mention of Amaryllis and Menalcas together is an implicit reminder of the bisexuality of pastoral love; cf. 7.59, 67, 10.37.

16 esses sc. 'on the occasion when I saw you'. As a *uerna* Alexis would more easily retain the fair colouring which was so highly esteemed in antiquity (10.38–9).

17 Corydon's reflections lead not to praise of Alexis but to a warning not to set too much store by his *color*.

18 The homodynes give an appropriately emphatic tone to the warning after the uncompromising *ne* + imperative.

   cadunt: the tiny white flowers of the privet 'are left unpicked to fall'.

   uaccinia: the Latin word seems cognate with Greek *huákınthos* and the present passage recalls Th. *Id.* 10.26–9: 'Pretty Bombyca, they all call you Syrian, lean and sunburnt, but I alone call you honey-coloured. The violet is dark and the inscribed hyacinthus too, yet these are the first to be gathered in garlands.' However, *uaccinium* and *hyacinthus* were apparently distinguished (Plin. *Nat.* 16.77, 21.170). The former is probably the bilberry, Vaccinium Myrtillus, *nigra* referring not to the pink flowers but to the berries, which were a cheap source of purple dye. For *hyacinthus* see 3.63n.

19 After the warning a recital of his own credentials as a farmer (19–22), a musician (23–4) and a handsome suitor (25–7).

   despectus tibi 'contemptible in your eyes' or 'despised by you'; cf. *contemptus exercitui inuisusque* (Tac. *H.* 1.60).

   qui for *quis*; see 1.18n.

20 diues has a genitive (either of reference or by extension from the partitive) in *A.* 9.26, an instrumental abl. at *A.* 4.37–8. Both usages occur chiefly in poetry.

   niuei is taken with *pecoris* by Servius and the Berne Scholiast; cf. *G.* 3.391 *munere sic niueo lanae.* But the reference to 'snow-white milk', if somewhat commonplace, is supported by Th. *Id.* 5.53 and Ov. *M.* 13. 829 (Polyphemus' serenade) *lac mihi semper adest niueum.* With *abundans* the abl. is usual, e.g. Cic. *Off.* 1.78; but Nepos has the gen. at *Eum.* 8.5. Cf. Th. *Id.* 11.34–6 'Yet even as I am, I have a herd of a thousand cattle, and from these I draw and drink the finest milk. My supply of cheese never fails, no, not in summer nor autumn nor the depths of winter.'

21 meae, unlike e.g. *mihi*, makes the lambs unequivocally his own. If he were a free man, a flock that produced a thousand ewe-lambs would make him wealthy indeed; if he is a slave, then to claim such numbers as his own, even for use *precario* in gathering his *peculium* (1.32n.), is preposterous. Similarly exaggerated is his boast not just of a continual supply of cheese, like Polyphemus, but of fresh milk right through the winter and the summer, when *lac praecipit aestus* (cf. 3.98). Once again suitor's licence.

Siculis: this is the only Eclogue specifically set in a traditional Greek pastoral location; cf. 4.1, 6.1, 10.1.

23 In *Id.* 11.38-40 Polyphemus claimed to be the foremost piper among the Cyclopes – in itself no great accomplishment – but then went on, as Corydon does not, to pay his beloved the compliment of being the inspiration of his music. Corydon's musicianship, unlike Polyphemus' (*ibid.* 13-15), is not dependent upon the occasion but part of his normal life, and one to which he attaches great importance; see 31ff., esp. 37-9.

24 Amphion with Greek *ī* is of course required by the metre.

Dircaeus, though often used by metonomy for 'Theban', e.g. Hor. *C.* 4.2.25, here alludes to the punishment of Dirce and Lycus by Amphion and his brother Zethus, when they returned to Thebes to avenge their mother and claim their inheritance. Cf. Propertius 3.15.11-42. The magical power of Amphion's music in rebuilding the walls of Thebes was proverbial (Hor. *C.* 3.11.2) and he is coupled with Orpheus as an exemplar of the civilizing power of poets at Hor. *A.P.* 391-6. The association with Orpheus led to the attribution to Amphion of the Orphean power to charm animals (Paus. 9.5.8), and this may be referred to in *armenta uocabat*. Obscure herdsmen, having learned the divine power of music from Hermes or Pan, may live to become builders and rulers of famous cities. Urban sophisticates should not be too hasty to despise the humble rustic and his music.

Actaeo Aracyntho 'Attic Aracynthus'. Servius' gloss *Thebanus* may be just an inference from the context. However there is evidence (Stephanus Byzantinus, s.v. Ἀράκυνθος and the scholiast on Stat. *Theb.* 2.239) for a mountain of this name on the borders of Boeotia and Attica, presumably in the same range as Mount Cithaeron. For the better known Aracynthus in Acarnania see Plin. *Nat.* 4.6. Propertius mentions Aracynthus in the context of Amphion's triumph: *uictorque* *canebat | paeana Amphion rupe, Aracynthe, tua* (3.15.41–2); the connection probably dated back to the years of Amphion's exile, when he lived as a humble shepherd. *actaeus* (from Greek *aktaîos* 'coastal') is inappropriate. The adj. is not attested in Latin, though *aktế* 'promontory', 'coast-line' occurs in a Latin form at *A.* 5.613. Moreover while Mt Cithaeron itself is conspicuous along the Corinthian Gulf, there is no evidence that Aracynthus was. However, *Aktế, Aktaía* was an ancient name for Attica (Strabo 9.1.3) and Ovid in *M.* 2.720 has *arces...Actaeae* of Athens. 'Attic' accords with the evidence set out above, and there is no need to assume that Vergil has made Corydon perpetrate a geographical blunder in order to show that he is out of his depth. Corydon is certainly preening himself, but the absurdity here lies rather in the breach of *decorum* he commits by introducing this incongruously learned piece of Alexandrianism.

Actaeo Aracyntho shows hiatus without correction of the unelided vowel, a recurrent Graecism in the Eclogues, mostly in hellenizing contexts; see 3.6n. The line has four heterodyne feet, including the fifth, and a major pause after the third foot trochee: − − − − $\overset{\angle}{\cup}$ ‖ $\cup$ − − − $\cup\cup$ $\overset{\angle}{-}$ − . The result is a laboured portentous tone that is grotesquely incongruous in its context. The line could be transposed directly from the Greek Ἀμφίων Διρκαῖος ἐν Ἀκταίῳ Ἀρακύνθῳ, as *G.* 1.437 was from Parthenius' Γλαύκῳ καὶ Νηρῆι καὶ Ἰνώῳ Μελικέρτῃ (Gell. 13.27, Macrob. *Sat.* 5.17.18). An Alexandrian source is suggested but by no means certified by the allusive obscurity of the line.

25–7 Cf. Th. *Id.* 6.34–8 'For truly I'm not ugly in appearance, as they say I am. For I recently looked into the sea, and it was calm, and my beard showed up handsome and my one eye handsome too –in my judgement'; a context where Polyphemus is much more a straight figure of fun than he is in *Id.* 11. After 24 the prosaic phrases and uncouth verse rhythm of 25 bring us back to earth with a jolt.

26 uentis is instrumental abl. either with *staret*, cf. *uento rota constitit* (G. 4.484), or less likely with *placidum* 'calm because of the winds, without any wind to disturb it'. Winds were commonly said to calm the sea, presumably by relaxing their force on it, e.g. 9.57, *A.* 5.763, where *sternere* is the active correspondent to the passive *stare* here.

  mare, like Greek πόντος in the Theocritean passage translated in 25–7n., suggests the open sea, though Seneca seems to have understood it to mean a pool in the rocks, which would certainly make a more plausible mirror (*N.Q.* 1.17.5). A calm sheltered inlet of the sea might just reflect the huge image of a Cyclops or at its edges even a shepherd. But the detail is meant to be grotesque in both contexts.

non ego Daphnin: the normal homodyne cadence ($\underline{} \cup \cup \underline{} -$) is slightly roughened by the presence of a pyrrhic word ($\cup \cup$) in the fifth foot. The effect is common in Lucretius. Though it recurs in the present Eclogue at 37, 42, 53, 60, it becomes less frequent in the later poems. A major pause at the bucolic diaeresis is of course usually followed by enjambement. Vergil often employs the sequence in excited passages; so the disruption of the normal pausal patterns may be expressive. For Daphnis, the archetypal singing herdsman of the pastoral, see 5.20n. The comparison here is as foolish as Corydon's in Th. *Id.* 5.80–1 (3.62n.). Its pathetic ineptness is intensified by that apologetic *adeo* in 25, its lack of conviction by the final conditional clause, and its naivety by the appeal to the very person who rejects him.

28 After his own credentials an invitation to Alexis to share the simple pleasures of the country. The corresponding appeals to Galatea in *Id.* 11.42–4, 63–6 are dissimilar in tone and detail.

sordida, the opposite of *nitida*, reflects like *humilis* and *sordent* (44) the fastidious view of an *urbanus*; cf. Mart. 10.96.4, 12.57.2.

29 habitare as the frequentative of *habeo* must originally have been transitive, as it is in Cic. *Verr.* 4.119 and often in poetry, e.g. *A.* 3.106.

casas: typically these consisted of a wooden frame covered with boughs and foliage (Sen. *Ep.* 90.10).

figere ceruos: hunting which appears only on the fringe of the Greek pastoral world (e.g. Th. *Id.* 1.115–17) was of course a feature of the real countryside (cf. *G.* 3.409–13) and references to it recur in the Eclogues; cf. 41, 3.12–13, 5.60–1, 7.29–30. Moreover, it is an aspect of country life sure to appeal to a city dweller (cf. 10.55–60), though whether the pampered Alexis would have relished such robust pastimes is something Corydon has, perhaps significantly, not stopped to consider.

30 hibisco 'with a green marsh mallow switch'. The tough mallow rushes were pliant enough to be used for baskets (10.71) and the flowering stem, which grows to upwards of a metre, would also make a supple switch, especially when it was fresh-cut (*uiridi*) Servius took this as dative; but although *compellere* + dat. is found at Hor. *C.* 1.24.18, Corydon is unlikely to have driven his goats 'to the mallows', which would be unattractive fare even for such omnivorous animals and grow only on treacherous marshy ground.

haedos here, following *agnae* (21), shows that Corydon like Tityrus in *Ecl.* 1 (cf. 1.9n.) has a mixed farm.

32 pluris for *compluris* is already found in Cic. *Fin.* 2.93. A comparison is however often implied in the usage, as here between Pan-pipes and the single rustic pipe. Pan-pipes were made up of a number of separate hollow reed or hemlock stalks (cf. *cicutis* in 36) of differing lengths (*disparibus*), usually between seven and twenty-one in number, and joined together with beeswax. See [Th.] *Id.* 8.18–19. The alliteration of *p* and *c* probably reflects heightened emotion.

33 instituit: either 'began the practice' with the normal infinitival construction (cf. Cic. *Rep.* 2.12) or 'taught men to', where the inclusion of the personal object (cf. *G.* 1.148) is usual. See 5.29–30. For the story of Pan and Syrinx see Ov. *M.* 1.689–712.

ouis ouiumque magistros: for the phrase pattern cf. 3.101 and [Th.] *Id.* 8.48 χὠ τὰς βῶς βόσκων χαὶ βόες 'both the one who herds the cows and the cows'. Though a relative latecomer to the Greek pantheon (Aesch. *Pers.* 448–9, Pi. fr. 89B), Pan, the god of song and dance, is already associated with idealized landscape in *h. Hom.* 19, Eur. *Hel.* 167–90. In Hellenistic epigram he appears in various contexts relevant to the pastoral; e.g. as the lover of Daphnis (*A.P.* 9.338, 341, 7.535), the recipient of a dedication by Glaucon and Corydon (*A.P.* 6.96) and associated with love and music making (*A.P.* 5.139).

34 nec te paeniteat: the subjunctive may be hypothetical in sense: 'nor would you be repentant', or hortatory: 'do not be...' (cf. 8.89).

triuisse is either perfect or more likely aoristic-present in meaning; cf. *nec te paeniteat duros subiisse labores | aut opera insuetas atteruisse manus* (Tib. 1.4.47–8). Unlike Tibullus Vergil retains the older form of the perfect of *terere*. For the movement of the pipes to and fro across the lower lip cf. Lucr. 4.588 of Pan, *unco saepe labro calamos percurrit hiantis*, and 5.1407 of primitive music-makers.

labellum: the diminutive, though perhaps literally appropriate for the boy, has emotive connotations of tender affection.

35 Amyntas: a companion of Simichidas in Th. *Id.* 7.2; cf. *Cous*...
Amyntas (Hor. *Epod.* 12.18). In 3.66, 10.37–8 the name is given to a
favourite, in 5.8, 15, 18 to a vain and jealous rival.

37 fistula is emphatically placed in enjambement before a diaeresis
which is also the major pause in the line. The explosive succession of
dentals and the jerky final cadence (cf. 26n.) suggest a self-assertive
tone.

   Damoetas occurs in Th. *Id.* 6 and again in *Ecl.* 3.

38 ista is probably for *haec*, as often in vulgar Latin, rather than in
its normal classical use as second-person demonstrative 'that...by
you'.

   secundum stresses the value of the pipe, as having had only one
owner and an expert musician at that. The implication is *tu nunc eris
alter ab illo* (cf. 5.49).

38–9 dixit...dixit: the colloquial naivety of the immediate repetition of the verb underlines Corydon's pride in his music.

40 nec rather than *non*, though going closely with *tuta*, shows that
what follows is parenthetic. Corydon is characteristically explicit
about the hazards of acquiring his gift, unlike Polyphemus in *Id.*
11.40–1 who merely says 'And I'm rearing for you eleven fawns, all
with collars, and four bear-cubs'.

41 capreoli 'roebucks', kids of the wild she-goat *caprea*. The white
spots on their necks disappear after six months, according to Servius;
which is consistent with the fact that they are here still unweaned.

43–4 So too the goatherd of Th. *Id.* 3 uses the occasion to remind his
beloved of others more appreciative of his gifts: 'Indeed I'm keeping
for you a white she-goat with two kids, which that swarthy girl who
works for Mermnon wants me to give her; and I will too, since you're
so haughty to me' (34–6). For *orare* + infinitive with the same subject
implied cf. *A.* 6.313. The same construction occurs with *postulare* in
Pl. *Rud.* 394, with *poscere* in Ov. *M.* 8.707–8.

44 faciet 'she will do so'. Though no doubt colloquial in origin, the
usage is paralleled at *A.* 1.58 and Cic. *T.D.* 5.90.

45 Corydon's account of his gifts is interrupted by a sudden urgent
invitation to Alexis.

huc ades: for this conflation of *hic ades* and *huc adueni* cf. 7.9, 9.39, Tib. 1.7.49.

46 Nymphae: spirits of mountains, woods, springs and meadows (Hom. *Il.* 20.8–9, *Od.* 6.123–4), they were worshipped as patrons of particular localities (Hom. *Od.* 13.351). They play an integral part in the religion of the pastoral, e.g. Th. *Id.* 5.53–4, where their worship is associated with the cult of Pan (*ibid.* 58–9), and *Id.* 7.153–5, where they assist in the harvest festivities. Elsewhere in the Eclogues they are depicted as lamenting Daphnis (5.21), controlling the woodland pastures (6.55–6) and escorting Gallus in the mountains (10.55). They are the subject of pastoral song (9.19) and their cult is alluded to in 3.9 and 5.74; cf. 1.52n. Like Pan they not only protect the herdsmen but also inspire their music (cf. Th. *Id.* 7.91–3), and so become indistinguishable from the Muses; see 4.1, 7.21n.

calathis: the loan-word from Greek *kálathos* 'a bucket-shaped basket' is not recorded in Latin before Vergil, who uses it of a wine-vessel (5.71), a cheese-basket (*G.* 3.402) and, instead of the native *quasillus*, a wool-basket (*A.* 7.805). For the present use cf. Prop. 3.13.30. Polyphemus in *Id.* 11.56–9 imagines himself offering the simplest of posies to Galatea, 'I would have brought you white snowdrops or soft poppies with red petals'; only to remember that 'the one comes out during summer, the other in winter, so I couldn't have brought them all to you at once'. Meleager's more elaborate garland to Heliodora (*A.P.* 5.147) includes a number of the flowers mentioned here by Corydon.

candida Nais: one of the nymphs of the sacred springs (1.52). The realistic picture of the *sordida rura* (28–30) has been transformed by way of the reflections on Pan and pastoral music into an Arcadian landscape, rich in flowers and fruits, with its own deity – fair like Alexis (*candidus* in 16) but a friendly and willing helper to the humble shepherd.

47 uiolas: like Greek ἴον the noun is used of various flowers and Pliny mentions three distinct colours, *purpureae, luteae, albae* (*Nat.* 21.27). The distinction between *pallentis* and *luteola* (50) and the implied contrast with (*lutea*) *papauera* suggest that this is the hoary stock, Matthiola Incana, Greek λευκόϊον, which flowers in spring.

48 narcissum: there are two varieties, the yellow and white Narcissus Serotinus, which flowers in September, cf. *sera comantem | narcissum* (G. 4.122–3), and the Narcissus Poeticus or pheasant's eye, which has a white flower and crimson corona and blooms in late spring. The latter is probably meant here, as in 5.38 *purpureus narcissus*.

bene olentis anethi 'dill', Anethum Graueolens, Greek *ánēthon*, was a common garden herb in antiquity, used in garlands (Th. *Id.* 7.63, Sappho fr. 81LP) and in cooking (Apicius *passim*). Its small yellow flowers appear in midsummer. The epithet adds an explicit olfactory ingredient to what has hitherto been primarily a visual composition.

49   casia: a Semitic word imported via Greek *kasía* and originally used of cinnamon (G. 2.466) but extended in Latin to members of the Daphne or garland-flower family. Here probably the Cneorum, an evergreen trailer (G. 4.30) whose pink flowers appear in spring. It was noted for its fragrance; hence *suauibus herbis. casia* and *suauibus herbis* are instr. abl., *uaccinia* dir. obj. accus. to *intexens*.

50   luteola...caltha: the African marigold flowers in July. The adjective is from *lutum*, the yellow weed Reseda Luteola, which is still used to make dye. That the flower is chosen for its colour, not its scent, is confirmed by the adynaton at Ov. *Pont.* 2.4.28 *calthaque Paestanas uincet odore rosas*.

pingit uaccinia 'picks out, sets off, the bilberries' (18n.). *luteola* implies a colour contrast with the darker hue of the bilberry; *mollia* which introduces a tactile element into the imagery implies a contrast with the firm bunched petals of the marigold. The interweaving word order of the so-called golden line (adj. *A*, adj. *B*, verb, noun *A*, noun *B*) reflects the complex visual pattern.

51   ipse ego: after Nais' basket of flowers Corydon himself will bring fruit decked with herbs.

mala: like Greek *mâlon*, *mêlon* the word was used of any hard fruit. Here *lanugine* suggests quinces, which when fresh are covered in white down. *cana* too probably refers to the down rather than the actual colour of the fruit, *aurea* in 3.71.

52   castaneas...nuces again implies a contrast in colour and texture (cf *castaneae hirsutae* in 7.53) with the preceding quinces. Unless these were last season's chestnuts, they could not be available with the quinces or plums. *mea* is somewhat presumptuous, applied to the girl with the fiery temper (14). For the naivety of the recommendation cf. 45.

53 cerea: either of the smooth texture of the plums, cf. *cerea...
bracchia* (Hor. *C.* 1.13.2–3), or of their colour, cf. *Priap.* 51.9B *magisque
cera luteum noua prunum.* The line is metrically grotesque. The diaereses after every foot save the third and fourth and the frequent homodyne entailed by the diaereses together emphasize the rhythmic shape of each individual foot and give a dismembered effect to the line. Even more remarkable is the hiatus between *pruna* and *honos.* Long vowels are sometimes left unelided, with or without correption (24 and 3.6; 65 and 8.108); but Vergil's only other certain example of a normally short vowel unelided is in *A.* 1.405: *et uera incessu patuit dea. ille ubi matrem.* In both instances the hiatus coincides with the line's major pause.

54 o lauri: the personification expresses the sympathetic relation that Corydon feels with his natural surroundings.
   murte: the myrtle was sacred to Venus as the bay was to Apollo. The combination of the two, e.g. 7.62, Th. *Ep.* 4.7, Hor. *C.* 3.4, 18–19, represents the union of love and music.
   The elaborate catalogue of flowers and fruits is now complete. Although all the ingredients are commonplace in the Italian or Sicilian countryside and there is nothing rare or exotic, it is nevertheless a highly polished set-piece, often rehearsed no doubt, as Corydon vainly sought his next meeting with Alexis. However, unlike Meleager *A.P.* 5.147, where the posy- or garland-motif is associated with the thought 'fair flowers for the fairest', Corydon's praise here is exclusively for the produce of his land. Allusions to the *sordida rura* have now given way to eloquent and fanciful *laudes ruris.* Yet unlike Theocritus' Polyphemus (46n.) he does not destroy the effect he has just created by recalling – as he could well have done – that all the ingredients of his catalogue were not in season together. Like Meliboeus' *locus amoenus* in 1.51–8 the passage shows that ordinary countrymen, aware of the realities of country life, can still be inspired by their surroundings to flights of poetic fancy. This truly Arcadian quality is something that no alien, whether it is the *barbarus miles* of *Ecl.* 1 or *formonsus Alexis* here, can fully comprehend or share.

56 An abrupt change of mood: in a flash of self-awareness and disillusion he sees the hopeless absurdity of his passion.and the alienation that it has imposed upon him.

rusticus is sharply contrasted with *urbanus* in both senses: 'a country-dweller' and 'a boor'; cf. the contemptuous words of the urbane Eunica to her rustic suitor in [Th.] *Id.* 20.3–4 'Cowman as you are, do you desire to kiss me, you wretch? I've not learnt to love rustics but to press the lips of well-bred townsmen.'

57 Iollas: the name, which is not Theocritean, recurs in 3.76, and is given to one of Aeneas' men in *A.* 11.640. Whatever his legal relationship to Corydon and Alexis (see 2n.), he is here a *diues amator*, the stock villain of comedy and elegy: cf. Tib. 1.5.47–8, Prop. 4.5, and Thraso in Ter. *Eun.*

58 heu heu: without elision or correption (see 53n.). Monosyllabic exclamations must obviously be a special case in metrical matters.

58–9 floribus Austrum...fontibus apros: flowers such as those depicted in 46ff. would need protection from strong winds, especially the summer south wind, *Scirocco*, for which cf. Ov. *M.* 7.532 *letiferis calidi spirarunt aestibus Austri*. For the enjambement after a diaeretic pause see 26n. The wallowing wild boars bring us back with a jolt to *sordida rura*. The whole sentence is no doubt intended as a rustic proverb of incompetence, though *perditus* 'ruined' has overtones of the lover's plight; cf. *peribat* (10.10). For 1st sg. *inmissi* see p. 39.

60 One last desperate appeal to Alexis.

di: besides the gods especially associated with the countryside – Pan and the Nymphs, Apollo, Ceres, Silvanus etc. – there were also those who had come to dwell in the country in pursuit of mortal loved ones. Attis, Adonis, Endymion and Ganymede had all roused divine passions; cf. Th. *Id.* 3.46–51 and [Th.] *Id.* 20.34–43.

61 Dardaniusque Paris: a modest piece of erudition after 24. Paris is called *Phrygius...pastor* at *A.* 7.363, and his fateful judgement of the goddesses, which gave the prize for beauty to Aphrodite, was made when he was a shepherd on Mt Ida. The epithet reminds us that the lowly shepherd became not only one of the great lovers but also like Amphion the prince of a great city, which was finally destroyed by his love. The contrast with *Pallas* is piquant: the virgin goddess

Πολιοῦχος 'Keeper of the citadel', whom with Hera Paris rejected, can stay in the city. The countryside is the place for lovers.

nobis 'you and me'. Corydon himself could already have said with Moschus (fr. 1.7) 'to me the land is welcome and the shady wood a delight'.

63 The rustic analogy is a conventional pastoral figure; cf. 5.32–4, 7.65–8, [Th.] *Id.* 8.57–9, 9.31–6. The present example is modelled on Th. *Id.* 10.30–1. 'The goat runs after shrub-trefoil, the wolf after the goat, the crane after the plough, and I am wild over you'. Vergil's organization is more mannered, even if the contents are no less naive. It begins somewhat fancifully; for lions do not prey on wolves, and in any event had been extinct in Europe since pre-historic times.

leaena: the choice of the feminine may be metrical, since *toruos leo* would be less tractable; but it also contributes to the chiastic gender pattern: *leaena, lupum, lupus, capellam*.

64 lasciua: the randiness of goats is proverbial and perhaps conveys an implicit boast into the following line, combined with something of the wistfulness of Th. *Id.* 1.87–8 'The goatherd's eyes, whenever he sees how the nannies are being mounted, dissolve in tears that he was not born a goat himself.'

65 ŏ Alexi: see 58n.

trahit sua quemque uoluptas underlines the ineptness of the detail in the analogy. For the wolf would presumably be terrified of the lion, as the goat certainly would of the wolf, while the shrub trefoil would be but the passive and unfeeling object of the goat's attentions. The *uoluptas* is thus very onesided. For the same unintentional admission of the real feelings that the lover inspires in his beloved cf. Th. *Id.* 11.24 'Why do you flee, like a sheep in terror of the grey wolf?'

66 aspice may still be addressed to the absent boy, but is more likely to himself in another moment of self-awareness. For the picture of the oxen returning from the fields with the inverted plough hanging from the yoke cf. Hor. *Epod.* 2.63–4. It is a detail from the real, not the idyllic, countryside; see 1.2n.

67 The slow succession of heavy syllables, seven of them with long vowels, is reinforced by the concluding triple homodyne. The tranquil evening scene marks not a reconciliation of conflict, as in 1.82–3, but a bitter contrast to the shepherd's own feelings.

68 Like the image of Love's fire itself the thought that passion burns continually, even when the heat of the day is past, was a commonplace; e.g. Hor. *C.* 2.9.10–12; cf. also Th. *Id.* 2.38–40 'Look, the sea is silent, the winds silent too; but the torment in my breast is not silent. No, I am all on fire for him.' But Meleager's epigram (1n.) is of course closest to Vergil's treatment.

modus: cf. 10.28, Prop. 2.15.29–30 *errat qui finem uesani quaerit amoris;* | *uerus amor nullum nouit habere modum.*

69 For the lover's recollection of his neglected tasks cf. Th. *Id.* 11.72–4 'Oh Cyclops, Cyclops, where have your wits flown off to? If you were to go and plait some cheese-crates and gather greenery to bring to the lambs, you'd maybe show a lot more sense.' At last Corydon realizes that the *dementia* which he attributed to Alexis (60) is in fact his own.

70 semiputata 'half trimmed' occurs only here in Latin and looks as if it is a technical term. As the grapes ripened, it was important to keep the foliage of both the vine itself and the tree to which it was trained so trimmed as to allow plenty of light but not too much of the direct rays of the sun to reach the ripening clusters; see 1.56n. and Colum. 4.27. As the *frondatio* was best done *antelucanis et uespertinis temporibus* (cf. Colum. 11.2.55), Corydon's observation of his neglect is timely.

tibi indicates interest, specifically either agency or disadvantage. Although it is possible that *-i* is short here (see 1.7–8n.) and the heavy syllable produced by the syllable division *ti-bif-ron-* (cf. Tib. 1.6.34 *seruare frustra*), it is more likely that *-i* is long, an archaism for which see 4.23n.

71 quin 'why not?' < *quī*, the old abl. of *quid*, +*nē*, the original negative particle (*nōn* < *ne* + **oinom*, viz. *unum*).

aliquid saltem: even if he does not resume work on the vines, at least he might do something useful. The pronoun is object to *detexere.* The antecedent to *quorum*, viz. *eorum* (with *aliquid*) is, as often, omitted: 'of those tasks that practical considerations demand'. For the partitive genitive with *indigere* cf. Cic. *Att.* 12.35.2. The prosaic tone of the lines is appropriate to his return to ordinary rustic tasks.

72 uiminibus: any pliant boughs suitable for the ribbing of a basket, to which the softer rushes (*iunco*) were plaited horizontally (Var. *R.* 1.23.5). The prefix of *detexere* is probably completive: 'to plait to the end', 'to finish plaiting'. For basket-making on the farm cf. 10.71 and Tib. 2.3.15 *tunc fiscella leui detexta est uimine iunci.*

73 In Corydon's final words there is none of the wounded vanity and vindictiveness of Eunica's suitor in [Th.] *Id.* 20.44–5 nor any threats to do away with himself, like the self-dramatizing goatherd in Th. *Id.* 3.9 (6n.), 25–7, 53, let alone the actual suicide of [Th.] *Id.* 23.49–53. Instead the mood is one of resignation, bolstered by the reassurance that he will find not just a more appreciative loved one, but another Alexis without the disdain. The poem ends as it began with Alexis. The obsession recalls Polyphemus' words in *Id.* 11.75–9 'Why pursue one who flees from you? Perhaps you'll find another Galatea, even more beautiful. Many girls invite me to play with them at night, and they all giggle whenever I give ear to them. It's obvious that on land even I seem to be somebody.' But Corydon has not even a flattering interpretation of girlish laughter to console himself with; he has not found contentment in love even among his own folk, and *fastidit* here ironically echoes the *fastidia* (15) of Amaryllis.

The poem is rich in echoes of earlier pastoral. Th. *Id.* 11 provides the theme of 'the passionate shepherd' and much of the detail (see the notes on 4, 20, 23, 40, 46, 69, 73). The debt is emphasized by the explicit Sicilian setting, and perhaps by the Galatea-quatrain assigned to the Corydon of 7.37ff. The idyll was ostensibly didactic, an illustration (1–3) of the 'medicine of the Muses', but Theocritus leaves us in no doubt that the remedy was short-lived, and needed frequent repetition. The didacticism in Vergil's poem is left implicit.

In replacing the monster by the more Arcadian figure of a human shepherd Vergil has deprived himself of a source of comedy. But the humour, muted to be sure, is there in the boasts of 20–6, 36–9, the naive commendations of 43–4, 52, and the inept analogy of 63–5. It is reinforced by echoes in 6, 43–4 from the absurd goatherd of *Id.* 3. The incompatibility of land and sea, so important in *Id.* 11, is replaced by the antipathy of town and country already remarked in *Ecl.* 1. To

this antipathy, for which Eunica's petulant suitor in *Id.* 20 provides
something of a precedent, the elegiac theme of the *diues amator*, the
rival Iollas, for whom there is no pastoral model, can easily be related.
The lover's alienation from the normal pattern of life, though it has
Theocritean precedent in *Idd.* 11 and 10 (for echoes of which see the
notes on 18, 63), was a prominent theme of Roman elegy. Yet, just as
Propertius could say *ingenium nobis ipsa puella facit*, so too in Polyphemus and Bucaeus love can be seen as a catalyst to the poetical powers
latent in the humble countryman, and the singer, though he finds the
medicine ineffectual, can still take pleasure in his new-found talent:
'In this way Polyphemus went on shepherding his love in music-
making and found life easier than if he had paid out gold' (*Id.* 11.80–
1). What is peculiar to Corydon is that, like the elegists again, his
flights of poetry are much more self-centred; moreover they reach
their heights in the idealizing contemplation of his beloved countryside, not in praise of the boy Alexis. In this most elegiac of pastorals
the Arcadian mood thus comes through strongly.

The monologue itself is but a sample extract; for the recital continued from noon till sunset (9ff., 66–7). It is uneven in structure, as
haec incondita has indeed led us to expect. Its divisions – at 19, 28, 45,
56, 60, 66 – correspond to violent and abrupt changes of mood, passionate appeals to Alexis alternating with *laudes ruris* and with moments
of disillusion and realistic self-awareness. This exploration of the complexity of the lover's state gives dramatic mobility to the poem and
again recalls the elegiac rather than the pastoral tradition.

Finally there is the choice of a homosexual love – Alexis instead of
Theocritus' Galatea or Amaryllis. Bisexuality was an accepted feature
of the Arcadian myth, as in classical love poetry, e.g. Catullus' Lesbia-
and Iuuentius-poems and the epigrams of the Greek Anthology.
The theme of homosexuality appears both in the pastoral *Id.* 7 of
Theocritus and in the non-pastoral *Id.* 23; but the immediate formative influence on Vergil's poem is of course from Meleager's epigram
cited on line 1.

There was an ancient tradition, explicit in Don. *Vit.* 28–31 and
Serv. *ad* 2.15 but already familiar to Martial (6.68.5–6, 8.55.12) and
Apuleius (*Apol.* 10), that Vergil had fancied a young slave Alexander
belonging to his patron Pollio (Maecenas in some versions!) and,
when he was presented with the boy, wrote this poem in gratitude to

the donor. Nothing in the text provides a starting point for such a story, and it would be a strange act of gratitude to depict the lover's rejection by his favourite, unless of course Alexander did repel Vergil's advances – the one detail on which the tradition is silent. Donatus reports that the poet was rustic in appearance, shy and hesitant in manner and bisexual (*Vit.* 25; 38f., 50; 28, 32) – in fact very like Corydon, so it is conceivable that some youthful disappointment in love led him to choose this theme for his first pastoral (for the date see pp. 17–18) and to project something of his own experience into the treatment of it. This does not mean that Corydon is a 'mask' for Vergil any more than Tityrus or Meliboeus are in *Ecl.* 1. The fact that Pollio was his patron at the time (3.84ff., 8.6–13) would account for the later form of the tradition. Whatever views we take of the poem's genesis do not affect our appreciation of it as a literary creation, in which Vergil's originality has blended a number of traditional elements to form a truly elegiac pastoral.

ECLOGUE III

1 For the opening cf. Th. *Id.* 4.1–3 'Battus "Tell me Corydon, whose cattle are these? Are they Philondas'?" Corydon: "No, they're Aegon's; he gave them to me to graze." Battus: "And I dare say you're milking them on the quiet in the evenings".' *Damoetas* in Th. *Id.* 6, *Menalcas* in [Th.] *Idd.* 8 and 9 are the names of competitors in friendly singing contests with Daphnis.

quoium: the adjective occurs often in comedy, e.g. Pl. *Rud.* 745, Ter. *Eun.* 321, and once in a legal formula at Cic. *Ver.* 2.1.142. It survived in popular Latin (cf. Span. *cuyo, cuya*) but its subliterary character – here deliberately employed for rustic colour (see p. 25) – was satirized in Numitorius' *Antibucolica* (Don. *Vit.* 171ff.) *dic mihi Damoeta; 'quoium pecus' anne Latinum? | non, uerum Aegonis nostri; sic rure loquuntur.*

an Meliboei: the polysyllabic ending to the verse, though sanctioned by Greek metrical practice, blurred the usual Latin homodyne cadence; cf. 2.24, 3.37, 6.53. The particle, as often (e.g. 21), introduces an animated question.

2 Aegon, who is again associated with Damoetas at 5.72, is evidently, like Meliboeus, of superior status to the two speakers. The combination in these two lines of lively Latin colloquialism and Greek proper names with their Greek sounds and inflections, voc. -*ā*, nom. -*ōn*, must have been very piquant to contemporary readers; cf. 9.1–2.

3   oues is either nom. or voc. The reading *ouis* would be collective singular like *pecus*. The jibe is from *Id.* 4.13 'And wretched beasts at that, to have found such a bad herdsman.'

Neaeram: though a common name for nymphs in mythology, e.g Hom. *Od.* 12.133, this is its first appearance in extant pastoral.

4   fouet 'fondles' attributes to Aegon a trait that apparently belonged to his father in *Id.* 4.58–63.

ac occurs only here and at 4.9 in the Eclogues, in both instances avoiding *et* in successive syllables.

5   bis mulget in hora: the charge of dishonesty (cf. *Id.* 4.3) is compounded by technical incompetence.

6   pecori et: hiatus after a long vowel without correption is a Graecism. It is found before both heavy syllables and light ones; cf. *pecori, armentaque* (*G.* 3.155), *pecori, apibus* (*G.* 1.4). The former is the more frequent in the Eclogues; cf. 2.58, 3.63, 100, 7.53, 8.41, 44, as against 2.24, 10.12 (10.13 being ambiguous, viz. *etiam* or disyllabic *etiam*).

subducitur: not only is Aegon being robbed but the unweaned animals also, robbed of their 'vital juice'; suckling ewes ought not to be milked except for their surplus.

7–8 'All the same (*tamen*) such accusations as yours (*ista*) should be made less wildly when you're talking to *men*; remember that!' The implied contrast in *uiris* is not with boys; for though Menalcas seems the younger of the two herdsmen (32–3), he is still old enough to claim that Galatea, and perhaps Phyllis too, fancied him. The contrast is with passive homosexuals. For, though homosexuality was accepted among the Arcadian shepherds, who shared the natural amorality of their flocks, there was always as in the bisexual tradition of ancient literature generally an attitude of contempt for the male who played the passive or 'female' role in a homosexual act, as the acc. *te* here indicates that Menalcas had done; cf. Th. *Id.* 5.41, Cat. 16.

qui may be singular (see 1.18n.) or plural. The ellipse of the verb is an instance not of *uerecundia* but of colloquialism, like the parenthetic *sed…risere* in the next line.

transuersa tuentibus: either literally 'peeping out of the corner of their eyes' or figuratively 'looking askance'; cf. Greek λοξὰ βλέπειν. This was too much even for the lusty goats, but not for the 'easygoing' nymphs, who might have been expected to frown on such a desecration of the shrine.

risere: *-ere* is not much commoner than *-erunt* in the Eclogues, but becomes overwhelmingly so in Vergil's later works.

10 credo unlike *ut credo* is usually sarcastic.

arbustum, the only instance of the singular in Vergil, is a plantation of trees, e.g. elms, to which the vines were trained; cf. 1.39n.

Miconos: the name, already found at Th. *Id.* 5.112, occurs again in 7.30.

11 Cutting other people's trees was already a punishable offence in the Twelve Tables (Plin. *Nat.* 17.7); young vines, which needed careful handling anyway (*G.* 2.362–70), would be especially damaged by such treatment.

13 calamos is frequently used by synecdoche for *sagittas*, e.g. *A.* 10.140. This meaning is guaranteed here by the collocation with *arcum*, though the sense 'pipes' is common elsewhere in the Eclogues, e.g. at 1.10, 2.32.

14 puero: the implication seems to be that Daphnis is younger than the two speakers.

15 aliqua sc. *ratione*.

16 fures: the contrast is with the rightful owners of the flock, so the normal sense seems appropriate. Servius says *pro seruo furem posuit*, and this meaning is well attested in comedy. However, the servile status of the herdsmen is explicit only in contexts where it is essential to the dramatic situation, 1.27, 32, 40 and 2.2 (and perhaps implied in 9.10).

17 Damon, whose flock is here being tended by Tityrus (20), does not appear in earlier pastoral, though the name is common in Greek generally. It is given to one of the singers in *Ecl.* 8.

18 excipere is often used of a hunter catching his prey, e.g. Hor. *C.* 3.12.12.

Lycisca is found as a canine name at Ov. *M.* 3.220. Pliny (*Nat.* 8.148) mentions mongrels bred from wolves and dogs, which Servius says were known as *lycisci* 'wolflings'.

21 an again introduces an indignant question; cf. 1n.

redderet is the past-tense equivalent of a deliberative subjunctive; cf. *quid facerem?* (1.41).

22 meruisset: the subjunctive is either by attraction to *redderet* or to indicate that the *quem* clause is causal.

24 posse negabat: for the simple infinitive as complement to a verb of saying cf. *A.* 3.201, Cic. *T.D.* 2.40 *ferre non posse clamabit.*

25 The ellipse of *uicisti* is colloquial and the use of the abl. of the gerund here as in 21, though common enough in literary Latin, was especially favoured in popular speech. For the jibe that follows cf. Th. *Id.* 5.5–7 'Have you, Sibyrtas' slave, ever acquired a pipe of your own? Why aren't you content any more to tootle away on a straw pipe with Corydon?'

26 tu is emphatic.

in triuiis: cf. *carmen triuiale* 'a vulgar ditty' (Juv. 7.55).

27 stipula: a single pipe made from a 'corn-stalk' (1.2n.), perhaps with a vibrating reed over the mouthpiece.

disperdere 'to murder'. The onomatopoeia is striking, with its sequence of *s* and *r* sounds and constricted *i* and *e* vowels. Damoetas, having been accused of theft and ineptitude as a farmer (5–6), is now charged with musical incompetence.

28–9 uicissim 'taking turns' in an amoeboean contest.

The paratactic use of *experiamur*, the interjected *ne* clause and the disturbed word order, expressive of Damoetas' excitement, are all features of the vivid colloquial style, reminiscent of Plautus and Terence.

uitulam 'female yearling' instead of *iuuencam* may also be colloquial.

30 bis uenit ad mulctram 'comes to the milking-pail twice a day'. Cf. Hor. *Epod.* 16.49 *ueniunt ad mulctra capellae.* According to Pliny (*Nat.* 8.177) it was rare for a heifer to produce twin calves, so *binos...fetus* would be a special commendation. The detail may have been influenced by Th. *Id.* 1.25–6 'And I'll give you a goat that has borne twins for you to milk three times over, one who even with two kids yields two buckets of milk besides.'

depono: like the bull in line 100 the heifer belongs to himself and not like the sheep to Aegon. For the wager before a singing contest see Th. *Id.* 5.21ff., [Th.] *Id.* 8.13ff.

32–4 Menalcas' animals by contrast belong to his parents. For the fear of their wrath cf. *Id.* 8.15–16 'I shan't ever wager a lamb, since my father's stern and my mother too, and they count all the sheep every evening.' Vergil has introduced the proverbial *saeua nouerca* (cf. *G.* 2.128). The prosaic vocabulary and colloquial syntax continues into 35–6 with its anticipatory *id quod* and the disturbed word order of the parenthetic *quoniam* clause. *ausim* may have had an archaic flavour. Though found in *G.* 2.289 and in Livy and Augustan poets, it was avoided by Cicero, who preferred *ausus sim*.

alter 'one or the other', though Servius took it as common gender for *altera*, referring to the step-mother.

36 For Menalcas' stake cf. Th. *Id.* 1.27–56 '. . . and I'll give you a deep cup . . . with two handles, freshly made and still smelling of the knife. At its lips a trail of ivy stands out, ivy dotted with clustered gold, and all along it winds the tendril rejoicing in its yellow fruit . . . And all over the cup spreads the pliant acanthus . . . ' Vergil has substituted two cups and provided them with altogether different scenes; see 40n.

37 fagina: beech-wood is appropriately humble material for herdsmen's cups; cf. Ov. *M.* 8.669–70. Nevertheless their society can boast an 'inspired' craftsman. For this common meaning of *diuinus* cf. 5.45, Cic. *de Or.* 1.40. There is a contrast here with *Id.* 1.57–8, where Thyrsis 'paid the ferryman at Calydna a goat and a large white milk cheese' for his cup, and *Id.* 5.104–5, where Corydon boasts of 'a bowl that is the work of Praxiteles': both the Theocritean artifacts are imported.

Alcimedontos: the name seems to be fictitious, and like *Delia* (67), *Alcon* (5.11), and *Mnasyllos* (6.13), is without precedent in extant pastoral. For the Greek flavour of the polysyllabic cadence see 1n.

38 lenta 'pliant', 'supple'; cf. 5.16 and 1.3n.

torno 'with a chisel'; the loan-word from Greek *tórnos* is used both of carving chisels and of the lathes to which they were fitted.

superaddita presents the visual effect as the actual process of

manufacture; the outlines of the vine, grapes and ivy were left in relief
by chiselling away the surface of the cup around them (*exsculpere*).

39 'clothes its scattered clusters with pale ivy'. This seems preferable
to understanding *corymbos* as *hederarum bacas* and taking *hedera...
pallente* with *diffusos*.

pallente (cf. *alba* at 7.38) probably refers to the colour of the ivy
leaves, which in one variety have light yellow markings, though the
rare Hedera Chrysocarpa has yellow berries, in contrast to the black
berries of the common Hedera Helix. At *G.* 2.258 *nigrae* may refer to
the leaves or the berries. Ivy, like vines, was associated with Bacchus
(Prop. 3.3.35) and poetic inspiration (7.25, 8.13, Hor. *C.* 1.1.29),
hence an appropriate decoration for drinking cups to be wagered
in a singing contest. The intricate word-order of the couplet,
with a variant form of the 'golden line' in 39, is expressive in itself
and also places the 'pliant vine' and 'scattered clusters' in emphatic
position.

40   duo signa: either one on each cup or one on either side of each
cup, for which *bina* would be more precise. The vine and ivy form the
frame, as in Theocritus, *loc. cit.* There, however, there are three scenes:
a beautiful woman and her two love-lorn suitors, an old fisherman
casting his net from a rock, a boy plaiting while the foxes plunder his
vines and his lunch-bag. Only the last of these, probably an allusion
to some rustic moral fable, has obvious links with pastoral; the other
two scenes, recalling the fisherman in *Id.* 21 and the urban setting of
love's cruelty in *Id.* 2, take us for a while outside the specifically
pastoral context.

Conon: the famous third-century astronomer *qui stellarum ortus
comperit atque obitus* (Cat. 66.2). He was credited with naming the
constellation *Coma Berenices* (*ibid.* 1-7) and his scientific discoveries like
those of Archytas seem to have been incorporated into the lore of
divination and prophecy (Prop. 4.1.77-8).

quis fuit alter: another characterizing colloquialism; for Vergil's
herdsmen must not in general appear too erudite. The reference is
either to Conon's friend Archimedes, whose name is unmetrical, or
more likely to the fourth-century astronomer Eudoxus, whose *Phaenomena* was the source of Aratus' didactic poem. The latter was trans-

lated into Latin hexameters by the young Cicero and much used by Vergil himself in the astronomical passages of the *Georgics*.

41 Astronomers' diagrams (cf. *A.* 6.849-50) were marked out on a table (*abacus*) sprinkled with sand or powdered glass.

orbem is either 'the vault of heaven' or, more likely in view of the next line, 'the cycle of the seasons'.

42 curuos: the ancient plough, being light in weight and with only one handle, required heavy pressure: *arator nisi incuruus praeuaricatur* (Plin. *Nat.* 18.179). For the agricultural allusion see 1.2n.

haberet: the subjunctive denotes purpose: 'for the ploughman to keep'.

43 Cf. Th. *Id.* 1.59-60 'it has never yet touched my lips, but is still lying there without a mark on it'.

45 molli...acantho: the cultivated varieties of 'bear's-breech', Acanthus Mollis, lack the characteristic prickles of the wild variety, Acanthus Spinosus. The luxuriant foliage of both is dark and soft, hence *molli* here; cf. ὑγρός 'pliant' in Th. *Id.* 1.55 (36n.). It is said to have inspired the form of the Corinthian capital.

circum is adverbial: 'all around'.

46 The miraculous power of Orpheus' music in charming animals, trees and rocks, rivers and even the elements is often alluded to: e.g Aesch. *Ag.* 1630, Eur. *Ba.* 562-4, Hor. *C.* 1.12.8-12. For his brief triumph over death itself see Eur. *Alc.* 357-62 and *G.* 4.467ff. Mythological and cosmogonical verses (see O. Kern's *Orphica*) were attributed to him by tradition as the archetypal poet-seer, and his role as a civilizer of mankind is stressed in Hor. *A.P.* 391-3. As the 'celebrated father of songs' (Pi. *P.* 4.176-7) he represents the whole range of poetic achievement, just as Conon and Eudoxus represent the range of scientific discovery. He occupies the central position, *in medio*, on both Damoetas' cups. The exact repetition of Menalcas' words from 43, the emphatic repetition of Alcimedon's name and the triumphantly brief description of Damoetas' own cups are calculated to deflate his rival's fulsome praise of the stake that he has offered.

48 ad uitulam spectas: though the construction occurs in Enn. *Ann.* 85V *spectant ad carceris oras*, it probably had a colloquial flavour at this time; cf. Var. *R.* 3.6.1 *si ad fructum spectes*. There is no need to understand *pocula* as the object of the verb with *ad* meaning 'in comparison with'.

nihil est quod 'there is nothing in respect of which', viz. 'there is no reason why'.

49   numquam hodie 'never in your life', 'not on your life'. The phrase is attested not only in comedy (Pl. *As.* 630, Ter. *Ad.* 570) but also in Naev. *trag.* 15R with the same verb *effugies* (Macrobius *Sat.* 6.1.38); but it was probably colloquial at this period.

ueniam quocumque uocaris: cf. Ov. *H.* 13.163. The phrase suggests that Menalcas has conceded Damoetas' point and will wager a heifer after all (32). This accords with Palaemon's judgement in 109, where cups are not mentioned.

50   Vergil does not extend the wrangling to the choice of a judge, as in Th. *Id.* 5.62-5, but adapts [Th.] *Id.* 8.25-6 'But who is going to judge us? Who'll be our auditor? That goatherd there perhaps, look, let's call on him.'

audiat haec... 'Just let this contest be heard by, say, the person who's coming now...Ah, it's Palaemon': taking *tantum* with *audiat*, cf. *tantum...reponas* (53-4), and *uel*, originally the imperative of *uolo*, in the sense that it commonly bears with superlatives. The style is vividly colloquial.

Palaemon: not in Theocritus or elsewhere in the Eclogues. It is the name of a sea-god in *A.* 5.823, Pl. *Rud.* 160; cf. Ov. *M.* 4.542.

52   si quid habes (sc. *quod dicas*): this colloquial phrase recurs at 9.32 (cf. 5.10-11).

54   sensibus...imis: cf. Hor. *Epod.* 14.1-2.

res est non parua: the parenthesis is colloquial.

55   Palaemon's decision avoids any dispute of the kind that Lacon and Comatas have over the choice of setting in Th. *Id.* 5.31-4, 45-61.

56   parturit: cf. Bion fr. 2.17 'In spring all things are pregnant, throughout spring everything delightful is in bud.' The season when 'the year is at its most beautiful' is the season when nature comes to life again; cf. *G.* 2.323-45. The association between nature's revival and human sexuality, implied in *parturit* as in the Bion passage, is often explicit in descriptions of spring; cf. Lucr. 1.10-20.

58 Cf. [Th.] *Id.* 9.1–2 'Make rustic music, Daphnis. You begin first: begin singing, Daphnis, and let Menalcas follow.' In *Id.* 8 the two singers drew lots and Menalcas began. Here Damoetas begins, no doubt because he proposed the contest, though Palaemon in nominating him could hardly be aware of this.

sequĕre: the future indicative often has hortative force. The imperative *sĕquĕrĕ* would be metrically more difficult.

59 alternis sc. *uicibus*. The contests are usually amoebaean, *di' amoibaiōn* ([Th.] *Id.* 8.61), hexameter couplets here as in *Id.* 5.80ff., quatrains in *Ecl.* 7, elegiac quatrains in *Id.* 8.33ff. In *Idd.* 6 and 9 the competition consists of just one pair of lengthier songs.

amant alterna Camenae: cf. Hom. *Il.* 1.604 'the Muses singing with beautiful voices in alternation (*ameibómenai*)'. The identification of the Italian (perhaps Etruscan) *Camenae* with the Greek Muses is as old as Livius Andronicus. Unsuccessful attempts have been made to connect the name with *carmen* (cf. Var. *L.* 7.26).

60 ab Ioue principium Musae: a sentiment as old as Alcman (fr. 29P) and Terpander (fr. 1D). More immediate precedents occur at Th. *Id.* 17.1 'Let us start from Zeus, and return to Zeus, ye Muses, when you cease'; and especially (see 40n.) Arat. *Ph.* 1–5 'Let us start from Zeus, whose name men never leave unspoken; all the streets and market-places of mankind are full of Zeus...Everywhere we are dependent on Zeus, all of us. For we are even his offspring.'

Musae is probably genitive; cf. Cicero's translation of Aratus' first line (*Leg.* 2.7) *a Ioue Musarum primordia* and perhaps *A.* 7.219 *ab Ioue principium generis*. It could, however, be vocative; cf. Ov. *M.* 10.148 *ab Ioue, Musa parens*.

Iouis omnia plena: no Stoic overtones need be seen here; the immanentism is adequately motivated by Palaemon's preceding eulogy of spring.

61 colit 'cares for', 'sustains' rather than merely 'dwells in'. The divine source of nature's fertility and man's music is one and the same.

62 et me Phoebus amat answers the immediately preceding phrase. The responsion pattern is thus not as symmetrical as Th. *Id.* 5.80–2 'Corydon: "The Muses love me far more than they love the poet Daphnis..."'. Battus: "And indeed Apollo loves me greatly..."'

sua 'those appropriate to him'.

63   lauriet: for the hiatus without correption see 6n. Combined with the polysyllabic ending (see 1n.) it gives an appropriately Greek tone to the line.

hyacinthus is depicted with lily-like petals (Ov. *M.* 10.212), rich red in colour – *suaue rubens* here, *ferrugineus* (*G.* 4.183), *purpureus* (Ov. *ibid.* 213) – and marked (cf. Th. *Id.* 10.28) with the letters *AI* (Euphorion fr. 40P, Ov. *ibid.* 215) or *Υ* (Philargyrius on the present line). It is not clear that all the Greek and Latin references to *hyacinthus* are to the same flower. Identifications by modern authorities include the corn-flag (Gladiolus Segetum), martagon (Lilium Martagon), and red asphodel. The *hyacinthus* like the bay-tree *laurus* had its mythological origin in the thwarted passion of Apollo; cf. the tales of Daphne and Hyacinthus in Ov. *M.* 1.452–567, 10.162–219. The associations of the two plants bring a touch of sorrow to the joyous picture of spring.

64   malum (2.51n.) was used like Greek *mâlon* of apples, peaches, quinces and pomegranates (Plin. *Nat.* 15.39), all of which were dedicated to Venus by her worshippers and offered as gifts to loved ones, e.g. Th. *Id.* 11.10, Prop. 1.3.24. Throwing the fruit was a conventional courtship signal; e.g. Ar. *Nub.* 997, Plato *A.P.* 5.78, 79, and especially Th. *Id.* 5.88–9 'With apples too Clearista pelts the goatherd as he goes by with his flock, and whistles sweetly to him', *Id.* 6.6–7.

66–7   ignis 'flame'; cf. Hor. *Epod.* 14.13. Amyntas unlike Galatea in *Id.* 6 does not tease the lover. Menalcas' choice of a homosexual theme accords with Damoetas' jibe in 7–9.

Delia is probably his *contubernalis*. The existence of a wife is not incompatible with homosexual proclivities. The name *Delia* commonly belongs to Diana (7.29), who as hunting goddess might be regarded as *nota canibus nostris*; it does not occur as a woman's name in earlier pastoral or elsewhere in the Eclogues. However Tibullus used it as a pseudonym for his mistress and the comparison of Amyntas here to another mortal seems more appropriate. Moreover the ascription of a divine name to a rustic girl adds witty point to Damoetas' use of *Venus* in the next line.

68   meae Veneri 'the girl who inspires love in me', cf. Pl. *Cur.* 191, Lucr. 4.1185.

69 aeriae...palumbes 'wood-pigeons nesting high in the air' like the turtle doves in 1.58, rather than 'high flying', its normal sense, attested in Lucr. 1.12 etc. The epithet emphasizes the hazards of the capture in contrast to Th. *Id.* 5.96–7 'And I shall give my girl a ring-dove presently, one that I've caught in the juniper – for that's where it perches.' Cf. 2.40.

congessere: the omission of *nidos* or the like (cf. *nidamenta congeret* in Pl. *Rud.* 889) is paralleled in Gell. 2.29.

70–1 quod potui is at first sight more modest, but *siluestri* indicates that the fruit was gathered in the wild wood, not the domestic orchard, and Amyntas has already received the first instalment.

aurea mala: either 'apples' or 'quinces' (2.51n.).

altera sc. *decem* (cf. Cat. 5.8) or *totidem* (cf. Hor. *Ep.* 1.6.34). For the promise cf. Th. *Id.* 3.10–11 'Look, I'm bringing you ten apples. I gathered them from the place you told me to gather them. Tomorrow I'll bring some more.'

73 diuom...ad auris: either because he wants the whole universe to know the cause of his joy or to ensure that, once the gods have heard Galatea's pledges, she will henceforth be bound by them – by no means an infallible guarantee: cf. 8.19, 35.

74 ipse animo: a double contrast seems implied. Watching the nets while the hunters pursued the quarry (75) was a menial task undertaken as proof of devotion to the beloved; cf. Tib. 1.4.49–50, Ov. *H.* 5.19. Amyntas himself (*ipse*) does not despise him in this humble role even though others may. Moreover the knowledge that Amyntas feels (*animo*) as he does even when they are separated is nothing compared to the joys of his *physical* presence (66–7).

76 Phyllida: the name, from Greek *phullis* 'foliage', is not found in earlier pastoral but is frequent in the Eclogues (5.10, 7.14, 10.37).

Iolla: probably as in 2.57 a person in authority, perhaps even the *dominus* of the two singers.

77 faciam uitula: for *facere* 'to sacrifice' with the instr. abl. cf. Pl. *St.* 251, Col. 2.21.4.

pro frugibus refers to the private *Ambarualia* celebrated just before the harvest (the state festival was fixed on three days in May). The victim to be sacrificed to Ceres was taken in procession *circum arua*

(Macrob. *Sat.* 3.5.7). For the ritual and its subsequent merry-making see *G.* 1.338–50, Tib. 2.1.1–26. During the official ceremonial period there was a strict taboo on sexual activity; hence the point of Damoetas' jest.

78 Menalcas may be speaking in his own person, and like Damoetas addressing the absent Iollas. This seems the better sense, but it does require the dissociation of *formonse* from *Iolla*, as in the text printed here. Alternatively he may be answering Damoetas, as if in Iollas' person; in which case the two vocatives go together as part of Phyllis' reported farewell. Neither interpretation is incompatible with the implication of 107 that both singers fancied Phyllis, nor with Menalcas' homosexual preferences, since *alias* would not include Amyntas.

   me discedere: for the acc. + inf. complement to *flere* cf. Prop. 1.7.17–18. It is probably by analogy with *dolere*.

79 longum: internal acc. with *inquit*, cf. *longum clamet* (Hor. *A.P.* 459–60).

   ualē ualĕ inquit: *ualē* like *mihī* (1.7), *tibī* (2.70) and other originally iambic words would have been somewhat old-fashioned at this period, when *ualĕ* was the normal pronunciation; cf. *tibī* (1.47), *duŏ* (2.40), *mihī* (3.1). Nevertheless *ualĕ* here is probably to be regarded as a variation on the preceding *ualē*, with correption of the vowel in hiatus (cf. *Hylă omne* in 6.44) rather than as a normally short vowel left unelided (2.53n.). The diminuendo effect of *ualē ualĕ* is onomatopoeic.

80 Present love affairs are reverted to in a pair of neatly balanced rustic analogies (cf. 2.63n.). Unlike Damoetas, who after Galatea (64) now sings of Amaryllis (81), Menalcas remains faithful to his homosexual love (66, 83).

   triste is substantival; cf. [Th.] *Id.* 8.57–9: 'To trees a storm is an evil to be feared, to waters drought, to birds a trap, to wild animals a net, to a man the desire for a tender maid.' For the threat to ripening crops and fruit from *imbres* and *uenti* see *G.* 1.316–24, 443–4.

82 satis 'recently sown' contrasts with *maturis frugibus.*

   depulsis 'newly weaned' (1.20n.).

   arbutus is the arbute or 'strawberry tree', Arbutus Unedo, which grows to a height of four metres and is ample enough to provide shelter from summer heat (7.46). The scarlet fruit, which has given the shrub its English name, is too dull for most human palates (Plin. *Nat.* 15.99) and in any case appears too late in the summer for newly weaned kids to sample; so presumably the thick evergreen foliage is meant here. For the arbute as goat-food cf. *G.* 3.300-1.

83 feto pecori refers either to the pregnant animals or to the young kids; cf. *fetas* (1.49). For the supple willow see 1.54n.

84 Pollio: the final syllable is always elided in the Eclogues, cf. 86, 88, 4.12. Cretic words are rarely elided in classical verse and Vergil restricts the licence to two categories: (i) final vowel + *m*, e.g. *Ilium in Italiam* (*A.* 1.68), *abluam et extremus* (*A.* 4.684). Such syllables are metrically anomalous since the *m* was pronounced strongly enough to check the preceding vowel before a consonant, e.g. *nostram quamuis*, but not so strongly as to prevent elision with a following vowel. (ii) final -*o*, e.g. *nuntio et in tutum* (*A.* 1.391), *audeo et Aeneadum* (*A.* 11.503). At this period -*ō*, already common in words like *ego* (17), *scio* (8.43), cf. 79n., was being extended by analogy, e.g. *nescio* (103), *desino* (Tib. 2.6.41) and later *findo* (Prop. 3.9.35). *Polliŏ* occurs at Hor. *S.* 1.10.42, *C.* 2.1.14.

C. Asinius Pollio, a politician of Caesarian sympathies whose career culminated in the consulship of 40 B.C., was also prominent in the literary life of the time. Fragments of his *declamationes* and History of the Civil Wars are preserved by the Elder Seneca, his erotic *nugae* are mentioned by the Younger Pliny (*Ep.* 5.3.5) and his tragedies (8.10n.) by Horace (*S.* 1.10.42-3, *C.* 2.1.9-12). To judge from his strictures on Cicero, Livy and Sallust (Quint. 12.1.22, 8.1.3, Suet. *Gramm.* 10), he was a severe critic; but he appears to have been a generous patron of young poets, including Vergil, Gallus and Horace. See also 4 fin. n.

quamuis est rustica: the only certain example of the indic. with *quamuis* in republican prose is Nep. *Milt.* 2.3, though it is found in Lucretius, e.g. 3.403. Vergil's only other instance is at *A.* 5.542, so it is just possible that here, as in Cat. 12.5, it has a hint of the colloquial.

85 Pierides: although the Muses, daughters of Zeus and Mnemosyne, were νύμφαι χθόνιαι 'nymphs of the land' at Mount Helicon in Boeotia, their original home was Pieria near Mount Olympus (Hes. *Th.* 52-3; 7.2n.). Like the humbler country nymphs they watched over the fortunes of their devotees, poets – as in Th. *Id.* 7.78-83, [Th.] *Id.* 9.31-6, Hor. *C.* 3.4.1-36 – and their patrons too.

uitulam: the sacrificial heifer that Pollio will offer in their honour.

lectori...uestro: either 'for the one who reads what you inspire' or 'for the reader who is devoted to you'. Pollio is thanked as an appreciative reader; in 86-7 he is praised as a poet himself.

86   noua carmina 'new poems'. If this refers to Pollio's tragedies, then *taurum* could have been chosen for its associations with Dionysus, patron of tragedy and dithyramb (cf. Simonides *A.P.* 6.213 and *schol. ad* Ar. *Ran.* 357). But the bull in contrast to the heifer of 85 need signify no more than the superior status of poet to patron in the worship of the Muses. The reference might be to Pollio's poems 'in the neoteric style'; not his tragedies, which seem to have been redolent of Pacuvius and Accius (Tac. *Dial.* 21), but short poems on personal themes in the Alexandrian manner (84n.).

87   iam cornu petat: cf. Lucr. 5.1034-5. The subjunctives are generic. The whole line recurs at *A.* 9.629.

88   te quoque gaudet sc. *uenisse.* Pollio like Thyrsis in Th. *Id.* 1.20 has 'arrived at the fullness of a pastoral musician's art'. Praise of the patron is neatly combined with good wishes for his admirers, among them Vergil himself.

89   The Golden Age imagery (cf. 4.25, 30) has Theocritean precedent in the wishes expressed by the singers in *Id.* 5.124-7 'Comatas: "Let Himera flow with milk instead of water, and you, Crathis, I pray, grow dark with wine and let your reeds bear fruit." Lacon: "Let Sybaris flow with honey for me."'

mella fluant 'let streams of honey flow'. Also relevant here are the symbolic associations of honey. The comparison of the poet to a bee and his verse to honey is as old as Pindar, e.g. *P.* 10.54, *O.* 10.98-9, and was a commonplace already for Plato (*Ion* 534a); see also Lucr. 1.947, Hor. *C.* 4.2.27-32, *Ep.* 1.19.44. At Th. *Id.* 1.146, 7.84 honey is the food with which outstanding pastoral singers are rewarded. The plural of bulk nouns like *mel* and *nix* (cf. 10.47) regularly denotes concrete instances: hence 'draughts of honey'. The alliteration of the liquid *l* is expressive.

amomum: the oriental shrub 'cardamom', Amomum Cardamomum, was unknown in Italy, though the spice made from its seeds was highly prized already in Plautus' time (*Truc.* 540). Its appearance on the common bramble is like the flowing honey an adynaton (cf. 1.59) whose realization belongs to the Golden Age transformation of nature; cf. 4.25.

90 Of the poetry of Bavius and Mevius nothing is known. The latter incurred the hatred of the young Horace (*Epod.* 10.2), and their carping at *hordea* (5.36n.) suggests a pedantic conservatism.

91 iungat sc. *aratro.* For *mulgeat hirquos* cf. Greek τράγον ἀμέλγειν 'to milk the billy goat' at Lucian *Demon.* 28. Both expressions may have been traditional metaphors of incompetence in popular speech.

92 The homely tone of the preceding line provides a transition to practical matters. Like the singing herdsman of Th. *Id.* 4.44-9, 5.100-4, Damoetas and Menalcas are not neglectful of their more routine duties.

   nascentia: although this verb had become restricted generally to human and animal birth, it is still sometimes used like its cognates *gigno* and Greek γίγνομαι of any process of natural reproduction, as here of strawberries (cf. Ov. *M.* 13.815 *siluestri nata sub umbra*) and in 107 of the *hyacinthus.* Cicero has *frumenta nata sunt* (*Ver.* 2.3.147).

93 frigidus: the displacement suggests the incoherence of colloquial speech. Damoetas' excitement is reflected in the succession of shrill *i*-sounds, the frequency of light syllables and the staccato effect of the three pauses that break up the dactylic flow.

94 parcite...procedere: this form of prohibition occurs in comedy and still has a colloquial flavour in Hor. *C.* 1.28.23-5, Liv. 34.32.20 *proinde parce, sis,...iactare,* and perhaps even at *A.* 3.42.

94-5 non...creditur: the enjambement, intensified by the preceding and following diaeretic pauses, gives an impression of breathless excitement. For the impersonal use of *credere* cf. Hor. *S.* 2.4.21, again colloquial.

96 For the subordinate status of Tityrus see 1.1n.
   pascentis: like English *feed* the verb may be either causative (e.g. 1.45) or intransitive.
   reice: compounds of *iacere* were regularly written with one *i* but

pronounced with -*ii*-, e.g. *obicio*, pronounced *obiicio* (see Gell. 4.17.1–8). Synizesis of prefixes ending in a vowel occurs already in Plautus, e.g. *eicis* beside *ēici* in *As.* 161, 127; so *eicit* (Lucr. 4.1272), *deicere* (Hor. *S.* 1.6.39). The older forms survived as variants, e.g. dactylic *reice* at *G.* 3.389, viz. *rēiice*, with the regular pronunciation of intervocalic *i*. For the meaning 'drive back' cf. *in bubile reicere* (Pl. *Pe.* 319), *reicitque canes* (Stat. *Theb.* 4.547).

97 Cf. Th. *Id.* 5.145–6 'Take heart, my horned goats; tomorrow I'll wash you all in Sybaris' lake.'

erit, omnis: the normal syllable division -*ri-tom-nī*- would give ∪ – – where – – – is required. Hence we must assume either that the *i* of *erit* was here lengthened by analogy with genuinely archaic forms like *uidēt* (*A.* 1.308), *fuīt* (Prop. 4.1.17) or that the punctuation abnormally affected the syllabification; viz. -*rit-om-nī*-. Cf. *frater erit? o quae* (*A.* 12.883), *manusque sinit. hinc* (*A.* 10.433) and see 1.38n.

98 cogite sc. *in umbras* (cf. anon. *Culex* 108). In *G.* 3.331ff. the animals are to be gathered into the shade at noon and dispersed to graze in the cool of the early evening.

lac praeceperit refers to the effect on the ewes' dugs. For *praecipere* of heat cf. Lucr. 6.1049–50, Col. *Arb.* 2.2.

100 Cf. Th. *Id.* 4.15–20 'Indeed there's nothing left of that calf except the bones. She doesn't live on dew-drops like the cicada, does she?...the bull's thin too, the reddish one.' Damoetas' diagnosis (101) however is novel.

heu heu: for the hiatus see 2.58n.

pingui macer: for the effective juxtaposition cf. 2.1n.

eruo: a variety of vetch, Vicia Ervilia, akin to the lentil but with pinkish flowers. It is still cultivated as cattle-food in Italy.

101 pecori pecorisque magistro: for the sympathetic association of herd and herdsman cf. 2.33.

102 Two constructions of the line are possible: (i) with the punctuation adopted in the text: 'These lambs are certainly – and love is not the cause – just clinging to their bones.' So Donatus, who on *hisce* at Ter. *Eun.* 269 says *pro* '*hi*' *uetuste; Vergilius* '*his certe...haerent*' *quia* '*hice*' *debebat dicere.* *s* is attested in the second declension nom. pl. in comedy, e.g. *hisce* at Pl. *Mil.* 374, and on inscriptions, e.g. *eis, magistris* on *CIL*

1.582, 2.3433. Like *quoium* (1) it is a bold colloquialism in formal poetry, which particularly suits the subject matter at this point. (ii) *his certe neque amor caussa est; uix ossibus haerent* 'As for these lambs I'm sure love isn't the cause; they're only just clinging to their bones.' *nec* for *non* occurred in early Latin, e.g. Pl. *Ba.* 119, Enn. *A.* 403V, Twelve Tables 8.16, and survived in legal and religious formulae, e.g. 9.6, Cic. *Leg.* 3.6, as well as in compounds, e.g. *necopinatus, neglegere.* There is no evidence that it survived in colloquial usage, but it may have in rural areas.

103 nesciŏ: cf. Cat. 85.2 and 79n.

fascinat: the nouns *fascinus, fascinum* seem to have been used originally of any magical charm but especially phallic emblems, which were believed then as now to be effective antidotes to evil spells (cf. Plin. *Nat.* 28.39 and *schol. ad* Hor. *Epod.* 8.18, where the word means simply 'penis'). The verb *fascinare* was applied to any evil spell which good fortune might attract (Cat. 7.12), in particular the 'evil eye'. *oculus,* for which cf. Hor. *Ep.* 1.14.37-8, guarantees the reference here.

104 The riddles, though appropriate in a rustic singing match, are unprecedented in extant pastoral. Their content is distinctly sophisticated and no answers or even attempts at answers are given.

105 Various solutions have been proposed for Damoetas' riddle: they are set out here in order of descending probability, but it would indeed require the god of prophecy *magnus Apollo* himself to certify the answer. (i) A celestial globe or model of the heavens like those attributed to Archimedes (Cic. *Rep.* 1.22) and Posidonius (Cic. *N.D.* 2.88). By this date there must have been a number of such *sphaerae* in different places – in fact wherever astronomy was practised (cf. Prop. 4.1.76). This would suit the plural *quibus in terris.* It would also provide an interesting link with the astronomers on the cups (40-1) and perhaps too with the echo of Aratus (60-1). (ii) The opening in the roof of the Capitoline temple of Jupiter, immediately above the deified boundary-stone *Terminus* (Ov. *F.* 2.671-2). There would then be a pun in *tris...non amplius* on the god's name, *ter minus,* as in the old riddle quoted by Gellius, 12.6. (iii) A well or pit, from the bottom of which the width of the sky would appear no more than *tris ulnas* viz. 1.5-1.8 metres. Servius even mentions a particular pit at Syene in Egypt, which was used for astronomical experiments. (iv) The *mundus*, a sacred pit in the Comitium, regarded as the entrance to the Underworld (Macrob. *Sat.* 1.16.16–18, P. Festus 156M). The semantic connection between *mundus* and *caelum* is obvious enough. (v) According to Servius Vergil told the grammarian Asconius that this was a trap for readers. The answer was 'the tomb of Caelius', a Mantuan waster who was left with nothing but a plot of land large enough to bury him when he died. Even if the tradition is authentic (and the Berne Scholiast makes Cornutus the recipient of this information), ancient poets like modern ones may not have been above having a joke at the expense of troublesome enquirers.

106–7 Menalcas' riddle is more straightforward in that the reference is clearly to the *hyacinthus* (63n.). Mythology provided a choice of two origins for the flower. One was from the blood of the Spartan prince Hyacinthus who was accidentally killed by his lover Apollo (Ov. *M.* 10.162ff.), and the markings on the flower formed *AI* the Greek expression of grief *aî aî*. The other origin was from the blood of Ajax. Defeated by Ulysses in the contest for the arms of Achilles (Ov. *M.* 13.382ff.) he committed suicide, and the markings represented the first two letters of his name *AI*. *regum* could apply equally well to Hyacinthus or Ajax. *quibus in terris* seems at first sight more restricted than in Damoetas' riddle, viz. either the plain between Troy and Cape Rhoeteum (Ajax) or the banks of the Eurotas outside Sparta (Hyacinthus). If *nascantur* is for *nati sint* 'they are natives, they originated' (cf. the use of *generat* in *A.* 8.141 and *creat* in Prop. 4.1.77) the restriction remains. But if it is taken literally 'they are being produced now', then the number of answers is indefinite, since the *hyacinthus* grew in many parts of the Mediterranean countryside. There is again a possible link with earlier lines – Menalcas' own mention of Apollo and the *hyacinthus* in 62–3 and perhaps even the figure of Orpheus on the cups (46). For the archetypal poet like his father Apollo had lost a loved one through his own rashness, and like the god (cf. 6.82–3) had sought solace in music. The tale of Hyacinthus forms part of Orpheus' recital of self-consolation in Ov. *M.* 10.

inscripti nomina...flores: unlike e.g. *crinis ornatus* (6.68) or *chlamydem circumdata* (*A.* 4.137), where the participle has a middle sense, the subject of the participle here is the patient not the agent of the verbal action (see 1.54n.). Hence *inscripti* is best taken in a passive sense with *nomina* as a Greek acc. of reference; cf. Tac. *H.* 3.74 *aram . . . casus suos in marmore expressam.* A less likely possibility is that the construction is conflated from the passive transformations of two distinct active constructions: (*a*) *inscribere nomina floribus* (dat.); cf. *ipse suos gemitus foliis irscribit* (Ov. *M.* 10.215); (*b*) *inscribere nomine flores*; cf. *aedis uenalis hasce inscribit litteris* (Pl. *Trin.* 168). On either analysis the construction shows the influence of Greek, where the accusative is common with middle participles of transitive verbs and not abnormal with passive participles expressing state. The Greek colour is appropriate to the Greek myth.

108 For the drawn contest cf. Th. *Id.* 6.41–6.

109 et uitula tu dignus et hic confirms that Menalcas staked a heifer after all (49n.), though Palaemon has not actually been told this. The phrase has sometimes been taken – unnecessarily – as evidence of Palaemon's distracted state of mind.

109–10 et quisquis amores... is explained by Servius: *et quicumque similis uestri est . . . namque hic Menalcas et amabat et metuebat ne umquam posset amor ille dissolui. contra Damoetas amaritudinem amoris expertus fuerat ex amicae Amaryllidis iracundia.* It is remarkable that Palaemon seizes upon the theme of love's bitter-sweet from 74–5, 80–1 and 100–1 rather than any of the others that have appeared in the contest, when he makes his final generalization: 'anyone will win a poet's prize who either fears love when it is flourishing or comes to know its bitterness'. That love was γλυκύπικρον 'a sweet-bitter thing' was a commonplace from Sappho (fr. 130LP) onwards and is a recurrent theme of Greek pastoral (see p. 10). But the explicit doctrine that the sorrows of love in particular make men into poets is a new refinement on Euripides' 'Truly Love teaches a man poetry even if he has hitherto been unmusical' (fr. 663N), and one which Catullus and Propertius would have endorsed. Palaemon's verdict brings the contest to a melancholy close. The lines have been needlessly corrupted by editors. Both Graser's *haud . . . haud* and Ribbeck's *hau temnet . . . haut*, with a punctuation between *hic* and *et*, turn the sentence into a generalization that is patently untrue. On the other hand Wagner's *haud metuet, dulcis aut . . .* makes it an empty platitude. Ebert's interchange of *amores* and *amaros* weakens the sense; for who has never feared the bitterness of love?

111   riuos: the irrigation channels referred to in *G.* 1.106, 269; cf.
Digest 43.21.2.1 *riuus est locus per longitudinem depressus, quo aqua decurrat.*
Palaemon's injunction marks a return to the workaday world. It may
also be taken metaphorically: *iam cantare desinite, satiati enim audiendo
sumus* (Serv.); cf. Cat. 61.231–2 *claudite ostia, uirgines; | lusimus satis.*

One of the earliest Eclogues (see 5.86–7), this poem is heavily indebted
to Theocritus. Its form – a conversation leading to a singing match –
recalls Comatas and Lacon in *Id.* 5, the detailed reminiscences of
which (25n., 62n., 64n., 69n., 89n.) are combined with those of other
relevant poems in the Theocritean corpus: the acrimonious conversation of Battus and Corydon in *Id.* 4 (1–2n., 100n.), and the friendly
singing contests of Daphnis with Damoetas in *Id.* 6 (64n.) and especially with Menalcas in *Id.* 8 (32–4n., 50n., 80n., 85n.). The association of the latter two names with Daphnis in Theocritus can hardly be
accidental to Vergil's choice of them as participants in the present
poem.

   Some of the passages recalling Theocritus are almost straight trans-
lations, others original though not in general very adventurous
variations on the Greek pastoral material. The themes of the singing
contest are for the most part conventional: rustic piety (60–3), the
joys and sorrows of rustic love and courtship (64–83), an interlude of
gentle banter at the absent Iollas (76–9), and concern for the welfare
of their animals (92–103). Nevertheless there are some interesting
innovations:

   (i) The speech of the herdsmen is characterized by colloquial and
occasionally even archaic features (see notes on 1, 7–8, etc.) that may
well be intended to suggest rural dialect.

   (ii) The single cup in *Id.* 1 was a prize promised to Thyrsis for
singing the Daphnis-dirge, and its scenes extend into the non-pastoral
world (40n.). Vergil's two cups are offered as the stake in a contest.
Their scenes, though much less elaborate and picturesque, have a
symbolic significance beyond the pastoral, but one that links them
with the opening dedications (60–3) and closing riddles in the actual
contest (104–7). Vergil seems thus concerned to integrate the descriptive set-piece more fully into the structure of his poem.

   (iii) The riddles themselves may be imported from popular culture
but their content is learned. With the preceding bull in love (101) the

sad overtones of the *hyacinthus* riddle set the mood for Palaemon's melancholy judgement.

(iv) The appearance of Pollio, Bavius and Mevius (84–91) reveals that Vergil was already attempting to relate the pastoral conventions more closely to contemporary realities. But the intrusion is clumsy and abrupt. All the innovations have something of the experimental and tentative about them, and the Eclogue as a whole is probably the least successful of the ten.

ECLOGUE IV

1 Sicelides Musae: the nymphs of Sicily – among them Arethusa (10.1) – inspired the work of native poets like Theocritus and Bion, and so are equated with the Muses. They are addressed explicitly in the refrain of *Epit. Bion.* 8 etc. Metrical considerations determined the vowel length in the initial syllable; cf. *Sĭkelĭdān* also in Th. *Id.* 7.40 but *Sĭculis* in 2.21, *Sĭkeloús* at Hom. *Od.* 20.383. The short vowel was probably original. In view of Vergil's fondness for Greek inflection the *e* of the nom. pl. is almost certainly short.

paulo maiora: an understatement, though not ironical from a poet who had already published *Ecl.* 5. *paulo* is not found elsewhere in Vergil but is often attested elsewhere with comparatives, e.g. Lucr. 2.137 *paulo maiora lacessunt.* The epithet *magnus* is very frequent in this poem: 5, 12, 22 etc.

2 arbusta: either in its strict sense 'forests', as a synonym for *siluae* in the next line, or for the unmetrical *arbores* (1.39n.).

myricae: the dense tamarisk bushes with their delicate foliage and pink flowers were common in the coastal lowlands of ancient Italy and Sicily and so became a feature of the pastoral landscape; cf. Th. *Id.* 1.13 and *Ecl.* 6.10, 8.54, 10.13. In all the Vergilian passages, except perhaps the last, *myricae* typify the humble and unpretentious.

3 consule: Pollio, consul in 40 b.c. with Domitius Calvinus. There is a close metrical correspondence between 1 and 3, and the homodyne cadences *maióra canámus* and *cónsule dígnae*, though normal in themselves, are each thrown into emphatic relief by the markedly heterodyne character of the rest of the line.

4 Cumaei...carminis 'of Cumaean prophecy'. For *carmen* as a

vehicle of prophecy cf. Cic. *Div.* 2.111-12, Prop. 4.1.51. The reference
is to the Sibyl of Cumae. The official collection of her oracles, written
in Greek hexameters, was kept by the *XVuiri sacris faciundis* who super-
vised all foreign cults, including that of Apollo with whom the Sibylline tradition was closely associated. The oracles were regularly con-
sulted at times of crisis. The earlier books were destroyed in the fire on
the Capitol in 83 B.C., and a new corpus subsequently gathered from
various sources, including Sibylline oracles outside Italy (Tac. *A.*
6.12.4). Like the mass of Sibylline prophecies in private circulation
(Suet. *Aug.* 31.1) this must have included material from the 'Orphic'
traditions and from oriental Apocalyptic, as the extant *Oracula Sibyllina*
certainly do, though most of these date from the Christian period. It is
probable that the appearance of the famous comet, *sidus Iulium*, in
July 44 B.C. (5 fin.n., 9.47n.) led to an official consultation of the
Sibylline books as well as a wave of unofficial prophetic speculation.
For comets were usually taken as portents (see Plin. *Nat.* 2.91-4,
Lydus *Ost.* 10), especially of impending national disaster (*G.* 1.488,
Tib. 2.5.71). Some of the optimistic interpretations current may well
be alluded to in the apocalyptic imagery of 5-10, and the Golden Age
symbols of *caduceus*, *cornu copiae* and *Sol* are common on coins of the late
40s. There was an ancient conjecture, found already in Probus' commentary and no doubt associated with a variant spelling *Cymaei*, that
Hesiod's *Works and Days* is meant, Hesiod's father having come from
Cyme in Asian Aeolis. But such a recondite use of the epithet is implausible, and *uenit iam* is totally incompatible with Hesiod's *ultima
aetas*, the Age of Iron, which had already gone on for too long when he
himself wrote *c.* 700 B.C.

The 'golden line' pattern here, with *ultima...aetas* enclosing
Cumaei...carminis and *uenit iam* in central position, suggests the cyclic
symmetry of the ages.

5 magnus...saeclorum ordo seems to allude to two distinct
doctrines of the sequence of ages. The first is the astronomical concept
of the *magnus annus*, defined by the period between successive occurrences of the same disposition of all the heavenly bodies in the sky
(Cic. *Rep.* 6.24). This was identified in Stoic thought with the *periodos*
between the successive conflagrations that dissolve the universe into
its original 'creative fire' (Cic. *N.D.* 2.41, 118). Unlike the Christian

dies irae, which destroys the world as a punishment for its corruption, the Stoic conflagration is the consummation of the world's essential divinity. This concept, which may be alluded to in the reign of the Sun-god Apollo (10), is not developed in the poem, and Vergil, while indicating the cosmic reverberations of the new age (50-1), clearly does not envisage any such catastrophic event in the sequence that he depicts. Secondly there was a tradition – probably Etruscan (Censorinus *D.N.* 17.5) – that a nation's life-cycle consisted of ten *saecula* (cf. the cycle of ten cosmic ages in *Orac. Sib.* 4.47, 8.199R). That the doctrine of *saecula* was in some form incorporated into the Roman Sibylline tradition is clear from the fact that the dates of *Ludi Saeculares*, e.g. in 249 and 149 B.C., were fixed after consultation of the Sibylline books (Hor. *C.S.* 5). If the length of a *saeculum* was officially recognized as 110 years at this time (Hor. *ib.* 21), then there would have been an expectation that 40/39 B.C. would begin a new age. In fact Servius on 9.46 says that an Etruscan diviner Volcatius interpreted the *Iulium sidus* as a sign that Rome's tenth *saeculum*, the Age of Apollo Helios (10n.), was about to begin. The idea that Rome was entering its final *saeculum* is in strict logic incompatible with the optimism of the poem, and the allusion is not pursued.

ab integro for the commoner *de* or *ex integro* is slightly archaic; it is found at Cic. *Verr.* 2.1.147 and in a phrase of Cato cited by D. Servius here. The normal Latin treatment of a mute + liquid cluster *in-te-gro* (cf. Lucr. 6.348 *in-te-grā*) would be unmetrical. *in-tég-ro* like *ag-ros* (5.35), *ap-ri-cis* (9.49) is supported by Greek metrical precedent. Its effect here may have been archaic.

nascitur, like *redit, demittitur*, indicates a process now going on, not an accomplished state of affairs.

6 Virgo: Aratus took up a hint from Hes. *Op.* 200-1, 'Aidōs (Shame) and Nemesis (Righteous Wrath) will desert mankind and go off to join the race of the immortals', and marked the transition from Silver to Bronze Age by the departure from the earth of Astraia, the virgin patron of Justice (*Ph.* 133-6). There is no suggestion there or in Ov. *M.* 1.149-50 or even in *G.* 2.473-4 that she is destined ever to return. The constellation Virgo, into which she was transformed, rises in early October, and some scholars have therefore seen here a reflection of the optimism that followed the pact of Brindisi in September/October

40 B.C. (Appian 5.64). Pollio played a prominent part in effecting this short-lived rapprochement between Octavian and Antony and the poem is dedicated to him; so in a passage of such allusive complexity the reference, implausible though it might seem in any other context, cannot be dismissed. More important however is the role of the Virgin in oriental Apocalyptic (7n.).

Saturnia regna for *Saturnium regnum*, as in 6.41, is probably a metrical variant; but see 1.6n. There was a tradition that Italy, especially Latium, had once been called *Saturnia terra* (Var. *L.* 5.42, Dion. H. 1.18.2). The god Saturnus was perhaps Etruscan in origin, though he was worshipped *Graeco more* (Fest. 322M). He seems from the date of his festival – 17 December, midway between the Consualia and Opalia – to have had some connection with the sowing of crops. But the early equation of him with the Greek Kronos who ruled in the Golden Age (Hes. *Op.* 111) led to the belief that after his overthrow by the Olympians he fled to Latium, which thus became the last outpost of the Golden Age (*A.* 8.319-27, Dion. H. 1.36.1). The Hesiodic doctrine of metallic ages is one of the two major thematic elements in the poem. However, unlike Aratus (*Ph.* 114-32) and Ovid (*M.* 1.89-150), Vergil omits the Silver and Bronze Ages, so reducing the Hesiodic sequence to three: Golden (here and in 9), Heroic (16, 35), Iron (8). Moreover there is no extant precedent for the idea that the metallic sequence could be repeated or reversed. Hesiod himself clearly hoped that the Iron Age would end and conditions improve (*Op.* 175, 180) but his faith that sin will be punished on earth and the just rewarded (*Op.* 225-37 contains a number of Golden Age details) is not given any clear chronological context. Here Vergil has adapted the doctrine of metallic ages to the repetitive model of the *magnus annus*.

7 noua progenies is prepared for by the metaphoric *nascitur* in line 5. The phrase can be reconciled with the Hesiodic tradition, in which each new age is marked by a newly created race of men (*Op.* 128, 143-4, 158). However, the birth of a child is a widespread apocalyptic symbol in Near-Eastern religion. Macrobius refers (*Sat.* 1.18.10) to an Egyptian winter-solstice cult of the Sun as a child, and the Alexandrian festival of Aion ('The Era' cf. *aeui* in 11) on 5 January included the liturgical formula 'Today the Virgin has given birth to

Aion' (Lyd. *Mens.* 4.1, Epiphanius *Panarion, haer.* 51.22.10). More familiar to us is the passage in Isaiah, 'Behold, the Virgin shall conceive in her womb and give birth to a son; and you will call him by the name Immanuel, God with us' (Isaiah 7.14 translated from the Septuagint version, which might well have been accessible to a *doctus poeta* of Vergil's time). The Virgin-and-Child motif appears, with a Christian interpretation, in the later parts of the extant *Oracula Sibyllina*; but it is likely to have entered the oracular tradition along with other parallels with Hebrew Apocalyptic at a much earlier date (there seems an allusion to it already in the pre-Christian *Orac. Sib.* 3.785–7), and so found its way into unofficial Roman collections and even into the new state corpus. If so – and Vergil cannot have found the motif in Greco-Roman literary or religious sources – the question is raised whether *Virgo* is in fact the mother of the *noua progenies*. For the indications of the Child's parentage are notoriously vague (49n., fin. n.). Certainly the assimilation of the Virgin Mother of the Wonder Child from oriental prophecy to the virgin Dike–Astraia of Greek mythology would provide a plausible starting point for the complementary development of the poem's two dominant themes – the return of the Golden Age and the birth and growth of the Child.

caelo demittitur alto: cf. *Orac. Sib.* 3.286 'And then indeed will God send down from heaven a King.' For the older more concise use of the bare ablative with *demittere* cf. *A.* 9.803–4.

8 modo adds a note of urgency to an imperative; cf. *G.* 3.73, *A.* 4.50.

nascenti is contemporaneous with *faue*, not with the poem's notional present.

quo: viz. as instrument of Divine Providence.

9 toto...mundo 'in all the world'. The noun was probably formed from the masculine of the adjective 'neat', 'elegant' on the analogy of Greek *kósmos* (Plin. *Nat.* 2.8). Used by Ennius of the heavens (*mundus caeli* in *var.* 9V), it was extended to mean the 'universe' (e.g. Cic. *N.D.* 2.154) and finally the earth, *orbis terrarum* (e.g. Hor. *C.* 3.3.53).

gens aurea: cf. Hes. *Op.* 109–10 'It was a golden race of mortal men that the deathless gods made first.'

10 Lucina, the goddess who brings children *ad lucem*, was identified sometimes with Juno (e.g. Pl. *Aul.* 692), more often, as here and in

Cat. 34.13–14, with Diana, the Latin counterpart of Artemis Εὔλοχος, the goddess 'who blesses childbirth'.

tuus: since Apollo was her brother.

regnat Apollo: the reign of Apollo thus precedes the return of *Saturnia regna*. D. Servius quotes from Nigidius Figulus an account of the Orphic doctrine of world ages. Each age was presided over by a god – Saturn, Jupiter, Neptune, Pluto – with an age of Apollo including the great conflagration still to come, at least in some versions of the doctrine. If this is alluded to here, a cyclic repetition of the sequence must be assumed, but the allusion is not developed further. It is clear that throughout 4–9 Vergil is exploiting the emotive connotations of a variety of apocalyptic images, all perhaps current in the prophecies surrounding the *Iulium sidus*. The swiftness of the succession leaves us with no time to follow out the logically irreconcilable elements in the various doctrines referred to, but the excitement and optimism evoked provide the appropriate emotional background to the two images that he does develop in full: the Golden Age and the Miraculous Child.

11 The brief address to Pollio serves to place the Messianic expectations precisely in history.

adeo emphasizes the preceding word; cf. 9.59, *G.* 1.24.

decus hoc aeui is the subject of *inibit*. If it were the object, the verb would have to refer to Apollo, the last-named subject. For *inire* 'to begin' cf. *ex ineunte aeuo* (Lucr. 5.859). The phrase itself may mean (i) 'this glorious fulfilment of time', with *aeuom* in the sense of Greek *aiōn* as in Lucr. 1.952, or with *aeuom* in its normal, more restricted sense as in Lucr. 5.1440, (ii) 'this glory of the (new) age' or (iii) 'the glory of this new age' (= *decus huius aeui*). *decus* refers to the marvels of the preceding line and a half. For although it can be used of persons, e.g. 5.34 and *A.* 11.508 *o decus Italiae uirgo*, it is unlikely to refer to the Child, since *inibit* for *ingredietur* 'he will make his entry' would be very unusual.

12 **Pollio** is named at last. The preceding *te consule inibit* provides the notional date for the poem, between the consular elections in 41 B.C. and Pollio's early resignation (there were two suffect consuls in 40 B.C.).

incipient...procedere underlines the gradualness of the transformation. The Golden Age will not return overnight; an important qualification to the poet's optimism.

magni: as belonging to the *magnus ordo*.

13 sceleris like *priscae...fraudis* (31) recalls Hesiod's picture of the Iron Age when 'there will be no favour for a man who keeps his oath or is just or good, but men will rather pay honour to the doer of evil and outrageous deeds' (*Op.* 190–2). There is also a more immediate reference to the *scelus* of civil war (cf. Hor. *Epod.* 7.1–2, 17–18) and indeed of war in general, the enemy of rural peace and prosperity (1.6n., *G.* 1.505–11).

14 inrita 'once they are nullified, erased', recalling the original participial sense *in + ratus* 'unratified'.

15–16 diuisque...permixtos heroas recalls Catullus' Heroic Age, when *domos inuisere castas | heroum et sese mortali ostendere coetu | caelicolae nondum spreta pietate solebant* (64.384–6). But the reference here is to the Child's maturity, when he has entered into his kingdom (*reget* in 17). Hence the allusions in *deum uitam accipiet* to Hesiod's Golden Age are more significant: 'They lived like gods, with hearts free of sorrow' (*Op.* 112), 'At that time banquets and assemblies were shared in common by immortal gods and mortal men' (fr. 1.6–7 MW; cf. *schol. ad* Arat. *Ph.* 103).

illis: the dative of interest connoting agency is widely attested not only with gerundival and perfect passive constructions but also with present and future passives; e.g. 6.72, *A.* 1.440, Cic. *Tusc.* 5.68, *Inv.* 1.86.

heroas: for the Greek acc. pl. in this word cf. Hor. *S.* 2.2.93, Manil. 5.483.

17 patriis uirtutibus could be taken with *reget* or *pacatum* or both. The adjective may mean 'belonging to his father or ancestors' (if the phrase goes only with *pacatum*) or 'characteristic of, inherited from, his father or ancestors'. For the general sense cf. Isaiah 9.6–7 'For a child has been born for us...the symbol of government has been placed upon his shoulders and he will be called Wonderful in counsel, God-like in battle, Father of a Wide Realm, Prince of Peace'; *Orac. Sib.* 3.755ff. 'But a great peace will exist over all the Earth...and the immortal god in the starry heavens will establish a common law over all the earth'; 652ff. 'And then God will send a King from the sun, who will put an end to evil war in all the Earth, killing some, to be sure, but fulfilling the hopes of those who have kept their word.'

18 munuscula: as in Hor. *Ep.* 1.7.17, the diminutive connotes tenderness, appropriately in the apostrophe to the new-born Child. The intricate word order of 18–20 is expressive.

nullo...cultu: the sociative abl. may be adnominal (abl. of description) with *munuscula* or adverbial (abl. of attendant circumstances) with *fundet*. The miracle itself was a traditional feature of the Golden Age; cf. Hes. *Op.* 117–18 'And the grain-giving earth brought forth fruit of its own accord in plenty and without stint', Lucr. 2.1158–9. In traditional hymnody such manifestations of joy in nature usually accompany the birth of a god, e.g. Apollo in Theogn. 5–10 and Limenius 5–10P.

19 errantis hederas: cf. Cat. 61.34–5. For the Bacchic connotations of ivy see 3.39n.

baccare: the plant is again associated with ivy in 7.25–8. *baccar*, from Greek *bákkaris*, may well have been given a false etymology from *Bacchus*. Although Pliny lists a variety of medicinal uses (*Nat.* 21.132–3), Servius' attribution of magical properties – *herba est quae fascinum pellit* – may be merely an inference from 7.28. Identification is uncertain; modern guesses include a species of cyclamen and Gnaphalium Sanguineum, a relative of the edelweiss.

20 colocasia 'Egyptian beans' are usually identified as the subtropical Caladium, which was especially associated with the Nile region whence its edible roots were exported. Although cultivated in Italy in Pliny's time (*Nat.* 21.87), it was not found wild *nullo cultu* except in parts of Sicily. This is in fact the only one of the plants here mentioned that does not grow wild in Italy. The miracle lies in their spontaneous appearance all over the world, *passim*; cf. Dion. Per. 941 'At the birth (of Dionysus) all things fragrant were growing.'

ridenti acantho: bear's-breech (3.45n.) like *baccar* was employed medicinally (Plin. *Nat.* 22.76). Although *ridere* is often used metaphorically of visual effects (e.g. Hor. *C.* 4.11.6, Lucr. 2.502), it is especially appropriate here in a context of rejoicing.

21 ipsae 'of their own accord'. Though not unknown in less miraculous contexts (e.g. *G.* 3.316–17, Th. *Id.* 11.12), the detail was a commonplace of Golden Age descriptions; cf. Hor. *Epod.* 16.49–50 (The Isles of the Blest), Tib. 1.3.45–6 *ipsae mella dabant quercus ultroque ferebant | obuia securis ubera lactis oues.*

distenta...ubera is a frequent image of normal pastoral prosperity, e.g. 7.3, 9.31, Lucr. 1.258–9.

22 Lions were of course unknown in Italy in historical times, but Vergil has in mind here the world-wide transformation of nature; cf. Hor. *Epod.* 16.33 *credula nec rauos timeant armenta leones,* and in association with the image of the Child Isaiah 11.6 'The calf and the young lion will grow up together and a little child will lead them'; *Orac. Sib.* 3.791–3 'And the lion, devourer of flesh, will eat husks in the stall like an ox, and tiny children will lead them in chains.'

23 ipsa: the emphatic repetition of the pronoun from line 21 marks an even more impressive portent.

blandos 'to charm and delight you', though *tibi* is to be construed strictly with *fundent.* As for metre *ti-bī-blan-dōs* with the archaic form of the pronoun as at 5.79, 8.93 is preferable to *ti-bib-lan-dōs,* since this treatment of initial mute + liquid clusters is extremely rare (e.g. Cat. 4.9 *Propontida trucemue* and the special case in 51 below). The miracle consists in Nature's spontaneous homage to the Child. The repetition *fundet* (20)...*fundent* here underlines the abundance of this new growth.

24 serpens: a familiar hazard to countrymen (3.93, 8.71). For the miraculous disappearance of snakes cf. Hor. *Epod.* 16.52. In Isaiah 11.8 they have merely been rendered innocuous: 'the infant child will play at the serpent's hole and put his hand into the den of the serpent's offspring'; cf. *Orac. Sib.* 3.794–5.

ueneni is gen. of reference with *fallax*; the sense is either 'which deceives us as regards its poison' (cf. the gen. with *audax, procax*) or 'which conceals its poison' (cf. *fallere* 'to conceal' in Prop. 4.5.14 and the gen. with *capax, tenax*). For the removal of these two threats to rural comfort cf. *G.* 2.152–4 in Vergil's idealized picture of Italian country life.

25 Assyrium: though not grown in Italy Cardamomum has no peculiarly Assyrian connections and the epithet seems chosen primarily to evoke oriental luxury. The plant is associated with Pollio in 3.89.

nascetur: the immediate contrast is with *occidet*; the destruction of *fallax herba ueneni* will be accompanied by the proliferation of *fallax herba unguenti* (for in appearance Cardamomum is not at all attractive). But in the wider context the verb associates the transformation of nature with the birth of the Child; cf. *nascitur* (5).

26 With the Child's boyhood will come an intensification of the Golden Age signs.

simul for *simul ac* (< *simul...ac...*) is common even in prose; e.g. Caes. *Gal.* 4.26.5, Cic. *Fin.* 3.21.

heroum laudes: cf. Hom. *Il.* 9.524.

parentis: in view of the supernatural background to the Child's birth and the miracles surrounding his life it is difficult to believe that this is a human father. See also 49n.

27   uirtus: perhaps still 'manliness', though the word had long since been extended to other qualities (e.g. Pl. *Mil.* 728, Cato *Agr.* 1.2) and Cicero defined it (*Leg.* 1.25) as *nihil aliud quam in se perfecta et ad summum perducta natura.*

28   molli: either of the softly waving stalks or of the actual ears of corn, which will no longer need their hard protective cover.

paulatim flauescet campus: grain will now spring up on any flat land, not just *in aruis*; so the arts of agriculture will be redundant. For the miracle cf. Hes. *Op.* 117–18 (18n.); *G.* 1.125–8, *Orac. Sib.* 3. 620–3 and 744–5 'And indeed Earth the mother of all things will give to mortals the best of its fruits, an unending supply of corn, wine and olive oil.' A return to the acorn-diet of the original Golden Age (*G.* 1.7–8) is not envisaged. The line is expressively enclosed by *molli... arista*, but both *paulatim* and the inchoative verb emphasize once more the gradualness of the transformation.

29–30 For the Golden Age flowing with honey and wine cf. 3.89, *G.* 1.131-2.

29   incultisque...sentibus is probably abl.; cf. 7.24, *A.* 2.546. The omission of the preposition with *pendere* is an archaism of a kind often found in the concentrated style of poetry. The phrase could however be dative; cf. perhaps *capiti...pendere corymbos* in Prop.

2.30.39. The 'golden line' word order emphasizes *incultis* and effectively juxtaposes *sentibus* and *uua*.

30 sudabunt...mella: the idea may have been suggested by the observation that honey was sometimes found in hollow tree-trunks (*G.* 2.452–3). The miracle itself is associated with (i) the Golden Age in Hes. *Op.* 232–3 'And on the hills the oak brings forth acorns on top and bees from half-way down'; cf. Tib. 1.3.45; (ii) the Isles of the Blest in Hor. *Epod.* 16.47; (iii) the New Age in *Orac. Sib.* 3.746–7 'But from heaven a pleasing draught of sweet honey and trees bearing crops of hard-skinned fruit and rich apples.' *sudare* normally takes an instr. abl., e.g. *G.* 1.117. The accusative complement, which is perhaps not attested earlier, is probably, as with *manare* and *stillare* in Hor. *Ep.* 1.19.44, *A.P.* 429, the product of two different uses, one signifying the external object as with *effundere*, *emittere*, the other the internal object, as in *sudorem sudare*. For *mella* 'streams or beads of honey' see 3.89n.

roscida refers to the surface texture, also perhaps to the belief that honey fell as dew and was merely gathered by the bees; cf. *G.* 4.1, Plin. *Nat.* 11.30-1.

31 tamen abruptly interrupts the process described in the preceding lines, which is resumed in 37ff.

priscae uestigia fraudis echoes *sceleris uestigia nostri* (13); cf. Catullus' *tellus scelere...imbuta nefando* (64.397).

32 temptare Thetin: the sea-nymph Thetis was the daughter of Nereus and Doris. For the metonymy of *Thetis* for *mare* cf. *Neptunus* in *G.* 4.29, Cat. 31.3 and perhaps 'the mighty wave of dark-eyed Amphitrite' at Hom. *Od.* 12.60. It is especially effective here, for it enables Vergil to exploit the full semantic range of the verb, the bold endeavour of *insanientem nauita Bosphorum* | *temptabo* (Hor. *C.* 3.4.30–1) and the criminal violence of *Iunonem temptare Ixionis ausi* (Tib. 1.3.73). With all their wants supplied Golden Age men had no need of sea travel; 'The troublesome sea lay undisturbed; not yet did ships bring back a livelihood from abroad' (Arat. *Ph.* 110–11; cf. Ov. *M.* 1.94–6). A return to this condition is one of the rewards promised to the just in Hes. *Op.* 236–7 'They do not travel on ships but the grain-giving earth bears fruit for them.' However, sea-travel was not just a last resort when Nature withheld her bounties from a sinful world; it was itself a symptom of that sinfulness, *fraus*. Commercial greed and lust for conquest had driven men to violate the natural order which had assigned all creatures their appropriate habitat; cf. Lucr. 5.1006, Tib. 1.3.37–40, Hor. *C.* 1.3.21–4 *nequiquam deus abscidit | prudens Oceano dissociabili | terras si tamen impiae | non tangenda rates transiliunt uada.* Moreover *Thetin* prepares for the reference to the two great expeditions of the Heroic Age, to Colchis and Troy. For Thetis became the wife of the Argonaut Peleus to whom she bore Achilles, the Greek champion at Troy. See Cat. 64, especially 1–21, 338ff.

cingere muris: it was well known in antiquity that human society had passed from a rural to an urban stage; cf. Var. *R.* 3.1.1–4, Cic. *Sest.* 91–2. In the Hesiodic tradition followed here by Vergil this sequence marked a decline: the fortification of cities went with bellicose aspirations and the extension of 'reckless hubris', which had already appeared in the Silver Age, to 'works of Ares' which flourished among the men of Bronze (Hes. *Op.* 134, 145–6). For the new corruptions that came with cities see also Lucr. 5.1105–35.

33   telluri infindere sulcos: agriculture like sea-travel and city-building is one of the symptoms of human sinfulness that is destined still to survive for a short while. Within the anaphoric sequence *quae…quae…quae* it is given not only the climactic position but also more space than the other two. The invention and use of the plough was a commonplace of the passing of the *Saturnia regna*; cf. *G.* 1.121–5, Tib. 1.3.41. The spontaneous growth of corn (28) may not yet have become universal, but in any case human impiety will for a time distrust the new bounties of nature and human greed still reach beyond the satisfaction of life's bare necessities. On the phrase itself see also 35n.

iubeant and *uehat* (34) denote purpose.

34   alter 'a second': the new Heroic Age will correspond closely to the first.

Tiphys was the helmsman of the Argo (A.R. *Arg.* 1.105–8). The rough cadence *quae uéhat Árgo* (2.26n.) is perhaps meant to bring an archaic flavour to this evocation of the heroic past.

35   delectos heroas: cf. Th. *Id.* 13.16–18 'Jason, son of Aeson, sailed in quest of the golden fleece, accompanied by the princes chosen from every city', Enn. *sc.* (*Med.*) 250–1V, Cat. 64.4.

altera bella after *alter...altera...* suggests a parallelism with the triple *quae* of 32–3; but the correspondence would be imprecise, since only two events are referred to in 34–5. The Argonautic reference can clearly be linked to *temptare Thetin ratibus*, the Trojan one to *cingere muris oppida. infindere sulcos* (cf. 33n.) perhaps contains a secondary allusion to the ritual in which the site of a conquered city was ploughed over to seal its annihilation; cf. Hor. *C.* 1.16.18–21 and Prop. 3.9.41–2 (of Troy) *moenia cum Graio Neptunia pressit aratro | uictor Palladiae ligneus artis equus.*

36 Troiam, after *Thetin* (32), *Tiphys* (34), prepares for the entry of Achilles. The innocence of the Golden Age was incompatible with heroic action. The great deeds of the 'nobler and more righteous race of men, the divine race of heroes' were inextricably associated with human sin: 'Evil war and the dread din of battle destroyed a part of them, some in the shadow of seven-gated Thebes...others when it brought them over the great gulf of the sea to Troy...' (Hes. *Op.* 158–9, 161–5). The barbarity of Achilles' glorious deeds is clearly recognized in Cat. 64.348–70. Now the *priscae uestigia fraudis* will inspire epic deeds of valour once more. The reference to this second Heroic Age is prepared for by *heroum laudes* (26). It may reflect the more pessimistic interpretations of the Comet's significance (4n.) as portending war and suffering.

Achilles is a somewhat ambivalent hero in this context. He is the prototype of epic heroism, to whom Aeneas, armed with his divine shield, is compared by Turnus in *A.* 11.438. But as the champion of Troy's enemies he might also be seen as representing the forces hostile to the triumph of the new Troy, imperial Rome; cf. the description of Turnus himself in *A.* 6.89 as *alius Latio iam partus Achilles.* The slow murky ominous tone of the line – with its *m*-alliteration, early elisions, central spondaic sequence and prevalent heterodynes – is resolved in the homodyne cadence *mittétur Achílles*, which is thereby thrown into emphatic relief (3n.). The regression from Iron to Heroic to Golden Age in this part of the poem does not belong to the cyclic conceptions of history alluded to earlier but recalls rather the pendular movement of the world to and from God, which is depicted in the myth of Plato's *Politicus* 269Dff. The end-point of the swing towards God is portrayed by Plato very much in terms of the Hesiodic Golden Age (*ib.* 271E–

272B). But logically the Age of Heroes ought to precede the Golden
Age in this scheme and not break into it as it does here. Vergil has
conceived the return of the Golden Age as a gradual process, with the
second Heroic Age as a last dying manifestation of *prisca fraus* intervening before that process is brought to its triumphal fulfilment. The
optimism generated by the *Iulium sidus* had been disappointed by
immediately subsequent events. Here in the very centre of the poem
is a warning that, though the prophecies will indeed be fulfilled, a
further period of discord and war must first be endured. Whether this
dark note of pessimism belongs to the original conception of the poem
or to a late stage of its composition can only be guessed at. Certainly
the worsening relations between the triumvirs in 40 B.C. and the continuation of Sextus Pompey's war (Dio 48.31.2) made undiluted
optimism difficult at this time.

38 mari with *cedet* may be dative (cf. Liv. 3.17.9) or ablative (cf.
Cic. *Mil.* 68).

uector is used to mean both *is qui uehit* (rare) and *is qui uehitur*,
especially a sea-passenger; cf. Cic. *Phil.* 7.27. Not only sailors and
military heroes but also passengers, *mercatores* (cf. 39), will forsake the
sea.

nautica pinus: the paradox of a nautical pine-tree emphasizes the
unnatural character of sea-travel; cf. Cat. 64.1-2 *Peliaco...prognatae
uertice pinus | dicuntur...nasse per undas.*

39 In Hor. *S.* 1.4.25-32 the man who *mutat merces* in far-off lands
exemplifies the plight of those who *aut ob auaritiam aut misera ambitione
laborat*; cf. *G.* 2.503.

omnia tellus: again (3n., 35n.) the regular homodyne cadence
stands out from the preceding heterodyne sequence.

40-1 For the untended crop-lands and vines cf. Cat. 64.39-41 (the
neglect of the land during the wedding of Peleus and Thetis), Hor.
Epod. 16.43-4 (the Isles of the Blest). In Lucretius' picture of primitive
rural life *nec robustus erat curui moderator aratri* (5.933).

tauris is either dative of interest (cf. Prop. 2.9.39) or less likely
ablative of separation (cf. *A.* 1.562). See 29n., 38n.

42 nec...mentiri: the personification, paralleled in Plin. *Nat.*
35.48, is especially appropriate where the contrast is between nature's

spontaneous bounties and the interference of sinful man with nature's normal processes, which is represented by *rastros, falcem, iuga*. It is continued in *uestiet* (45) and perhaps *mutabit* too (44), echoing *mutabit* in 39. The use of dyes was a symptom of civilized decadence; cf. Lucr. 5.1423, Tib. 2.4.28 and *G.* 2.465. The paradox of the Golden Age is that man, now free of his obsession with luxury, is surrounded by it and does not need to transgress nature's bounds to obtain it.

43   suaue rubenti: cf. 3.63.

44   murice: instrumental ablative. The famous 'Tyrian purple' (*A.* 4.262), extracted from a Levantine shell-fish, was a commonplace for expensive self-indulgence.

    luto 'dyer's weed' when boiled yields a yellow dye. Unlike *murex* and *sandyx* it was native to Italy and relatively inexpensive.

45   sandyx was used both of the red oxide of lead and of the red sandalwood, Pterocarpus Santalinus, which yielded a similar pigment. Although *pascentis* was taken by Pliny (*Nat.* 35.40) and Servius to prove that *sandyx* here is a plant, Vergil may be using the noun simply as a colour term.

    uestiet: Pliny reports (*Nat.* 8.191) that *nigri uelleris praecipuas* [sc. *oues*] *habet Pollentia iuxta Alpes, iam Asia rutili quas Erythraeas uocant, item Baetica, Canusium fului, Tarentum et suae pulliginis*, and Martial addresses Corduba *albi quae superas oues Galaesi,* | *nullo murice nec cruore mendax,* | *sed tinctis gregibus colore uiuo* (12.63.3–5). Juvenal (12.40–2) suggests three possible causes for the tinted fleeces: the character of the grass, some special quality in the spring-water or *Baeticus...aer*. In the New Age these localized phenomena, no doubt enhanced, will become universal. Servius claims a reference to Etruscan prophetic lore here and quotes a passage on Etruscan portents, which is preserved more fully by Macrobius (*Sat.* 3.7.2), who attributes it to a certain Tarquitius: *purpureo aureoue colore ouis ariesue si aspergetur, principi ordinis et generis summa cum felicitate largitatem auget, genus progeniem propagat in claritate laetioremque efficit.* This doctrine was surely known to Vergil and may even have formed part of the oracular material in general circulation at this time.

46–7   Cf. Cat. 64.321–2 of the song of the *Parcae* at the wedding of Peleus and Thetis *talia diuino fuderunt carmine fata,* | *carmine perfidiae* *quod post nulla arguet aetas*; 326–7 *sed uos quae fata sequontur | currite ducentes subtegmina, currite, fusi*; 382–3 *talia praefantes quondam felicia Pelei | carmina diuino cecinerunt pectore Parcae.* The song grimly foretold the violent deeds and early death of Achilles (338ff.), and was followed by an expression of Catullus' own wistful longings for the innocent days when gods and men mingled freely together (397ff.). Now the valour of a second Achilles will form the prelude to the fulfilment of Catullus' nostalgic wish.

46 talia saecla is either vocative or more likely accusative of the space traversed (cf. *A.* 3.191), with *currite* addressed to the spindles *fusis*. The incantatory effect of the five homodyne feet is striking even after the frequent homodynes of the preceding couplet.

47 stabili fatorum numine: the phrase (cf. Cic. *Tusc.* 1.115) suggests the decrees of a providential deity rather than the mechanical working of an impersonal fate; cf. *stabilisque rerum | terminus* in Hor. *C.S.* 26–7. The genitive is probably therefore a defining one: 'in the steadfast will (of Jupiter) consisting of the decrees of Fate'.

Parcae: the three Fates or *Moîrai* of Greek mythology (Hes. *Th.* 904–5) were Clotho, Lachesis and Atropos. They seem to have been in origin birth-spirits, who fixed a person's destiny at the moment he was born. Spinning, which must have been Clotho's specific activity at first (cf. Greek *klôthein* 'to spin') was already attributed to all three in our earliest records of them. Their distinctive iconography in post-classical art is already attested in *Anthol. Lat.* 1.792 *tres sunt fatales quae ducunt filia sorores. | Clotho solum baiulat, Lachesis trahit, Atropos occat.* The Latin *Parcae* may also have begun as birth-spirits; cf. Varro's etymology from the root of *pario, partus* (Gell. 3.16.9–11). Their names *Nona, Decuma, Morta* are obscure (cf. the fanciful explanations in Gell. *loc. cit.*) but their assimilation to the *Moîrai* is illustrated by *fusis* (46). The chiastic word order places the emphasis on *concordes* and *Parcae*.

48 adgredere...magnos...honores is best taken not as a continuation of the message of the Parcae but as resuming Vergil's own apostrophe to the Child. *honores* is to be understood in a general sense. The chronological progression of 18–45, presented in future indicatives throughout, is complete, the message of the Parcae in 46–7 provides a coda; and 48–62 with its sequence of singular imperatives is a

personal exhortation to the new-born Child, interrupted in 53–9 by
Vergil's own poetic aspirations regarding this advent. Alternatively
48–52 could form the conclusion to the unfolding of the New Age
expounded in 18–45. For there has been no explicit statement of the
Child's activities *ubi iam firmata uirum te fecerit aetas* (37), only an account of the miracles that will attend his maturity; and *magnos honores*
might be taken to refer to this stage of his life. But this is less likely.

49 deum suboles does not necessarily imply that the Child is
divine but it suggests at least the status of a demi-god, comparable to
Bacchus, Hercules or Aeneas, *deum certissima proles* (*A.* 6.322).

   magnum Iouis incrementum with its sonorous *m*-alliteration
and spondaic cadence gives a majestic climax to the sentence. Two
meanings are possible: (i)'a mighty addition to Jupiter', viz. his offspring – like Bacchus or Hercules – or his adjutant, the representative
of his power on earth, as Augustus is depicted in Hor. *C.* 1.12.57–60,
3.5.1–4. For *incrementum* of the process of addition or of what is added
cf. Cic. *Fin.* 2.88, Var. *L.* 8.17, *R.* 2.4.19 and especially *CIL* 10.5853.14
puer(is) curiae increment(is). (ii) 'that which will grow into (a second)
Jupiter'. This sense of the noun is found in Ov. *M.* 3.103 *uipereos dentes
populi incrementa futuri*. Whichever meaning Vergil had in mind, the
phrase can hardly refer to posthumous deification, such as Julius Caesar had recently been awarded, or to the divine titles conferred on
living dynasts by admirers and grateful beneficiaries, e.g. *Iuppiter
Iulius* of Caesar in 44 B.C. (Dio 44.6.4), 'Dionysus gracious and gentle'
of Antony at Ephesus in 42 B.C. (Plut. *Ant.* 24); cf. *filius Maiae patiens
uocari | Caesaris ultor* of Augustus (Hor. *C.* 1.2.43–4). Honours of this
sort came from political and military achievements. By contrast the
Child here is to be *magnum Iouis incrementum* from birth; as *noua
progenies* sent down from heaven he is to be born into a quasi-divine
status, which will not depend upon the admiration and esteem of
others. For this supernatural messianic role cf. the 'Son of Man' in
Daniel 7.13–14.

50–1 conuexo nutantem pondere 'with all its rounded mass
vibrating'. For the concept of a spherical *mundus* with its heavier
elements, *terrasque tractusque maris*, concentrated at the centre and the
aether located in the *caelum profundum* at the periphery see Cic. *Tusc.*
1.40, *N.D.* 2.115–18. *conuexo* is in fact more accurate than *globoso* or

rotundo since the interior of only one hemisphere could be visible at a time. *nutare* is used of any strong swaying or vibration (cf. *A.* 9.682) and even sometimes implies imminent collapse (e.g. *A.* 2.629). Like the tremors that precede the advent of a god to his temple (e.g. *A.* 3.90–2) these signs would be terrifying to those who had not learnt to read them. For their apocalyptic connotations cf. Haggai 2.6–7 'Thus speaks the Lord of the Hosts: "One thing more. I will shake heaven and earth, sea and land, and I will shake all nations"'; *Orac. Sib.* 3.675–9 'And in those days Earth, mother of all things, will be shaken by an immortal hand... and the souls of all men and all the sea will tremble before the immortal face and there will be fear.'

terrasque tractusque maris: the metrical variation in the treatment of *que*, viz. -*quet-rac*- but -*que-ma*-, is a feature of elevated verse-style, modelled on the frequent Homeric variation in ...τε...τε phrases. Some of the Latin instances are extensions of normal Latin phonology; e.g. *Drymoque Xanthoque* (*G.* 4.336), *Antheusque Mnestheus-que* (*A.* 12.443), where -*quek-san*- and -*quem-nes*- accord with the regular treatment of *x* and *mn* internally (neither cluster occurs initially in Latin). Others, like the present instance and *aestusque pluuiasque* (*G.* 1.352) with *quep-lu*- instead of *que-plu*, involve a mute + liquid cluster, on which see 5n. A few are pure Homerisms, alien to the native phonology, e.g. *liminaque laurusque* (*A.* 3.91), *Chloreaque Sybarinque* (*A.* 12.363), where the continuants *l* and *s* are presumably lengthened; the present example, unique in the Eclogues, recurs at *G.* 4.222.

profundum 'high' shows a rare, perhaps innovatory, use of the converse to its normal meaning; cf. the more frequent use of *altus* to mean 'deep' as well as 'high'.

52   laetantur: this reading has been preferred to *laetentur* as being the more likely to have been emended in the tradition. For the rare use of the indicative cf. 5.7n., *A.* 6.855–6.

53 Vergil's hopes expressed here contrast with the disconsolate pessimism of Hesiod: 'Would that I might live no longer among the fifth race of men who came thereafter, but had died before or been born afterwards' (*Op.* 174–5). They recall the joyous expectancy of *Orac. Sib.* 3.371ff. 'Blessed the man or woman who will be on earth then...'

54   spiritus: both 'breath', with reference to the preceding line, and 'inspiration', with reference to what follows. For the latter sense cf. Hor. *C.* 2.16.37-9.

dicere: although the infinitive is commonly found with impersonal *sat(is) est* (10.70), it is very rare with *satis sum* etc., the normal construction of which is with a gerund or gerundive, e.g. Liv. 9.43.19, Ter. *An.* 705-6. The assimilation of the relative (sc. *tantus* with *spiritus*) to the neuter *sat* suggests that the personal construction has here been influenced by the impersonal.

55 uincat: less arrogant than *uincet*, which also has good manuscript authority. The hypothetical sense of the subjunctive accords better with the preceding optative *maneat* and the subjunctives of 58, 59.

nec...nec for *aut...aut* reinforce the initial *non*. This use of a double negative is more characteristic of Greek than of Latin formal style: cf. 5.25.

Thracius Orpheus: the archetypal poet (3.46n.).

56 Linus: there were various local cults and myths relating to this mysterious youth and his violent death. His name has been connected with Greek *línos*, the lament sung at vintage festivals (Hom. *Il.* 18.569-72), and with the dirge-refrain *aílinon* (Pi. fr. 126.5, Ov. *A.* 3.9.23). Like Orpheus, with whom Ovid (*loc. cit.*) also associates him, he came to be regarded as 'learned in every kind of wisdom' (Hes. fr. 306MW), was the subject of many dirges (Hes. fr. 305MW) and had a number of apocryphal works attributed to him, including a *Theologia* (D. Servius). He appears again at 6.67.

adsit: the verb is commonly used both of a supporting friend or witness in a legal action and of a god who appears to bring help in time of need; cf. *G.* 1.18, *A.* 4.578.

57 Orphei with diphthongal *-ei*, following Greek *Orpheî* rather than *Orphëï*, is confirmed by *G.* 4.545. It is normal for Greek proper names in *-eus* in Latin; cf. 6.78.

Calliopea...Apollo: the explicit mention of the Muse of Epic poetry and the patron god of minstrelsy emphasizes the divine inheritance in the two poets' musical talent. Various parentages were reported for both Orpheus and Linus; in some accounts both were the sons of Calliopea and Apollo (Apollod. 1.3.2).

58-9 The repetition of *Pan etiam Arcadia* and the similarity of *si* *iudice* to *se iudice* arouse strong suspicions of textual corruption, especially as both *P* and *R* present garbled versions of the couplet.

The self-confidence inspired by expectations of the New Age goes far beyond even what is claimed for Bion in the panegyric which it recalls in part: 'Am I to take the pipe and give it to Pan to make music with? Perhaps even he would be afraid to press his lips to it lest he come off second best to you' (*Epit. Bion.* 55–6). If Orpheus and Linus bring intimations of poetry outside the pastoral, Arcadian Pan takes us back again. The fulfilment of the New Age will inspire Vergil to transcend his present achievements in poetry, just as the expectation of it has inspired him to go beyond the *humiles myricae* of conventional pastoral.

60–3 The high proportion of homodynes produce an incantatory effect, as in 46.

risu cognoscere: probably 'to acknowledge with a smile', which goes well with the reading *qui non risere parenti* and with the insistent repetition of *incipe parue puer*. For this sense of the verb, more often associated with *agnoscere* (e.g. Ov. *M.* 13.27–8), cf. Cic. *Cat.* 3.10. Less likely 'to identify by her smile', with the verb in its normal sense 'to get to know'; this would perhaps go better with the reading *cui non risere parentes* in 62.

61 decem...menses: the average gestation period is within two or three days of ten lunar months; cf. Gell. 3.16.

tulĕrunt: but *tulērunt* at 5.34. *-ĕrunt*, the older form, is more frequent in iambic and other metres, but rare in hexameters owing to the preponderance of perfect stems ending in long vowels; cf. *miscueruntque* (*G.* 3.283), *constiterunt* (*A.* 3.681).

fastidia 'qualms', 'periods of squeamishness', as in Colum. 10.180 *longi fastidia morbi*. For the plural see 1.6n.

62 incipe parue puer: the urgent repetition is reinforced by the close metrical correspondence between this line and 60.

qui non risere parenti: the reading *cui non risere parentes* gives easy grammar but feeble sense; a mother's smile hardly characterizes her child as exceptional nor would the absence of it, however unnatural it seems, obviously disqualify him from future greatness. Quintilian

(9.3.8) cites this passage as an instance of *figura in numero*, and although his MSS give it in the same form as Vergil's, it is clear from his comment that he read *qui non risere* and *hunc*, and accepted the harsh syntax as Vergilian. (It is impossible that, having been taught to spell the dative '*quoi*' *tantum ut ab illo* '*qui*' *distingueretur* (1.7.27) he would have mistaken *qui* for *quoi*.) A plural relative occurs with a singular antecedent in *A.* 8.427–8 *fulmen erat...quae plurima...deiecit*, Pl. *Curc.* 494–5 and Liv. 22.57–3; in all three instances the relative clause defines a larger group to which the antecedent belongs. So here: the Child is one of a select company who have smiled at birth upon their mothers. It was observed in antiquity that babies do not normally smile before the age of six weeks (Plin. *Nat.* 7 *pr.* 2, Censorinus *D.N.* 10.1). Exceptions included Hermes and Perseus (Lucian *D. Deor.* 11.220, *D.Mar.* 12.319), Beroe the daughter of Aphrodite (Nonn. *D.* 41.212) and Zoroaster (Plin. *Nat.* 7.72). The *risus praecox* here is thus a sign of the Child's supernatural character.

parenti: *ridere* with the accusative regularly means 'to laugh at', 'make fun of', e.g. Cic. *Quinct.* 55, Prop. 2.16.47; with the dative or *ad* + accusative 'to greet with a kindly laugh', 'to laugh for', e.g. Cat. 61.219 (see below), Lucr. 1.8 (with the verb used metaphorically, as in line 20 cf the present poem); cf. the use of *subridere* in *A.* 1.254. Hence 'to greet with a laugh', 'smile upon' is the sense here.

63 *proinde nobilibus pueris editis in atrio domus Iunoni lectus Herculi mensa ponebatur* (D. Servius). If this custom actually existed, an allusion to it here would be very flat; for what was commonplace among the Roman gentry would hardly be an honour worthy of this miraculous Child. In fact the *risus praecox* that announces the Child's supernatural status portends honours for him comparable to those of Hercules in Hom. *Od.* 11.602–4: 'He enjoys himself at feasts with the immortal gods and has as his wife Hebe with the fair ankles, child of great Zeus and of Hera with the golden sandals' (cf. Hor. *C.* 4.8.30, Ov. *M.* 9.400–1). In these closing lines Vergil's imagination, playing around the concept of the Wonder Child, has formed an intensely realistic image reminiscent of Catullus' picture of the infant son of Torquatus in 61.216ff. *uolo paruolus | matris e gremio suae | porrigens teneras manus | dulce rideat ad patrem | semihiante labello.* But the apocalyptic overtones are not thereby excluded; the vivid realism emphasizes Vergil's conviction

of the coming actuality of the *nouom saeculum*; cf. the vivid anthropo-
morphism of Lucretius' presentation of Venus and Mars in his proem
to Book 1.

The identification of the Child in this poem has been the subject of
endless debate. A number of human candidates have been proposed;
none has won general acceptance among scholars.

(i) The prominence of Pollio in the poem and the belief that
pacatum. . .patriis uirtutibus (17) could refer, somewhat extravagantly,
to his mediation in the Pact of Brindisi led to the suggestion that a son
of Pollio is meant. Servius mentions two sons, Saloninus and Asinius
Gallus. There is no other evidence that the former ever existed. The
latter was born in 41 B.C., too early for the notional date of the poem.
He became consul in 8 B.C. and seems to have boasted of being the
Child, a fact which at least indicates that the identity of the Child
was open to doubt even in Vergil's own lifetime. In any case it is
remarkable that while Pollio's consulship is mentioned explicitly, his
paternity is nowhere even hinted at.

(ii) A child of Mark Antony has also been suggested. He was unquestionably the senior partner of the triumvirate at the time and his
military record might be thought to justify the expectation (cf. 17)
that he would bring peace to the world. The twins Alexander Helios
and Cleopatra Selene whom Cleopatra bore to him about this time,
possibly in 40 B.C. itself, were apparently invested with the titles and
apocalyptic insignia associated with Hellenistic royal houses. But this
superficial link with the poem's imagery cannot outweigh the fact that
Antony's liaison with Cleopatra was an affront to orthodox Roman
sensibilities. The suggestion that their children might preside over a
new age of concord uniting East and West could only have been a
perverse fantasy or a tasteless joke, and is entirely inconsistent both
with the tone of the poem itself and with the political climate of
opinion in 41–40 B.C.

(iii) The pact of Brindisi, made between the two triumvirs in early
autumn 40 B.C., was sealed by a dynastic alliance between Antony
and Octavian's sister Octavia, which was arranged with callous haste
after the death of her former husband Claudius Marcellus. Some have
seen in the echoes of Catullus 61 and 64 an allusion to the marriage, but

these can all be explained in other ways (see the notes to 15-16, 19, 32, 46-7, 63) and in any event could not outweigh the absence of any of the usual nuptial commonplaces. Moreover it would be rash indeed to celebrate a marriage by eulogizing an offspring from it that might not – and as it happened did not – materialize.

(iv) A similar objection could be made to treating the poem as a marriage-hymn for Octavian and Scribonia. They were married in the summer of 40 B.C. and did in fact produce a daughter Julia, whose arrival the triumvir promptly greeted by divorcing her mother. Vergil could hardly be blamed for Julia's subsequent career of notoriety; but again one may ask whether he would have risked having his prophecy nullified by future events.

(v) Subsequent history did in fact throw up two further candidates. The son of Octavia and Marcellus, M. Claudius Marcellus, who had been born in 42 B.C., was adopted by Augustus as his heir in 25 B.C. and married to Julia, an honour that he lived to enjoy for no more than a couple of years. The famous reference in *A.* 6.855 to the young Marcellus as heir to the Augustan throne seems to have led to his identification with the Child in the poem, which is mentioned in the Berne Scholia. But any reference to Marcellus in the circumstances of 40 B.C. would have been astoundingly tactless and wholly unmotivated.

(vi) Lastly the Berne Scholia also mention the identification with Augustus himself. It is undeniable that Vergil professed to see the fulfilment of the poem's aspirations in the *pax Augusta*: *Augustus Caesar, diui genus, aurea condet | saecula qui rursus Latio regnata per arua | Saturno quondam, super et Garamantas et Indos | proferet imperium* (*A.* 6.792-5). But apart from the fact that the Child in the poem is not yet born, this subsequent allusion to the present context cannot be used to establish Vergil's intentions at the time when the future emperor was still a minor, if up-and-coming, partner to Mark Antony. It is true that the young Octavian had professed belief in the special patronage of Apollo (Suet. *Aug.* 94) and exploited his own physical resemblance to the Sun-god (*ib.* 70, Serv. on line 10 here). But in the present poem Apollo's reign (9-10) is but the prelude to the *Saturnia regna*. He is not presented as its presiding deity. The Apollonian patronage, like the deifications referred to in the note on 49, while important for the development of the ruler-cult, can only be applied to the interpretation of the Eclogue by hindsight. Moreover, even the most fulsome praise of the *princeps* in Augustan poetry does not approach the apocalyptic heights of lines 7, 49–51 or 63 here; as early as 40 B.C. no mortal – whether political leader or dynastic child – could have been so depicted in a Latin poem. Vergil prophesies that the Child will rule a world at peace and surrounds his prophecy with a rich complex of highly emotive apocalyptic imagery. Would he have risked the possibility of having such a noble prophecy nullified, if not reduced to ridicule, by attaching it not just to an unborn child but to *any* human being?

(vii) The most famous identification of the Child is with Jesus Christ, son of the Virgin Mary. Its first authentic appearance is in the writings of St Augustine (*Epist. ad Rom. inc. expos.* 3, cf. *Epist.* 137.12), who attributes the prophecy not to Vergil himself but to the Sibylline oracle by which the poem was inspired. Now the recognition of parallels between Sibylline oracular material alluded to in the Eclogue and the prophetic books of the Old Testament does not entail a Christian interpretation for the former. After all there is no compelling reason for taking even the Old Testament passages themselves as a prophecy of the birth of Christ.

We may thus accept the messianic character of the apocalyptic imagery that Vergil has adopted in this poem without giving it a specifically Christian reference. Just as in the fifth Eclogue Vergil alludes to the deification of the mortal Julius Caesar, so he proclaims here a divine incarnation that will follow it. The *noua progenies* sent down from heaven, offspring perhaps of Jupiter and Virgo (see 7n., 49n.), will rule a world that is pacified by Jupiter's powers, *patriis uirtutibus,* and reflects among men the concord re-established among the gods themselves in the new reign of Saturn in heaven. But Vergil is a poet, not a theologian, and the oriental apocalyptic imagery, like that of the Hesiodic Golden Age, is for him essentially metaphoric. The Child is for Vergil a symbol of the divine forces that will bring the *nouom saeculum* to pass.

The style of the poem is very mature. Its concentrated verbal texture and imagery set it apart from all the other Eclogues save the sixth. So too does its hexameter technique, with a relatively high incidence of spondaic rhythms and a tendency to exploit the expressive possibilities inherent in the interplay of accent and quantitative metre, which foreshadows Vergil's epic hexameter.

Structurally the poem divides after the three-line prologue into three major sections: *A* (4-17), *B* (18-47), *C* (48-63). Within *A* we have (i) a complex of apocalyptic allusions culminating in the Birth of the Child (4-10), (ii) the placing of this event in time – Pollio's consulship (11-14), (iii) the Child's future life depicted in terms reminiscent of Catullus 64 (15-17). In *B* the two complementary themes are developed – the infancy, youth and maturity of the Child, corresponding to the gradual emergence of nature's Golden Age. The three stages, (i) 18-25, (ii) 26-30, (iii) 37-45, concluding with an allusion to Etruscan divination, are interrupted by (iv) the return of the Heroic Age (31-6). The Catullan echoes in the latter are intensified in (v), the coda containing the message of the *Parcae* (46-7). In *C* the poet (i) addresses the new-born Child, proclaiming his cosmic significance (48-52), (ii) expresses his own poetic aspirations in relation to the New Age (53-9), (iii) returns to address the Child in vividly realistic and emotive terms (60-3).

Although there is no neat mathematical symmetry here, the structure is tight and effective. The significance of the pessimistic prophecy of another Heroic Age, disrupting the progression within *B*, has already been remarked (36n.). The historical point of departure for the gradual emergence of the *nouom saeculum* is marked by a personal reference – to the statesman Pollio in *A* (ii), the point of its fulfilment by a reference to the poet himself in *C* (ii), and the concluding scene in *C* (iii) takes us back to the dominant image of *A* (i).

The conception of the poem may date from the appearance of the *sidus Iulium* itself. It certainly brings together in the conception of a Golden Age that is to be preceded by an Heroic Age within the lifetime of a wonder-child both the optimistic and pessimistic lines of interpretation of the comet (see 4n., 36n.). Since the triumvirs had fixed the consular lists for some years in advance at their meeting in Bononia in 43 B.C., it is likely that Vergil, who was close to Pollio, would have known that he was to be consul for 40 B.C. in plenty of time to elaborate the theme in all its detail. Indeed Pollio's own Jewish contacts (Josephus 15.10.1) may have provided Vergil with some of the background to the oriental material in the Sibylline oracles. But poems are not always published in advance of the events they purport to herald, Pollio certainly did not hold office for his full term, and the warning of heroic wars to come, though likely to have formed part of the original conception of the poem, would have had a particularly topical relevance if the date of publication was some way into 40 B.C., when relations between Antony and Octavian were rapidly deteriorating again. The pessimism of Horace's sixteenth Epode is relevant here. The detailed parallels between the two poems do not enable us to establish priority, and if much of the Golden Age imagery of the Eclogue – traditional in any case – was current in contemporary oracular material, then the similarities may signify nothing more than the use of a common source by the two poets. What is certainly clear is that whereas Horace read the signs of continuing strife as a refutation of the prophecy of a new Golden Age, Vergil saw them merely as evidence that it would not come to pass overnight, while nevertheless retaining his faith in its eventual fulfilment.

ECLOGUE V

1-2 Mopse: unlike Menalcas (2.15n.) Mopsus does not appear in extant Greek pastoral. Two seers bore the name, one a Lapith and Argonaut (Hes. *Sc.* 181, A.R. 1.65-6), the other a son of Apollo and Manto (9.60n.), who founded the oracle at Mallos (Strabo 14.642). A courteous dialogue between the two herdsmen here leads not to a contest as in *Ecl.* 3 and 7 but to a friendly exchange of songs (20ff.) comparable to [Th.] *Idd.* 8 and 9, in which both Menalcas and Daphnis, who is the subject of the two songs here, were the participants.

boni...inflare...dicere: the infinitive with verbal adjectives is probably by analogy with the corresponding verbs; e.g. *nescia fallere* (*G.* 2.467), *nescit fallere*. With non-verbal adjectives, as here, it is a residue of dative and locative functions denoting purpose and field of reference. Both types occur in Plautus and are probably native, but their increased currency from the first century B.C. onwards especially in poetry, where they provided a concise alternative to more cumbersome constructions, can be attributed to Greek influence. Cf. 54, 10.32 and [Th.] *Id.* 8.4 (7.5n.).

3 consedimus is either preterite 'Why didn't we sit down?' or perfect (= *sedemus*) 'Why aren't we seated?' *considimus* would mean 'Why aren't we seating ourselves?' For the invitation to sit and sing in the cool shade cf. Th. *Idd.* 1.21, 5.31–3. The whole phrase is expressively enclosed by *corulis* and *ulmos*.

4 maior: *id est uel natu uel merito* (D. Serv.). For the former sense cf. Caes. *Civ.* 3.108.3. The ellipse is colloquial in origin.

5 sub incertas...umbras: with *sub* the verb normally means 'to come close up to', e.g. Caes, *Civ.* 1.45.2; in the sense 'to go underneath' it normally has a datival complement, e.g. *G.* 3.464, Cic. *Dom.* 116. The variation between 5 and 6 may therefore be significant. The fine image of flickering shadows is suggested rather than depicted by the addition to the vague *incertas*, which could by itself be derogatory, of the cause of this uncertainty, the movement of cool westerly breezes.

6 antro 'to the cave' or 'to the hollow in the rocks' tactfully suggests an alternative spot. See 1.75n.

7 sparsit: although the indicative in indirect questions is usually colloquial, its occurrence with *aspice ut* in *A.* 6.855–6 and probably *Ecl.* 4.52 indicates that in some stereotyped phrases the interrogative force of the subordinate clause was no longer prominent. In prose *spargere* is normally constructed as 'to sprinkle *x* on or over *y*' (e.g. Cic. *Sen.* 77). The construction 'to sprinkle *y* with *x*' is common in poetry from Ennius (*sc.* 363V) onwards and is also implied in e.g. *maculis sparsum* (Liv. 41.21.13).

labrusca 'the wild vine' (Plin. *Nat.* 23.19). For the descriptive detail cf. Calypso's cave in Hom. *Od.* 5.68–9, the prototype of all classical *loci amoeni*.

racemis: originally of the stalks on which the clusters of grapes grew, then commonly as here of the clusters themselves scattered (*raris*) over the vines. The 'golden line' word order suggests the intertwining of the vines; cf. 3.39.

8 Amyntas was the jealous rival to Corydon in 2.35 and Menalcas' favourite in 3.66ff.

tibi certat: the verb is regularly constructed with *cum*, rarely *contra*. The dative is also found in 8.55, Hor. *Epod.* 11.18; like that with *pugnare* (*A.* 4.38, Cat. 62.65) it may be extended from *resistere* etc.

However it could well have been influenced by the Greek dative with verbs like μάχεσθαι 'to fight'.

9 quid si idem certet 'What if he were also to strive...?' i.e. 'I suppose he would also strive...' The usage is colloquial; cf. Pl. *Po.* 330 '*eunt hae.*' '*quid si adeamus?*' '*adeas*'. The sarcastic tone, though clear from line 15, is not inherent in the form of the question itself.

superare: the infinitive with *certare*, common in Vergil (e.g. *G.* 2.99–100, *A.* 2.64) occurs already in Enn. *A.* 445V, Lucr. 5.393. Cf. 1–2n.

10–11 Phyllidos ignes 'the flames of love kindled by Phyllis'; cf. Ov. *Tr.* 2.537–8 *Phyllidis hic idem* [sc. *Vergilius*] *teneraeque Amaryllidis ignes | bucolicis iuuenis luserat ante modis*. Phyllis appears in 3.76ff., 7.59.

Alconos...laudes 'the praises bestowed on Alcon': Alcon does not appear elsewhere in the Eclogues or earlier pastoral, and this may simply be an *ad hoc* phrase to complete the trio of pastoral themes.

iurgia Codri: although *Codrus* does not appear in earlier pastoral, it is the name of a rival poet in *Ecl.* 7, where Thyrsis (26) indulges in some 'invective against Codrus'.

ignes, laudes, iurgia of various kinds comprise almost all the personal themes of pastoral singers in the conventional genre. Servius took all three characters to be from mythology: *Phyllis* the Thracian princess whose ill-fated love for Theseus' son Demophoon is the subject of Ov. *Her.* 2; *Alcon* the Cretan archer (cf. *A.P.* 6.331) who shot a snake coiled about his son without harming the boy; *Codrus* the king of Athens at the time of the Dorian invasion who, inspired by an oracle that *illos posse uincere quorum dux periisset*, entered the enemy camp in disguise and was killed in a quarrel (cf. Lycurg. *Leoc.* 84–7). *ignes...laudes... iurgia* would thus refer to 'the passion of Phyllis, the praises bestowed on Alcon, the taunts made by Codrus'. But *si quos...habes* would then be an odd expression and it is hard to see why such a trio of subjects should be chosen to typify a herdsman's repertoire and referred to so elliptically.

12 pascentis but *pastos* (24). For the syntax of this verb see 1.54n.

Tityrus is left to mind the animals, as in Th. *Id.* 3.1–2 'my goats are grazing on the hill and Tityrus is leading them'. For his generally subservient role among the herdsmen see 1.1n. The line, besides revealing that Mopsus is a goatherd like the singer of the Daphnis-dirge in Th. *Id.* 1, reminds us that these recitals are but an interlude in the routine of pastoral life. So too Thyrsis in *Id.* 1.12–14 reassures the goatherd that he himself will mind the goats while their master makes music.

13   immo is colloquial and dismisses the subjects proposed in favour of something more important, something that has actually been composed beforehand, like Thyrsis' and Lycidas' pieces in Th. *Idd.* 1.19, 7.51, and also written down. This is the first reference to writing of any kind in extant pastoral, Th. *Id.* 18.47–8 being outside the genre. The only other ones in the Eclogues are at 42 and 10.53.

in uiridi . . . cortice: *cortex* (6.63) is the bark proper, the protective covering to the soft moist rind, *liber*, that encloses the trunk. The bark of the beech-tree is very smooth and, when fresh, easy to inscribe. Vergil is unlikely to have permitted his countrymen the barbarism of stripping fresh bark from a tree, so we must assume that Mopsus' *carmina* like Gallus' *amores* in 10.53–4 are carved on the trunk. Twenty-five lines (20–44) written out in full would make an implausibly long inscription, though Calpurnius *Ecl.* 1 has a poem of fifty-six lines (33–88) supposedly inscribed on a beech tree (20, 25).

14   carmina: the plural must refer to the individual sections of the song.

modulans alterna notaui is obscure but is likely to mean 'I noted the alternations of flute and voice as I played' rather than 'I noted the music and words on alternate lines'. *modulari* is used of marking rhythmic or accentual patterns (Cic. *Or.* 58), of singing (Quint. 9.2.35) and of tuning or playing an instrument (Hor. *C.* 1.32.5). As Mopsus has been praised for his piping (2), the reference of *modulans* is probably to this. The separate sections of the song would be marked by a change of melody which the singer would play over before he sang (cf. 87). We are perhaps to imagine Mopsus writing down the words and music alternately, pausing after each section of the song was written (*describere*) to compose and play through the melody (*modulari*) and then inscribe it (*notare*).

15   iubeto certet Amyntas: the colloquial parataxis with the bucolic diaeresis falling sharply after the homodyne spondee gives an aggressively emphatic tone. It is more likely to have been emended in

the scribal tradition by the addition of *ut* than vice versa. Menalcas'
reference to Amyntas' rivalry still rankles with Mopsus, whose mind
is perhaps finally put at rest by the verdict of 18.

16   lenta begins another of Vergil's rustic analogies (2.63n.). The
suppleness of the willow (3.83) contrasts with the more rigid olive
wood. *pallenti* could apply to the leaves of either tree; cf. *glauca* of the
willow in *G.* 2.13, *glaukḗ* of the olive in Soph. *O.C.* 701. Though hardly
the more beautiful of the two, the olive was unquestionably the more
valuable.

17   puniceis: the adjective must originally have been applied to
Phoenician (Tyrian) *murex*. It is applied to blood (Ov. *M.* 2.607),
roses (Hor. *C.* 4.10.4), and even crocuses (Ov. *F.* 5.318).

   saliunca, probably the 'Celtic nard', Valeriana Celtica, was a
native of the Alpine regions of Italy (Plin. *Nat.* 21.43). It was highly
scented, but its stems were too brittle to be used in garlands. But the
comparison here is rather in terms of colour, the small yellowish
flowers of the *saliunca* against the rich red blooms of the rose-beds.
Both *saliunca* and *rosetum* are rare in classical Latin and do not occur
elsewhere in Vergil. The artful juxtaposition of the two epithets
puniceis humilis, balanced chiastically by their respective nouns in
another of Vergil's 'golden line' effects, implies the complementary
contrast *nobilibus pallens*; cf. 2.50n.

19   desine plura: the confusion of *desine loqui* with *parce plura loqui*
and the ellipse of the infinitive are both colloquial, and the tone is
matched by the metre, with the line fragmented by the diaereses after
tu and *desine* and the caesural pause after *puer*. For *antro* see 6n.

20   exstinctum placed first asserts the character of the song: it is a
lament for the dead Daphnis, not like *Id.* 1.64ff. an account of his last
moments.

   Nymphae: cf. Th. *Id.* 1.141 of Daphnis, 'the man who was dear to
the Muses and hated not by the Nymphs'.

   Daphnin: unlike the other pastoral characters Daphnis belongs to
earlier mythology; see Parth. *Erot.* 29, Aelian. *V.H.* 10.18. The son of
Hermes and a nymph, he was exposed as a baby under a bay-tree
(Greek *dáphnē*), whence his name. Brought up by the Sicilian herdsmen, he adopted their way of life and excelled in pastoral music, of

which in some accounts he was the inventor (see p. 1). He pledged life-long fidelity in love to a Naiad but was tricked into breaking his vow and punished with blindness. Philargyrius on the present line says that he consoled himself with song; Servius that he invoked his father's aid and was raised to heaven. Other tales of Daphnis' love-life are reported from Hellenistic poets in the scholia to Theocritus, and a Sicilian Daphnis-cult is reported by Servius here and by Diodorus, 4.84. In *Id.* 6 and in the post-Theocritean *Idd.* 8, 9, 27 he is hardly distinguishable from the conventional herdsmen of the genre. However, in *Id.* 5.20 he is cited as a proverbial example of suffering. The reference may be to his pining for Xenea (*Id.* 7.73-7) who apparently rejected his love (Ov. *A.A.* 1.732). In *Id.* 1.64–145 he is reminiscent of Hippolytus, defiantly taunting Aphrodite as he goes to his death. Although the Theocritean picture of the handsome cattle-herd and musician doomed to untimely death is clearly one of the models for Mopsus' lament, Vergil has erased all traces of the traditional erotic background to his suffering and of the Theocritean motif of hostility to Venus. See also 2.26n., 7.1n., 9.46n.

21 flebant completes the succession of heavy syllables in the preceding line. Followed by a diaeresis coinciding with a sense-break, it has a tone of grim finality. For a similar rhythmic effect see *A.* 6.212-13.

23 atque...atque...: in most other instances of this sequence (e.g. *G.* 3.257, Tib. 2.5.73-4) the first *atque* can be treated as a conjunction with the preceding clause. This is possible here only by understanding *est* with *complexa*. But the omission of the auxiliary verb would be surprising in a phrase co-ordinating perfect and present tenses. Better therefore to take this as an early example of *atque...atque* in the sense of *et...et* or *-que...-que* (28) 'both...and', which is attested clearly in Sil. 1.93.4 *hic crine effuso atque Ennaeae numina diuae | atque Acheronta uocat Stygia cum ueste sacerdos.*

    crudelia qualifies both *deos* and *astra*. It may also be predicative, intensifying the reproach: 'his mother invoked the gods and stars, calling them cruel'.

    mater is probably the nymph of the traditional tale (20n.). The delay in her entry not only heightens the drama of the opening lines but also emphasizes the contrast with the Theocritean situation.

Although like Daphnis in *Id.* 1 and Bion in *Epit. Bion.* Mopsus'
Daphnis is invested with super-human, heroic status by the fact that
he is mourned by nature and the gods, the opening and closing lines
of the dirge depict him in vividly human terms, the object of normal
human sorrow. The image of the grief-stricken mother belongs to a
theme recurrent both in ancient epitaphs and in literature (e.g. Thuc.
2.44.1, Juv. 10.240–2), the disconsolate plight of parents who survive
their children.

24 The herdsmen and their animals who came in sorrow to the
dying Daphnis in Th. *Id.* 1.74–5, 80–1 now mourn his death. The slow
sequence of heterodyne spondees is expressive.

25 Daphni...Daphni (27) **...Daphnis** (29) **...Daphnis** (30):
the insistent repetition is emotive.

nulla neque amnem: following the pause at the bucolic diaeresis,
the enjambement with the next line is hastened and brings a note of
urgency to the statement. For the emphatic double negative cf. 4.55.

26 quadrupes usually refers to horses in Vergil. Achilles' horses
wept for the dead Patroclus in Hom. *Il.* 17.426–8. But horses do not
belong to Theocritean pastoral and are mentioned explicitly in the
Eclogues only in the figure at 8.27. *quadrupes* is used of a stag in *A.*
7.500, so it may here refer to sheep or goats or even Daphnis' heifers,
the fem. *nulla* contrasting with the masc. *pastos* in 24. In Th. *Id.* 1.113,
6.1 Daphnis is also a cattle-herd.

graminis...herbam 'the grass of their pasture'. *gramen* was
originally 'fodder', 'pasturage'; cf. Greek *gráō* 'I gnaw'. The phrase
recurs in Liv. 1.24.5, Ov. *M.* 10.87. Aegon's herd pines for its absent
master in Th. *Id.* 4.12–14; even more relevant is *Epit. Bion.* 20–4 'He
who was beloved of the herds sings no more...and the cows that
wander with the bulls moan and refuse to graze.'

27–8 Poenos...leones: cf. *Id.* 1.72 'for him even the lion from the
forest wept when he died', implying not necessarily that there were
lions in Sicily in Daphnis' time but that the mourning for him was
universal. Vergil's similar intention here is underlined by the epithet.
The setting of the Eclogue is vaguely Italian, cf. *Pales* (35), *Ceres* (79);
but even the wild beasts in lands once hostile to Rome lament the
Italian herdsman. The universality of the mourning is expressed too

in the contrasting landscape of *graminis...herbam* and *montesque feri siluaeque*. For the latter phrase cf. Lucr. 5.201 *montes siluaeque ferarum* and Th. *Id.* 7.73-4 'the mountain was troubled about him [sc. Daphnis] and the oaks sang laments for him...', Bion *Adon.* 32ff. where mountains, woods and rivers cry out 'Alas for Adonis.'

locuntur: for *loqui* with the acc. + inf. construction of *dicere* cf. *A.* 1.731.

29 Armenias...tigris: proverbially savage (Prop. 1.9.19), they were said to have been tamed by Bacchus (*A.* 6.805) and yoked to his chariot ([Tib.] 3.6.15-16).

curru: dat. as in *A.* 3.541 rather than instr. abl. -*uī* was impossible in hexameters if the preceding syllable was heavy; hence dat. *uenatu* (*A.* 9.605), *uisu* (Lucr. 5.101) and even *manu* (Prop. 1.11.12). The form though rare in the MSS of prose authors, was favoured by Caesar (Gell. 4.16.8-9).

30 instituit: either 'instituted the practice' or 'taught (men) to'; see 2.33n.

thiasos: although Greek *thíasos* is sometimes used of other religious guilds or even secular companies, its earliest and most common application is to troops of Bacchants, and the Latin word is exclusively used of orgiastic worshippers, e.g. of Cybele (Cat. 63.28) or Bacchus (Cat. 64.252).

31 lentas...hastas 'languid spears', a strange description of the Bacchic *thyrsus*, which consisted of a fennel staff crowned by a bunch of ivy and in Hellenistic times by a pine-cone with ivy and vine leaves entwining the stem (*foliis...mollibus*). Fennel is not supple, so *lentas* must refer either to the languid movement of the wands (cf. 1.3 and *lenta...manu* in [Tib.] 3.5.30) or to the optical illusion of suppleness produced by the movement of the foliage around it. Cf. *mollis... thyrsos* (*A.* 7.390). *hastas* too is remarkable. For though the use of the word in *Priap.* 43.4 makes it appropriate for a phallic symbol, its connotations are essentially military (cf. Gell. 10.27), and the combination with *lentas* rather than *duras* is in the nature of an oxymoron. Daphnis the lover of peace (61) converted the weapons of war to symbols of peace. Even to attribute the introduction of Bacchic rites to him is surprising. For Bacchus, wine and orgiastic cults are alien to conventional pastoral. Nevertheless the worship of Bacchus belongs to the religion of the countryside; he is complementary to Ceres as patron of nature's abundance (79, Eur. *Ba.* 274ff.) and the ecstasy of the Bacchants is a temporary return to the Golden Age, which has close links with the pastoral myth (see 71n. and p. 6).

intexere: for the construction with acc. + abl. rather than dat. + acc. cf. *G.* 2.221. The 'golden-line' word order is again expressive of the meaning.

32   The vine of Bacchus becomes the first member of another rustic analogy; cf. 16-18. The form of the analogy recalls Th. *Id.* 18.29-31 'As a large cypress adorns the fertile land or garden where it springs up...so also does rosy Helen adorn Lacedaemon'; the detail recalls [Th.] *Id.* 8.79-80 'To the oak its acorns bring decoration, to the apple-tree its fruit, to the cow her calf, to the herdsmen the cows themselves', evoking a panorama of nature's prosperity.

arboribus: although Pliny includes the vine among *arbores* (*Nat.* 14.9), it is usually distinguished from them; e.g. Cato. *Agr.* 32. Hence the reference is probably to the trees on which the vines were trained; see *G.* 2.290ff.

33   **aruis:** for this non-pastoral detail see 1.2n.

34   **decus omne** 'all that is glorious', 'their whole glory'.

35   **ipsa...ipse** are emphatic. The very patrons of pastoral life forsook the earth through grief, perhaps also to punish those who had caused Daphnis to perish *crudeli funere*; in which case Vergil may be thinking of the departure of the divine patrons of justice which marked the advent of the Iron Age (4.6n.). Meleager *A.P.* 7.535 has Pan deserting to the city in grief at Daphnis' death.

Pales: an Italian goddess (or god: see Serv. *ad G.* 3.1) of shepherds and rural life, depicted with a pruning hook. Her festival, the *Parilia* (21 April), was celebrated as the official birthday of Rome, the anniversary of Romulus' foundation on the Palatine (Ov. *F.* 4.721ff.).

Apollo: as *Apóllōn Nómios* he was patron of the pastures, *nomoí*. Although he was one of the earliest Greek immigrant deities at Rome, his cult remained under the jurisdiction of the *XVuiri sacris faciundis*, and in *G.* 3.1-2, where he is coupled with Pales and Pan, Vergil indicates his alien origin by the phrase *pastor ab Amphryso*. So perhaps

the pair represent Italian and Greek divine patronage of the countryside – an indication like the Punic lions (27) that the mourning is
universal. Moreover Apollo was the patron of music (3.62, 4.57, 6.3),
and in the death of Daphnis the world has lost a herdsman not only of
exemplary *pietas* but of supreme musical skill (48–9).

36 In Th. *Id.* 1.132–6 the dying Daphnis prayed for confusion in
nature: 'Now brambles, bear violets I pray, and thorns bear violets
too, and let the fair narcissus cover the junipers with its blooms and all
things go topsy-turvy and the pine bring forth pears, since Daphnis is
dying...' Now that he is dead, a blight has actually descended upon
the countryside.

grandia: large grains were regularly selected from the harvest to
provide seed for the next crop (*G.* 1.197–9).

hordea may be used, as Servius claims, *metri causa*. However, the
plural, as in *G.* 1.210, can denote individual 'grains of barley' in
contrast to barley in bulk; cf. *frumenta* (*A.* 4.406) and see 1.6n.
Quintilian (1.5.16) characterizes the use of *hordea* with a singular
meaning as a barbarism, and it may be for this reason that Vergil's
usage attracted the jibe *hordea qui dixit superest ut tritica dicat* attributed
by Servius (*G.* 1.210) to Bavius and Mevius, by Cledonius (*G.L.*
5.43.2) to Cornificius.

37 **infelix** has the same root as *femina, fecundus*; cf. P. Festus 92M
felices arbores Cato dixit quae fructum ferunt, infelices quae non ferunt. But
lolium 'darnel', believed in antiquity to be a degenerate form of wheat,
is not so much barren as a bearer of 'un-nourishing', 'harmful' seeds,
and this is probably the meaning here, as in *A.* 3.649 *uictum infelicem*.
The more general sense of the word 'unlucky', an extension of the
original biological meaning, is of course relevant too. The appearance
of darnel is another token of calamity.

auenae are here 'wild oats', strictly the *auena agrestis* which was
believed to be a degenerate form of oats or barley (Plin. *Nat.* 18.149).
infelix lolium et steriles...auenae are listed among crop-weeds in *G.* 1.154.

nascuntur: for the metaphor see 3.92n.

38 **purpureo,** like Greek *porphúreos* from which it is borrowed, is
used of various rich or brilliant colours, e.g. black grapes (Plin. *Nat.*
14.15), poppies (Prop. 1.20.38), and even swans' plumage (Hor.
C. 4.1.10). Here it could refer to either the deep yellow calyx of the

Serotinus or the crimson corona of the Poeticus (see 2.48n.). The spondaic ending, as in 4.49, underlines the solemnity of the portent.

39 carduos 'the common thistle', Carduus Arvensis, is listed among the crop-weeds in *G*. 1.152.

paliurus 'Christ's thorn', Paliurus Aculeatus, though recommended by Columella as a hedge plant (11.3.4), was a menace to farmers and gardeners because of its rapid proliferation. Leonidas describes a tomb as 'all overgrown with sharp paliurus and bramble' *(A.P.* 7.656.3–4). So here the thistles and thorns are a sign both of nature's grief and of the neglect that results from Daphnis' departure.

40 foliis: *florentibus herbis* in 9.19, a clear echo of this line, suggests that *folia* here are 'flower petals'; cf. φύλλα in Th. *Id.* 11.26. For the ritual scattering of flowers over the grave see Leonidas *A.P.* 7.657.7–8; cf. *A.* 6.883–5. For the abl. with *spargere* see 7n.

inducite...umbras: at the festival of the *Fontanalia* each October *in fontes coronas iaciunt et puteos coronant* (Var. *L.* 6.22). But here the shrouding of the springs, presumably with branches and foliage, is a sign not of thanksgiving but of mourning. Servius' suggestion of a monumental planting – *facite nemora circa fontes* – seems improbable.

41 mandat fieri...talia: for the acc. + pass. inf. forming a single direct object complement to a verb of command cf. *has omnis actuarias imperat fieri* (Caes. *Gal.* 5.1.3), *signa quae...tolli procul...mandauerat* (Suet. *Tib.* 65.2). For similar constructions with the active infinitive cf. Sall. *Iug.* 47.2, Tac. *A.* 15.2.5, and see 1.9–10n., 1.55n. The repetition of *inducere* and *mandare* in quite different senses from 30, 36 is somewhat infelicitous.

42 tumulum...tumulo: for the emotive repetition cf. *A.* 6.380. The *carmen* is presumably to be inscribed on the *cippus* set up on the mound, implying once more literacy which is novel to the world of pastoral; see 14n.

43–4 The epitaph is not necessarily part of Daphnis' *mandatum* (41) to the herdsmen; it was usual for sepulchral verses to be expressed in the person of the deceased. All Daphnis' qualities are summed up in the couplet. His skill as a herdsman (cf. Th. *Id.* 1.120–1 'I am that Daphnis who pastured his cows here, the Daphnis who watered his bulls and calves here') is implied in *formonsi*, his diligence in *custos*.

For his beauty – and *formonsus* is one of the characteristic terms of praise in the Eclogues – cf. [Th.] *Id.* 8.72–3 'It was I whom a maid with meeting brows saw yesterday from her cave as I drove my heifers past and exclaimed "He's handsome, handsome".' Even *in siluis*, though it echoes *Id.* 1.116–17 'No longer shall I, the cattleherd Daphnis, go to your woods, your thickets and your groves', has in the Eclogues associations with pastoral music-making (1.5n.).

ad sidera notus, recalling Hom. *Od.* 9.20 'and my glory reached the heavens' (cf. *A.* 1.379 *fama super aethera notus*), suggests heroic stature as well as the success of poets whose works 'perchance fame has brought even to the throne of Zeus' (Th. *Id.* 7.93).

45 Another rustic analogy (cf. 16–18, 32–5) evokes the familiar association of pastoral music with relaxation in the cool shade.

diuine 'inspired'; cf. Th. *Id.* 7.89 θεῖε Κομᾶτα, also 3.37, 6.67, 10.17.

46 per aestum explains *fessis*. Cf. 2.10 and [Th.] *Id.* 8.78 'It is pleasant in summer to lie down and sleep beside running water.' For the pause at the bucolic diaeresis followed by enjambement in a context of excitement cf. 2.26n.

47 sitim restinguere 'to quench one's thirst'. The inf. is subject like *sopor* to *est* understood. Cf. Th. *Id.* 1.7–8 'More pleasant is your music, shepherd, than that water which gushes down from the rock high above.'

48–9 magistrum: as there is no hint that Mopsus is Menalcas' pupil, this must be Daphnis. Having already won fame as a piper (2) Mopsus has now surpassed both Menalcas himself and the rival Amyntas in singing. Hence *alter ab illo* is 'successor to Daphnis'; cf. *alter ab undecimo... annus* at 8.39–40. For the general sense cf. *Epit. Bion* 95–6 'inheritor of the Doric music which you taught your pupils' and Corydon's boast in 2.38 *te nunc habet ista secundum*. Not 'ranking second only to Daphnis' (cf. *ab Achille secundus* of Ajax in Hor. *S.* 2.3.193), which would correspond to the tribute paid in *Id.* 1.3 'You will carry off the second prize after Pan.'

50 quocumque modo is a further mark of his modesty.

51 tollemus ad astra: after 43 the natural sense is 'I shall extol to the stars'; cf. 9.27–9 and *rusticus urbem | tollis ad astra* in Hor. *S.* 2.7.28–9. The stars to which Daphnis' mother addressed her sorrowing protest (23) are now to hear Menalcas' panegyric of him. But once the song begins, a second meaning is revealed: 'I shall raise him [i.e. 'sing of his elevation'; cf. the use of *circumdat* in 6.62] to the stars.' As in 25ff., 41ff., the repetition of the name is emphatic.

53 an as often introduces an emotionally charged question.

54 puer by making the youth of the dead *magister* explicit heightens the poignancy of 22–3.

cantari dignus: see 2n.

ista: not just 'those songs of yours' but 'your songs on this theme', referring specifically to 51–2.

55 Stimichon like *Alcon* (11) does not occur before in extant pastoral.

56–7 candidus...Daphnis: the emphatic separation underlines the contrast with *exstinctum...Daphnin* (21). For the distinction between *candidus* 'radiant' and *albus* see 7.38n. Though applied to mortals, e.g. Dido in *A.* 5.571, Jason in Hor. *Epod.* 3.9, it is especially used of divinities, e.g. Galatea in 7.38, Nais in 2.46, Venus in *A.* 8.608, and heavenly bodies like Taurus in *G.* 1.217, *luna* in *A.* 7.8. It thus marks the transformation from *formonsus pastor* to celestial deity.

Olympi: *caelum dicunt Graeci Olympum, montem in Macedonia omnes* (Var. *L.* 7.20); but the metonymy, which is as old as Homer, *Od.* 20.103, is not uncommon in Latin; cf. Cat. 62.1, *G.* 1.450.

58 alacris is probably nom. sg. rather than acc. pl., since the contrast is between nature's joyous activity and her earlier sad lethargy (25–6, 37, 39). The epithet, unique in the Eclogues, may be intended also to contrast with the normal *otium* of the pastoral *siluas*.

59 Panaque...Dryadasque: the traditional divine inhabitants of the woodlands. Their Greekness is emphasized by the Greek inflections.

60 For these symptoms of a new Golden Age, contrasting with the injurious transformations of nature in 36–9, cf. 4.22 and Th. *Id.* 24.86–7 'That will be the day on which the jagged-toothed wolf sees a fawn in her lair without wanting to savage it.'

61 otia: socio-political as well as pastoral connotations are relevant here. See 1.6n. and cf. Cic. *Sest.* 98–9.

62–3 ipsi...ipsae...ipsa (64) 'spontaneously', 'of their own accord'. The wild wooded hills that were filled with cries of grief (28) now echo with shouts of joy, themselves sharing in the *laetitia*. For the image cf. Lucr. 2.327–8 *clamoreque montes | icti reiectant uoces ad sidera mundi*; but Vergil's personificatory treatment of the echo-phenomenon anticipates the distinctive form of the sympathy-figure in 1.5, 1.39.

   intonsi: *siluosi, incaedui* (Serv.); cf. *A.* 9.681–2.

63–4 carmina...sonant: all nature proclaims its jubilation. For the apocalyptic sign cf. Isaiah 55.12 'The mountains and hills shall break forth before you into singing and all the trees of the field shall clap their hands.' In the phrase itself, for which cf. Hor. *Epod.* 9.5, Prop. 2.31.16, the acc. may denote either the internal object, as in *nec mortale sonans* (*A.* 6.50), where it is simply the nominalization of the verbal activity 'sounding a mortal sound', or the external one, as in Hor. *C.* 2.13.26–8: *sonantem...dura belli*, where the direct object exists independently of that activity.

64 Cf. Lucr. 5.8 *deus ille fuit, deus, inclute Memmi*, of Epicurus.

65 sis bonus...felixque tuis 'May you be well-disposed towards your people and bring them prosperity.' For the ritual phrases cf. *A.* 1.330 to Venus, *A.* 12.646–7 to the Manes.

66 duas...duas: although both nom. and acc. are found with *ecce* in early Latin, the former is usual in classical Latin (e.g. 3.50), the latter very rare. Unlike Semele in Th. *Id.* 26.5–6, who has three altars to Dionysus' nine, Daphnis is to share the four equally with the god who mourned him (35). However *altaria*, in apposition to *aras*, is perhaps meant to distinguish the Olympian god from the deified mortal (1.43n.).

67 bina: i.e. one at each festival (cf. 70). As a minor deity Daphnis will receive libations rather than sacrifices; cf. Th. *Id.* 5.53–4 'I shall set up a large bowl of white milk for the Nymphs and another of delicious oil.'

68 duo: the distributive meaning, having been made explicit in *bina* (67), is not repeated. It is not clear whether Servius' note '*duo*' *uetuste* *dixit* refers to the indeclinable form or to an assumed *-ō. duŏ*, though attested alongside *duŏ* in Pl. *Mil.* 1384, was already an archaism then and recurs only in late texts, e.g. Prud. *Perist.* 11.89, Avian. 29.22. Hence *duŏ* is probably the form here and the heavy syllable results from the combination with initial *st-* in *statuam. -ŏs-tā-*, which would be the normal syllable division within a word, is paralleled at Tib. 1.5.28 *pro segete spicas*; but *-tĕ-spē-* occurs in *A.* 11.309 *ponite. spes* and *-tă-skȳl-* at Prop. 3.19.21 *uenumdata Scylla*. Catullus has both treatments: *nulla spes* and *unda Scamandri* (64.186, 357). But classical poets seem in general to have avoided these sequences. See also 9.57n.

   oliui: appropriate to a winter ceremony, as fresh milk is to a summer one; cf. *frigus* and *messis* in the next line. For the archaic *oliuom* cf. Lucr. 2.850.

69   multo...Baccho 'with lots of wine'. For the metonymy cf. *G.* 2.190-1, and *Thetin* (4.32). Pride of place in the celebrations will be given to the produce of the god whom Daphnis introduced to his people (29-30).

   hilarans conuiuia 'enlivening the festivities'. The scene recalls the thanksgivings in Th. *Id.* 7.63ff. 'and on that day...I'll draw the wine of Ptelea from the bowl...and two shepherds will play their pipes to me...and Tityrus nearby will sing how Daphnis the cattle-herd once fell in love with Xenea', and the rustic festivities of the *Ambarualia* in Tib. 2.1.

71   calathis: like Greek *kálathos* the Latin loan-word is used of baskets (2.46n.) and of vessels for carrying wine (cf. Mart. 14.107) or milk (*G.* 3.402). It is not clear whether the latter were wicker-covered jars or vessels shaped like tapered baskets.

   Ariusia: although Chian wines were well enough known in Rome at this time (cf. Hor. *Epod.* 9.34, *S.* 1.10.24), those from Ariusia in the north of the island were especially prized (Plin. *Nat.* 14.73). Unlike the local reference in Th. *Id.* 7.65 (see 69n.), which is set in Cos, this one breaks the pastoral illusion by its hint of imported luxury.

   nouom...nectar: the epithet may refer to the novelty of wine, as perhaps introduced by Daphnis himself with the rites of Bacchus, or to the fact that a fresh wine is to be opened at each festival. *néktar* is used of wine, e.g. in Callim. fr 399Pf. either because of its pleasing taste or because it was a 'medicine for pain and trouble' (Eur. *Ba*

283), which enabled men to experience the carefreeness of gods. In the pastoral world, as in the Golden Age, the solace of drunkenness was not needed; shepherds soothed their pains with the 'medicine of the Muses' (Th. *Id.* 11.1–3).

72 Damoetas appeared with Daphnis in Th. *Id.* 6 and with Menalcas himself in *Ecl.* 3, where Aegon too is mentioned (3.2).

Lyctius: Lyctus was one of the most important Dorian settlements in Crete and was apparently associated with the cult of Apollo (Callim. *H.* 2.33). Nearby was Mount Aegaeon, in one of whose caves Rhea gave birth to Zeus (Hes. *Th.* 477), and this may have suggested the birthplace for Aegon here.

73 Satyros: part man, part goat, satyrs are described by Hesiod as a race of worthless layabouts (fr. 123MW); they were notorious for their bibulous and lecherous habits (e.g. Th. *Id.* 4.62–3). They commonly appear in the retinue of Bacchus or singing and dancing with Pan and the nymphs (e.g. Lucr. 4.580–5, Hor. *C.* 2.19.3–4). Figures of awe and amusement to countrymen, they seem almost a bestial parody of the *uoluptates* of the pastoral myth.

Alphesiboeus: the name, which recurs in *Ecl.* 8, is not found in earlier pastoral. Greek *alphesíboios* 'producing a good yield of oxen' is used both of a girl with many suitors (Hom. *Il.* 18.593) and of the river Nile (Aesch. *Supp.* 855). *Alphesiboia* occurs as a mythological name in Th. *Id.* 3.45.

74 sollemnia 'regularly enacted', 'performed at fixed intervals'; cf. Festus 298M *sollemne quod omnibus annis praestari debet.*

75 lustrabimus probably refers to the Ambarvalia, celebrated in late July or early August when the crops were cut (3.77n.), rather than to one of the lesser *lustrationes* like that of the newly sown fields at the Paganalia in January (Ov. *F.* 1.669–72). There was no distinct festival of nymphs in the Roman calendar. They no doubt shared in the festivals of associated deities, e.g. Faunus at the February Lupercalia or Flora at the April Floralia, as well as having a place of honour in such celebrations as the Fontanalia in October. But *uota... reddemus* probably implies a more local cult, related to their patronage of a particular grove or spring (cf. 2.46n.).

76–7 After the disruptions of nature, first in mourning then in rejoicing for Daphnis, comes a return to the normal pattern of life. For the belief that cicadas lived on dew-drops see Hes. *Sc.* 395, Th. *Id.* 4.16. The catalogue proceeds from the contexts of hunting and fishing to the more specifically pastoral images of the bee and the cicada.

78 This line recurs in *A.* 1.609, addressed to Dido, and is preceded by a similar series of *dum*-clauses depicting the changeless phenomena of nature.

79 Baccho Cererique: as the patrons of liquid and solid nutriment respectively (30n.) the two deities are frequently coupled (e.g. *G.* 1.7, Var. *R.* 1.1.5), though their festivals were always kept distinct.

80 damnabis...uotis 'you too will hold them to their vows': the petitioner made his vow to the god (*uouere, uoto uocare*; cf. *G.* 1.42, *A.* 1.290); if the petition was granted, then the god obliged him to keep the vow (*damnare uoti*, e.g. Nep. *Timol.* 5.3, or more rarely *damnare uoto*, e.g. here and Sisenna *hist.* 100P) and he became *uoti reus* (*A.* 5.237) until it was fulfilled (*uotum soluere, reddere*; cf. 74–5). The phrase, conferring a divine prerogative on Daphnis, perhaps marks him off from the ordinary recipient of a hero-cult. He is moreover to be worshipped by *agricolae* generally, not just by *pastores*.

82 sibilus Austri: cf. Lucr. 5.1382–3 *et zephyri caua per calamorum sibila primum | agrestis docuere cauas inflare cicutas*. Menalcas' song has surpassed even nature's prototypes. However, the south-east wind, unlike the gentle west wind rustling in the pines or the reeds (5, cf. Plato's epigram *Plan.* 13), is usually associated with storms: 2.58n., *G.* 3.278–9, 429. So the image together with those in 83–4 has an exciting, awesome quality which expresses Mopsus' delight (*iuuant*) at Menalcas' jubilant song as aptly as Menalcas' evocation of the idyllic scene in 45–7 had expressed the soothing, consolatory effect of Mopsus' lament.

83 percussa...fluctu: from Homer and Hesiod onwards the sea is a hostile element and mention of it is rare in the pastoral. Polyphemus speaks like a true pastoral shepherd when he bids Galatea 'leave the grey sea to beat on the shore' (Th. *Id.* 11.43). For breakers as an image of violent and relentless power see 9.43, *G.* 3.237–41.

84   decurrunt flumina: again a Theocritean image (47n.) has been transformed into something more awe-inspiring; cf. *A.* 12.523–4, Hor. *C.* 4.2.5–7. The weighty spondaic rhythms of the line reinforce the aural image.

85   ante 'first, before you give me anything'. In Th. *Id.* 6.43-6 Damoetas and Daphnis exchange presents, a Pan-pipe and an oboe (*aulós*), at the end of their drawn contest.

   cicuta is the single pipe made from a hollow hemlock stalk. For the multiple Pan-pipes see 2.36 and 1.2n.

86–7 Menalcas is thus identified as the author of the second and third Eclogues.

   docuit implies that the melody was formed first and inspired words to match; cf. 14n.

88   pedum: *baculum incuruum quo pastores utuntur ad comprehendendas oues aut capras* (Fest. 249M). The crook is given none of the symbolic associations of Lycidas' staff in *Id.* 7, which is 'a token of friendship in the Muses' (129) offered to Simichidas 'because you are a sapling fashioned by Zeus wholly for truth' (43–4); but we are clearly meant to recall it. For the name *Antigenes*, which does not recur in the Eclogues, was that of the host at the harvest celebration (*Id.* 7.3–4).

89   tulit: the verb is used both of bringing gifts (e.g. *A.* 2.49) and, as here, receiving them (cf. Hor. *Ep.* 1.17.44). For the meaning 'to take away forcibly' see 34. For the infinitive with *dignus* cf. 54 and 2n.

90 The crook has symmetrical knots in its wood (*paribus nodis*) and bronze sheaths (*aere*), at the foot to prevent wear and higher up to add strength. In Th. *Id.* 17.31 Hercules' iron club had imitation knots cut into it, but it is improbable that Vergil's phrase is a hendiadys referring to bronze studs in the form of knots. Though a handsome object (*formonsum*) it brings us back to the workaday world of the herdsmen. The two gifts sum up the *ludus* and *seria* (7.17) of Arcady.

This poem on the death and deification of Daphnis is like *Ecl.* 2 and 3 rich in echoes of earlier pastoral, in particular of the Daphnis-dirge in *Id.* 1 (see 20, 27–8, 36, 43–4, 47), the partly autobiographical *Id.* 7 (see 27–8, 43–4, 69), the friendly singing-match of Daphnis and Menalcas in *Id.* 8 (see 32, 43–4, 46), and the *Lament for Bion* (see 26,

48–9). The landscape is conventional – the cool shade of elms and beeches (3, 13), hollow rocks (6) and grassy river-banks (46–7), in the background mountains, woods (43, 84) and even sea (83). Hints of the real countryside are provided by the agricultural references (36, 80), and specifically of Italy in the allusions to the Ambarvalia (75) and the mention of Pales (35) and Ceres (79). The courteous and affectionate tone of the herdsmen's conversation, which recalls *Id.* 8, is enlivened now and again (4–6, 15, 19) by colloquial touches.

The two songs that are framed by the conversation pieces (1–19, 45–55, 81–90) are equal in length – twenty-five lines each – and are linked by a number of detailed echoes: 20 ∼ 59, 75; 28 ∼ 62–3; 30 ∼ 69, 79; 35 ∼ 66. They exhibit a close parallelism in their thematic progression: (*a*) The grief of the nymphs and Daphnis' mother, the mourning of the animals (20–8) ∼ The joy of Pan and the nymphs, all nature jubilant (56–64); (*b*) Daphnis' piety towards Bacchus and the grief of Pales and Apollo, who forsook the land that he had once adorned (29–35) ∼ The divine honours he will receive in association with Apollo (65–71); (*c*) Plant-life awry, the funeral rites and epitaph (36–44) ∼ Shepherd celebrations and the promise of annual homage to the new god, patron with Bacchus and Ceres of nature's renewed prosperity (72–80).

Thus far the poem can be read as a self-contained and homogeneous pastoral; indeed the distinctive pastoral tone is reiterated by the vivid rustic analogies placed at significant structural points (16–18, 45–7, 82–4). The details of Daphnis' life and character – his beauty (44), his prowess as a countryman (34, 44) and a musician (48–9), his piety (30) and love of peace (61) - and the pathos of his untimely death, intensified by the presence of a distraught mother, can all be related to the traditional pastoral hero of that name. Yet the situation has been altered in two respects: in contrast to *Id.* 1 and *Ecl.* 8 and 10 the erotic background to the catastrophe has been totally suppressed and attention is focused not on the spectacle of the dying herdsmen but on the situation after his death. These changes in themselves hardly bear out the expectations of 13–15, where Mopsus seems to be rejecting the conventional themes of pastoral and clearly regards his lament as important enough to have been written down – an unprecedented reference to literacy in the world of pastoral.

The inspiration of Menalcas' song is partly from the *Lament for Bion*, where the universal mourning is transcended by the eulogy on the dead poet as a peer of Homer himself. But Bion is not deified. In deifying Daphnis Vergil has gone back beyond Theocritus to the myth of the Sicilian cult-hero (see 20n.). Yet the revelation in 86–7 that Menalcas is Vergil's own *persona* indicates that this is not just a piece of literary antiquarianism; it asserts the relevance of the myth of Daphnis' death and apotheosis to Vergil's own time. We see now the point of Mopsus' obscure advertisement in 13–15.

Julius Caesar was assassinated in March 44 B.C. Four months later there appeared in the northern skies a comet which was widely believed to signal his assumption into heaven (for the ambiguity of such a portent in itself see 4.4n., 9.47n.). In 9.46–9 Daphnis contemplates *Caesaris astrum* as a portent of rural prosperity, and there can be little doubt that Vergil, whose *patria*, Transpadane Gaul, had been enfranchized by the dictator (Dio 48.12.5), shared the hopes that the comet portended a return to the peace and prosperity which his rule had abortively promised. Mopsus no doubt represents those poets who shared Vergil's Caesarian sympathies, though whether any detail in the poem would have served to identify him specifically –with Varius for instance (8.88n.), Domitius Marsus or Aemilius Macer, all of whom have been suggested as candidates – is now impossible to ascertain. Divine honours seem to have been granted to Caesar by the triumvirs in 43 B.C., and on 12 July 42 B.C. his birthday was celebrated with religious solemnity and the month of Quintilis itself renamed in his honour (Suet. *Iul.* 81, 88). It is incredible that anyone in the late 40s could have read a pastoral poem on this theme without thinking of Caesar. The references to Italian religion, the suppression of the erotic motivation of Daphnis' sufferings, the statements given to Mopsus and Menalcas in 13–15 and 86–7 all cumulatively indicate that Vergil intended readers to make just this association.

The reference of Daphnis to Caesar was already accepted by some in antiquity. Servius rejected it, though not totally, in favour of a fictitious brother of Vergil, by name Flaccus. He does however note on line 20 that *multi 'matrem' Venerem accipiunt*. It is true that in 44 B.C. Octavian instituted a cult of *Venus Genetrix*, the mythical ancestor of the *gens Iulia*, that Vergil himself refers to *Dionaei Caesaris* in 9.47, and that Ovid in *M.* 15.761ff. depicts the goddess pleading for the life of her illustrious descendant. But there is no hint that the mother here is a goddess, like the mourner over the young shepherd in Bion's *Adonis*; she is portrayed in very human terms, as an actual mother, not a remote divine ancestor. At 29 Servius says *hoc aperte ad Caesarem pertinet, quem constat primum sacra Liberi patris transtulisse Romam*, a statement hard to reconcile with the antiquity of the Liberalia at Rome or the introduction of the Greek worship of Bacchus in private cults more than a hundred and forty years before Caesar's reign. Some modern commentators have seen in 26–7 a reference to the story that just before Caesar's death he found the herds of horses which he had consecrated and left at the Rubicon *pertinacissime pabulo abstinere ubertimque flere* (Suet. *Iul.* 81). Similarly line 57 has been taken to refer to Caear's vision on the eve of his death when *ipse sibi uisus est per quietem interdum supra nubes uolitare, alias cum Ioue dextram iungere* (*ibid.*). But the grief of a dead herdsman's animals is a conventional feature of pastoral laments and the slight verbal similarity between the poet's and historian's description of apotheosis surely need not mean that the former has a specific historical incident in mind. Finally on the coupling of Daphnis' cult with Apollo's (66) it has been observed that Caesar's birthday coincided with the *ludi Apollinares* (and for that reason was officially celebrated on the preceding day). But the connection between the mythical Daphnis and the divine patron of herdsmen and musicians needs no historical point of reference to support it here (cf. 35).

In short there are no adequate grounds for seeing the poem as a detailed allegory. Indeed its distinctive quality is that while clearly alluding to contemporary history and revealing unequivocally the poet's political sympathies, it preserves throughout its pastoral integrity.

ECLOGUE VI

1 Vergil begins by excusing himself for offering to Varus a poem somewhat different in character from what he had expected.

Prima is to be taken with *Syracosio...uersu*, as the adjectival equivalent of the more usual *primum*, 'it was in Syracusan verse that my Muse first deigned to play'; not with *nostra*, 'my Muse before anyone else's deigned to play...'. Latin poets were given to boasting their priority in adapting Greek genres (e.g. Lucr. 1.926–30, *G.* 2.174–6) and Vergil's claims in the pastoral were certainly stronger than those of Horace in Aeolic metres (*C.* 3.30.12–14) or Propertius in elegy

(3.1.3–4); but the sequence *prima, cum canerem* (3), *nunc* (6) confirms the first interpretation.

Syracosio: cf. Greek *Surakósios*; *nam latine 'Syracusanus'* (Serv.). As in 4.1, Vergil delights in recalling the Theocritean origin of the genre at the start of an un-Theocritean piece.

ludere: see 1.10n. Here the contrast with *canerem reges et proelia* suggests distinctly neoteric associations; cf. Cat. 50.2, *G.* 4.565.

2   nec is the spelling in R and V; P and γ have the usual pre-vocalic *neque*. If *nec* is what Vergil wrote, it must have been to avoid a sequence of *u*- and *w*- sounds (cf. *erubuit, siluas*); cf. *G.* 2.287, where a similar choice of variants is offered by the manuscripts, and *A.* 2.432.

erubuit + inf. is probably by analogy with the construction of e.g. *non recuso* (Caes. *Gal.* 3.22.3) and *dignata est* (a usage itself not attested in prose before the Empire).

siluas: the Muse need not feel ashamed of the humble woods (1.5n.) or the poetry associated with them. For *habitarunt di quoque siluas* (2.60), and *siluae* may on occasion be *consule dignae* (4.3).

Thalea: the Muse *Tháleia* had comedy for her province; cf. Greek *thalía* 'good cheer', 'festivity'; but *thálos* 'a shoot', *thállein* 'to bloom' clearly suggested associations with the countryside (Plut. *Mor.* 9.744F), and her iconography includes both an actor's mask and a shepherd's crook. The extension of her jurisdiction from comedy through mime to pastoral is intelligible enough.

3   canerem reges et proelia: epic themes; cf. *A.* 7.41–2 and Hor. *A.P.* 73 *res gestae regumque ducumque tristia bella.* Servius refers the phrase to either a premature start on the Aeneid or a poem on *gesta regum Albanorum, quae coepta omisit, nominum asperitate deterritus*; cf. Don. *Vit.* 19 *mox cum res Romanas incohasset, offensus materia ad Bucolica transiit.* However, the phrase could apply equally to the epic treatment of recent historical events; cf. Horace's words to Augustus in *Ep.* 2.1.250ff. *nec sermones ego mallem | repentis per humum quam res componere gestas | …et barbara regna tuisque | auspiciis totum confecta duella per orbem*; and in the present context the reference is more likely to an epic poem on Varus' military exploits comparable in scope to Cicero's poem on Marius or Furius Bibaculus' on Julius Caesar. Whether Vergil ever seriously contemplated such a poem is very doubtful indeed. Although *laudationes* of famous men and their deeds were literally sung in olden times (Cic. *Tusc.* 4.3), the use of *canere* of such compositions had long since become metaphorical; e.g. Lucil. 621M, Cic. *Q.Fr.* 3.5.4. The *carmina* of the herdsmen in pastoral were certainly sung; cf. the musical contexts of *canere* and *cantare* in 2.31-3, 5.9, 14, 3.21-2. So there is a threefold contrast here: between *ludus* and *seria* (1), actual singing (3, 8) and ordinary verse composition, the themes of *siluas* and *reges et proelia* (2-3).

Cynthius refers to Mount Cynthus in Delos, the birthplace of Apollo and one of his most important cult-sites. In the Eclogues the god is called either *Phoebus*, as elsewhere generally in this poem and in 3.62, 5.9, 7.22, or *Apollo* as in 73, 3.104, 4.10, 10.21, always at the end of a line. The epithet, unique in the Eclogues, has solemn non-pastoral overtones; cf. *Troiae Cynthius auctor* (*G.* 3.36). Callimachus, whose rejection of epic provides the model for Vergil's *recusatio* here, uses a similarly solemn epithet of the god, *Lúkios* 'The Lycian god' (*Aet.* fr. 1.22Pf).

3-4 aurem uellit: though a conventional way of reminding a person of something, the gesture was also a ritual method of summoning a witness who had promised to testify at the *antestatio* in a legal action; cf. Pl. *Per.* 749, Plin. *Nat.* 11.251. Vergil seems to prefer the older forms of the perfect of *uellere*, e.g. *conuellimus* (*A.* 2.464), *reuelli* (*A.* 4.427), even though the sigmatic forms are well attested elsewhere; e.g. *deuolsit* (Cat. 63.5), *reuulsi* (Ov. *M.* 8.585); see Prisc. *G.L.* 2.526.

Tityre: Vergil is addressed by the name of the typical lowly herdsman; cf. 8.56 and 1.1n.

pinguis, as Servius notes, is predicative with *pascere*. For the thought cf. Apollo's injunction in Callim. *Aet.* fr. 1.23-4 Pf. 'Poet, ⟨feed⟩ the victim as fat as possible, but keep the Muse slender, there's a good fellow', and see p. 5.

5 deductum: *translatio a lana quae deducitur in tenuitatem* (Serv., cf. Macrob. *Sat.* 6.4.12). The metaphor is commonly used of literary style, e.g. Hor. *Ep.* 2.1.225 *tenui deducta poemata filo*, Cic. *Or.* 20, Quint. 10.1.44. As a term of approval the adjective connotes the polish and refinement of neoteric personal poetry in the *genera tenuia* of elegy and lyric, e.g. Prop. 3.1.7-8 *a, ualeat Phoebum quicumque moratur in armis. | exactus tenui pumice uersus eat.* Servius, who assigned the poetry of *tenuis auena* to the same stylistic category (see p. 5 n. 1), here observes *allēgorikōs autem significat se composuisse hunc libellum tenuissimo stilo.* As in Callim. *loc. cit.*, the mock-modesty of Vergil's *recusatio* of epic themes and style is revealed by the contemptuous implication that epic *carmen* is not *grande* but *pingue.* For other metaphors employed in *recusatio* see Prop. 3.3.17–24, Hor. *C.* 4.15.1–4.

6 super...erunt 'there will be a surfeit of them'. For this sense o *superesse* see Cic. *Fam.* 13.63.2. For the tmesis cf. *praeque...ueniens* (8.17), *super unus eram* (*A.* 2.567, in the commoner sense of *superesse*).

7 Vare: two men of this *cognomen* are known to have been connected with Vergil. Quintilius Varus from Verona may have been a fellow pupil of his in the Epicurean 'garden' of Siro (so the *Vita Probiana*) and was certainly a friend of both Vergil and Horace (Hor. *C.* 1.24.9–10, *A.P.* 438–41). He was an eminent literary critic but had no military career, so cannot be the addressee of this poem. Alfenus Varus, who came perhaps from Cremona (*schol. ad* Hor. *S.* 1.3.130), was a notable jurist (Gell. 7.5.1), hence well qualified to serve on the land-commission that dealt with the settlement of veterans in Cisalpine Gaul in 41 B.C. He was consul suffect in 39 B.C. Servius on line 6 says *Germanos uicerat et exinde maximam fuerat et gloriam et pecuniam consecutus.* Agrippa is known to have campaigned as propraetor in 38 B.C. (Dio 48.49.3) along the German frontiers of the new province of Gaul. Whether Varus' exploits belong with this campaign or not, they were certainly not important enough to earn him a triumph – or even perhaps a set of laudatory verses. If he was directly responsible for including Mantuan land in the confiscations (see 9.28n.), this would have been an additional reason for Vergil's reluctance. However, we cannot be sure whether the *recusatio* is motivated by distaste for the bellicose theme, estrangement from Varus or simply preoccupation with the subject matter that he finally treated in this poem.

condere bella: cf. *Caesaris acta | condere* (Ov. *Tr.* 2.335–6). The phrase is a conflation of *condere carmen* (cf. 10.50–1) and *dicere* or *canere bella* (cf. *A.* 7.41–2).

8 agrestem...Musam: emphatically placed in another of Vergil's 'golden line' arrangements. Cf. 1.2 and Lucr. 5.1398, referring to the *securitas* of primitive man, *agrestis enim tum Musa uigebat.* In disclaiming serious subjects in favour of the *lusus* and *otium* of the pastoral shepherd Vergil ironically echoes the opening of one of his most profoundly serious and topically relevant poems; cf. *G.* 4.564-5.

9 non iniussa cano 'I do not sing songs that I have not been commanded to sing.' Varus might request a poem (*poscere*) but could hardly command one. Moreover the following *tamen* confirms that the reference is to Apollo's admonition in 4-5: 'This is not what you expected, Varus, but it is what Apollo ordered me to write.'

quoque 'in addition to the laudatory poems that others may write for you', referring to 6-7. The prosaic wording of this first conditional clause goes with the affectation of an *humile genus*.

10 captus amore: either 'himself a captive of love' or more likely 'attracted by the subject of love'; cf. *G.* 3.285 *dum capti circumuectamur amore*, referring to the theme of *Venerem et caeci stimulos...amoris* (*ibid.* 210). 'Those who are captivated by the subject of love will find this humble (cf. 4.2 for *myricae*) pastoral treatment of it a worthy tribute to you, Varus.' The noun cannot refer to love of Varus; for even with *te...te...* following we should then expect an explicit *tui* as in *A.* 12.29 *uictus amore tui*; still less to love of the poet and his genre, since the required connection with *haec* in the preceding line would be obscure.

11 te nemus omne canet recalls both Tityrus' praise of Amaryllis (1.5) and Menalcas' of Daphnis (5.64).

12 praescripsit pagina: the noun probably refers to publication of the poem on its own individual sheet; the verb confirms that the title of the poem included Varus' name.

13 Pierides: for the appeal to the Muses cf. 3.85, 8.63, 10.72.

Chromis et Mnasyllos: the former is the name of a Libyan in Th. *Id.* 1.24. The latter does not occur in earlier pastoral, though *Mnásylla* occurs in a sepulchral epigram, *A.P.* 7.730. The three proper names give a distinctively Greek colouring to the line. Servius believed that both characters here are fauns or satyrs and they certainly seem very familiar with Silenus (17-18). However, *timidis* (20), *pueri* (24), the apotropaic painting of Silenus' face (22n.) and the reference to evening pastoral tasks (85) all suggest that they were ordinary shepherd-boys. Mnasyllus is an ordinary shepherd in Calp. 6.28, and in Ov. *M.* 11.91 as in Aelian *V.H.* 3.18 it is *ruricolae* that bind Silenus.

13–14 in antro Silenum: *silēnoí* seem originally to have been the older, as *saturiskoí* were the younger, satyrs (see 5.73n.). One of the sileni at least was credited with arcane knowledge (see 19n.) and became the tutor to Dionysus (Diod. 4.4.3), with whom he and Pan both appear in the fragmentary *Pap. Rainer* (*Buc. Gr.* 168–70). In the human part of his body Silenus is represented as old and bald, with an ugly snub-nosed face, a shaggy beard and a fat paunch. He shared with the other satyrs a taste for music and dancing (Pi. fr. 142B) and the pleasures of wine and sex. However, his sensuality seems to have been good-humoured, and he is often, as here, indistinguishable from the Old Man of the Forest found in other folk-traditions, a figure both amusing and awesome. Plato's Alcibiades in his famous eulogy of Socrates as 'the complete lover' compares him to grotesque statuettes of sileni, represented with Pan-pipes or oboes, which open to reveal beautiful 'images of gods' inside (*Symp.* 215a and especially 216d). It is likely that Vergil had this passage in mind and saw Silenus as embodying, for all his grossness, natural wisdom and a devotion to music and love. The cave in which Propertius receives his Callimachean initiation as a poet is decorated with *orgia Musarum et Sileni patris imago | ficitilis et calami, Pan Tegeaee, tui*; also present are *Veneris dominae uolucres, mea turba, columbae* (3.3.29–31). Servius, believing Varus to be Quintilius Varus and a fellow-pupil of Vergil and Gallus in the Garden of Siro, sets forth at this point on another of his allegorizing flights: Silenus is Siro, the two shepherds Vergil and Varus, Aegle the Epicurean doctrine of *uoluptas*.

15 inflatum...uenas 'with his veins swollen'. The participle may be middle or passive, depending on whether we regard Silenus as agent or patient; cf. 1.54–5n., 3.106–7n.

ut semper: the first of many delightful touches that convert the gross sensualist into an amusing and endearing figure.

Iaccho: for the metonymy cf. 5.69. Drunkenness was not a feature of Arcadian life, but then Silenus is not a typical Arcadian. *Íakkhos* commonly has solemn ritual connotations in Greek (e.g. Ar. *Ra.* 398; cf. *G.* 1.166) and there may be a light-hearted allusion to the tradition that Bacchus inspired poets, which is put to both serious and jocular use by Horace, e.g. *C.* 2.19, *Ep.* 1.19.1–11.

16 serta: garlands were often worn at drinking parties; e.g. Pl.

Symp. 212e (Alcibiades' entry), Hor. *C.* 4.1.32. Ovid at *M.* 11.91 describes the captured Silenus as *uinctum coronis.*

procul, 'at a distance', not 'far off', goes with *iacebant.*

tantum 'only' probably goes with *delapsa.* The garland has merely slipped off; he had not had time to cast it aside before falling asleep. It could also be taken with *serta*: 'all that was with him were the garlands, lying as they had fallen'.

capiti: verbs of separation have either the ablative, denoting originally the physical effect, or the dative, denoting the abstract relationship of interest. With animate nouns both constructions are regular, with inanimates only the former is common; e.g. with *detrahere* Cicero has both *parenti* and *ab homine* but *de curru*, never *currui* (*Off.* 3.29, 30, *Cael.* 34). So perhaps there is a hint of mock-pathos here: Silenus' head had suffered a loss. However, there was often no formal differentiation of the two cases, e.g. *caelo facies delapsa* (*A.* 5.722, probably abl.), *Romanis dubitationem...exemerunt* (Liv. 34.37.6, probably dative); and the semantic distinction itself became blurred, e.g. *non noxae eximitur Q. Fabius* (Liv. 8.35.5). Metrical considerations are relevant: *capite* would have to be elided into a following heavy syllable.

iacebant: the variant *iacebat* is probably due to scribal anticipation of *pendebat*, though its Latinity is confirmed by the use of a feminine *serta* at Prop. 2.33.37.

17 grauis attrita: the 'golden line' word order effectively juxtaposes the two adjectives: in spite of the great weight of the bowl, its handles showed the signs of excessive use: *frequenti scilicet potu* (Serv.).

pendebat: *manibus non emissa* (Serv.).

cantharus: the loan-word from Greek *kántharos* 'a large bowl with handles' is already found in Plautus. Macrobius, *Sat.* 5.21.1, notes Vergil's liking for Greek names of drinking vessels; cf. *calathis* (5.71). The whole line adds a colourful piece of characterization.

18-19 ambo: the archaic dual form of the accusative recurs in *G.* 4.88, *A.* 12.342, again at the end of lines.

spe...luserat 'had deluded...in respect of their hopes' or 'by holding out hopes'; cf. *A.* 1.352.

19 ipsis ex ulucula sertis: for the word order cf. Lucr. 4.829 *ualidis ex apta lacertis.* The capture of a supernatural being who is compelled to tell his secrets is a common folk-tale motif. It appears in the capture of Proteus by Menelaus (Hom. *Od.* 4.363ff.) and Aristaeus (*G.* 4.315–558) and in Numa's deception of Picus and Faunus (Ov. *F.* 3.285ff.). More relevant here is Midas' capture of Silenus, alluded to in Hdt. 8.138.3. Different versions of the old satyr's revelations to Midas are reported (cf. Cic. *Tusc.* 1.114); D. Servius on line 13, citing Theopompus' *Thaumasia*, says *liberatum* [sc. *Silenum*] *de rebus naturalibus et antiquis Midae interroganti disputauisse*; cf. Aelian *V.H.* 3.18.

20   Aegle 'The shining one' (Greek *aiglē* 'a gleam'), a common nymph-name, e.g. the mother of the Graces (Paus. 9.35.5), one of the Hesperides (Serv. *ad A.* 4.484). As a supernatural being she is able to give moral support to the boys' audacious plan. In all the tales mentioned in 19n. except that of Midas the aid of a goddess or nymph is an essential element of the plot.

22   sanguineis...moris: the black mulberry, Morus Nigra, was introduced to Italy from the Near East. In colour its berries resemble congealed blood (see Ov. *M.* 4.121–7). The painting of Silenus' face by Aegle is not just a comic prank. Gods associated with the fertility of the land are often depicted with their faces painted with berry-juice or vermilion; e.g. Pan in 10.27, Priapus in Tib. 1.1.17–18, Ov. *F.* 1.415. Statues of gods were painted at festivals, e.g. Jupiter in Plut. *Q.R.* 98; and the practice was extended to their worshippers, e.g. Tib. 1.7.5–8 the festival of Bacchus, and to generals celebrating a triumph (Plin. *Nat.* 33.111). In origin this was clearly an apotropaic ritual. Aegle's action can therefore be seen as a way of subduing the supernatural creature to the will of mortals and pacifying his wrath.

23   dolum ridens: Silenus gives proof of his supernatural constitution by waking without any trace of a hang-over, and promptly shows his good humour – or perhaps the effects of the painting – by sharing the joke with his captors and granting their request at last.

quo uincula nectitis 'to what end...', 'why...?'; for the possible magical connotations of the phrase see 8.78n.

24   satis est potuisse uideri: in view of 14 we should probably understand *mihi*, 'it is enough that you have been able to see me (viz. against my will)', *quod ideo dicit quia hemithei cum uolunt tantum uidentur* (D. Serv.); cf. *A.* 8.604–5 *uideri | iam poterat legio*. Less likely, understanding *uobis*, 'it is enough that you are seen to have been capable (of capturing me)'; cf. *A.* 5.231 *possunt quia posse uidentur*.

25-6 cognoscite is perhaps just a synonym for *audite*, but there may be a suggestion that Silenus' song is intended to instruct as well as to entertain; see 82-3n.

carmina uobis: the preceding pause at the bucolic diaeresis emphasizes the chiastic antithesis with *huic aliud mercedis*. The latter phrase = *huic alia merces* 'for *her* there'll be another reward', with the genitive by analogy with the partitive in *aliquid mercedis* etc. It is a tactful allusion to Silenus' sexual appetite, which can hardly have been unforeseen by the *Naiadum pulcherruma* when she joined in the prank. Her presence thus enables the old satyr's character as himself *captus amore* to be exemplified.

ipse 'of his own accord'. He does not wait for them to renew their request (18-19).

27 So far Silenus has been the centre of a charming rustic comedy, for which the nearest pastoral precedents are *Pap. Rainer* (13-14n.) and the Polyphemus of Th. *Id.* 6.6-19. But the portentous Orphean imagery that follows prepares us for the altogether more serious tone of Silenus' recital.

in numerum 'in time to the rhythm'; cf. *G.* 4.175, Lucr. 2.631.

Faunosque: in origin Faunus, whose name is cognate with Greek *thós* 'jackal', *thaûnon* 'wild beast', seems to have been an Italian forest-god, part man part wolf; hence his connection with the Lupercalia (Ov. *F.* 5.101). The ancient etymology from *faueo* (cf. Serv. *ad G.* 1.10) reflects a desire to emphasize the beneficent aspect of a potentially hostile power. In humanized form he appears in legend as Faunus king of Latium (*A.* 7.48) and Daunus king of Apulia (Hor. *C.* 3.30.11). The god was assimilated to Pan and the satyrs (Hor. *C.* 1.17.2, Ov. *M.* 6.392-3), the goat replaced the wolf in his iconography, his more sinister aspects were suppressed and he was pluralized. Fauni were often associated with the nymphs (*G.* 1.10-11, *A.* 8.314-16). Besides their patronage of country life and hunting they possessed the power of prophecy (Var. *L.* 7.36, Cic. *Div.* 1.101; cf. *A.* 7.81-101). Here they are clearly the Italian counterpart to the Greek Silenus and his satyric kind: even Italian ears are charmed by Greek music.

27–8 ferasque...quercus: cf. Prop. 2.13.5–6 (64n.). For the Orphean powers thus attributed to Silenus see 3.46n.

29 Parnasia rupes, towering above Delphi, evokes the prophetic as well as the poetic powers of Apollo.

30 Rhodope, the mountain range separating western Thrace from Macedonia, the modern Despoto-Dagh, was associated not only with Orpheus (cf. G. 4.461) but also with the earliest worship of Dionysus (Hdt. 7.111).

Ismaros was a mountain of southern Thrace which also had Orphic (cf. Prop. 2.13.6) and Dionysiac (Ov. F. 3.410) associations, being famed for its vines (G. 2.37–8). For the traditional links between Orpheus and Bacchus cf. Eur. Hipp. 953–4, also G.4.520–2 on the death of Orpheus.

Orphea is disyllabic, with synizesis of -ea. The acc. of Greek names in -eus is normally -ĕă in Latin verse, e.g. Nerea (35), Eurysthea (G. 3.4), Thesea (A. 6.122) and probably Orphea (3.46). Rare metrical variants are Idomenĕā (A. 3.122), reflecting the archaic Greek form, and Typhōĕā (G. 1.279) parallel to Orphĕā here. Although the comparison to Apollo in the preceding line is reiterated in 82–3, Orpheus is here given the climactic position in the sentence. As the poet of science and mythology, res naturales et antiquae, Orpheus provides the model for Silenus in this recital.

31ff Silenus begins with a cosmogony, recalling Orpheus' song to the Argonauts in A.R. Arg. 1.496–502. The verbal echoes of Lucretius in 31–40 (see Macrob. Sat. 6.2.22–4) are perhaps intended to evoke the grand didactic manner of the de Rerum Natura rather than its specific doctrine. For there is almost nothing exclusively Epicurean here (but see 31n., 33–4n.). In any event the accounts given by the different philosophical schools of the cosmogonical process had much in common, however much they differed over causative principles. Silenus' cosmogony like that in Ov. M. 1.5–88 is sufficiently general to be appreciated by readers of many different philosophical and religious persuasions.

31 magnum per inane coacta: cf. Lucr. 2.109–10 multaque praeterea magnum per inane uagantur, | conciliis rerum quae sunt reiecta and 2.935 non fieri partum nisi concilio ante coacto. Although kháos ' the yawning void' figured in earlier cosmogonies (Arist. *Phys.* 208b), the phrase certainly suggests atomist doctrine (cf. D.L. 9.31). By contrast Ovid's *chaos*, which is *rudis indigestaque moles* (*M.* 1.7), belongs rather to the Stoic system (cf. D.L. 7.140, 150).

coacta fuissent: for the use of the pluperfect of *esse* to distinguish past-in-the-past from perfect-in-the-past (*coacta essent*) cf. Cic. *Div.* 1.74 *fixa...fuerant*, Liv. 29.6.4 *abstracti fuerant*.

32 semina terrarumque: Lucretius often refers to his atoms as *semina rerum*, the combinations of which *magnarum rerum fierent exordia semper,* | *terrai maris et caeli generisque animantum* (2.1062-3). However, Ovid uses *semina rerum* (*M.* 1.9) without any particular Epicurean connotations, 'the seeds or particles from which things are formed', and this is all that Vergil's phrase need mean. Indeed there may be a deliberate ambiguity; for the genitives could also be taken as defining: 'the seeds consisting of earth...', which would be a reference to the Empedoclean system of the four primary elements, earth, air, water and fire.

animae: like *animus* the word is cognate with Greek *ánemos* 'wind' and was used by Lucretius (e.g. 1.715) for Greek *aér*. Ennius had used *uentus* in this sense (*Ann.* 147V, cf. Var. *L.* 5.65); Cicero accepted the already current *aer* (*N.D.* 2.91).

33 liquidi...ignis: cf. Lucr. 6.205. For the traditional purity of fire see e.g. Hor. *C.* 2.20.2. Though especially important in the Stoic system (Cic. *N.D.* 2.39-44), the doctrine of a spherical *mundus* surrounded by fiery *aether* was also Epicurean (D.L. 10.88, Lucr. 5.495-508); so the phrase need have no specific doctrinal overtones.

33-4 his exordia primis omnia presents a very Lucretian doctrine, with *primis* referring to the atoms, which he himself had called variously *corpora prima, primordia, semina rerum*; cf. *ex illis omnia primis* in Lucr. 1.61. *exordia* refers to the primitive *concilia* of atoms from which more complex objects are formed; cf. Lucr. 2.1059-63, 3.378-80. The cosmogonical sequence in 32-4 is from *semina* to *exordia*, including initially the four elements, to the synthesis of *exordia omnia* to form the globe of the universe *mundi orbis* itself. Nettleship's *ex ordia* is unnecessary: *concrescere* occurs with the plain abl. at Lucr. 4.1261-2, and it is unlikely that Vergil would have introduced a technical term that has only one certain occurrence in Lucretius (4.28). The alternative reading is *his ex omnia primis omnis*, with *ex* placed as in 19. Although this phrase is close to Lucr. 1.61, cited above, the cosmogonical sequence is less distinctively Lucretian: first the *semina*, then the four elements, finally *omnia, omnis . . . orbis* 'everything, even the entire globe itself'. The latter phrase, emphatically placed to enclose the line, would reinforce the implications of *omnia*. The choice of reading turns on the crucial question: was *his exordia primis* corrupted by a scribe unfamiliar with Lucretius and *omnia* in the next line thereupon replaced by *omnis* or was *his ex omnia primis* 'corrected' by a scribe who *was* familiar with Lucretius and *omnis* thereafter replaced by *omnia*? The choice is a difficult one.

34 ipse tener: the adjective refers to the period before things had settled into the relatively stable and solid state represented by *durare solum*; cf. Lucr. 5.780–1. It therefore goes closely with *ipse*: the globe of the universe was itself still soft at that stage. This interpretation slightly favours the reading *exordia . . . omnia*. If however *tener* referred rather to the continuing fragility of the world, this would suit the other reading better.

  concreuerit 'grew together', 'cohered'. The process is described in Lucr. 5.465–71.

  mundi orbis: Lucretius sometimes uses *mundus* of the heavens (e.g. 1.788 *sidera mundi*), more often (e.g. 1.1054) of the spherical world as ordered by natural law – not of course 'the universe' as in the Stoic system, since there were countless other *mundi* and infinite atoms and void outside them – which is sometimes actually distinguished from *caelum* in the immediate context (e.g. 5.65, 68). Vergil has the word in both senses: 'the world or universe' in 4.50, 'the heavens' in *G.* 1.5. The former seems more appropriate here, whether in its Epicurean or its Stoic connotation.

35 durare: the subject of *coeperit* (36) is not *solum* 'dry land' but *mundi orbis*. Hence the infinitive can be taken in its normal sense 'to make hard' rather than as a synonym for *durescere*.

  discludere: for the separative process referred to see Lucr. 5.443–5 (437–9) and especially 480–2.

  Nerea ponto '(to shut off) Nereus in the sea'. The local ablative without *in* is archaic and compact. Although the context implicitly

7   CVE

rejects the prescientific cosmogony that made the old sea god the son of Pontos (Hes. *Th.* 233), this phrase acknowledges the existence of the gods even in a thus demythologized universe. The allusion thus prepares for the abrupt thematic transition to mythology at 41.

37 iamque nouom... solem: viz. after the stage at which earth, the densest of the four elements, has gravitated to the centre of the sphere, and fire, the lightest of them, floated outward to the periphery (Lucr. 5.449-70, Cic. *N.D.* 2.115-18). The formation of the heavenly bodies is now complete also, assuming that Vergil accepts the role of the sun's rays in the separation of land from water (Lucr. 5.483-5). The stage marked by *iamque* is therefore probably not the emergence of the sun from the creative process and the end of primaeval darkness (i.e. *lucescere* in contrast to *obscurari*) but rather its appearance in the heavens after the mists had lifted – *submotis nubibus* – moving in a higher trajectory than before – *altius* in contrast to *ex inferiore loco* (cf. Lucr. 5.471ff.).

stupeant: the insertion of a personifying verb (or adjective, cf. *ignaros* in 40) into a passage of objective scientific exposition prepares for the transition at 41 to a more empathetic style, as *Nerea* (35) had prepared for the change of theme.

38 cadant... imbres: now that the sun was in its familiar place and the mists had risen to form clouds (for the formation of *nubila*, *nubes* see Lucr. 6.451-526), the water-cycle began and with it the emergence of animate creatures.

40 ignaros... montis: for the setting cf. Lucr. 5.822-5. The reading *ignotos* replaces the empathetic adjective by a more prosaic one. The pattern of enjambement in 33-40 and the restriction of major pauses to the line-ends of 34, 36 and 38 are perhaps expressive of the continuity of the cosmogony.

41ff *relictis prudentibus rebus de mundi origine subito ad fabulas transitum fecit* (Serv.). The combination of themes recalls D. Servius' summary of Silenus' revelations to Midas (19n.) and Orpheus' song to the Argonauts (A.R. *Arg.* 1.496ff.), which passes from cosmogony to the reigns of Ophion and Kronos and the childhood of Zeus. At Ov. *M.* 1.89ff. there is a similar shift from quasi-scientific cosmogony through the Hesiodic Ages of Metals to myths of human metamorphosis.

Pyrrhae is dative of agent with *iactos*; see 4.15–16n. Like Noah and his wife in the Book of Genesis 6.8–9 Deucalion and Pyrrha escaped from the great flood because of their exceptional piety in a degenerate age. They re-created the human race by casting stones over their shoulders in obedience to an oracle of Themis, which Deucalion's father Prometheus had interpreted for them. The story, alluded to in Hes. *Eoiae*, fr. 2–4MW, is told at length in Ov. *M.* 1.313–415. It is referred to here in a single phrase depicting the miraculous event, itself an allusive device that depends for its effectiveness on the reader's prior knowledge of the tale. Although Vergil has not mentioned the creation of Man in the succinct cosmogony that precedes, it is not necessary to assume that he has arbitrarily converted Pyrrha from the role of Noah's wife to that of Eve, as the mother of the whole human race. Nevertheless the apparent chronology of 41–2 is very awkward. Thus in the traditional version (cf. Ov. *M.* 1.86–112) the Golden Age of the *Saturnia regna* precedes the Fall of Man and the great flood that was its punishment, and Deucalion and Pyrrha were the grandchildren of Iapetus, Saturn's brother.

Saturnia regna is probably a necessary metrical variant for *Saturnium regnum* (see 1.6n.). In the war of the gods that brought the reign of Kronos to an end Prometheus, though a Titan and nephew of Kronos, supported the Olympians. He incurred Zeus' anger however by deceiving him in the arrangement of sacrifices and by the theft of the sun's fire as a gift to mankind (Hes. *Th.* 535ff., 562ff.). As a punishment for this last act of defiance he was bound to a remote mountain in the Caucasus and had his liver eaten out daily by an eagle (Hes. *Th.* 521–5); as he was immortal, the liver grew again each night. Propertius (2.25.14) and Seneca (*H.F.* 1209) follow Vergil in referring to more than one eagle, the plural being intended, no doubt, to intensify the horror of the punishment (cf. the tortures of Tityos in Lucr. 3.993). As in 41 the details are highly allusive, with the one word *furtum* and the powerful image of *Caucasiasque...uolucres*. The mention of the crime after the punishment indicates that the sequence in the preceding line need not be chronologically significant. In fact the rhythmic correspondence of *furtumque Promethei* with *Saturnia regna*, both preceded by the major pause of the line, suggests that the two phrases have been deliberately placed to contrast with each other: the Age of Innocence and the Age of Deceit. Prometheus' gift of fire was moreover directly connected with the development of metalworking – the manufacture of ploughshares and swords – which characterized the Hesiodic Ages of Bronze and Iron.

42   Promethei: the monosyllabic *-eî* reproduces the normal post-Homeric contraction in the Greek forms; cf. *Tereî* (78).

43-4   Hylan: the Heroic Age is represented not by one of the great exploits of the Argonautic or Trojan expeditions (cf. 4.34–6) but by a minor, decidedly unheroic interlude in the former. The story of how Hercules carried off Hylas to be his minion on the voyage and then lost him to the river-nymphs of Propontis is told in A.R. *Arg.* 1.1207–355, Th. *Id.* 13, Prop. 1.20. Its current popularity is attested by *G.* 3.6. The accusative is probably direct object to *clamassent*, with the indirect question alone dependent on *adiungit*, and *Hylan* and *nautae* both displaced for dramatic effect – Hylas, sailors, fountain: 'Next Silenus told them at which spring Hylas was left behind when the sailors called out for him.' Alternatively *Hylan* and the *quo fonte* clause may be in apposition as objects to *adiungit*, the noun being placed proleptically as in *nunc rem ipsam ut gesta sit...attendite* (Cic. *Tul.* 13). But this is less likely.

   quo fonte 'at which spring' i.e. 'the name of the spring at which'; cf. Prop. 3.1.5 *dicite, quo...in antro?* In A.R. 1.1222 it is called Πηγαί 'The Springs'.

   ut litus...sonaret is probably a result clause with *clamassent*. It could perhaps be another indirect question in asyndeton after *quo fonte* etc., the tense shift indicating the continuation of the echo when the shouting had finished. To construe it as the object clause to *adiungit* with *quo fonte* etc. as a relative clause within it yields odd sense: 'how at the spring where the sailors had called Hylas when they left him behind the shore re-echoed'. In Th. *Id.* 13.58ff. only Heracles is involved in the searching and calling.

   clamassent: six of the eleven syncopated perfect forms that occur in the Eclogues are found in the present poem: *implerunt* (48), *quaesisset* (51), *uexasse* (76), *lacerasse* (77), *pararit* (79). See 1.23n.

   Hyla, Hyla omne: for the Greek flavour of the hiatus cf. 2.24n. For the fading effect of *-ă...-ă* cf. 3.79n. For Greek proper names in *-ās* Vergil usually retains the Greek voc. *-ă*; cf. *Damoeta* (3.1), *Menalca*

(5.4), *Lycida* (7.67). Once again Vergil has taken the narrative for granted and focused attention entirely on the pathetic situation of the drowning boy, who left behind by his comrades hears his name being called yet is unable to answer.

45 From the Argonauts to Minos' kingdom in Crete. Minos refused to sacrifice to Poseidon a white bull which the god had sent from the sea. To punish him Poseidon inspired in his wife Pasiphae a violent passion for the animal. The child born of this fantastic union was the Minotaur. The story was treated in a dithyramb of Bacchylides (26Sn.) and in Euripides' *Cretes*. Although later demythologizers made Taurus a human lover (Plut. *Thes.* 19), the unexpurgated version like other pathological tales appealed to the imagination of the Alexandrians (cf. Callim. *H.* 4.311) and their Latin disciples; e.g. Ov. *M.* 8.136–68, *A.A.* 1.289–326. Vergil returns to it again at *A.* 6.24–30. Pasiphae's *pathos* is treated more elaborately in 45–7, 52–60 than any of the other tales referred to.

fortunatam si: for the compressed apodosis cf. *A.* 4.657–8 *felix, heu nimium felix, si litora tantum | numquam Dardaniae tetigissent nostra carinae.*

46 solatur 'comforts' in contrast to *canebat* (31), *refert* (42), *adiungit* (43) indicates the singer's more sympathetic involvement in the story that he is telling. He breaks off from the narrative to interpose words of pity and comfort addressed to the suffering heroine directly (47, 52); cf. the address to Nisus and Euryalus in *A.* 9.446. Alternatively the verb may mean 'tells how she was comforted', cf. *circumdat* (62); but this is less likely.

amore: the simple abl. with *solari* is normally instrumental, e.g. *G.* 1.293 *longum cantu solata laborem.* Here it indicates the reason for the consolation, usually expressed by *in* or *de* + abl., e.g. Ov. *Tr.* 4.6.49, Cic. *Tusc.* 3.71. For *in* omitted cf. 35n.

47 a uirgo infelix is an echo from Calvus' *Io* (fr. 9M) *a uirgo infelix, herbis pasceris amaris,* cited here by Servius. Such exclamations were a feature of subjective narrative style. Pasiphae cannot have been a virgin at this time; nor was Io at the time of her metamorphosis (cf. Ov. *M.* 1.600, 610–11). But *uirgines nuptae* is used of faithful young wives at Hor. *C.* 2.8.23, *adultera uirgo* of Medea in Ov. *H.* 6.133. The implication is perhaps no more than that Pasiphae was a young and chaste wife to Minos before Poseidon's intervention.

quae te dementia cepit recalls Corydon's realization (2.69) of the hopeless incongruity of his passion for Alexis and the alienation from normal life that it had brought him.

48 Proetides: the Greek nom. pl. in *-ĕs* is compelled by the metre; but see p. 39. The daughters of Proetus king of Tiryns or Argos were punished for insulting Hera or Dionysus by an hallucination that they were cows. In contrast to Pasiphae however, the affliction did not extend to sexual desire for bulls (49–50). The story was treated by Hesiod (*Eoiae*, fr. 131–3MW) and Bacchylides (11.43–58) and alluded to in Ov. *M.* 15.326–7. Whether it formed an inset in Calvus' *Io*, as the tale of Io herself did in Europa's story at Mosch. 2.44–60, cannot be determined from the meagre fragments that survive. By inserting the Proetides into his account of Pasiphae Vergil is certainly alluding to the tale-within-a-tale structure, which was a form of narrative much favoured by the Alexandrian poets, e.g. Callim. *Hecale*, Cat. 64. Usually the two stories chosen had a complementary relationship. So here: a king's daughters who deserved their punishment and absurdly imagined themselves beasts, a king's wife who was punished for her husband's offence, and being afflicted with unnatural lust pathetically longed to be a beast.

falsis mugitibus: for *falsus* 'counterfeited' cf. Hor. *Ep.* 2.1.212 and the use of *fallere* in *A.* 1.683–4. The contrast between this bizarre and comical detail, reinforced by those in 50–1, and the depravity of Pasiphae's desire for *turpis...concubitus* vividly sums up the antithesis of mood between the two stories.

50 collo timuisset aratrum: the first word is dative; cf. *A.* 2.130. The phrase is almost Ovidian in its suggestion that in the midst of their hallucination they retained their royal sense of *decorum* and so feared the indignity of having to perform like a poor farmer's heifers a task that normally belonged to oxen.

51 lēui: *humana scilicet* (Serv.). Again an Ovidian touch, adding a further comic detail to the situation.

quaesisset: i.e. they had sought but not found. The absurdity of this last symptom of their hallucination contrasts with the pathos of Pasiphae's equally fruitless search, depicted in the following lines.

52 in montibus erras: viz. like an animal; cf. *errare* in 1.9, 2.21. The verb also suggests the *malus error* of disastrous love (cf. 8.41), which sent Corydon to the lonely *montibus et siluis* (2.5) and Minos to the Cretan hills in vain search for the Gortynian nymph Britomartis (Callim. *H.* 3. 189ff.). The close connection with line 47, immediately before the *Proetides* inset, is underlined both by the repeated *a uirgo infelix* and the exact metrical correspondence of the two lines.

53 niueum: the bull's radiant colour, already mentioned in 46, is enhanced now by the setting, with the *suaue rubens hyacinthus* (3.63), the thick dark green foliage of the holm-oak and the lighter green texture of the grass. With such an idyllic spot to rest and graze in and plenty of heifers (*magno* in 55) among whom to select a mate, he is the very picture of contentment; a bitter contrast to Pasiphae's own wretchedness, as her own words in 59–60 emphasize.

   latus. . .fultus hyacintho 'with his snow-white flank supported on soft hyacinths'. The verb *fulcire* most commonly means 'to support, press from beneath'; e.g. *A.* 4.247. *fultus* occurs with the passive meaning 'supported' at Lucil. 138M *et puluino fultus*, cited here by D. Servius, and at Prop. 3.7.50, Juv. 3.82 – all contexts of luxury and comfort; cf. *effultus* in *A.* 7.94. It is true that the verb can sometimes mean simply 'to press against', e.g. Cels. 7.19.5 *linamenta super non fulcienda*, and in Prop. 1.8.7 *pedibus. . .positas fulcire pruinas* the sense is either 'to push against' or 'press down'. However, a middle meaning for *fultus* here, viz. 'pressing down on', would probably require *latere. . .fultus hyacinthum*. The metre of *fultus hyacintho* is unusual. Normally *h* is not treated as a consonant, so that the syllable division here would be *-tu-shy-a-*, $\cup\cup\cup$; cf. *lī-tu-shy-la-* (43). Instead the division here must be *-tus-hy-a-*, $-\cup\cup$; cf. *languentis hyacinthi* (*A.* 11.69). Like the polysyllabic ending to the line itself (see 3.63n.) this treatment of *h* as a full consonant is an imitation of Greek epic metrical practice, as Velius Longus remarks (*G.L.* 7.52); cf. *Il.* 11.624 εὐπλό-καμος Ἑκαμήδη 'Hecamede of the fair tresses'.

55 claudite, Nymphae: Pasiphae's opening words are marked off by the major pause at the bucolic diaeresis (cf. *forsitan illum* 58) and the urgency of her address is expressed by the repetition of *Nymphae* in the next line.

56 Dictaeae: the nymphs of Mt Dicte in E. Crete were said to have nursed the infant Zeus (Callim. *H.* 1.46, Apollod. 1.1.6–7). Hence the epithet, though often used by synecdoche for 'Cretan', may have specific associations with the god; cf. *Dictaei regis* of Jupiter at *G.* 2.536. In Mosch. 2.158–9 Zeus stresses that he is taking Europa to the Cretan land that nurtured him. Pasiphae's plea to the nymphs who had once nursed the god to aid her in capturing the wandering bull would then recall that other bull whose *color niuis est* (Ov. *M.* 2.852) and who captured a princess and brought her to the *Dictaea...rura (ibid.* 3.2). So oblique an allusion would not be out of place in this richly Alexandrian context; it is thematically relevant and belongs too to the royal family history, Minos being the son of Zeus and Europa (Hom. *Il.* 14.321–2).

saltus: originally a verbal abstract from *salio* meaning 'a leap'; cf. *G.* 3.141. By metonymy it had come to be used of mountain passes and defiles, whether open or wooded (e.g. *A.* 11.904, Var. *R.* 2.3.6). Here it refers to the forest glades in the hills where cattle were pastured in the hot season; cf. Festus 302M *saltus est ubi siluae et pastiones sunt.*

claudite: one of the hunting techniques described in *G.* 1.140, *A.* 4.121.

57 si qua forte 'in case anywhere by chance'; a common meaning of *si forte.*

58 errabunda...uestigia: cf. Cat. 64.113 *errabunda regens tenui uestigia filo,* of Theseus hunting the Minotaur. Like Theseus it is Pasiphae who is really wandering (cf. 52). The tracks of the bull, for whom *errare* is part of normal life (cf. 1.9), mock the woman who is now alienated from her own way of life, wandering like Corydon when he said *tua dum uestigia lustro* (2.12).

60 aliquae...uaccae sadly echoes *aliquam* (55). All Pasiphae's schemes (55–8) are futile; only his natural mates can bring him in; *trahit sua quemque uoluptas* (2.65).

Gortynia: Gortyn not far from Minos' capital, Knossos, was throughout antiquity one of the most important cities of Crete. Servius' statement that the sun-god Helios, who was Pasiphae's father, kept his herds near Gortyn seems unparalleled; but many localities boasted this honour and Gortyn may have been one of them. For the miraculous plane tree there, beneath which according to *Graeciae fabulositas* Zeus made love to Europa (cf. 56n.), see Plin. *Nat.* 12.11. Throughout 45–60 the actual narrative has again been omitted in favour of its more picturesque and dramatic details: (i) the contrasting images of the wandering Pasiphae and first the ridiculous Proetides, then the snow-white bull in his idyllic contentment; (ii) Pasiphae's pathetic appeal for divine aid and its unconscious expression of the hopeless realities.

61 Hesperidum miratam mala: for the story of how the beautiful Boeotian princess Atalanta, who had outrun all her other suitors, was defeated in the final challenge by the subterfuge of the golden apples see Ov. *M.* 10.560–680, Hyg. *Fab.* 185. A different account of how she was finally won is implied in Prop. 1.1.9–16. The 'apples' (for the indeterminate meaning of *mala* see 2.51) of the Hesperides were originally presented by Gaia to Hera on her marriage to Zeus (Hes. *Th.* 215ff.). In Ovid's version the golden fruit given to Hippomenes by Venus are from the goddess's own sacred lands in Cyprus (*M.* 10.644–50). None of the later versions that describe the fruit as Hesperidean are certainly independent of Vergil; but it is unlikely that he himself introduced the variant in what clearly was already a richly varied tradition. The story is here represented by a single vivid image: the fateful moment when the girl paused to marvel at the tempting fruit (cf. Th. *Id.* 3.40–2). The image is enhanced phonetically by the labial alliteration of *p* and *m*.

62–3 Phaëthontiadas: Phaethon's disastrous attempt to emulate his father Helios in driving the sun-chariot across the heavens was treated by Hesiod (see Hyg. *Fab.* 154) and in Euripides' *Phaethon*. It is often referred to in later literature; e.g. A.R. *Arg.* 4.597–611, Lucr. 5.396–405. The metamorphosis of his grief-stricken sisters, though it is given equal prominence in Apollonius' account and presumably formed the climax to Aeschylus' *Heliades*, must originally have been a coda to the story, as it is in Ov. *M.* 2.340–66. The sisters are usually called *Heliades* 'daughters of the Sun'. A patronymic interpretation of *Phaethontiades* might be supported by the fact that *phaéthōn* 'shining', used to describe the sun from Homer onwards, occurs as a proper name 'The Sun' in *A.* 5.105, Nonn. *D.* 5.81. But this would be per-

verse in a context where the distinction between Phaethon and Sol is
crucial. Priscian (*G.L.* 2.65) understood the usage as a semantic extension by *poetica licentia* from patronymic to adelphonymic function:
'the sisters of Phaethon'. Apparent parallels exist for this usage: Greek
meleagrides 'guinea-fowls', sisters of Meleager (cf. Var. *R.* 3.9.18,
Ov. *M.* 8.533–46), and *Titanida Tethyn* (if this is the right reading) in
Ov. *F.* 5.81. However, the patronymic sense of the *-ides -ades* suffix is
itself only a specialization of the originally more general meaning
'belonging to, connected with', which is still common enough in
Greek and in Latin, e.g. *Libethrides* (7.21), *Calydonides* (Ov. *M.* 8.528)
and especially *Phaethontide...gutta* (Mart. 4.32.1) referring to amber.
This general sense 'associated with Phaethon' suits Sen. *H.O.* 188
Phaethontiadum silua sororum and would be appropriate here too,
especially as Phaethon himself has not been mentioned. The word
could be taken substantivally as the object of *circumdat* and *erigit*, with
alnos in predicative apposition: 'he surrounds the women associated
with Phaethon...and raises them up...as alders'. It is less likely to
be an adjective with *alnos* 'the alders connected with Phaethon'. The
choice of it here in preference to *Heliadas* inserts into the description
of the final metamorphosis a concise allusion to the narrative background, a device reminiscent of Callimachus or Propertius.

   circumdat...erigit: by making Silenus responsible for what
actually happens in the story Vergil draws attention to the descriptive
skill of the recital, by which the whole transformation from the initial
Phaethontiades to the final *alnos* is vividly recreated; cf. Serv. *mira autem
est canentis laus ut quasi non factam rem cantare sed ipse eam cantando facere
uideatur.*

   amarae corticis 'that grows on the bitter bark'. The noun occurs
in both masculine (e.g. *A.* 7.742) and less often feminine (cf. Lucr. 4.50)
gender; cf. Quint. 1.5.35.

   alnos: in other versions, e.g. *A.* 10.190, the sisters of Phaethon are
turned into poplars. Alders like poplars were common along river
banks (*G.* 2.110–11) and Vergil associates them especially with the
river Po (*G.* 2.451–2), which was usually identified with the Eridanus,
traditional site of the metamorphosis.

64 The initiation of Gallus comes abruptly into this mythological
catalogue; cf. Pollio's intrusion in 3.84. C. Cornelius Gallus was like

Alfenus Varus of provincial origin, having been born in 69 B.C. at
Forum Iulii (Fréjus) in Narbonensis. Like Pollio he combined active
careers in politics and literature, being however a supporter of Octavian throughout and much more closely identified with the neoteric
movement in poetry. He is named with Tibullus, Calvus and Catullus
by Ovid (*A.* 3.9.59–66), and his four books of elegies to Lycoris (see
10.2n.) established him as the first of the line of Latin elegists (Ov. *Tr.*
4.10.53–4). For his aetiological poem in the manner of Euphorion and
Callimachus see 72n. Of his work all is lost save the line *uno tellures
diuidit amne duas.* Together with Vergil (cf. Macrob. *Sat.* 5.17.18) he
was a disciple of Parthenius of Nicaea, who had come to Rome as a
prisoner-of-war in 73 B.C. and remained to become one of the most
influential figures in the Latin Alexandrian movement. Parthenius
himself wrote some poetry, also two prose works in Greek, *Metamorphoses* and περὶ Ἐρωτικῶν Παθημάτων 'on disastrous experiences in
love'. The latter, containing excerpts from Hellenistic poets, is still
extant. It was dedicated to Gallus with the express intention that
'you will have at hand a supply from which to draw whatever suits
your purpose best, whether it is epic or elegiac' (*prooem.* 2). This
suggests a range of poetic theme and technique more like Propertius'
than Tibullus'.

errantem Permessi ad flumina: the river Permessus rose from
the spring Aganippe (10.12) and flowed down Mount Helicon and
around its base. It was one of the bathing places of the Muses (Hes.
Th. 5). *errantem...ad flumina* 'wandering by' (rather than 'to') 'the
streams' may imply that Gallus has lost his way and is uncertain
about his vocation as a poet, but it also suggests the movement of the
shepherd following his flock and so recalls the setting in which the
Muses 'once taught Hesiod fair song as he pastured his lambs at the
foot of sacred Helicon' (Hes. *Th.* 22–3). The Hesiodic initiation-
dream recurs as a motif in Callimachus *Aet.* fr. 2 (cf. *A.P.* 7.42.1),
Ennius *Ann.* 1–12V, *var.* 45V (cf. Lucr. 1.117–26) and in 3–9 of the
present poem. Propertius in 3.3 brings together a rich complex of
imagery inspired by all these contexts to depict his own initiation as a
love-poet in the tradition of Philetas. In an earlier poem, singing
Augustus' praises, he had excused himself from the more appropriate
epic manner with the words *nondum etiam Ascraeos norunt mea carmina
fontes | sed modo Permessi flumine lauit Amor* (2.10.25–6). Access to the

heights of Helicon is by divine invitation only; poets whose aspirations outrun their powers, like Mamurra in Cat. 105.2, are rudely turned back. Yet the poet of Love may hope for a place on Helicon's slopes even if a little lower than that of the Hesiodic company: *hic* [sc. *Amor*] *me tam gracilis uetuit contemnere Musas* | *iussit et Ascraeum sic habitare nemus,* | *non ut Pieriae quercus mea uerba sequantur* | *aut possim Ismaria ducere ualle feras* | *sed magis ut nostro stupefiat Cynthia uersu;* | *tunc ego sim Inachio notior arte Lino* (Prop. 2.13.3–8); he may not be vouchsafed the powers of Orpheus, but still may follow in Linus' footsteps. The Propertian passages, clearly echoing the present lines, provide a commentary upon them. Gallus in writing his new poem has graduated from the humbler regions of erotic elegy to the heights of the more serious impersonal genres, just as Catullus had risen above the *nugae* of personal poetry by composing works like the *Peleus and Thetis* (64) to become a truly *diuinus poeta*.

65 Aonas: the Aones were an ancient people settled near Thebes (Strabo 9.401). *Aonia* is used by synecdoche for *Boeotia* perhaps first by Callimachus (*H.* 4.75), who also has the adjective *Aónios* (fr. 572Pf.), attested in Latin already at Cat. 61.28. In Prop. 1.2.28 *Aonius* refers particularly to the Muses (cf. 10.12), who are called *Aonides* in Ov. *M.* 5.333. The adjectival use of *Aōn* seems unparalleled, but presumably had some Alexandrian precedent. The Greek acc. pl. like *Phaethontiadas* (62) enhances the exotic flavour of the context. The proper name provides the specification for *sororum*; cf. Prop. 2.30.27, Ov. *M.* 5.255.

66 Phoebi chorus: cf. Hes. *Th.* 7–8 'on the heights of Helicon [the Muses] performed their lovely choruses'.

uiro...adsurrexerit: *honorem praebuerit* (Serv.); cf. *G.* 2.98, Cic. *Inv.* 1.48. The noun emphasizes the rarity of such a tribute from deities to mortals.

67 diuino carmine pastor 'the shepherd with the divine power of song': Linus (4.56n.) is represented as a shepherd in Callim. *Aet.* fr. 27Pf. For his association with the Muses see Paus. 9.29.6–9. The reference to him in Prop. 2.13.8 (64n.) indicates a particular connection with the elegiac genre.

68 apio...amaro: wild celery, Apium Graveolens, with its long-lasting foliage (*uiuax* in Hor. *C.* 1.36.16), was often used with the evergreen ivy and myrtle for festive garlands (Th. *Id.* 3.22–3, Hor. *C.* 2.7.24–5). However, it was also used to adorn tombs (Plut. *Timol.* 26.1); Hesychius, s.v. σελίνου στέφανος 'celery garland', says that it was because of its mournful associations that it was used to crown the victors at the Isthmian games, and D. Servius on the present line that the celery crown worn by the Nemean victors was in memory of the premature death of one Archemorus. So *amaro* here, in contrast to Theocritus' 'fragrant celery' (*loc. cit.*), may refer not just to its taste but also to its sad associations – appropriate to the wearer (see 4.56n.).

ornatus: for the middle sense 'having adorned himself' cf. 1.54n. The repetition of this Hellenizing construction so soon after 53 is perhaps a deliberate evocation of neoteric style. See also 75.

70 Ascraeo...seni: Hesiod was born at Ascra near Helicon (*Op.* 639–40) and the adjective suffices to identify him; cf. *G.* 2.176, Prop. 2.10.25. The noun like *pater* sometimes indicates venerable antiquity rather than old age; e.g. Hor. *S.* 2.1.34 of Lucilius.

quos ante: in fact the Muses presented Hesiod not with pipes but with a staff plucked from a bay tree (Hes. *Th.* 30–1). For the symbolic presentation from the Muses cf. Ennius' garland in Lucr. 1.117–18 and the *mollia serta* of Prop. 3.1.19–20.

71 cantando...deducere...ornos: the power that magicians claimed to charm mountain-ashes from the hillsides (*A.* 4.491) was traditionally attributed also to Orpheus' music (*G.* 4.510; see 3.46n.). As a singer of *res prudentes* and *fabulae* Hesiod was in the Orphean tradition, scientific teacher and myth-maker. Indeed he is sometimes coupled with Orpheus, e.g. Ar. *Ra.* 1032–3, and was even said to be descended from him (Hellanic. fr. 5J). Many so-called Orphic fragments are in fact based on lines of Hesiod.

72 tibi: for the agential dative see 4.15n.

Grynei...nemoris...origo: Gryneia was one of the ancient towns of Aeolis in Asia Minor, near the coast north-east of Cyme. According to Servius it was the site of Mopsus' victory over Calchas in a divination contest (cf. Hes. fr. 278MW). There was an oracular cult of Apollo there (Strabo 13.622; cf. *A.* 4.345). Servius' description of the sacred grove is very like the *locus amoenus* of pastoral: *arboribus*

*multis iucundus, gramine floribusque uariis omni tempore uestitus, abundans
etiam fontibus.* Cf. Paus. 1.21.7. In the same note Servius remarks *hoc
autem Euphorionis continent carmina quae Gallus transtulit in sermonem
Latinum*; from which we need infer no more than that Gallus' poem
contained some passages adapted from or modelled on different parts
of Euphorion's work. The Chalcidian poet was notoriously obscure,
so if Gallus was a true *cantor Euphorionis* his new aetiological poem must
have been a worthy successor to Calvus' *Io*. That Apolline cult-sites
were fashionable subjects for poets at this time is suggested by the
reference in *G.* 3.6 to *Latonia Delos*. Parthenius' *Delos* in fact contained
a reference to *Grúneios Apóllōn* (Steph. Byz. 213.10). The following
line here clearly echoes Callim. *H.* 4 (*Delos*). 268-70 'By me shall
Apollo be called Delian, nor shall any other land be loved so much by
any other god'; which reminds us that such subjects were particularly
Callimachean. We need not infer from the present passage that Hesiod,
whose father was from Cyme, also treated the Grynean grove in
detail.

74 Silenus now reverts from allegory to mythology. Scylla the
daughter of Nisus king of Megara betrayed her father and his kingdom
to Minos by cutting a talismanic lock of hair from his head during a
siege of the city. The story occurs in various forms; e.g. Aesch. *Cho.*
614ff., Apollod. 3.15.8, Prop. 3.19.24-8. In the most familiar version
she was subsequently changed into a sea-bird, the *ciris*, and her father
into a sea-eagle; see *G.* 1.404-9, Parthen. fr. 20M, Ov. *M.* 8.145-51,
anon. *Ciris* 493ff. The latter narrative poem, which is probably post-
Ovidian, has been attributed both to the young Vergil (Don. *Vit.* 57)
and to Gallus.

aut Scyllam goes closely with *aut ut...narrauerit* as direct object to
loquar: 'Why need I mention either Scylla...or how Silenus
narrated...?' Alternatively it could be taken with *aut...mutatos...
artus* as direct object to *narrauerit*: 'how he narrated either ⟨the tale of⟩
Scylla...or the metamorphosis...'; but this is less likely. The actual
question, breaking the illusion of the recital, implies as usual that the
reason for mentioning Scylla is obvious. Like much else in the poem it
is not so to the modern reader.

74ff amalgamate Megarian Scylla with the monster of the Straits
of Messina, described in Hom. *Od.* 12.85-100 (cf. Hes. *Eoiae* fr.

262MW). In each of the various versions of the latter Scylla's story a sea-god fell in love with her and a jealous rival poisoned her bathing pool. As a result the lower part of her body was changed into a hideous monster with six raging dogs' heads and a dozen feet; see Ov. *M.* 14.1–74. The two Scyllas are kept distinct by Apollodorus (cf. *Epit.* 7.20) and Hyginus (*fab.* 198, 199); and the many poets who confused the two are rebuked by the author of *Ciris*, 54ff. Vergil himself, Propertius and Ovid all have both the 'pure' version of Megarian Scylla (*G.* 1.404–9, Prop. 3.19.24–8, *Met.* 8.6–151), and also the conflated one (here, Prop. 4.4.39–40, *A.* 3.12–21–2 and *F.* 4.500). Now the association between Greek *Skúlla* and *skúlax* 'yelping', implicit in the Sicilian heroine's transformation, is already explicit in Hom. *Od.* 12.85-6. A different connotation of *skúlax*, viz. 'bitch', seems to be the point of Callimachus' 'Scylla, a whore not falsely named, cut the purple lock' (*Hecale*, fr. 288Pf.). So it may be that Callimachus himself or one of his followers – Parthenius for instance – was responsible for the conflation of the two stories, by which the metamorphosis of the one became the finale to the disastrous love affair of the other (see 64n.), and the woman whose bitch-like lust had turned her into a shameless criminal received a grimly appropriate punishment in having her sexual organs turned into a lair for raging dogs.

74–5   quam fama secuta est... uexasse is difficult. *sequi* may be taken intransitively, 'to come later', with *quam...uexasse* dependent on a verb of saying implied by *fama*: 'who, as the story was subsequently, ...attacked'. This might be intended to indicate that the present version was not the original one. Alternatively *sequi* may be transitive, 'to pursue', with *quam* as dir. obj. and an *eam* understood as subject to *uexasse*: 'who has been pursued by the story that she... attacked'.

candida succinctam... inguina may be taken descriptively, with the participle as a perfect passive and the acc. as one of reference: 'being surrounded as to her groin'; cf. Lucr. 5.892–3 *rabidis canibus succinctas semimarinis | corporibus Scyllas*. Alternatively the phrase may be narrative, with the participle preterite middle and the acc. one of direct object: 'once she had surrounded her groin'. For a similar ambiguity cf. Lygd. [Tib. 3.]4.89 *Scyllaque uirgineam canibus succincta* *figuram.* Ovid's horrifying account of her metamorphosis depicts in detail the corruption of her sexual organs (*M.* 14.60–6). In Vergil's image the preservation of Scylla's *candida inguina* after the metamorphosis cruelly mocks her with the evidence of what she had once been; cf. Prop. 4.4.40 *candidaque in saeuos inguina uersa canis.*

76 Dulichias 'of Odysseus'. Dulichium was part of Odysseus' kingdom in Hom. *Od.* 1.245–6, but the reason for its special association with Odysseus in Latin poetry, e.g. Prop. 2.14.4, Ov. *M.* 13.107, is not known. It is mentioned with the Echinades islands in Hom. *Il.* 2.625–6 and was identified with one of the latter by Strabo (10.453). But the description of *Doulikhion* as 'rich in wheat and grass' at Hom. *Od.* 16.396 suggests a region in the alluvial plain of the Achelous river opposite the Echinades rather than any of the barren islands themselves (cf. Thuc. 2.102.3–5).

rates: Homer's Odysseus had only one ship left when he ran the straits between Scylla and Charybdis (*Od.* 12.205, 245).

uexasse: Gellius (2.6.1ff.) defends Vergil against the charge made by Cornutus and other first-century Vergilian commentators that the word was too mild to be appropriate here (*nec tantae atrocitati congruere*) by pointing to the more violent sense which it had as an intensive derivative of *uehere* in older authors, e.g. Cic. *Verr.* 4.122, Cato *de Achaeis* (fr. 177M) *quomque Hannibal terram Italiam laceraret atque uexaret.*

77 a timidos: the exclamatory intrusion by the poet, like the emotive apostrophe to characters (47, 52), is a feature of the subjective narrative style; cf. *G.* 4.525–6 *Eurydicen...* | *a miseram Eurydicen...* *uocabat.* It is especially notable here in the retelling of an actual Homeric incident.

78 Terei is disyllabic; cf. *Promethei* (42). The heavy spondaic rhythms of the line introduce an even more fantastic and horrible tale. In Ovid's version of the myth (*M.* 6.424–674) Philomela on her way to visit her sister Procne was raped by Tereus, who then had her tongue torn out and shut her away in solitary captivity. He returned to his kingdom in Thrace and reported that Philomela was dead, but Procne learned the truth from a tapestry her sister made and sent to her. The two sisters punished Tereus by killing Itys, the son of Procne and Tereus, and serving him to his father at a banquet. Tereus pursued the sisters and all three characters were changed into birds. For a different and somewhat confused version see Apollod. 3.14.8. The grisly story is treated or alluded to in many places, e.g. Hom. *Od.* 19.518–23, Aesch. *Ag.* 1140–9, Thuc. 2.29. In the Greek versions Procne became the nightingale, Philomela the swallow, Tereus the hawk, or more commonly the hoopoe, perpetually crying *poû? poû?* 'Where? Where?' The Latin tradition, though not always clear (cf. Ov. *M.* 6.668–9), seems to make Procne the swallow, *hirundo* (*G.* 4.15, Ov. *F.* 2.853–6), and Philomela the nightingale, *luscinia* (*G.* 4.511; cf. Ov. *A.* 2.6.7–10). This may be simply due to a false etymological connection between *Philomēlē* and *philoûsa mélē* 'delighting in songs' which is more appropriate to the nightingale's 'amorous descant' than to the swallow's twitterings.

78–81: the narrative sequence is severely distorted: the chronological order is *dapes* and *dona* (79), *mutatos...artus* (78), *uolitauerit* (81, with *ante* underlining its priority), *petiuerit* (80). Once again description takes precedence over narration, as the successive interrogatives *quas, quae, quo, quibus* emphasize. We are given only two narrative details. The first is the climactic horror of *dapes* and *dona*, which depend for their impact on our prior knowledge of the fable, viz. that the women served up the body during the meal and presented the head and limbs to the father when he had eaten. The second is Philomela's escape from Tereus afterwards.

80   deserta petiuerit sc. *Philomela.* Although the hoopoe frequents lonely spots, *deserta*, the verb suggests flight from a pursuer (cf. Ov. *M.* 6.668) and is therefore more appropriate to Philomela than to Tereus. In any event it would be normal to assume no change of subject from the preceding line.

80–1   quo cursu...quibus...alis 'with what flight...with what wings' i.e. 'what was the name of the bird in whose form...'; cf. *quo fonte* (43).

81   super: for the anastrophe of the preposition cf. 8.59, 9.40–1.

   uolitauerit: *sua tecta* requires the reference to be either to Tereus or his queen. Although Vergil has given Philomela the major role in the revenge, this is consistent with her role as the sister-in-law in the

traditional version. For she had suffered far more horribly than
Procne. In fact the sequence of interrogative clauses referring to her
is broken after *petiuerit* by the insertion of *et* (80), trivial in itself but
emphasized by the disruption of the normal homodyne cadence to the
line. Moreover *infelix* 'the ill-fated one' suits the victim Tereus more
than either of the avengers. It is true that in Ov. *M.* 6.669 *altera* [sc.
soror] *tecta subit* refers to the swallow and its habit of nesting under the
eaves of buildings. But the image of a bird hovering above its own
roofs is surely appropriate to the hoopoe into which Tereus had been
turned. He then must be the subject of *uolitauerit*. The reason for disruption of the narrative sequence now becomes clear. Vergil begins
and ends with the king: his *artus* (78) are now replaced by *alis* (81),
and the image of him vanquished and transformed into humiliating
impotence encloses the allusions to Philomela's vengeance and escape.

82   omnia quae: the implication is perhaps that the synopsis of
Silenus' song has not been exhaustive; for the recital lasted all day,
from the satyr's awakening till nightfall (85-6).

  Phoebo...meditante expands the comparison to Apollo in 28.
For the verb 'to practise', 'rehearse', significantly echoing line 8, see
1.2n.

82-3   beatus audiit Eurotas: for the epithet cf. *gaudet* (29) of
Parnassus. *hunc fluuium Hyacinthi causa Apollo dicitur amasse* (D. Serv.).
The reference then is to the god consoling himself in song for the death
of a loved one, just like Orpheus in Ov. *M.* 10.143ff., whose recital
actually includes the tale of Apollo and Hyacinthus (162-219). The
further personification in *audiit* is maintained in *iussitque* and *ediscere*:
the trees are not merely to hear but also to learn the stories (cf.
cognoscite in 25). *diuinum carmen* can charm even brute nature into
animation; cf. 28-30, 70-1. For the comparison to the god cf. Prop.
2.34.79-80 of Vergil himself.

84   For the reminiscence of Lucr. 2.327-8 cf. 5.62n.

85   referre: the repetition of the verb in a different sense in successive lines ('reflect' in 84, 'bring back home' or 'reckon up' here)
seems somewhat inelegant. Both infinitives in the line are direct
complements to *iussit*, each with its own direct object: 'ordered the
gathering in of the sheep and the counting up of their number'. For

comparable constructions with *mandare* and *permittere* see 5.41n., 1.9n.
The variant reading *referri* would provide a syntactic variation, with
ouis as object to *cogere* but *numerum* as subject to *referri*, for which there
are parallels at *A.* 5.772–3, 11.83–4.

86 inuito...Vesper Olympo: for the rising of Venus, which *ab
occasu refulgens nuncupatur Vesper, ut prorogans lucem uicemque lunae reddens*
(Plin. *Nat.* 2.36), cf. Cat. 62.1–2, *A.* 8.280. Here, as in both those
passages, *Olympo* is used by metonymy for *caelo* (cf. *Olympi* in 5.56).
The improbable alternative is that the poem is set in the borderland
of Thessaly and Macedonia west of Olympus; cf. 8.30n. Silenus' song
has re-echoed *ad sidera* (84); the heavens are delighted by it, as the
creatures of earth had been (27–8) and are reluctant, *inuito*, when the
shadow of night, which is *grauis cantantibus* (10.75), brings the recital
to a close.

Much in this fascinating poem must remain obscure, so long as we
know so little of the occasion for which it was composed and the background of contemporary literary history against which it needs to be
placed. There are virtually no echoes of Theocritus. The image of
poet as shepherd (3–5), though complementary to the pastoral figure
of shepherd as poet, is Hesiodic and Callimachean. Even the bucolic
mime (13–30) introduces a motif not from the pastoral tradition but
from folk-tale, with precedents in Homer and Herodotus. The central
character, the bibulous monster Silenus, whose supernatural status is
stressed throughout the incident, is an intruder in Arcady. Theocritus
in *Id.* 6 and 11 had purged the Cyclops Polyphemus of most of his
traditional monstrosity and assigned him a role that assimilated him
to the ordinary love-sick shepherd of the pastoral. But Silenus' song is
quite unlike anything else in the genre. There is plenty of rustic
imagery – *fonte* (43), *armenta* (45), *aratrum* (50), *hyacintho* (53), *herbas*
(54), *nemorum...saltus* (56), *stabula* (60), *mala* (61), *alnos* (63), *floribus*,
apio (68); but it all has a localized significance within the tales where
it occurs. It does not, as in the other Eclogues, cohere to form a single
evocative landscape.

True to his prophetic character Silenus holds forth to his captors
de rebus naturalibus et antiquis (see 19n.). The opening cosmogony (31–
40), though Lucretian in style, is too general to be labelled exclusively
Epicurean. It is the prelude, as in Ovid's *Metamorphoses*, to a series of

myths, which after the transitional *Saturnia regna* and *furtum Promethei*
are dominated by the themes of disastrous love and fantastical transformation. The distinction between *res prudentes* and *fabulae* (see 41n.)
was perhaps less sharp in an age that had demythologized much of its
thinking about the physical world but still regarded human pre-
history as *poeticis magis decora fabulis* (Liv. *praef.* 6). The myths and
legends of the heroic age were accepted partly as a kind of history,
partly as the repository of traditional wisdom concerning the human
condition. For Callimachus and his disciples, however, both Hellenistic
and Latin, it was the sub-heroic side of the heroic age, the sensational
tales of love and fantasy that were of most interest. The style of
Silenus' mythology is very much that of neoteric narrative. In each
case the story is treated very allusively on the assumption that it is
already well known. In fact the contents of Silenus' programme are all
familiar even to us from a number of Greek and Latin sources (see
42n., 43–4n., 46n. etc.). None of the tales is as obscure as the thematically similar selection that Parthenius put together for Cornelius
Gallus (see 64n.; only Megarian Scylla occurs in both places; see 74n.).
All through we are given instead of a dynamic story-line one or two
static tableaux, which focus attention on a particular picturesque or
dramatic moment. Sometimes the impersonal narrative texture is
interrupted by exclamatory asides (47, 52, 77), by which the poet
establishes a direct relationship with the reader, inviting him to share
the appropriate emotional response. Lastly, one of the favourite
patterns of Hellenistic narrative poetry, the tale enclosing a tale, is
represented here, in the most elaborate piece in the recital: *Pasiphae*
(45–60) encloses *Proetides* (48–51), with which it contrasts both in tone
and in theme.

   Two particular neoteric subjects, metamorphosis and love, give
unity to the whole poem. Thus Silenus' potential antipathy is quickly
transformed (24–5) and his grossness falls away to reveal a poetic soul
capable of transforming even brute nature (27–30); the metamorphosis of the raw elements into an ordered world leads to the mythical
metamorphosis of Pyrrha's stones, Philomela etc. and the symbolic
metamorphosis of Gallus. Love is prominent throughout the Eclogue
– in the reference to the reader who is *captus amore* (10), in the character of Silenus, whose traditional lustiness, tactfully recalled in 26, had
been elevated to a higher status in the famous passage in Plato's

Symposium (see 13–14n.), and in the final image of Phoebus beside the Eurotas (see 82–3n.). Traditional cosmogonies had often assigned an important role to Love, whether as a divine being like Pherecydes' *Érōs*, a more abstract cosmic principle like Empedocles' *Philótēs* and the *sacer orbis amor* (Luc. 4.190–1) of Stoic thought, or even as a poetic symbol for the continuous creation of atomic *concilia*, which *alma Venus* has become in Lucretius' famous proem. There is therefore an implicit contrast between *Amor* as a principle of creative concord in the natural world and *Amor* as a discordant and destructive force in human affairs – Pasiphae, Scylla etc. The latter theme is of course recurrent in the Eclogues; c.g. 2.68–9, 8.43–50, 10.28–9. It is combined with the metamorphosis motif again in the Ovidian Orpheus' recital (*M.* 10.155–739).

Gallus' initiation (64–73), besides being a tribute to a friend and fellow-poet, must clearly have some special relevance to the mythological catalogue into which it breaks so abruptly. The details of his commission from the Muses associate him with Orpheus, as Silenus had been earlier (30), and with Hesiod. Now the Muses had declared at Hesiod's initiation (Hes. *Th.* 27–8) 'We know how to say many things that are fictitious but just like fact; but when we choose, we know how to utter things that are true.' For the creative artist the boundaries of fact and fiction, of *mímēsis* 'imitation' and *poíēsis* 'invention', are always fluid. Hesiod like Orpheus (see 3.46n.) took the whole range of human thought and experience, both *res prudentes* and *fabulae*, as his province. Silenus' recital reasserts this Hesiodic concept of the universality of poetry. But it is reasserted in specifically neoteric terms. The choice of themes is Alexandrian: scientific didacticism (for after the fifth century poems *de rerum natura* belonged more to the literary than the philosophical tradition) and tales of mystery and imagination. As we have seen, the style of presentation is Alexandrian too. The Callimachean form of Vergil's opening *recusatio* to Varus (see 3–4n.) now assumes its full importance: Callimachus, not Theocritus, is now the dominant influence in his poetic thinking. He is nearing the end of his career in pastoral. It is significant therefore that Gallus has earned the right of succession to Orpheus and Hesiod not by the love elegies on which his later fame was based (see 10.6n.) but by the aetiological poem on the Gryneian grove of Apollo (72–3), which he had just published or was expected soon to publish. For it is the impersonal, not the personal, genres of poetry that are held up to admiration, genres in which – as Vergil's own pastoral, didactic and epic poetry demonstrate – an intense personal commitment is not of course excluded but must be mediated obliquely.

This interpretation is confirmed by the character of the three excerpts that are elaborated most fully: the Cosmogony (31–40) = scientific didacticism; *Pasiphae* (45–60), with its inset *Proetides* (48–51) = mythology cast in a neoteric narrative form; *Gallus* (64–73) = the Latin neoteric movement and his aetiological poem the Hesiodic synthesis of science and mythology.

In proclaiming in illustrative form Vergil's allegiance to the poetic principles of Hesiod and Callimachus the Eclogue corresponds to Theocritus' literary manifesto in *Id.* 7. The recital *de rebus naturalibus et antiquis* may or may not include references here and there to works of Vergil's neoteric colleagues that are lost to us, and presumably were to Servius, who quotes only one such example (see 47n.). It certainly provides the appropriate setting for a tribute to their acknowledged leader. Moreover the choice of the Dionysiac Silenus as the singer, reinforced by the comparison with Orpheus and Apollo (29–30, 83–4), confers a prophetic status on the song that raises it above the level of ordinary pastoral. But then the poem has little to do with the orthodox pastoral genre at all. Little either, so far as we can tell, with Varus. What he made of it all or was intended to make of it is beyond even conjecture.

ECLOGUE VII

1 Forte: even a casual meeting of Arcadian herdsmen, as they gather together to rest and shelter with their flocks from the heat of the day, is seized upon as an opportunity to make music. 1–20 set the scene for a singing contest between Corydon and Thyrsis. For a similar chance encounter leading to a singing contest between Daphnis and Menalcas cf. [Th.] *Id.* 8.1–2.

arguta is regularly used of high-pitched notes – the squeak of a lock (*G.* 1.143), the twittering of swallows (*G.* 1.377), a swan's song (9.36), or, as here, in 24 and 8.22, the rustle of the wind in the trees. It is used of clear-voiced poets in Hor. *Ep.* 2.2.90. For the aural image itself cf. 5.82n.

Daphnis, a spectator and perhaps even the judge of the competition, is silent throughout, and the whole incident is reported in the person of Meliboeus (9).

2 compulerantque...in unum: cf. Th. *Id.* 6.1–3 'Damoetas and Daphnis the cattle-herd once brought the herd together into one place, Aratus;...and by the spring they both sat down at midday in the summer, and this is what they sang...'

Corydon et Thyrsis: for the former see 2.1n. The latter name is perhaps intended, from its resemblance to Greek *thúrsos*, which is used of the Bacchants' wand (5.31n.), to suggest devotion to Dionysus. It was given to the singer of the Daphnis-dirge in Th. *Id.* 1.64ff. The names in the first two lines thus recall Theocritean contexts linking Daphnis and Thyrsis and exhibiting Daphnis' own prowess as a singer.

3 distentas suggests spring or early summer, and this fits well with the rustling of the leaves (1), the young myrtles (6), the kids and lambs (9, 15) and the swarming bees (13). It also indicates the prosperity of the flocks. With characteristic economy Vergil uses the gathering of the animals to reveal that Corydon is a goatherd and Thyrsis a shepherd; for the *tauri* and *iuuenci* of 38, 44 belong to their adopted roles as wooers of the sea-nymph. Daphnis is presumably in his traditional role of cattleherd (5.25n.). For Meliboeus himself see 11n. The whole range of herdsmen's activity is thus represented in the scene.

4 florentes aetatibus: cf. [Th.] *Id.* 8.3 cited in 5n.

Arcadēs ambo: the Greek nom.pl. here is required by the metre; see 6.48n.

This is the earliest reference to Arcady in connection with the pastoral myth. In Erucius, *A.P.* 6.96, which is close in date to the Eclogue, 'Glaucon and Corydon herdsmen on the hills' offer a sacrifice to 'Cyllenian Pan who loves the hills'. They are described as Ἀρκάδες ἀμφότεροι 'Arcadians both', presumably as fellow-countrymen of the god rather than as inhabitants of an idyllic Arcady. In Theocritus various pastoral settings are specified – south Italy in *Id.* 4.17, 5.72, Cos in *Id.* 7.1 – but Sicily, the country of Daphnis (*Id.* 1.117) and Polyphemus (*Id.* 11.7, Bion 2.1) as of Theocritus and Bion themselves, was the most favoured (*Id.* 8.56, 9.15, *Ecl.* 4.1, 6.1).

However, only one of Vergil's Eclogues (2) is explicitly set there. Perhaps for contemporary Latin readers Sicily was too near to be effectively idealized, and its associations in recent history – the slave revolts culminating with Spartacus, the depredations of Verres, the war with Sextus Pompey – too grim to sustain the idyllic image (but see Lucr. 1.726–8). Vergil might have chosen Cos instead or the Vale of Tempe, a traditional *locus amoenus* (Plin. *Nat.* 4.31, Aelian *V.H.* 3.1) which he alludes to himself at *G.* 2.469 in his famous praise of the countryside. Instead he chose Arcadia.

The Arcadians of real life lived in an isolated part of the Peloponnese and spoke an archaic dialect of Greek. They had, so it was believed (Thuc. 1.2.3), been untouched by population movements, and as 'acorn-eaters' (Hdt. 1.66.2) had preserved a primitive way of life, which could be represented in favourable or unfavourable terms (Theop. *ap.* Athen. 4.149d on the occasional relaxation of class-barriers, Paus. 8.2.6 on werewolves). Their economy was largely pastoral, and because of the low level of subsistence many of the younger men sought service abroad as mercenary soldiers (Xen. *H.* 7.1.23). In Ov. *F.* 2.289–302 they are exemplars of 'hard' primitivism. Even Polybius (4.19.13–21.6), who lays great stress on their devotion to music, sees this as the one civilizing influence in an otherwise brutal and grim environment. The only poetic genre that he mentions is the dithyramb, and the two dozen epigrams attributed to the Arcadian poetess Anyte, though many of them are on rural subjects, contain almost none of the specifically pastoral features.

In traditional mythology Arcadia was the homeland of Hermes, the inventor of the lyre and the shepherd pipe (*h.Hom.* 4.2, 39–67, 511–12) and father (at least in some accounts) of Pan, the patron of shepherds and their music; cf. 2.33n. and Erucius' epigram cited above. It is in association with Pan and Hermes that we find the earliest hints of an idealization of the Arcadian region: 'Arcadia with its many springs, the mother of sheep' (*h.Hom.* 19.30); cf. *h.Hom.* 4.2, Bacch. 10.95 and later Th. *Id.* 22.157 'Arcadia rich in sheep', which is hard to reconcile with Polybius' objective account of the region. A mythological link between Arcadia and Theocritus' Sicily is provided by the story of Arethusa (10.1n.). There was also a belief that Arcadian Greeks had settled prehistorically in Italy itself (Strabo 6.283), and Dionysius Hal. even identifies them (*A.R.* 1.13) with the aborigines from whom in some accounts the Romans were descended. Evander's Arcadian settlement on the Palatine, mentioned by Dionysius (*ibid.* 1.31), figures prominently in *Aeneid* 8, and in Ov. *F.* 2.267–82 is responsible for importing the worship of Pan.

In creating or confirming a new location for the pastoral Vergil has thus brought together a number of hitherto distinct traditions concerning Arcadia: the historical facts of its archaic pastoral economy and devotion to music, the mythological idea of its prosperity as the home of Pan and Hermes, the link with Sicily by way of Arethusa and the association of Arcadians with the origins of the Roman people themselves. However, in view of the importance of the innovation – for henceforth Arcady became *the* pastoral setting – it is worth noting that Vergil's references to it are infrequent and confined to the later poems; which incidentally suggests that the change is due if not to him then to one of his contemporaries. His first mention of *Arcadia* in 4.58–9 is specifically as Pan's country, not as an ideal pastoral setting. Damon's song (8.17ff.) seems notionally situated in Arcadia (27, 28–30), but the place of the herdsmen's recital is left quite vague. Only the last poem is set unequivocally in Arcadia (10.13–15, 31–3).

With the picture of Arcadian herdsmen singing beside the Mincio (13) the essentially mythical character of Vergil's Arcady is clearly revealed. It is not therefore just a remote region of the Peloponnese glamourized by the poetic imagination, but a truly ideal pastoral world, based to be sure upon elements in the various traditions regarding the actual Arcadia and its inhabitants, yet ultimately detached from any specific reality and enjoying an independent existence of its own. As such it could form the object of imaginative contemplation for the poet and his readers or even become identified for the time being with some particular part of the real countryside that was within the poet's own experience or had some special emotional appeal to him – the Mantua of his boyhood, the unspoiled parts of rural Italy or the first humble settlement at Rome.

5   Cf. the description of Daphnis and Menalcas in [Th.] *Id.* 8.3–4 'They were both in their teens, both were skilled in piping, both in singing too.'

   pares...parati: given the play on the two words and the fact that both are preceded by infinitives, the obvious sense is 'equally matched as singers and each ready to respond (to the other)'. However, the dependent infinitive, though common enough with other adjectives (4.54n., 5.2n.), seems rare with *par* (e.g. Pers. 5.6), and this has prompted alternative but less convincing interpretations. The first, already mentioned by D. Servius, is that *pares* and *parati* form a single phrase: 'equal and ready (i.e. equally ready) to sing and to respond'. The second is that both infinitives go with *parati* and *pares* is added predicatively: 'ready to sing and to reply on equal terms'.

6 mihi: the dative of interest with *caper deerrauerat* is a somewhat colloquial variant for *meus caper*. It is emphasized by its position in the sentence, and as the first indication of the narrator's participation in the incident brings a note of authenticity to his report. For a similar departure from the normal impersonal mode of narration cf. [Th.] *Id.* 9.22 'I clapped my hands for the singers and promptly gave each of them a gift.'

a frigore murtos shows the normal construction with *defendere* 'to defend'; cf. Cic. *Font.* 49. When the verb means 'to ward off' the nouns are of course transposed, viz. *a murtis frigus* (cf. Cic. *Off.* 3.74) or the object protected is put in the dative, as in 47 *solstitium pecori defendite* (cf. Hor. *C.* 1.17.3); cf. 4.41n., 6.16n. Pliny, *Nat.* 17.16, mentions the practice of laying straw around young plants to protect them from cold, especially during the spring frosts.

7 uir gregis: cf. [Th.] *Id.* 8.49 'Ho there goat, husband of the white nannies...' and the use of *maritus* in *G.* 3.125, Colum. 7.6.4.

ipse 'even he'. The flock usually stayed in sight of the leader, who kept them together and all moving in the right direction.

deerrauerat shows a common contraction in its first two vowels; cf. Lucr. 1.711, Ov. *M.* 1.77. For the sequence of tenses – pluperfect with historic presents – cf. *A.* 6.171-4.

atque ego Daphnin: the slight rhythmic unevenness produced by the pyrrhic word in the fifth foot (2.26n.) recurs in 21, 47. The use of *atque* rather than a temporal conjunction may have a colloquial flavour, though it is also found in *A.* 4.663.

9 Meliboee: for the name see 1.6n. Daphnis' words in 9-13 have a distinctively colloquial flavour: the ellipse of *est* with *saluos*, *tibi* echoing *mihi* (6) and the internal acc. *quid* with *cessare* 'to pause a while' (10). The supine *potum* (11), being somewhat archaic, perhaps gives the colloquialism as in 9.24 a specifically rustic character.

11   Since Meliboeus is being reassured, the *iuuenci* presumably belong to him in addition to the goats just mentioned. Alternatively he is like Damoetas, who tended Aegon's sheep as well as his own cattle (3.3, 29); or the bullocks may belong to Daphnis the cattleherd, whose prediction that they 'will come back through the meadows of their own accord' would then be a reassurance that he himself will not need to disturb the *otium* of the occasion. The first interpretation is the most likely.

12   **praetexit** 'provides with a fringe': the verb is used with a variety of constructions. The equivalents of *praetexit harundinem ripis* [dat.] *Mincius* and *praetexit harundo ripas* occur respectively in Val. Fl. 3.436 and *A*. 6.4–5. The 'golden line' order is again expressive, with *uiridis...ripas* enclosing *tenera harundine*. For the description of the Mincio cf. *G*. 3.14–15. The river rises in the Alps and flows through Lake Garda to join the Po near Governolo. Both *uiridis* and *harundine* are distinctive, since the river's course through the low-lying country-side near Mantua formed a series of water-meadows and swamps, which were often flooded.

13   **sacra:** the oak was sacred to Jupiter (*G*. 3.332).
   examina is regularly used of swarming bees (*G*. 4.21, Var. *R*. 3.16.29). The grassy banks, bordered by soft reeds, the shady oak and the buzzing bees form a *locus amoenus* fit for relaxation and music-making; cf. 1.50n.

14   **Alcippen:** the name occurs in Th. *Id*. 5.132–3 but not elsewhere in the Eclogues. For Phyllis see 3.76n. They are the 'wives' (*amicae* Serv.) of Corydon and Thyrsis (59). Meliboeus himself, as a bachelor apparently (cf. *Ecl*. 1), has no one at home to perform the urgent tasks while he is absent.

15   **depulsos...clauderet agnos:** the presence of newly-weaned lambs again indicates spring or early summer; cf. 4n. The verb refers either to their segregation from the ewes or more likely, since the ewes would be with the flock, to the need to keep them under shelter in the heat of the day. *agnos* itself might imply that Corydon as well as Thyrsis (3) kept sheep or even be understood summarily for *agnos, haedos, uitulos*. Most likely however the lambs are Meliboeus'. With all

three kinds of animal among his stock (11n.) he emerges as perhaps
the most accomplished and prosperous of the herdsmen present (see
p. 24).

16   et has an adversative force: 'on the other hand'.

Corydon cum Thyrside is to be taken as it were in quotation
marks, in apposition to *certamen*.

17   seria ludo: for the contrast cf. Hor. *S.* 1.1.27. Prosaic *negotia*
form the background even to Arcadian *otium*; but Meliboeus gets his
priorities right.

18   alternis...uersibus: cf. 3.58-9, [Th.] *Id.* 8.30-2 'The lot fell
to clear-voiced Menalcas and he sang first, then Daphnis took up the
answering strain (*amoibaiān*) of pastoral song'.

19   alternos...meminisse uolebant 'the Muses were wanting to
remember amoebaean verses'. To take *alternos* as the subject of
meminisse – 'The Muses wanted them to remember in turns' – would
be clumsy, since *alternis* and *hos, illos* all refer to the verses, not the
singers; it would also imply that the verses were not spontaneous but
prepared beforehand. The Muses were the daughters of Mnemosyne
'Memory' and their name *Moûsai* is etymologically connected with
moneo, memini; cf. *A.* 7.645 *et meministis enim, diuae, et memorare potestis.*
The songs that the Muses inspire a poet to utter are brought forth
from the store of their divine memories and transmitted to him. The
quaintness of this idea and the belief that there is a reference back to
this line in *memini* (69) led to the reading *uolebam*, which Servius explains as *optabam, o Musae, meminisse alternos*.

21   Nymphae...Libēthridēs: to find the Muses addressed as
Nymphae is not surprising in a genre where poetic inspiration is attributed indiscriminately to the *Númphai* of the pastoral landscape
(Th. *Id.* 7.92) and the *Boukolikaì Moûsai* ([Th.] *Id.* 9.28); cf. 2.46n.,
4.1n. That it was unusual, however, is indicated by the fact that
Servius here cites Varro for the view that *ipsae sunt nymphae quae et
Musae.* There was a town Libethrum or Libethra east of Mt Olympus
in the Pierian district, close to the so-called tomb of Orpheus (Paus.
9.30.9), and also a peak called Libethrium in the Helicon complex, on
which there were shrines to both the Muses and the *Númphai Libéthriai*
(Paus. 9.34.4, Strabo 8.410). The Muses themselves are called

Partheni[k]aì [Li]bēthrídes 'virgin Libethrides' by Euphorion (see *A.S.N.P.* 4 (1935) 7); cf. Κούρη Λειβηθρίας . . . Μοῦσα 'Libethrian maiden. . .Muse' (*Orph. fr.* 342K). The retention of Greek *-ēs*, required for the metre, produces an exotic effect.

aut mihi carmen: for the rhythm see 7n. For a pause at the bucolic diaeresis occurring in successive lines (*proxima Phoebi* in 22) cf. 7–8. In all four instances it precedes a rapid enjambement.

22 Codro: the Verona scholia quote some lines from Valgius here, *Codrusque ille canit quali tu uoce canebas | atque solet numeros dicere, Cinna, tuos...*, and suggest that *Codrus* is a pseudonym for Vergil himself. Modern scholars have proposed as alternative identifications Cornificius, Cinna and Messalla Corvinus. Without a context not much can be inferred from Valgius' lines, and Codrus may after all be simply another Arcadian herdsman (cf. 5.11).

proxima Phoebi: cf. Th. *Id.* 1.3 (5.82n.). The neut. pl. may be general 'things second only to Phoebus' verses' or in agreement with *carmina* understood from the preceding line.

23 facit–aut: the normal syllable division *-fa-ci-taut* would give ∪ ∪ – where the metre requires ∪ – –. Unless *facis ut* at Pl. *Amp.* 555 is evidence for a doublet *facīre*, we must assume *facīt* here not as an archaism but by analogy with archaisms like *uidēt, fuīt*. Alternatively the syllabification may have been abnormally affected by the punctuation, viz. *-fa-cĭt-aut*. See 1.38n., 3.97n.

si non possumus omnes 'if we aren't all capable of this'; cf. 8.63n.

24 pendebit fistula pinu: to mark the singer's retirement. Tib. 2.5.29–30 has *pendebatque uagi pastoris in arbore uotum, | garrula siluestri fistula sacra deo*, of an *ex uoto* offering. Both types of dedication occur in epigrams, e.g. *A.P.* 6.1, 2, 4 and 11–16. Theocritus *A.P.* 6.177 may belong to either; Hor. *C.* 3.26.3–6 combines the two. The pine was *grata deum matri* (Ov. *M.* 10.104) but the reference here is more likely to Pan. Pines were a feature of Mount Maenalus (8.22–3); and the pine's mythical origin was in the metamorphosis of Pan's beloved Pitys (Lucian *Dial. Deor.* 272, cf. *Arcadio pinus amica deo* in Prop. 1.18.20). *pinus* like Greek *pítus* and *peúkē* is used for both the stone pine, Pinus Pinea (65), and the Corsican pine, Pinus Laricio (4.38). If Corydon is forced to retire from the art of imitating Pan (2.31) he will hang his pipe on Pan's tree. The 'golden line' word order produces an emphatic juxtaposition of 'pipe' and 'pine'.

25 hedera: ivy was sacred to Bacchus and used both to adorn the thyrsus (5.31n.) and to crown successful poets (3.39n.). In contrast to Corydon, whose modest appeal for divine aid recognized the possibility of failure, Thyrsis demands the applause of the gallery.

crescentem suits the self-confident tone of the quatrain (cf. Hor. *C.* 3.30.8) better than the variant *nascentem*.

26 inuidia rumpantur...ilia Codro: the verb is colloquial in this usage; cf. Prop. 1.8.27, Mart. 9.97.1. But *ilia* adds a coarse note; cf. *ilia rumpens* of sexual excess in Cat. 11.20. Corydon was content to equal Codrus; Thyrsis hopes not only to surpass him but to see him bursting with envy.

27 ultra placitum 'beyond what is acceptable among ourselves', thereby inviting intentionally or accidentally an evil spell; less likely 'beyond what is approved by the gods' and so liable to attract their displeasure to the object praised. For the fear of excessive praise or prosperity cf. Cat. 5.10-13, Th. *Id.* 6.39-40.

baccare: for the uncertain identification of this plant see 4.19n., where it is also coupled closely with ivy. Servius' remark that *herba est ad depellendum fascinum* could be merely an inference from the context, and the reason for Thyrsis' choice of *baccar*, may be that it is less likely to attract malicious envy than the prestigious ivy. The succession of *r* and explosive *t* and *k* sounds gives the line a somewhat harsh tone.

28 uati...futuro contrasts with the more modest *poeta* (25). At 9.33-4 Lycidas disclaims the title of *uates*. The Greek loan words *poiētēs* and *poiēma* were already established in Latin before Ennius (*Ann.* 6V). *uates*, the native Latin word (Var. *L.* 7.36), like its Celtic and Germanic cognates had religious and prophetic as well as poetic associations; cf. *A.* 6.65-6 *sanctissima uates | praescia futuri* and the derivatives *uaticinari* etc. Hence the more prestigious connotations that *uates* sometimes has in contrast to *poeta*, e.g. Prop. 2.10.19, Hor. *C.* 1.1.35.

mala lingua refers not to the evil eye but specifically to a verbal spell or curse. *fascinare* is used of both; e.g. 3.103, Cat. 7.11-12.

29 tibi sc. *dedicat* with *Micon* (30) as subject.

Delia: chaste Artemis Πότνια θηρῶν 'Queen of the wild beasts' was born with her brother Apollo on the island of Delos. She was worshipped as the goddess of woods, waters and mountains, and with her the nymphs of Arcadia (Callim. *H*. 3.87ff.). Although she is the recipient of the hunting trophies here, she is not prominent in the religious life of Arcady, where neither chastity nor the hunt were conspicuous. Hunting, whenever it is mentioned, represents either a specially motivated excursion from the pastoral world proper, as in 2.29 and Th. *Id*. 11.40–1, or as here and in 10.55–7 an infusion of the real countryside into the myth.

29–30 paruos...Micon is Corydon's son or a young friend who has assisted him in the hunt (cf. 3.73). The phrase is often taken to refer to Corydon himself. Menalcas' reference to himself as *mikkós* 'tiny' in *Id*. 8.64 fits the description of the two herdsmen there (3) as ἀνάβω 'teenagers'; but it is hard to see why Corydon should adopt a pseudonym here or, *florens aetate* as he is (4), describe himself as *paruos*, which is surely incongruous even for a modest hunter. The epithet also dissociates Micon from the owner of the *arbustum* in 3.10.

30 ramosa: cf. *A*. 1.190 *cornibus arboreis*.

uiuacis...cerui: the longevity of the stag was proverbial; cf. Hes. fr. 304.1–2MW, Juv. 14.251. For Corydon's dedication cf. Leonidas *A.P*. 6.110.3–4, and Erucius *ibid*. 96 (see 4n.), where Glaucon and Corydon, having sacrificed a steer to Pan, fix its horns to a plane tree as 'a fair ornament for the pastoral god'.

31 si proprium hoc fuerit 'if it turns out that this properly belongs to you', i.e. 'if this is in fact an appropriate offering'. *hoc* refers either to Micon's dedication or to the statue promised in the following line. Diana would presumably show her approval of the present gift by granting further successes, which in turn would be rewarded appropriately. Alternatively the sense may be 'if this turns out to be a permanent possession of mine'; cf. Lucil. 701M *quom sciam nihil esse in uita proprium mortali datum*, also Hor. *S*. 2.6.4–5. *hoc* would then refer to Corydon's success as a hunter, implied in the preceding couplet; cf. *A.P*. 6.10. But this is less likely.

31–2 de marmore tota...stabis is virtually the passive equivalent of *te de marmore ponam*, for which cf. *G*. 3.13. The emphatically placed adj. implies a contrast with a *simulacrum deae acrolithum* (*CIL* 8.8309) in which the extremities were of marble and the body of the statue was in some cheaper material; cf. *A.P.* 12.40.2.

32 puniceo...coturno: statues were often gaudily painted. The high laced boots in red are part of Diana's hunting gear.

euincta is probably middle like *indutus, accinctus* etc., with the acc. as direct object: 'having bound her calves'; cf. the active construction in *A.* 1.337 and Liv. Andron. fr. 29B *et iam purpureo suras include coturno*. Diana is represented as having done for herself what the decorator does for her statue. Alternatively the participle could be passive with the acc. of reference: 'being bound as to her calves', i.e. 'with her calves bound'. See 1.54n.

33 sinum, attested in the masc. gender at Pl. *Curc.* 82, is glossed by Varro, *L.* 5.123, as *uas uinarium grandius...quod sinum maiorem cauationem quam pocula habebat.* The Verona scholiast, after quoting the grammarian Asper's gloss *uas patulum*, objects to the incongruous use of the word for a milk receptacle; but Vergil may have chosen it precisely to make Thyrsis a little absurd.

liba are cakes made of flour, eggs and cheese (Cato *Agr.* 75). Mixed or coated with honey, they were offered to Liber at the Liberalia (Ov. *F.* 3.735–6, 761–2).

Priape: this picturesque god was said to be a native of the Hellespont (*G.* 4.110–11) and the son of Dionysus and Aphrodite (Paus. 9.31.2, Tib. 1.4.7). He presided over the fertility of gardens (Ov. *F.* 1.415) and so of bees (*G. loc. cit.*), and was depicted as a grotesque little figure with a huge erect penis. His statues, painted red, served both as dedications and as scarecrows. His words of solace to the dying Daphnis (Th. *Id.* 1.81–91) are in keeping with the licentious Hellenistic and Latin verses known collectively as *Priapea*. In Tib. 1.4 he is *praeceptor amoris*. In all respects he offers a coarse contrast to Corydon's chaste Delian goddess.

34 exspectare sat est is impudent, even if the garden is in fact a poor one. The *s* and explosive *c p* and *t* sounds suggest an aggressive tone.

35 pro tempore 'in accordance with my present circumstances'; cf. Caes. *B.G.* 5.8.1. The extravagance of a marble statue – capping

Corydon's promise to Diana – is the more incongruous since *Priapi* were usually of cheap stone or wood; cf. Hor. *S.* 1.8.1. The division of the line into two metrically equal parts by the diaeresis – admittedly not a prominent one – after the third foot is an instance of the *metrum Priapeum*, not inappropriate in the context.

35–6 at tu...aureus esto: a ludicrously boastful promise. The peremptory tone of the first two words, which also disrupt the cadential rhythm, and of the concluding imperative, added to the prosaic – indeed colloquial – tone of the vocabulary throughout the quatrain – *sinum, sat est, pro tempore, fetura suppleuerit*, produces an unpleasant contrast to the style of Corydon's dedication.

37 Nereine 'daughter of Nereus': Corydon takes up a mythological theme, the wooing of the sea-nymph Galatea, which is well established in pastoral (e.g. Th. *Idd.* 6, 11, [Bion] 2) and is a major formative influence in *Ecl.* 2, Corydon's Alexis-monologue. The form of the name is strange. *Nerinas...aquas* at Nemes. 4.52 would provide support, if that reading were secure. Latin poets usually follow the normal Greek patronymic form *Nēreis, -id-*, e.g. Cat. 64.15, Tib. 1.5.45, with *Nereia* as a rare variant, e.g. *A.* 9.102. In Greek itself *Nērēínē* unlike *Ōkeanínē* etc. is late and rare, e.g. Opp. *Hal.* 1.386. If Haupt's conjecture *Nērēínē* is right at Cat. 64.28, then it is just possible that Vergil wrote *Nereine* with contraction of *ēí* to *eî*.

thymo: although the shrub flowered for only a short time in early summer, it was valued by apiarists both for the fragrance that it imparted to the honey and for its medicinal properties in the hive (*G.* 4.169, 241, 270).

38 hedera...alba: see 3.39. It was this variety (Plin. *Nat.* 16.147) that was used for the poet's garland (25). The contrast between the two colour-adjectives is relevant here: *albus* has the slightly wider chromatic range, being used not only of 'white' but 'pale' shades of green, grey etc., *candidus* connotes greater intensity, 'glowing', 'gleaming', and is therefore more emotive; cf. 5.56. The form, though not the content, of 37–8 recalls Th. *Id.* 11.19–21: 'O white Galatea, why do you rebuff your lover, you who are whiter than pressed milk to look at, softer than a lamb, friskier than a young calf and sleeker than an unripe grape?' The association is underlined by the accumulation of Greek sounds in *Nereine, Galatea, thymo, Hyblae, cycnis*.

39   repetent praesaepia: i.e. at sundown. The significance of the alliterations in the line is hard to specify.

tauri: in playing the role of Polyphemus he still retains his identity; cf. *Corydonos* (40). But as a goatherd (3) he is putting on airs in referring to these bulls, even though he does not explicitly claim ownership of them. Polyphemus was usually depicted as a shepherd, e.g. Th. *Id.* 6.10, 11.12.

40   cura: of the lover's concern for the beloved; cf. 10.22.

uenito: so Polyphemus in Th. *Id.* 11.42-4 invites Galatea to spend the night with him. The so-called future imperative < *ueni* 'come' + **tō* 'after this', the ablative of an old demonstrative pronoun. It is less peremptory than the simple imperative, e.g. *huc ades* in 2.45.

41   immo announces Thyrsis' intention of again outdoing Corydon.

uidear: *est* in the conditional clause (43) confirms that the subjunctive is volitional in answer to *uenito*, rather than potential.

Sardoniis...herbis: the celery-leaved crowfoot, Ranunculus Sceleratus, though not peculiar to Sardinia, was thought to be responsible both for the proverbial 'Sardonic smile' of those who ate it (Paus. 10.17.13) and for the acrid flavour of *Sardum mel* (Hor. *A.P.* 375). The phrase contrasts precisely with Corydon's in 37.

42   rusco: butcher's broom or box holly, Ruscus Aculeatus, is a short shrub with sharp spines and red berries, which flowers towards the end of winter. According to D. Servius it was commonly used to make besoms. The contrast in colour and texture with the swan's down in Corydon's comparison is neatly brought out by the antithesis of *candidior* (38) and *horridior*.

proiecta...alga 'sea-weed cast up on the shore' was considered worthless (Hor. *S.* 2.5.8, *C.* 3.17.10). Again the contrast with Corydon's phrase in 38 is precise, even to the implicit antithesis between *alba* and the dark brown hue of the sea-weed. Vergil has preserved the principle of responsion while assigning to Thyrsis a triple comparison which contrasts with Corydon's both in its repellent imagery and in its concern not with praise of Galatea but with her feelings for him.

43   toto iam longior anno est: cf. Ov. *Her.* 18.25 *septima nox agitur, spatium mihi longius anno,* Th. *Id.* 12.2 'those who desire grow old in a day', Dioscorides *A.P.* 12.171.3–4. Unlike Corydon he is not content to wait for nightfall, when the cattle would return of their own accord from the pastures. The sequence of monosyllables, disturbing the even flow of the line, perhaps reflects his agitation.

44 si quis pudor: the cattle should feel ashamed, either for keeping their master from his love-making or, less likely, for lingering to watch him while he is at it in broad day-light, like the goats who spied on Menalcas in 3.8.

iuuenci: Thyrsis is a shepherd (3), so he too is boasting – even more than Corydon (39) in that he presumes to direct the cattle.

45 muscosi fontes: cf. Cat. 68.58 *riuos muscoso prosilit e lapide.*

somno mollior herba: cf. Lucr. 5.1392 *prostrati in gramine molli* and *G.* 2.470 *mollesque sub arbore somni.* For the imagery of the couplet as a whole cf. Lacon's setting for the contest in Th. *Id.* 5.31–4 'you'll sing more pleasantly sitting here under the wild olive and these trees. The water drips cool here, there's grass growing here and this couch (of leaves)' and 50–1 'And look, you'll walk on lambskins here and fleeces softer than sleep.' For the suggestion of luxury in the last phrase cf. *Id.* 15.125: 'rich purple coverlets above, softer than sleep'. The slow spondaic rhythms from *muscosi* to *rara* depict the languor of the scene.

46 rara...umbra 'chequered shade'; cf. 5.7. The phrase in this variation on 'golden line' word order expressively encloses the scene.

uiridis...arbutus: cf. Hor. *C.* 1.1.21 in a similar context of rural *otium*. For *arbutus* itself see 3.82n. If *arbutus* with the vocatives *fontes* and *herba* provides the subject for *defendite* (47), the line must be equivalent to *et, arbute uiridis, quae ea* [sc. *fontes et herbam*] *rara umbra tegis.* Nom. for voc. is common enough, but the transposition of persons from *ea tegis* to *uos...tegit* is very strange. Easier syntax is got by taking *uos* as voc., referring to some unspecified features of the landscape and antecedent to *quae*, the object of *tegit.* But the inversion of *quae uos* is then awkward and the sense less satisfactory.

47 solstitium 'midsummer heat': for the metonymy cf. Hor. *Ep.* 1.11.18 and the similar use of *bruma* 'midwinter cold' in Prop. 1.8.10.

pecori defendite: for the construction see 6n.

47–8 aestas torrida: from *rara uiridis* (46) to *torrida* (48) the rhythm is markedly dactylic. The note of urgency is intensified by the rugged cadence to 47 (cf. 7n.) and the abrupt pauses at diaeresis after *defendite* (bucolic) and *torrida*. 'Fair summer scorches' (Th. *Id.* 6.16), but Corydon's image of scorching heat, introduced as a contrast to the cool shade, is immediately redressed by the detail of the ripening grapes. The parched landscape implied by the epithet contrasts with the green hues explicit in *uiridis* and implied in *muscosi* and *in palmite gemmae*.

48 lento 'pliant'; see 1.4n. and cf. *lenta...uitis* (3.38). Servius' note *bene tarde frondere uites commemorat in Venetia* implies that he had *lento* in his text. The variant *laeto* (< *leto* < *lento*) would not be inappropriate: 'joyous', 'happy' or in its original sense 'fruitful', 'flourishing'; cf. *G.* 1.1. *laetas segetes*, 2.262 *laetum...uitis genus*, also *laeto imbri* (60).

palmite 'vine shoot': *palmites uitium sarmenta appellantur quod in modum palmarum humanarum uirgulas quasi digitos edunt* (P. Fest. 220M; the definition seems sound, even if the etymology is not).

gemmae 'buds', 'eyes' of a plant, especially the vine (*G.* 2.335). In spite of ancient opinions, e.g. Cic. *Or.* 81, this seems to have been the original sense of the word.

49 focus is the source of winter heat as *fontes* (45) of summer cool. For the contrast between the comforts of summer and winter see [Th.] *Id.* 9.9–21, where however the details are quite different.

49–50 pingues: the image of 'pitchy', 'resinous' pine logs contrasts with the seductive *somno mollior herba* (45).

plurimus...semper...adsidua make Thyrsis' lines more boastful, since they represent not the bounties of nature but his own domestic energies. There was no chimney, so the smoke escaped either through a hole in the roof or, as *postes fuligine nigri* suggests here, through the open door. With the pine logs constantly burning Thyrsis' house must have been a grimy, stuffy place, and the colour contrast between *nigri* and *uiridis* (46) is therefore significant.

52 numerum: sc. *ouium uel similium* (D. Serv.). The wolf is not troubled by mere numbers but will attack the flock when and where he chooses. Alternatively the sense may be that the wolf does not care about the tally, which when the shepherds come to make it at the end of the day (6.85) will reveal his depredations. Finally, since *numerus* is often used later (e.g. Tac. *Agr.* 18) of a detachment of men, the reference could be to a band of hunters whom the wolf is confident that he can elude. On the whole the first interpretation seems best.

torrentia 'seething', 'raging', cf. *torrida* (48). The comparisons express defiance but their terms cannot be followed through effectively, since the raging North Wind naturally belongs with the attacking wolf and the rising torrents, and Thyrsis huddled over his fire sheltering from *frigora* 'the icy blasts' has more in common with the terrorized flock and the threatened river banks.

53ff The two preceding themes of love and the seasons are now brought together in the 'Where'er you walk' variation of the sympathy figure (p. 9): the presence of the beloved brings prosperity to the lover's world, absence or reluctance a barren desolation; cf. [Th.] *Id.* 8.41–8 'There the ewe bears twins and the she-goats too, bees fill the hives and oaks grow taller, where fair Milon's footsteps go. But if ever he departs, the shepherd there is withered and the pastures too . . .'; Meleager *A.P.* 12.159.5–6 'If ever you cast a clouded eye on me, I see winter; if your glance is gay, sweet spring is in bloom.'

53 stant 'stand erect'. Applied to slender junipers, the verb suggests that the air is calm and that the trees themselves are flourishing.

iuniperi et castaneae hirsutae: the two hiatuses without correption together with the spondaic ending produce a concentration of metrical abnormalities unparalleled in Vergil even by 2.24 and *G.* 1.437 *Glauco et Panopeae et Inoo Melicertae.* For what is remarkable here is the combination of native Latin words to create a distinctly Greek metrical effect. The versification, whether deliberately or not, is thus symptomatic of the passage as a whole: the Greek form, Theocritus' sympathy figure, has been given new Latin content.

hirsutae, whether or not it refers to both trees, describes the flourishing foliage rather than, as Servius thought, the prickly covering of the chestnuts.

54 iacent, which in another context might represent the farmer's neglect or indolence, here implies the sudden and unexpected prodigality of nature; cf. Th. *Id.* 7.143–5 'Everything smelled of rich summer and the fruit season. Pears rolled in abundance at our feet and apples by our sides.'

sua quaeque...poma 'their own particular fruit'. Attempts have been made to normalize the syntax by emending to *quaque* or by reading the first word as a monosyllable *sụā* to agree with *arbore*; cf. *sụo* in Lucr. 1.1022, *genụa* in *A.* 5.432. However, clear parallels for the construction occur at Cic. *Fin.* 5.46 *quia cuiusque partis naturae et in corpore et in animo sua quaeque uis sit*, Liv. 3.22.6 *equites item suae cuique parti post principia conlocat*. The association of *castaneae* and *poma* in the couplet recalls the gifts offered by Corydon to Alexis in 2.52-3.

55 omnia nunc rident: the personification, common elsewhere (4.20n.), here enhances the sympathy figure. All nature rejoices with Corydon at the coming of Alexis. Without him the *torrida aestas* would become barren and desolate.

55-6 formonsus Alexis montibus his: a clear allusion to 2.1-5, which, while it does not however justify imposing the situation depicted there on the present quatrain, certainly associates the two Corydons; cf. 37n. *montibus* cannot belong to a Mantuan location; cf. 12n.

56 abeat: the subjunctive implies that the event is unlikely.

57 aret ager takes up Corydon's final image to develop the converse figure: the rapid spread of drought in the *aestas torrida*, expressed here in the sequence of swift dactyls, will be dispelled by Phyllis' return.

uitio...aeris: *id est pestilentia corrupti aeris affligitur* (Serv.). *morbidus aer* is discussed by Lucretius, 6.1096–1102: *uis omnis morborum pestilitasque* either descends from the sky or rises from the earth *ubi putorem nacta est | intempestiuis pluuiisque et solibus icta*. But the reference here is rather to seasonal (in contrast to *intempestiuis*) drought produced by the imbalance between hot and cold, wet and dry. *aer* the vital element (Cic. *N.D.* 2.91, Plin. *Nat.* 2.10) is both hot and wet, in contrast to *aether* and *aqua*. An excessively hot summer by drawing too much moisture from *aer* diminishes its vital potency, and the resultant *uitium* can be remedied only by *laetus imber* (60).

moriens...herba contrasts with *somno mollior herba* (45) in Corydon's picture of summer shade.

58 Liber: an Italian god of fertility and especially wine, closely associated with Libera and Ceres (*G.* 1.7) and later assimilated to the

Greek Dionysus, cf. Cic. *N.D.* 2.62. The name is more likely to be connected with *libare*, Greek *leibein*, than with *liber* 'free', but the etymology is quite uncertain.

inuidit extends the sympathy figure to include even the gods. Offended by Phyllis' absence, Bacchus has begrudged the hills their shady vines – a contrast with Corydon's image of the budding vines in 47. The perfect tense indicates result: a state of desolation.

59 nostrae: probably for *meae*, indicating that Phyllis is Thyrsis' *coniunx* (14). For though Corydon's praise of her in the next quatrain might suggest that the plural is meant literally, he could simply be taking up the theme of his competitor's lines, as Menalcas did from Damoetas in 3.78.

uirebit echoes the *uiridis...arbutus* of Corydon's cool shade (46). There may be a play here on the meaning of *Phyllis* (3.78n.).

60 Iuppiter: the sky-father (3.61n.). The fructifying seed of Jove, following the reference to *Liber*, underlines the association between the sexual fulfilment of love and the fertility of nature that is implicit in the 'Where'er you walk' figure. In view of the parallel positions of *Iuppiter* and *Liber* here it is possible that they are being identified with each other (cf. *Iuppiter Liber* = Ζεῦς Ἐλευθέριος in *CIL.* 1.2.756); but this is not very likely.

laeto 'bringing joy and fertility', cf. 48n.

plurimus 'in abundance'; cf. *G.* 1.187.

61 populus Alcidae gratissima: Hercules' mother was Alcumena the daughter of Alcaeus. His father was not Alcumena's husband Amphitryo but the ubiquitous Jupiter. So *Amphitryoniades* is a somewhat imprecise patronymic for Hercules as well as metrically ponderous (cf. *A.* 8.214). *Alcides* 'grandson of Alcaeus' was more often used (e.g. *A.* 8.203, 219). It was no doubt also preferred for its metrical neatness and its association with Greek *alkē* 'strength'. It was the white poplar, *leukē*, that Hercules was supposed to have introduced into Greece (Paus. 5.14.2). Its Homeric name *akherōis* (*Il.* 13.389) may have suggested the other tale, recounted here by Servius: Pluto carried off Leuce to the underworld and on her death caused the white poplar to spring up beside the Acheron; Hercules on his way back from the underworld bound his head with a garland plucked from the tree. The garland is coupled with the 'fruit of Dionysus' in Th. *Id.* 2.120–1.

uitis Iaccho: cf. Thyrsis' reference to Liber in 58.

62 murtus: myrtle is a common seaside plant in Italy (*G.* 2.112) and is said by Servius to have covered the new-born Venus as she rose naked from the sea.

laurea: for the connection with Phoebus see 3.63n. In 2.54–5 the myrtle and the bay are coupled for their *suauis...odores.*

63 The conclusion to the rustic analogy places the humble hazel, which Phyllis admires, above even the trees that are esteemed by the goddess of love and the patron of shepherds and their music. Like Amaryllis in 1.5 Phyllis is given an almost divine status as the inspiration of rustic song.

65 fraxinus...pulcherrima: the ash, Fraxinus Excelsior, matches the poplar in height (cf. *ingens* in *G.* 2.65). The adjective, placed before the bucolic diaeresis, rhythmically balances Corydon's *gratissima* (61).

pinus in hortis is clearly the smaller variety, the Pinus Pinea; see 24n.

66 populus in fluuiis: poplars are especially associated with wet land (Hom. *Od.* 17.208, Plin. *Nat.* 16.77). Black poplars, αἴγειροι, and elms grow near the sacred spring in the *locus amoenus* of Th. *Id.* 7.136–8 (1.50n.).

abies in montibus 'the silver fir on the hills' completes the list of tall trees, associated not like Corydon's plants with different gods but with different parts of the landscape: forests, gardens, streams and hills.

67 saepius...me...reuisas contrasts somewhat coarsely with Corydon's less self-centred praise of Phyllis.

Lycida: the name of one of the participants in Th. *Id.* 7, [Bion] 2 and *Ecl.* 9, also of the loved one in Bion fr. 9.10. The amorous catalogue in the present poem, even if we omit the mythical Nereid Galatea (37), includes Alexis (55), Phyllis (59, 63), Lycidas (67) and also Alcippe (14), who is probably Corydon's *coniunx*, even though she is not deemed worthy of a poetic tribute. There is thus once more a suggestion of the promiscuity of Arcadian love and in the final sequence – Alexis and

Phyllis, Phyllis and Lycidas – a positive assertion of Arcadian bisexuality (2.15n., 10.37).

68   pinus in hortis: the repetition is less elegant than Corydon's variations, *sua laurea Phoebo* (62), *nec laurea Phoebi* (64). Moreover the comparison of Lycidas to a series of tall trees, however handsome, is less effective than the more complex comparisons of Corydon's quatrain, and the concluding line is relatively flat; for in spite of the formal similarity of *fraxinus in siluis cedat* to *nec murtus uincet corulos* (64), the latter transforms the analogic pattern, already complete in *Phyllis amat corulos* (63), into a far grander tribute to the beloved.

69   haec memini 'this is what I recall', coming after the abrupt ending to the contest, may imply what *haec tantum memini* would certify, that there were other quatrains which Meliboeus has forgotten. But we need not assume that these would have revealed Corydon's superiority more decisively. The grounds for the verdict, indicated in the details of the preceding notes and summarized below, are clear enough.

70   ex illo...tempore: cf. [Th.] *Id.* 8.91 'and from this time Daphnis became foremost among the shepherds', a final reminder of the silent presence at this Arcadian contest of the great singing herdsman himself (1). There is no indication however that he pronounced the judgement.

Corydon, Corydon est...nobis: the contest was *Corydon cum Thyrside* (16); but since then the Arcadians have heard nothing but 'Corydon, Corydon'. Servius took the second *Corydon* to mean *uictor, nobilis supra omnes* 'Corydon has been a Corydon indeed for us'; but it is unlikely that the name could be used like *Tityrus* in 6.4, 8.55 or *Orpheus* in 8.55 in such a generic sense.

Here Vergil has returned to conventional pastoral, specifically to the singing competition of *Idd.* 5, 6, 8, 9 and *Ecl.* 3. In contrast to the earlier Eclogue there is virtually no translation or paraphrase of Theocritean material, and the Theocritean themes and figures employed are handled with confident independence. Servius declared that *ecloga haec paene tota Theocriti est; nam et ipsam transtulit et multa ad eam de aliis congessit.* The last statement we cannot evaluate and Servius himself nowhere gives detailed specification of these *congesta*, but comparison with the four relevant Idylls of the Theocritean corpus (cf. the notes on 2, 5, 38, 45 etc.) shows that Servius' notion of *translatio* was somewhat imprecise. On the other hand there is none of the clumsy intrusion of contemporary realities like the praise of Pollio in 3.84ff. The pastoral myth is sustained throughout. The opening scene evokes the prosperity of the idyllic landscape. The singers are for the first time explicitly 'Arcadian' (4n.); yet the scene itself is located beside Vergil's native Mincio, the idealized memory of which contributes, no doubt, to the enrichment of the myth. Daphnis the archetypal pastoral musician presides in silence over the contest, and after *Ecl.* 5 this reversion to his traditional role is symptomatic of Vergil's temporary return, as in *Ecl.* 8, to a more orthodox conception of the genre. The realities of country life are not however suppressed, and we are made firmly aware that the *otium* that the herdsmen enjoy as the necessary setting for their music-making is only an interlude in their more menial routine.

The contest itself is equal in length to that in *Ecl.* 3 (48 lines); but the choice of quatrains rather than couplets, inspired perhaps by the elegiac quatrains of *Id.* 8, which Vergil obviously had in mind at a number of points in the poem, enables each theme to be developed more extensively. The effect is almost of six complementary pairs of epigrams. The themes are all conventional enough: initial dedications to patrons divine and human; pious offerings to Diana and Priapus; variations on a traditional theme, the wooing of Galatea; the comforts of summer and winter, praise of loved ones expressed in the 'Where'er you walk' figure and a pair of rustic analogies. But the presentation of these themes is subtle and concentrated and the progression from one to the next smoother and more articulated than in *Ecl.* 3. The singers are finely characterized through their quatrains: the arrogant and self-assertive Thyrsis contrasted with a gentle modest Corydon reminiscent of the pathetic lover of *Ecl.* 2. Here and there a slight coarseness in Thyrsis' language (e.g. 26) or versification (e.g. 35) stands out against Corydon's uniform elegance. Sometimes Thyrsis' figures are inept (51–2, 65–8) and his imagery more repellent (41–2), even where (49–50) it is intended to please. It is true that Corydon who sings first is able to preempt the best of the figures and images while Thyrsis, compelled by the rules to respond in kind, has the more difficult task. However, the advantage is bestowed by Vergil himself and the order of the quatrains could after all have been reversed. (In *Id.* 8 it is the respondent Daphnis who wins.) In any case the difference between the two singers, a matter of accumulated detail, must not be exaggerated. Both are true Arcadians (4); Thyrsis shows considerable ingenuity in the construction of his responses and it is no disgrace to have been defeated by a Corydon in such superlative form.

In contrast to *Ecl.* 3 the writing is more subtle, the texture richer and more delicate, the resources of pastoral figure and imagery are deployed with fine economy and the modulations of the hexameter rhythm characteristic of the poet's mature verse technique.

ECLOGUE VIII

1 Musam 'music': for the metonymy see 1.2n. The accusative is held in suspense until *dicemus* (5).

Damonos et Alphesiboei: for the mention of herdsmen's names in the first line of an Eclogue see 1.1n. For the names see 3.17, 23 and 5.73.

2 immemor herbarum: emphatically displaced to draw attention to what in normal circumstances would be a symptom of grief (5.26) or disease (*G.* 3.498) in the cattle.

est mirata: the personification, as in 6.30, indicates the supernatural power that music has to awaken a sympathetic response in all nature.

iuuenca may mean that both singers herd cattle; for the goats in 33 belong only to the *persona* of Damon's song.

3 certantis is the only indication that what follows is a contest and not just a recital as in Th. *Id.* 6 or in *Ecl.* 5.

lynces like the lions of 5.27 do not belong to the Italian or Sicilian countryside. In Greece they were found among other places in the Pindus range in Thessaly (Xen. *Cyn.* 11.1) and on Mount Maenalus in Arcadia (Callim. *H.* 3.88–9). Their traditional associations in mythology – with Pan (*h. Hom.* 19.24), the magic of Apollo's music (Eur. *Alc.* 579) and Bacchus (Ov. *M.* 3.668) – are appropriate enough to the pastoral.

stupefactae: cf. *quin ipsae stupuere domus...Leti* of Orpheus' song in
G. 4.481.

4 mutata is probably passive like *stupefactae*, representing the effect
of the magic. The acc. may be taken either as one of reference (cf. *A.*
1.658 *faciem mutatus et ora Cupido*) or as direct object to *requierunt*, which
is transitive in Prop. 2.22.25 and Calv. *Io* fr. 13M (cited by D. Servius
here) *sol quoque perpetuos meminit requiescere cursus.* Alternatively *mutata*
may be middle (cf. the deponent *est mirata* (2) and see 1.54–5n.) with
cursus as direct object and *requierunt* in its normal intransitive sense;
but this is less likely. The phenomenon is cited as an adynaton in Eur.
Med. 410, Hor. *C.* 1.29.10–12, and as a feat of magic in Val.Fl. 6.443
(Medea), Hor. *C.* 1.12.9–10 (Orpheus). The 'golden line' word order
perhaps suggests the pattern of the eddying currents.

5 The repetition of the two names brings us back to the starting
point after surveying the whole Orphean scene: the domestic animals,
then the wild beasts, finally inanimate nature all captivated by the
herdsmen's singing.

6 The dedication breaks the continuity between the announcement
of the contest's magical effects (1–5) and the description of its setting
(14–16). It is almost certainly addressed to Pollio. Servius and others
have believed Augustus to be the addressee. Octavian was certainly
campaigning in Illyria in 35–3 B.C. (App. *Ill.* 16–28, Dio 49.38),
whence he would have returned to Italy by the route implied in 6–7.
He is said to have tried his hand at writing tragedy, but the date of
this essay is unknown and it seems to have been taken light-heartedly
by his friends (Suet. *Aug.* 85). To see a serious reference to it in the
lavish praise of line 10 would be fanciful, if not perverse. Moreover
there is no evidence that Octavian was even indirectly one of Vergil's
patrons when the Eclogues were first published. By contrast Pollio had
been Vergil's patron in *Ecl.* 2 and 3 (cf. 11–12 here) and himself en-
joyed a reputation as a tragedian. He held a proconsular command in
Macedonia in 39 B.C. and although the coast of Illyria and the mouth
of the Timavo would be a very roundabout route for his return to
Italy, that is not to say he did not take it.

tu mihi...superas: the dative, placed close to the subject, indicates the poet's personal concern for his patron's return. For *superas*
'pass by on sea' cf. *A.* 1.244, Nep. *Them.* 3.3.

magni...Timaui: the river Timavo flows into the Gulf of Trieste not far east of Aquileia. About 1½ kilometres inland a number of underground streams (cf. *A.* 1.245) emerge from high cliffs – perhaps the *saxa* here – to form the *lacus Timaui* (Liv. 41.1). Most of the emergent streams appear to have been saline, whence the river was locally known as 'the source and mother of the sea' (Strabo 5.214 citing Polybius). *magni* therefore refers to its reputation rather than its size.

7 Illyrici...aequoris 'Adriatic Sea'. *Illyricum* was commonly used not only of the administrative province (Liv. 45.26) but also of the whole area from the coast between Venetia and Epirus eastward to the borders of Moesia and Macedonia (Strabo 7.313).

legis 'sail past', 'skirt': cf. *G.* 2.44, Liv. 21.51.7. For the related sense 'to pass over' see *A.* 3.706.

en erit umquam: for the slightly uneven cadence resulting from the fifth-foot pyrrhic cf. 48, 102 and 2.26n.

8 tua dicere facta: cf. 4.54. The reference here is probably specific, namely to Pollio's victory over the Parthini, for which he celebrated a triumph on 25 October 39 B.C. (*CIL.* 1.1. p. 50, Dio 48.41.7). As in 6.61–2, Vergil artfully excuses himself from writing up the military exploits of his addressee.

9 en erit ut liceat: although Horace in the mid-30s (*S.* 1.10.42–3) refers to Pollio's tragedies (for which see 3.84n.) as if they were already well known, this phrase suggests that not all of them were yet published. It may seem an odd compliment to a friend to hope that the fame of his poetry will be spread throughout the world by one's own verses; but a short pastoral is after all likely to travel more swiftly than a full-scale drama.

10 coturno 'the buskin' or 'raised boot' (Greek *kóthornos*, cf. 7.32) was commonly used by metonymy for 'the tragic genre or style', e.g. Prop. 2.34.41, as the 'slipper' *soccus* was for comedy; cf. Horace's famous pun, *hunc socci cepere pedem grandesque coturni* (*A.P.* 80).

11 principium: sc. *mihi est*, cf. *Il.* 9.97–8 'In you will I end and from you will I begin, since you are king of many peoples' (Nestor to Agamemnon), Th. *Id.* 17.1 (3.80n.). If Vergil means what he says, 'I shall conclude my pastorals as I began them, with you, Pollio', then

the present poem must have been intended to be his last in the genre
(see p. 18).

desinam. accipe ($- \cup \cup - \cup \cup$) is remarkable for the non-elision of
-*am*. The punctuation may have allowed the abnormal syllable
division -*si-nam-ac-ci*-, which also produces a bucolic diaeresis. The
heavy syllable *nam* would then be reduced by correption, leaving a
short (possibly nasalized) *a* in hiatus with *ac*-. For hiatus with correption see 108n. Less probably the non-elision may reflect an abnormally
distinct pronunciation of -*m* (Prisc. 2.29.15), *si-na-mac-ci* with no
correption required in the first *a*. For the rareness of elision in cretic
words see 3.84n. Of the 17 instances of non-elision in the Eclogues
twelve occur, equally distributed, in 2, 3 and 8. This may be evidence
that the poem is a reworking of early material written at the same time
as *Ecl.* 2 and 3. The variant reading *desinet* removes the metrical
abnormality but is more awkward grammatically, since we should
then have to understand *principium Musae est, tibi Musa desinet* or the
like. The effect of the diaereses after *te, tibi* and *accipe* is abrupt and
disjointed.

11–12 iussis...coepta tuis suggests that Pollio had commissioned
more than one poem (though *carmina* is used of one poem in 5.14).
Line 8 does not prove that the commission was for an epic tribute and
Pollio may have actually specified the Theocritean subjects of *Id.* 1
and 2. What Vergil has given him at any rate is a *retractatio* of these
two *carmina* in a single pastoral piece.

13 hederam...lauros: although both were traditional symbols of
poetry, there is here a contrast between the poet's ivy (7.25) and the
triumphant general's bay (Ov. *M.* 1.560–1). Pollio, poet and general,
will be crowned with both, and Vergil's lines will contribute a
specifically poetic honour to the poet rather than to the general.

serpere: the meaning is reflected in the word order of the two lines.

14–15 frigida...umbra...ros...tenera...herba: though the
setting is left vague, the three details suggest the spring season. The
time of day is precisely indicated (cf. *G.* 3.326) and leads directly into
the setting of Damon's song.

16 incumbens tereti...oliuae 'leaning on a smooth olive staff'.
The verb could of course be used of leaning against a tree, e.g. Ov. *M.*

6.335, and the goatherd in Th. *Id.* 3.38 declares 'I shall sing leaning
like this against the pine tree'; but the adjective could hardly refer to
an olive trunk, which is not normally, as Servius imagines, *rotundum et
oblongum, ut columna*. Damon is leaning on a smoothed *baculum de oliua*;
cf. Ov. *Pont.* 1.8.52 *ipse uelim baculo pascere nixus oues*. This was probably
a shepherd's crook (5.87n.), rather than a plain staff or the short
curved throwing-stick also used by herdsmen (Th. *Id.* 4.49), though
this too was often made of wild olive (*Id.* 7.18–19, 128–30).

17   nascere: the verb is used of the rising sun in *G.* 1.441, of the new
moon in Hor. *C.* 3.23.2.

praeque diem ueniens age 'and coming before lead out the day'.
prae is used not prepositionally, which would require *die*, but adver-
bially, as in Pl. *Am.* 543 *abi prae, Sosia*. The archaic tmesis *prae...ueniens*
is appropriate in a prayer. Although *praeuenio* is transitive in Sall. *Iug.*
71.5 and Liv. 8.16.13, *diem* here is better taken as direct object to *age*.
The usual sense of *agere* 'to drive' would be incongruous with *prae
ueniens*. For the meaning 'to lead' cf. *A.* 12.78 and Greek *ágein*. Lucifer
'bearer of light' leads forth the day as the herdsmen their cattle; cf.
A. 2.801–2 *surgebat Lucifer...ducebatque diem*.

almum: though often used of daylight, e.g. *A.* 5.64, Hor. *C.* 4.7.7,
the epithet here has a pathetic irony. For the benefits that this new
day will bring to pastures and herds are in contrast with the disaster
it threatens for the goatherd-lover in whose person Damon sings; like
Corydon in *Ecl.* 2 the goatherd is alienated from the normal pattern
of nature by his thwarted passion.

18   coniugis: though sometimes used proleptically of the betrothed,
e.g. *A.* 3.331, the word refers here to an 'Arcadian' wife, with whom
vows had been exchanged (19–20) but no formal union solemnized,
as Nysa's attachment to Mopsus will shortly be (26, 29).

indigno 'unworthy' either because it was fickle – taking the
genitive as subjective, or less likely because it was not properly requited – taking the genitive as objective.

deceptus, when we first come to it, seems to refer to Lucifer, and
the temporary ambiguity brings out Nysa's impiety in flouting the
pledges made before the gods (19–20, 35).

19   For the lover's complaint cf. Dido's words in *A.* 4.520–1.

20 extrema moriens...hora contrasts bitterly with *nascere* and *diem almum*; see 17n. There may also be overtones of the traditional antithesis between the recurrent life-cycle of the rising and setting sun and man's once-for-all journey through life from dawn to nightfall (Cat. 5.5–6, cf. *Epit. Bion.* 99–104, Hor. *C.* 4.7.12–16). See 58n. For the whole couplet cf. Cat. 64.190–1 *iustam a diuis exposcam prodita multam | caelestumque fidem postrema comprecer hora.*

21 Maenalios: Mount Maenalus is in Arcadia and a favourite haunt of Pan (Th. *Id.* 1.124); the sorrows of love are an Arcadian theme. The apostrophe to Maenalus in the following lines suggests but does not guarantee (see 30n.) a setting for the goatherd's lament. It certainly need not be taken to indicate where Damon is singing (see 3n.). For this refrain cf. Th. *Id.* 1.64 etc. ἄρχετε βουκολικᾶς, Μοῖσαι φίλαι, ἄρχετ' ἀοιδᾶς 'Begin, dear Muses, begin a pastoral song', from the Daphnis-dirge; also *Epit. Bion.* 8 etc. All three refrains exhibit the same metrical pattern (– ∪ ∪ – ∪ ∪ – – repeated) and divide their songs into unequal stanzas.

tibia, like the Greek *aulós*, was a reed instrument akin to the clarinet or oboe, usually made of cane or box-wood (Plin. *Nat.* 16.164–5, Ov. *F.* 6.697). In spite of Lucr. 5.1385, Th. *A.P.* 9.433 it has less specifically pastoral associations than the Pan-pipes, *fistula* (1.2n.). It was said to have been invented by Athena (Bion. fr. 10.7) and was employed regularly at concerts, funerals and sacrifices. *tibiae* were frequently played in pairs by one person. The murmuring *m*-alliteration of the refrain perhaps evokes their plaintive tone; cf. *dulcisque querelas* (Lucr. 4.584). For the alternation of pipe and voice see 5.14n.

22 argutum 'clear' (7.1n.).

pinus...loquentis: cf. Mosch. fr. 1.8, Cat. 4.11–12.

24 calamos non passus inertis: the play on the two senses of *iners* 'artless' and 'idle' concisely alludes to Pan's reaction to the metamorphosis of Syrinx. When the nymph was changed into a marsh-reed and her sighs replaced by the sighing of the wind in the reeds the frustrated god was captivated *arte noua uocisque...dulcedine* (Ov. *M.* 1.709) and taking the reeds made them into Pan-pipes. The monuments to the Arcadian god's unhappy love affairs, Maenalian pines (7.24n.) and Pan-pipes, enclose the reference to *pastorum... amores* in 23.

26 Mopso Nysa: *Mopsus* was the name of the singer of the Daphnis-lament in *Ecl.* 5. *Nysa* does not appear in earlier extant pastoral unless it is in the corrupt [Bion] 2.31. It was the name of a Bithynian princess (Suet. *Iul.* 49) and of Dionysus' birthplace (*h.Hom.* 1.8).

datur: sc. *nuptum*, 'is being given in marriage by her family'; cf. *ducitur* (29). Formal marriage, duly solemnized, belongs to the real countryside, not to Arcady (p. 24).

27 iungentur...grypes: gryphons were mythical creatures with a lion's body and an eagle's head and wings, believed to inhabit the Rhipaean mountains in the remote north (Hdt. 3.116). The Greek nom. pl. -*ēs*, guaranteed by the metre, gives an appropriately exotic tone. The verb refers to sexual union rather than, as in 3.91, to yoking for haulage. For the adynaton of incongruous matings cf. Ar. *P.*1076 'until a wolf marries a sheep', Hor. *C.* 1.33.8 *iungentur capreae lupis.* The marriage of Mopsus and Nysa will be a symptom of nature awry.

28 timidi: *damma* 'doe', 'hind' is usually feminine; the masculine here, though paralleled in *G.* 3.539, is noted as unusual by Quintilian, 9.3.6. Here it is not mating but the unnatural concord between normally hostile species that marks the next stage, *aeuo...sequenti*, in nature's disruption. The harmony between prey and predator is a mark of the Golden Age in 4.22, Hor. *Epod.* 16.32. The transforma-tions that reveal a world all topsy-turvy are usually the reverse of those belonging to the Golden Age. So in 5.36–9 barrenness replaces fertility and strife concord. Here the combination of fantastical matings and unprecedented harmony reveals the ambivalence of the situation: a lover's expectations (*speremus amantes* 26) can be of Golden Age happiness or of gloom and despair. The same event brings the one to Mopsus, the other to his rejected rival.

28a The two songs are presumably meant to be of equal length and similar stanzaic pattern. Hence we must either follow γ and include a refrain after 28 or reject the testimony of all the MSS and delete the refrain after 75. The latter course is the bolder, since a balancing refrain is more likely to have been omitted accidentally than a non-balancing one interpolated. The deletion of 76 would leave just nine refrains and also remove the only two-line stanzas (29–30, 77–8). A pattern for each song of $3^2 \times 5$ lines, comprising 3^2 refrains and

$3^2 \times 4$ stanzaic lines, divided into groups of three, four and five, would certainly have its admirers. A more important consideration, however, is the organic relation of 29–30 and 77–8 to the preceding stanzas. The protest at the ill-assorted marriage of Mopsus and Nysa (26–8) is followed by apostrophes to each of the two partners (29–30, 32–41). The first of these clearly gains in dramatic effect if like the second it is separated off by a refrain rather than tacked on to the initial protest of 26–8. The case for separating off 77–8 is less strong. The couplet continues the triple rituals of 73–5, but with a change from first person to imperative, though this is paralleled within other single stanzas, e.g. 64 and 67, 101–2 and 103. Moreover the obvious allusion in *Veneris...uincula necto* (78) to the wedding rites of Mopsus gains point from the isolation of the two couplets. After much hesitation the first course has been adopted in the text and the refrain inserted after 28.

29   incide faces: the pinewood torches were freshly cut to be carried in the bridal torch-light procession; cf. Cat. 61.77–8.
   tibi: for the dative of agent cf. 4.15n.
   nuces 'walnuts'. *nuces iuglandes* 'Jove's acorns', *Iouis glandes*, were the *nuptialium Fescenninorum comites* according to Pliny, *Nat.* 15.86, who after remarking the walnut's double protection of skin and shell adds *quae causa eas nuptiis fecit religiosas, tot modis fetu munito; quod est uerisi-milius quam quia cadendo tripudium soniuium faciant.* (Servius here gives the latter explanation.) Pliny's reference to *fetus* and the ritual dance in the context of Fescennine songs suggests that the walnuts were originally fertility symbols (for the walnut as a sign of fertility see *G.* 1.187–90) like the rice that is still sometimes scattered over bridal couples. But the fact that the bridegroom as well as the spectators threw walnuts suggests a different explanation. Nuts were common children's toys (Hor. *S.* 2.3.171, Suet. *Aug.* 83) and *nuces relinquere, ponere* is used of putting away childish things, e.g. in Pers. 1.10, Mart. 14.185.2. Servius, noting that both the *pueri* present and the *maritus* threw nuts, explained the ritual as symbolizing the rejection of pederasty by the bridegroom as he entered upon an adult sexual relationship. This would certainly give point to Cat. 61.121–7. The two explanations are not mutually exclusive: the nuts thrown by the boys and other guests are the relic of an old fertility ritual, those

thrown in return by the groom a symbolic indication that he has put away boyhood – whether this includes homosexuality or not – and is now entering an adult procreative relationship. In any case the allusion to a familiar Roman wedding ritual adds yet another touch of realism to the pastoral situation.

30 Hesperos: the Greek cognate of *Vesper*. Its identity with the morning star, Lucifer, the Greek Φωσφόρος, had long been familiar: Hesperos has the epithet ἑωσφόρος 'dawn-bearer' in Hom. *Il.* 23.226, his mother is Ἠώς ἠριγένεια (= *Aurora*) in Hes. *Th.* 381, Hyg. *Astron.* 3.42, where the identification of Hesperos as the planet Venus is attributed to Eratosthenes. As the herald of darkness *portans optata maritis* (Cat. 64.328) Hesperos was called the *sidus Veneris* (Plin. *Nat.* 2.36, Hyg. *loc. cit.*). Contradictory emotions are naturally aroused in lovers by the planet's different manifestations, e.g. Meleager *A.P.* 12.114 'Farewell Morning Star (*Phaesphóre*), herald of the dawn, and come as Evening Star (*Hésperos*), bringing back in secret her whom you are now taking from me.' But the normal pattern of responses is upset here. Lucifer, dolefully addressed at the start, is destined, when he next appears as Hesperos, not to banish but to intensify the goatherd's sorrow; cf. Cinna fr. 6M (Serv. *ad G.* 1.288) *te matutinus flentem conspexit Eous | et flentem paulo uidit post Hesperus idem.* For the astronomical solecism of the Morning and Evening Star appearing on the same day cf. Cat. 62.34–5, Hor. *C.* 2.9.10–12.

Oetan: the mountain, a south-east projection of the Pindus range west of Thermopylae, marked the southern limits of Thessaly. At *A.* 2.801–2 the rising of Lucifer above Mt Ida is appropriate to the geographical setting. Hesperos rising above Mt Oeta would only be visible in the area west of the mountain, viz. in southern Thessaly. So this could be a clue to the notional setting of the singing contest. However, the association between Hesperos and Mt Oeta is without such a geographical significance at Cat. 62.7 (a nuptial context) and Stat. *S.* 5.4.8. Servius here refers vaguely to an Oetaean cult of Hesperos, *qui Hymenaeum speciosum puerum amasse dicitur*, which may also be alluded to in Nonn. *D.* 38.137. There was moreover an old tradition (cf. Pi. fr. 126.6–7B) that the youthful Hymenaeus *die nuptiarum oppressus ruina est* (Serv. *ad A.* 1.651), and the possibility that this catastrophe was connected with the boy's grief at losing Hesperos would add point to *deserit* here and introduce an appropriately ominous note into this last address to Mopsus: 'Hesperos is deserting Oeta for you...as he did when Hymenaeus was married.' The phrase remains obscure. The Greek inflections again provide a sense of distance.

32 coniuncta: sc. *tu quae coniuncta es.*

   digno, which is explained by implication in the following lines, contrasts with the *indignus amor* (18) that formerly linked her to himself.

32–3 despicis... tibi est odio recalls *despectus tibi sum* (2.19). Only now is it revealed that the rejected lover is in fact a goatherd. Like the town-bred Alexis Nysa despises the goatherd's rough appearance, his way of life and his music. The implication is that Mopsus, like Iollas in that Eclogue, had none of these disadvantages in her eyes.

34 For the hirsute lover despised cf. Th. *Id.* 3.7–9 (2.6n.) and Polyphemus' 'shaggy brow' in *Id.* 11.31. The variants *demissa, prolixa* have crept into the text from Servius' gloss on *promissa*. The first phrase is expressively grotesque, with its two words spread over 3½ feet (two of them dactyls), divided after the second foot trochee and followed by the major pause at the fourth foot strong caesura.

35 Cf. Aesch. *Ag.* 369f., Enn. *trag.* 317V *sed eos non curare opinor quid agat humanum genus*, cited in Cic. *Div.* 2.104 on the Epicurean doctrine *quicquam deos nec alieni curare nec sui.* Returning to the charge of perfidy made in 19, he implies (*digno* in 32) that her insincerity is now well-matched in Mopsus.

37 The wistful memory of their first meeting is modelled on Th. *Id.* 11.25–8: 'I fell in love with you, maiden, when you came with my mother wanting to pluck hyacinth flowers from the hill, and I led the way.'

   saepibus in nostris makes the setting more intimate and domestic; instead of picking wild flowers on the hills Nysa was a family visitor gathering fruit in their orchard. For the realistic touch in *saepes* cf. 1.53n.

   roscida mala: for the erotic connotations of the fruit see 2.51n. The epithet indicates the early morning, the very time of day that he is now lamenting his loss.

38 matre: unlike Theocritus Vergil omits the specifying pronominal adjective. Servius' indecision – *uel huius uel puellae matrem intellegere* *possumus* – shows that the Latin was indeed as ambiguous as the English 'I saw you gathering fruit with Mother.' The boy's own mother is less likely to have needed a guide in the family orchard, and the contrast between *uester*, which normally implies plurality, and *nostris* favours *tua matre*.

39 alter ab undecimo is usually taken to mean 'twelfth'; cf. *alter ab illo* (5.49), *heros ab Achille secundus* (Hor. *S.* 2.3.193). The boy had had his eleventh birthday and was now in his twelfth year. However, Servius, who knew Latin as a living language, says *id est tertius decimus. 'alter' enim de duobus dicimus.* So we must at least recognize this as a possible alternative.

40 fragilis...ramos: the precision of the chronological detail – assuming it to have been unambiguous to Vergil himself – is vividly reinforced by this image of the boy standing tip-toe to reach the fragile branches all around him (the position of the two words is expressive). The beginning of puberty is thus evoked and the excitement of falling in love for the first time. But now the goatherd who was Nysa's *dux* at that first meeting *in saepibus* is to see her married to another – *ducitur uxor* (29). The memory of that first encounter mocks him in all its vivid detail. Vergil has added a new dimension to the Theocritean image.

41 ut uidi, ut perii: *unum 'ut' est temporis, aliud quantitatis* (D. Serv.); cf. Simaetha's love for Delphis in Th. *Id.* 2.82 χώς ἴδον ὡς ἐμάνην ὡς μοι πυρὶ θυμὸς ἰάφθη 'and when I saw, how frenzied I became, how struck with fire my heart!', and Atalanta's love for Hippomenes in Th. *Id.* 3.42 ὡς ἴδεν, ὡς ἐμάνη, ὡς ἐς βαθὺν ἅλατ' ἔρωτα 'and when she saw, how frenzied she became, how deeply plunged in love'. (Most modern editors read ὡς...ὡς...ὡς... 'when...thus... thus...' in both passages.) The unusual use of *ut* in two different senses indicates that Vergil has both passages very much in mind; the hiatus after *perii* (cf. 3.6n.) may also be a deliberate imitation of the latter line.

malus...error: the noun is coupled with *insania* in Hor. *Ep.* 2.1.118. It recalls the madness of Corydon (2.69) and Pasiphae (6.47), which drove them to forsake their normal lives and wander alone (*errare*) in hopeless quest of their loved ones (2.4–5, 6.52).

43-5 Cf. Th. *Id.* 3.15-16: 'Now I know Love. A cruel god. Surely he sucked the dug of a lioness and was reared by his mother in the wild wood', *Id.* 23.4. The cruelties of *Eros/Amor* and accusations concerning his parentage are a pastoral and elegiac commonplace; cf. Th. *Id.* 2.55-6, Bion fr. 14, Meleager *A.P.* 5.176, 180, Prop. 1.12.16, 2.12. In Meleager *A.P.* 5.177.5-6 Sky, Earth and Sea all disown him. For the figure here cf. Dido to Aeneas in *A.* 4.366-7 *duris genuit te cotibus horrens | Caucasus Hyrcanaeque admorunt ubera tigres.*

43 sciŏ: for 'iambic shortening' see 3.79n. In the first person singular of verbs it is common in Plautus, e.g. *sciŏ* (*Amp.* 1082) and even *intellegŏ* (*Rud.* 101), and in the more conversational parts of Catullus, e.g. *nesciŏquid* (2.6), *uolŏ* (6.16). Vergil confines it to *sciŏ*, *nesciŏ*, cf. *A.* 3.602; but its spread beyond iambic sequences is exemplified by *findŏ* (Prop. 3.9.35), *tollŏ* (Ov. *A.* 3.2.26), and became general in the spoken language (Charis. 13-14B).

44 Tmaros...Rhodope: the former was a mountain ridge in Epirus, now the Albanian Mitzikéli. For the latter range, dividing Thrace from Macedonia, see 6.30, where its association with *Ismaros* explains the variant reading here.

extremi Garamantes were an African tribe beyond the Gaetuli (Hdt. 4.174, 183), long believed to be at the border of the inhabited world; cf. *A.* 6.794. The versification is distinctly Hellenizing: hiatus without correption (3.6n.) in *Rhodope aut* and the quadrisyllable at the end of the line (which also contributes to its predominantly heterodyne character). This reinforces the Greek tone of the proper names and inflections (-*os*, -*ē* and probably -*ĕs*; cf. *delphinăs* at 56). Indeed the whole line could be a translation from Greek, e.g. ἢ Τμάρος ἢ Ῥοδόπη ἢ τηλουροὶ Γαράμαντες; cf. *G.* 1.332 *aut Athon aut Rhodopen aut alta Ceraunia telo*, adapted from Th. *Id.* 7.77 ἢ Ἄθω ἢ Ῥοδόπαν ἢ Καύκασον ἐσχατόωντα (see also 2.24n.). Its effect is to evoke the exotic and remote wilds.

45 nec generis nostri...nec sanguinis recalls Patroclus' words in Hom. *Il.* 16.33-5 'Pitiless that you are, the knight Peleus wasn't your father after all, nor Thetis your mother; it was the grey sea and steep cliffs that gave you birth, so harsh is your nature.' To say that Amor was not of human race and blood would in itself be platitudinous; but the goatherd is denying his 'inhuman' tormentor even those anthropomorphic attributes which convention (e.g. Mosch. 1, Meleager *A.P.* 5.178) bestowed on him. For an elaborate inversion of the present figure see Lygd. [= Tib. 3] 4.85–94.

edunt 'are the parents of' denotes the present state resulting from the past act (*ediderunt*); cf. *generat* (*A.* 8.141) and Greek ἐκφύει (Soph. *O.T.* 437).

47 saeuos Amor: cf. Enn. *trag.* 254V *amore saeuo saucia*, of Medea; see also 10.29n. Medea's murder of her children in revenge against Jason was a common subject for dramatists from Euripides to Seneca and for vase- and wall-painters; see *App.Plan.* 135ff. For the present passage cf. Prop. 3.19.17–18 *Medeae...quo tempore matris | iram natorum caede piauit amor.*

48 crudelis tu quoque mater: Servius took this to refer to Medea also: *sed et illam quae paruit et illum qui coegit incusat.* But the implication that no normal woman would have been driven to such a revenge even by Love detracts from the effectiveness of Medea as an instance of the *saeuitia Amoris.* The reference to Medea cannot be taken as a condemnation of the cruel nature of Nysa, since it is the goatherd himself whose situation might drive him to violence and revenge. D. Servius adds that *alii hoc loco cum Amore matrem Venerem culpari uolunt.* This certainly suits the contrast between *mater* and *puer* in 49–50, and a reference to Venus, herself *mater saeua Cupidinum* (Hor. *C.* 1.19.1), would be apposite. But the use of the same noun to refer both to Venus and Medea in successive lines without any more explicit definition would be very inelegant. The triple occurrence of *crudelis* and *mater* is very jejune and the rhetorical word-play of 49–50 has an irrelevant touch of Ovidian wit about it; so suspicions of textual corruption seem justified. Heyne's suggestion of bracketing 49–50 leaves the awkward *crudelis tu quoque mater* in 48 without any supporting elaboration. Hermann proposed replacing this phrase by *puer a puer improbus ille* and omitting 49; Ribbeck conflated 48–50 into *commaculare manus, crudelis! tu quoque mater | crudelis mater, magis at puer improbus ille.* None of these solutions is convincing in itself; all disturb the symmetry of the two songs by excluding one or two lines from the passage. It is likely that the corruption, which must have occurred very early, consisted in the total replacement of the original 49, perhaps even some modification in the latter half of 48, and that what Vergil wrote here provided a clearer transition from the mother who cruelly murdered her sons to the cruel mother whose son had inspired this action. *mater* in 50 would then refer unequivocally to Venus.

49   improbus: cf. *A.* 4.412 *improbe Amor, quid non mortalia pectora cogis?* The adjective is used of that which exceeds the bounds of what is normal or reasonable; cf. *G.* 1.119 of a greedy goose, 146 of excessive labour, 388 of a crow calling for rain, *A.* 2.80 of *Fortuna.* The line is ambiguous. *crudelis...magis* may be for *crudelior:* 'Is the mother or that wicked boy the more cruel?' But the anastrophe of *magis* is unusual, and it is preferable to take *magis* in the sense of *potius*, as in 1.11. Hence either 'Is it rather the mother or that wicked boy who is cruel?' or 'Is it rather that the mother is cruel or that that boy is wicked?' The order and rhythm of the last three words suggest that *improbus* is attributive, not predicative, and so support the former of these interpretations, but the answer in 50, 'that boy is wicked; but you too are cruel, mother', goes better with the latter.

52ff   The prophecy of nature's disruption (27–8) is now transformed into a prayer; cf. Th. *Id.* 1.132–6 (5.36n.).

52   ultro fugiat lupus would represent the reversal of roles in a still hostile relationship (cf. Th. *Id.* 1.135 'Let the stag drag down the hounds') not the Golden Age reconciliation of strife, as in 28 and 5.60 *nec lupus insidias pecori.*

52–3   aurea durae mala...quercus: the two epithets are emphatically juxtaposed. As Amor himself was brought forth from the *durae cotes* (43), so now golden fruit, which are the symbols of love (2.51n.), will appear instead of acorns on the hard oaks. In 4.30 *durae quercus sudabunt roscida mella.*

53   narcisso floreat alnus: cf. *Id.* 1.133 'Let fair narcissus blooms cover the junipers.' The unprepossessing alder, Alnus Glutinosa, is common in marshland and on river banks, especially in the Po region (*G.* 2.110, 451).

54   pinguia...electra: Greek *ēlektron* was used both of amber and of a gold–silver alloy that resembled it (Plin. *Nat.* 33.80, 37.31). The adjective here indicates that the former, Latin *sucinum*, is meant. The plural suggests amber drops. Amber was thought to be exuded by riverside trees like the alder (6.63) and poplar (*A.* 10.190, Ov. *M.* 2.364–5); but not, it would appear from this line, by the humble tamarisk (4.2,.6.10).

55 certent et cycnis ululae: cf. Th. *Id.* 1.135 'And let the owls from the mountains speak to nightingales'; *Id.* 5.136–7 'It isn't right for jays to contend with nightingales or hoopoes with swans.' The futility of competing with swans in song was proverbial, e.g. 9.36, Lucr. 3.6–7, 4.181–2. But the doleful swan-song just before death was particularly famous (Aesch. *Ag.* 1444–5, Cic. *T.D.* 1.73, Arist. *H.A.* 615b, denied by Plin. *Nat.* 10.63) and the cry of the screech owl was like the *ululatus* of mourners (Var. *L.* 5.75). So the contest of the two may be something of a deathly portent here. For the dative with *certare* cf. 5.8n.

Tityrus: *uilissimus rusticus Orpheus putetur* (Serv.). There is no need to take it as the goatherd's name. In nature's reversal even the humblest rustic (cf. 1.1n., 6.4n.) will become an Orpheus or Arion, capable of charming the elements as Damon has been doing with this very song (2–4).

56 delphinǎs: for the Greek acc. cf. *delphinĕs* in *A.* 8.673.

Orpheus...Arion: for the former see 3.46n. Arion was on the way from Sicily to Corinth when he was threatened with death by the sailors. He was allowed to play one last tune on his lyre and his music so captivated the dolphins that when he was thrown into the sea, one of them carried him safely to shore (Hdt. 1.23–4, Ov. *F.* 2.79–118). The chiastic pattern of the line throws emphasis on *Orpheus* and *Arion* as well as bringing dolphins and woods close together in anticipation of 58; cf. Ov. *M.* 1.302 *siluasque tenent delphines* of the great flood and 1.60n. The closing image of the rustic Tityrus at sea completes the sequence of nature's reversals and again leads neatly on to the next stanza.

58 omnia...fiat mare: for the singular verb cf. Ov. *M.* 1.292 *omnia pontus erat*, anon. *Dirae* 46 *cinis omnia fiat*.

uel medium '(Let everything become sea), yes, even mid-sea.' The first flood destroyed a corrupt and perverse world (Ov. *M.* 144–50); the goatherd now prays that the present perverse world in

which he has suffered so unjustly may complete its own disruption in
the same way. There is no justification for believing that Vergil has
mistaken ἔναλλα for ἐνάλια 'of the sea' in Th. *Id.* 1.134 πάντα δ' ἔναλλα
γένοιτο 'let all things become altered'.

   uiuite 'farewell'; cf. Hor. *S.* 2.5.110 *uiue ualeque*. The verb contributes a plaintive sequence of thin vowels to the cadence, which is
emphatically isolated by the pause at the preceding bucolic diaeresis
and the absence of enjambement. It also points a contrast with
morientis (60). The woods, like those that cover Maenalus (22) or were
charmed by Orpheus (56), will live on after the goatherd's death. The
antithesis between nature's continuity and human mortality (20n.) is
now more prominent. Daphnis' farewell to his environment (Th. *Id.*
1.115–18) is more elaborate and, coming early in his speech, lacks the
dramatic finality of the goatherd's gesture here.

   59   specula 'view-point', 'look-out post'; cf. *A.* 10.454. This detail
and the suicidal intent itself recall Th. *Id.* 3.25–7 'I'll take off my cloak
and jump into the waves from the spot over there from which Olpis
the fisherman watches for tunny; and if I kill myself, well, that has
done what you want at least.' However the absurd posturing betrayed
by Theocritus' opening phrase has no place in Vergil's sad bucolic
drama; and in so far as a poet can control the choice of precedents
available to the reader it is more likely that Vergil intended an allusion to the famous story of the love-sick Sappho's suicidal leap from
the Leucadian promontory (Strabo 10.452, Ov. *H.* 15.163f.). For the
anastrophe of *de* here cf. *flumina circum* (9.40).

   aerii...montis: cf. Cat. 68.57.

   60   deferar is future middle: 'I shall cast myself down' rather than
passive subjunctive: 'may I be cast down'.

   extremum hoc munus: although Mopsus and Nysa have been
apostrophized (29, 32), it is Lucifer who is now addressed once more,
the phrase being a clear echo of *extrema moriens tamen adloquor hora* in
the opening stanza. The goatherd ends where he began. His last
offering to Lucifer is this his swan-song. The phrase is often taken to
refer to his suicide; cf. *Id.* 3.27 (59n.), [Th.] *Id.* 23.20–1 (2.6n.). But
this is less likely. For it makes *morientis* otiose; *amantis* would have been
more effective; cf. *A.* 4.429 *extremum hoc miserae det munus amanti*, where
incidentally the verbal reminiscence like others from Damon's song

(43–4n., 48–50n.) reveals associations in Vergil's mind between the plights of the two rejected lovers.

61 For the variation here cf. Th. *Id.* 1.127 etc. λήγετε βουκολικᾶς, Μοῖσαι, ἴτε λήγετ᾽ ἀοιδᾶς 'Cease, Muses, come cease the pastoral song.'

62–3 Instead of a simple link like [Th.] *Id.* 9.14: 'Thus Daphnis sang for me and thus Menalcas' Vergil appeals to the Muses to report Alphesiboeus' song. The device may be intended to emphasize its literary novelty. For it is not like Damon's a *retractatio* of conventional pastoral themes but a pastoral adaptation of part of an urban idyll carefully shaped to balance its companion piece in the Eclogue. In it the herdsman is required to assume the role of a jealous woman who resorts to magic to bring back her lover. So there may also be a suggestion that the *arcana* of female magic rites are better left to goddesses to reveal. For the aid of the Muses in special circumstances cf. 6.13 *pergite Pierides*, *G.* 4.315, *A.* 1.8, 7.37. Although the Muses are often *Pierides* in the Eclogues (3.85n.), their Thessalian origin is especially relevant here in view of the traditional association of Thessaly with witchcraft (Ar. *Nub.* 749, Luc. 6.435ff.).

63 non omnia possumus omnes: the thought is as old as Homer, *Il.* 23.670–1. For its Latin proverbial form cf. Lucil. 218M. A more elliptical version occurs at 7.23 in a similarly modest appeal to the Muses by Corydon.

64 For the enchantress' instructions to prepare for the ceremony cf. Th. *Id.* 2.1–3 'Where are my bay-leaves? Bring them, Thestylis. And where are the charms? Wreathe the bowl with fine crimson wool, that I may bind my dear lover who is so cruel.' The addressee is not named till 76. It is natural in view of the role of Thestylis in the idyll and in the absence of clear indication to the contrary here to assume that she is an attendant. However, the parallel with Damon's song, which is a monologue, at least raises the possibility that she is talking to herself here and in 77–8 and 101–2, and that *Amaryllis* is her own name. This would resolve the problem of 106. The setting – probably in the *atrium* beside the *impluuium*, i.e. within the house walls but under the open sky – is left to be inferred from 101, 107.

molli: *lanea* (D. Serv.); cf. Prop. 3.6.30.

65 uerbenasque...pinguis: although English *vervain* is derived from *uerbena*, the latter seems to have been used not only of Rosmarinus Officinalis, but also of other plants with sacral associations, e.g. bay, olive and myrtle (Servius *ad A.* 12.120). Servius glosses the word here as *uirgulta quae semper uirent, iucundi odoris*, so it may be no more specific than 'sprays of fragrant evergreen'. The epithet implies that they were not yet dried but still green and juicy, *florentes, uirentes* (Serv.).

adole: *incende, auge* (Serv.). Another sacral word, originally meaning 'to burn'; cf. the non-ritual use in Ov. *M.* 1.492 *stipulae demptis adolentur aristis.* From such usages as *adolentque altaria donis* (Lucr. 4.1237) and a false etymological connection with *adolescere* 'to grow' it acquired a second meaning *augere, honorare, propitiare* (Non. 247 and 58M), which is clearly attested in Tac. *A.* 14.30 *cruore captiuo adolere aras.*

mascula: the best kind of frankincense, being shaped like round drops (cf. the Greek name σταγονίας) according to Plin. *Nat.* 12.61–2. It is produced from Arabian terebinthus. For the combination of *uerbenas* and *tura* cf. Hor. *C.* 1.19.14. The plural of *tus* may be literally 'grains of incense'; but *masculum* would be difficult metrically (1.6n.).

66 coniugis: cf. 18. The two songs exhibit different reactions to a partner's infidelity, *querelae* (19) and *magica sacra.*

66–7 sanos auertere...sensus: *a sanitate mutare* (Serv.). A true lover cannot be *sanus*; the enchantress is determined that he will feel the full *dementia* and *error* of love (41n.).

carmina for her are to be ἐπῳδαί 'spells', an instrument of her will, not a self-pitying lament; cf. *A.* 4.487–8 *haec se carminibus promittit soluere mentes | quas uelit ast aliis duras immittere curas.* The word is emphatically repeated not only in 69–70 but in the recurrent refrain (68 etc.).

desunt: for the violation of strict concord ('the only thing we need are songs') cf. 58.

68 The refrain this time is less reminiscent of its model, Th. *Id.* 2.17 etc. ἴυγξ ἕλκε τὺ τῆνον ἐμὸν ποτὶ δῶμα τὸν ἄνδρα 'Magic wheel, draw home to me that man of mine.' The urgent rhythm of the refrain, with five dactyls and five homodynes, the emphatic cadence

separated off by the bucolic diaeresis, and the explosive *d*-alliteration
are all expressive of determination and aggression; cf. 21n.

ab urbe...Daphnin introduces the town–country antithesis noted
in 1.34 and implicit throughout *Ecl.* 2. Theocritus' enchantress was in
the town (*Id.* 2.35), not far from the sea (*ibid.* 38). To emphasize the
rural setting here Vergil has replaced the Delphis of *Id.* 2 by Daphnis.

69 deducere lunam: instead of a helpless complaint to Lucifer
(17) she invokes the power to command the heavenly bodies to her
will. An art that can bring down the moon from the sky can surely
bring back Daphnis from town. For this traditional claim of witchcraft see Ar. *Nub.* 749–52, Hor. *Epod.* 5.45–6, Prop. 1.1.19.

70 Circe the archetypal enchantress is coupled with Medea in Th.
Id. 2.15–16. Yet Circe's magic like Medea's was unable to win back
her lover. She could change Ulysses' companions into swine (Hom. *Od.*
10.230–43), but only for a time; and after a year he deserted her,
taking them with him (*ib.* 483–9). Nor was she more successful with
Glaucus, having like Medea to console herself with vengeance (Ov.
M. 14.40–67).

71 frigidus...anguis: another traditional accomplishment of
magicians; cf. Lucil. 575M *Marsus colubras disrumpit cantu*, Ov. *M.*
7.203. It could also no doubt be beneficial to herdsmen as a form of
pest-control; cf. 3.93. The emphatic separation of the phrase makes
the epithet especially effective: incantations can break down anything that is cold, including a lover's heart.

cantando 'by the act of singing', 'by incantations'. The gerund
like other verbal nouns, e.g. *cantus*, is neutral as to the distinction of
active and passive voice; cf. *mansuescit arando* (*G.* 2.239). The three
examples of 69–71 represent the range of magical powers – to charm
the heavenly bodies, influence nature, and change human beings; cf.
Ov. *A.* 2.1.23–6, Tib. 1.8.19–21 *cantus uicinis fruges traducit ab agris,* |
cantus et iratae detinet anguis iter, | *cantus et e curru Lunam deducere temptat.*

73–4 For the use of thread in magic cf. Ov. *F.* 2.575, Plin. *Nat.* 28.48.
tibi: i.e. the image of Daphnis; cf. *effigiem* (75). For the use of images
in magic see Hor. *S.* 1.8.30 and cf. *A.* 4.508.
triplici...colore indicates that there were three different colours
of thread, white, red and black according to Servius; *terna...licia* that

the threads were taken in groups of three. The differentiation (*diuersa*) by colour implies three groups, each containing either a different colour – three white threads, three red and three black – or all three colours in a different order – the first consisting of white, red and black, the second of red, black and white etc. *ternos...colores* (77) would suit either interpretation but the strict sense of *triplici* perhaps favours the latter. For a more complex triple pattern of coloured threads in magic cf. anon. *Ciris.* 371–3.

altaria: see 1.43n.

75 impare for the more usual *impari* is required for the metre; cf. Luc. 7.682. For the ritual importance of 'three' generally cf. *A.* 6.506, Th. *Id.* 2.43, Tib. 1.2.54 and the Christian *Kyrie Eleison*. Odd numbers, especially primes like 3 and 7, have often been venerated.

deus: either generic 'a deity' or, like *daimōn* 'divine spirit' in Th. *Id.* 2.28, referring to Hecate. *deus* is used of Venus in *A.* 2.632. Hecate, patron of witchcraft (Eur. *Med.* 395–7, Hor. *S.* 1.8.33), was *triformis dea* (Ov. *M.* 7.94–5), being identified with Luna and Diana (*A.* 4.511) and worshipped *nocturnis triuiis* (*A.* 4.609).

76 For the textual problem of the refrain here see 28n.

77 Amarylli: the name whether it is her own or that of her attendant (64n.) again points to a rustic setting (see 1.5n.).

78 modo is commonly added to imperatives in conversation, meaning 'just', 'only', e.g. *quin tu i modo* (Pl. *Trin.* 583), *modo fac...ne quid aliud cures* (Cic. *Fam.* 16.11.1).

Veneris...uincula: cf. Lucr. 4.1202–5 *in uinclis communibus* and *ualidis Veneris compagibus, A.* 4.16 *uinclo...iugali.* See also 28a n.

80 limus...cera: both words refer either to pieces of clay and wax or more likely to images of Daphnis made from them; cf. the *effigies* of *lana* and *cera* in Hor. *S.* 1.8.30. The remarkable pattern of six homodynes, with the trochaic caesura after *durescit* dividing the line into two rhyming parts, seems intended to reproduce the jingle of popular charms, which preserved the characteristic stress metres of the native Latin verse tradition, e.g. *ego tui memini | medere meis pedibus. | terra pestem teneto, | salus hice maneto | in meis pedibus* (Var. *R.* 1.2.27). For the sympathetic magic of burning cf. Th. *Id.* 2.28–9 'As I melt this wax with the aid of the divine spirit, so may Delphis the Myndian melt with love right now'.

81 ēōdem: for the synizesis of *eo-* cf. *deínde* (5.15), *reíce* (3.96) and the contraction in *deērrauerat* (7.7), all of which probably reflect ordinary speech.

sic nostro...amore: cf. Hor. *Epod.* 5.81-2 *amore sic meo flagres uti | bitumen atris ignibus.* Fire can harden clay and melt wax; so the fires of love rekindled in Daphnis will melt away his hardness towards her and harden him against the attractions of others. Since representations of parts of the body are often employed in magic, there may be specific physical symbolism implied here, *cera* referring e.g. to an image of the heart, Greek *kêr*, and *limus* to a clay penis; cf. the homophone *limus* used of the 'apron' worn at sacrifices, *uestis qua ab umbilico usque ad pedes teguntur pudenda poparum* (Serv. *ad A.* 12.120).

82 molam: *far tostum et sale sparsum* (P. Fest. 141 M). It was sprinkled over the sacrificial victims (Cic. *Div.* 2.37, Serv. *ad A.* 2.133); hence *immolare.* Cf. Th. *Id.* 2.18 'Look, first the grains of barley smoulder in the fire'; 33 'Now I will burn the bran.'

fragilis...laurus: cf. Th. *Id.* 2.23-5 'I burn the bay against Delphis, and as it crackles loudly when it has caught fire and suddenly burns up and we don't see even its ash, so may Delphis' flesh waste away in the flame.' For the sense of the adjective 'crackling' cf. Lucr. 6.112 *et fragilis sonitus chartarum.* If the fire is extinguished by the *pinguis uerbena* (65), the omen is bad; cf. Prop. 2.28.36. If the fire burns the bay to ashes (105-6), the omen is good; cf. Tib. 2.5.81-3. The *Phoebi Delphica laurus* (Lucr. 6.154) naturally had prophetic properties. The following line indicates its particular relevance in the present magic ceremony.

bitumine: the mineral pitch with which the fire was kindled; cf. Ov. *M.* 14.792.

83 in Daphnide is either 'on Daphnis' or 'in the case of, with reference to, Daphnis'. For the rivalry of the latter construction with *in* + acc. 'against' cf. *in filio...suam uim exercuit* (Nep. *Dion* 6.2) but *uim...uelut in captos exercebant* (Tac. *A.* 6.1(7).5); *saeuus in hoste fuit* (Ov. *A.* 1.7.34) but *saeuissimo...in suos* (Liv. 34.32.3). As the bay is burnt, so the cold-hearted lover will be burnt and his *fragilitas* broken like the snake in 71. The etymological connection between *Daphnis* and Greek *dáphnē* 'bay' (cf. *Id.* 2.23) adds special significance to the sympathetic rite here.

85ff The following image of the forlorn Daphnis is modelled on Lucr. 2.355–65, where the uniqueness of every creature in spite of its common atomic composition is instanced by a heifer in search of her calf, which has been taken for sacrifice: *at mater uiridis saltus orbata peragrans* | ... | *omnia conuisens oculis loca, si queat usquam* | *conspicere amissum fetum...* | *nec tenerae salices atque herbae rore uigentes* | *fluminaque illa queunt summis labentia ripis* | *oblectare animum subitamque auertere curam...* | *usque adeo quiddam proprium notumque requirit.* For another recollection of this famous passage see Ov. *F.* 4.459–60, of Ceres seeking Proserpine. The uniqueness of the calf in the eyes of its mother is now made the exemplar of the uniqueness of the beloved in the eyes of a lover. See further 88n.

85–7 qualis cum...bucula...procumbit focuses attention less on the long hopeless search (as in Lucretius) than on the final state of exhausted despair and longing – the very state of helplessness to which the enchantress hopes to reduce Daphnis. The relevant simile in *Id.* 2, though more sensational, has none of the pathos: 'Hippomane is a plant among the Arcadians and all the young stallions and swift mares go mad for it over the hills. Even so may I see Delphis like a madman approaching this house...' (48–51).

86 per nemora recalls the lovesick wanderings of Corydon (2.3) and Pasiphae's final cry to the nymphs (6.56), *nemorum iam claudite saltus.*

    bucula: the diminutive in contrast to Lucretius' *mater* makes it clear that *iuuencus* here is the heifer's mate, not her calf. The onomatopoeia of *o* and *u* vowels in the latter part of the line is naive but effective.

87 propter aquae riuom: cf. Lucr. 5.1392–3 *prostrati in gramine molli* | *propter aquae riuom.* The archaic sense of the preposition is also found e.g. at Lucr. 2.30 and *G.* 3.14.

    uiridi...ulua: this marsh plant (*G.* 3.175), which is distinguished from *iuncus* in Ov. *M.* 4.299, is probably 'fen sedge', Cladium Mariscus. The lush surroundings mock the heifer's sorrow here as in Lucretius; cf. *herba...uiridi* in the images that mock Pasiphae (6.59).

88 perdita perhaps recalls Corydon (2.59) and Damon's goatherd (41). But the line itself is from a passage of Varius, *de morte Caesaris*, cited by Macrobius, 6.2.20, *ceu canis umbrosam lustrans Gortynia uallem,* | *si ueteris potuit ceruae comprendere lustra,* | *saeuit in absentem et circum uestigia lustrans* | *aethera per nitidum tenuis sectatur odores.* | *non amnes illam medii, non ardua tardant,* | *perdita nec serae meminit decedere nocti.* The hunting context of the Varian line, being more appropriate to the enchantress herself than to her victim, reinforces what is already hinted in the structural correspondence between *Daphnin* and *iuuencum* at 85: the heifer-simile applies only superficially to Daphnis. In depicting the pathos of Daphnis' plight, to which she professes indifference (89), she is unconsciously revealing her own feelings. The wistful longing and the weariness of the searcher belong to her; she is like the wandering Pasiphae (6.52). The use of this simile is thus a fine psychological stroke by the poet. For 87–8 cf. *G.* 3.466–7.

89 mederi: i.e. to cure him of the *insania* that her magic will have caused (66–7). But the madness will bring him back to his rightful place, with his *coniunx* in the country, since like is meant for like: in Lucretius' words *proprium notumque requirit*, in Corydon's (2.65) *trahit sua quemque uoluptas.*

91 exuuias is used of anything taken off (*exuere*), e.g. the spoils stripped from an enemy (*A.* 2.275), the sloughed skin of a snake (*G.* 3.437). In Th. *Id.* 2.53–4 the material is burnt: 'This is the fringe that Delphis has lost from his cloak, and now I tear it in shreds and cast it in the fire.' The sympathetic ritual of burning such material is intended either to rekindle the fires of passion in the beloved (Lucian *Dial. Mer.* 4.4–5) or to destroy him (*A.* 4.496–8). Here the enchantress' aim is not to destroy her lover but to bring him back (97n.); and the clothes, which have not been lost but merely left behind, are not burnt but buried.

perfidus: cf. the goatherd's complaints against Nysa (18–20, 35).

92–3 pignora...mando; debent...Daphnin: the clothes left behind are a guarantee that he will be back. The legal metaphor is sustained through the couplet. *pignus est quod propter rem creditam obligatur cuius rei possessionem solam ad tempus consequitur creditor. Ceterum dominium penes debitorem est* (Isid. *Orig.* 5.25.22). A creditor was therefore not permitted in law to use for his own profit a pledge given by a

9   C V F

debtor; *si pignore creditor utatur, furti tenetur* (*Dig.* 47.2.54). So the *exuuiae* that guarantee repayment of the debt (*debent*) are deposited (*mando*) with a third party (*terra*) for safe-keeping until the day of settlement, viz. Daphnis' homecoming. The *terra* in contrast to *urbs* (90, 94) is their native soil; *limine in ipso* locates the reconciliation at the domestic threshold. *mando*, besides its legal contexts (see Cic. *S. Rosc.* 111–13), is commonly used like *demando, commendo* in spells and curses, e.g. Audollent 228, 293; also of burying the dead, e.g. *A.* 9.214. So there may be a suggestion that the *perfidia* symbolized by the clothes will be destroyed by the magic. But the legalistic connotations of the verb, reinforced by *pignora* and *debent*, are dominant.

95 has herbas...atque haec...uenena: probably an hendiadys. Her last resort in magic is to 'herbal drugs'. *uenenum* (< *Venus*) seems originally to have meant 'aphrodisiac' (cf. Afranius 380–1R) but it was early extended to mean 'drug', 'poison' generally. That *uenena* were not always harmful is clear from *Dig.* 50.16.236 *qui uenenum dicit adicere debet utrum malum an bonum; nam et medicamenta uenena sunt;* cf. Pl. *Ps.* 870, Serv. ad *A.* 11.458.

Ponto: with *lecta* in either a locatival or ablatival sense. Pontus along the south coast of the Black Sea east of the river Halys was the home of the dreaded aconite (Plin. *Nat.* 27.4). But the name was sometimes applied to any region bordering the Black Sea, the original *Póntos* of the Greeks, e.g. Ov. *T.* 5.10.1, and in particular to Colchis, the country of Medea, east of Pontus proper, e.g. Cic. *Man.* 22. The most effective poisons were usually advertised as being imported from remote places (Hor. *Epod.* 5.21, Th. *Id.* 2.162).

96 ipse...Moeris: the name is not found in earlier extant pastoral but recurs in *Ecl.* 9. It would obviously be associated with Greek *moîra* 'fate' (cf. Th. *Id.* 2.160) and so be appropriate to the local expert (*ipse*) on magic.

nascuntur: see 3.107n. The sequence of nasals and back vowels in the latter half of the line gives a tone of awe and mystery.

97ff Moeris' three achievements, like the three in 69–71, illustrate the range of his powers. There is no suggestion that these herbal spells are intended to destroy her lover, like the poisons of the enchantress in Th. *Id.* 2.159–62, which reveal both a lack of faith in the efficacy of her magic (cf. 103 here) and a determination that if she cannot have him back, no one will: 'Now I'll bind him with love-charms; but if he goes on hurting me, by the Fates, it will be the gate of Hell that he'll be beating at. Such are the evil drugs, I tell you my Lady, that I am keeping for him in my box, having learnt the art from an Assyrian stranger.'

his...saepe: the repetition of the pronoun from 95 (*has, haec*) and of the adverb in 98 suggests insistence and agitation.

lupum fieri: Circe's *carmina* could change men into swine (70), Moeris with his *uenena* can change himself into a wolf. For the were-wolf, *uersipellis*, see Ov. *M.* 1.209–39, Petron. 62. The superstition was particularly associated with Arcadia and the worship of Jupiter Lycaeus 'Jupiter Wolf-god' (Plin. *Nat.* 8.80–3).

98 animas...sepulcris: *carmina* can bring down heavenly bodies to earth (69), Moeris' *uenena* can bring back the *Manes* from the under-world. This was also a traditional claim of witchcraft and especially associated with necromancy, cf. Hom. *Od.* 11.24–50, *A.* 4.490, Luc. 6.531ff.

99 alio goes either with *traducere*, meaning 'to another place' (ad-verb) rather than 'from another person' (abl.), or with *satas* where it will mean 'by another' (abl. or even dat., cf. Pl. *St.* 80, Sen. *Ben.* 4.32.3). This specifically rustic feat corresponds to the destruction of snakes (71). The spiriting away of crops, usually performed by spells, not herbal concoctions (Tib. 1.8.19), was subject to penalties in the Twelve Tables (*tab.* 8.8; cf. Plin. *Nat.* 28.17, Serv. here). As *deducere* (69) echoed *ducite* in the preceding refrain, so *traducere* here anticipates it in the next.

101 fer cineres: the ceremonies end with the scattering of the ashes over running water. The use of the plural *cineres*, already attested in Cat. 68.98 (of the relics of the dead), shows an assimilation of form to meaning; cf. *cinis* (106) and English *ashes* ~ *ash*. *cinerem* would be inconvenient metrically here.

riuoque fluenti: for the dative with verbs of motion see 5.6n.

102 nec respexeris has no particular relevance to the actual ceremony but refers to the taboo on viewing anything that has been employed for magic or sacral purposes; cf. Hom. *Od.* 5.349–50, Th.

Id. 24.93–6, Ov. *F.* 5.437-40. The harsh clusters of *s* with explosive *p* and *k* consonants give an aggressive vehemence to the line.

his (sc. *uenenis*) picks up the sequence of deictic pronouns in 95 and 97, where she had described their powers but not what she intended to do with them. Once the ashes are disposed of, she will make one last attempt on Daphnis with her drugs.

103 nihil ille deos, nil carmina: the first phrase echoes the goat-herd's charge against Nysa (19, 35). Daphnis is moved neither by the idea that his perfidy (91) may incur divine punishment nor by all these spells – a pathetic revelation of her lack of faith in the powers she has extolled; cf. Th. *Id.* 2.159–60 (97n.). The echo of Corydon's *nihil mea carmina curas?* (2.6) provides yet another link between the two poems.

105 tremulis: of flickering fires in Cic. *Arat.* 153 (*N.D.* 2.110), Lucr. 4.404.

altaria 'offerings on the altar'; so Servius, perhaps rightly. See 1.43n.

106 sponte sua...ipse: the sudden spontaneous blaze was a good omen, as smouldering was a bad one; cf. *G.* 4.385–6.

dum ferre moror 'while I was delaying the removal'. *ferre* is direct object to *moror* and neutral as to person like *referre...iussit* in 6.85–6 and the verbal noun in e.g. Caes. *Civ.* 2.26 *impetum sustineant ac morentur.* The implied subject of *ferre* could thus be herself or an attendant. However, it is more natural to understand the same subject for both verb and infinitive, as in Cic. *Phil.* 5.33 *quoi bellum moremur inferre*; in which case *fer cineres, Amarylli* (101) must be addressed to herself. The alternative is to adopt the suggestion of D. Servius: *hoc ab alia dici debet.* But the sudden emergence of an attendant from the role of silent partner is in itself improbable and disturbs the parallelism of the two songs.

107 nescio quid certe est is colloquial; cf. Cat. 80.5, Hor. *S.* 1.9.67. For -ŏ see 43n., 3.79n.

Hylax is a significant name; cf. Greek *hulakteîn* 'to bark'. The barking dogs in Th. *Id.* 2.35 herald the arrival not of the girl's lover but of Hecate.

108 qui amant: for the correption in hiatus see 2.53n., 3.79n. In this phrase it may be colloquial; cf. Pl. *Mer.* 744 *nam quï amat,* Cat. 97.1 *non ita me dï ament.*

somnia fingunt: a proverbial characteristic of lovers; cf. Publil. Syr. 16 *amans quod suspicatur uigilans somniat.* The colloquial flavour of these lines is accompanied by unusual metrical features: the diaeretic pauses after *aspice* (105) and *credimus?* (108), the abruptness of the caesural pause after the fifth-foot trochee *ipse* (106) and the frequent caesural pauses elsewhere – after *sua, moror* (106) and *certe est* (107) – all give a sense of breathless excitement and urgency.

109 parcite: for the use of the verb without a complement cf. *A.* 6.834.

ab urbe uenit: Daphnis' homecoming, whether or not it is due to the magic, at least rewards its exponent. The happy outcome contrasts both with the result of the *carmina* of Theocritus' enchantress and with the suicidal despair at the end of Damon's song. The contest ends as abruptly as it began: no exchange of presents, no mention of a verdict. However the dramatic effectiveness of the ending cannot be denied.

The dedication to Pollio (6–13) suggests a publication date for the Eclogue in the latter part of 39 B.C. But it is detachable from its context and may postdate the composition of the poem (see 11n.). The combination in Damon's song of themes and details from *Idd.* 1, 3 and 11 recalls the synthesis of Theocritean material in *Ecl.* 2 and 3, while Alphesiboeus' song could well have started as an adaptation of part of the second idyll, perhaps like Catullus' *incantamentorum amatoria imitatio* to which Pliny (*Nat.* 28.19) refers.

The chief models for the Eclogue, *Idd.* 1 and 2, may already have been adjacent in the ancient Theocritean corpus, though the latter of these could not have formed part of any purely bucolic selection. Both idylls depict the sufferings that love can cause, whether it is accepted or rejected. Both exhibit – the first only in part, the second throughout – a structure of stanza and refrain. Whatever *retractationes* Vergil may have made of the two before, his deployment of the material here has all the assurance of his mature pastoral manner.

Damon's goatherd has nothing of Daphnis' heroic defiance in *Id.* 1; the mood is closer to the unsuccessful suitor of Amaryllis in *Id.* 3. The monologue has much of the pathos, tinged now and then with absurdity, that characterized *Ecl.* 2. Yet unlike Corydon and the

Theocritean wooer the goatherd has known the joys of love requited. That love is now lost. Unlike Corydon and Polyphemus too in *Id.* 11 he can find no solace in the 'medicine of the Muses'; instead of creating an idyllic world into which he could temporarily escape, his poetic fancy forms a vision of the universe gone totally awry. At the approaching triumph of his rival he wilts, and the end of the song, though somewhat melodramatic, is forlorn and desolate.

Alphesiboeus' enchantress differs in many respects from her predecessor in *Id.* 2. She has been translated from the city to the country (68n.), and the names that Vergil has chosen – Daphnis instead of Delphis for her lover, Amaryllis for the witch or her attendant (Thestylis in Theocritus) – recall *Idd.* 1 and 3 respectively, and so link the magic rites more closely to the theme of Damon's song. There is nothing here of the sentimental but very moving nostalgia that is portrayed in the second half of the Idyll to balance the mood of the opening section, presumably because this would not have provided sufficient contrast to Damon's song. Instead our attention is focused wholly on the enchantress' passionate determination to bring her lover back – whether by *carmina* or *uenena*. In *Id.* 2.149–54 Delphis' infidelity was explicit; here the suggestion is rather 'Johnny's so long at the Fair', and we are left in doubt whether the girl's suspicions are well-founded and her magic necessary at all. What Vergil creates out of this *contaminatio* of the two Theocritean themes is a study in contrasts: between the jilted man who abandons all hope of regaining his beloved and the jealous woman whose reaction to the prolonged absence of her lover is positive, indeed aggressive – an instance in fact of that *furiosa libido* which Ovid claimed to be characteristic of women (*A.A.* 1.281, 341–2).

The contrast is sustained by a quite close structural correspondence between the songs: (i) 17–20: Lucifer, hear my dying *carmen* ~ 64–7: Amaryllis, prepare for magical *carmina*; (ii) 22–4: Arcadia is the home of lovers' laments ~ 69–71: Witches' songs can transform the world; (iii) 26–30: The incongruous union of Nysa and Mopsus signifies a world distorted ~ 73–8: The triple binding can bring Daphnis back to union with his true love; (iv) 32–5: Nysa's disdain of the goatherd ~ 80–3: The enchantress' power over Daphnis; (v) 37–41: A wistful recollection of the first falling in love ~ 85–9: A wistful prospect of the lover's renewed longings; (vi) 43–5: The grim birthplace of Amor

~ 91–3: The hopeful burial of Daphnis' pledges; (vii) 47–50: Medea's unnatural violence inspired by Amor ~ 95–9: The supernatural powers of Moeris' herbs; (viii) 52–6: All nature will go awry and the humble herdsman become an Orpheus ~ 101–3: The magical songs are over; the enchantress will become a Moeris; (ix) 58–60: The second Flood will come and the goatherd will drown himself ~ 105–8: The fire's omens are good: here comes Daphnis.

The central images of the two songs (stanzas v) are modelled on the two poets whom Vergil admired most at this time, the Greek creator of the pastoral and the Latin exponent of Epicureanism. But the implicit tribute is incidental. For the images of the two stanzas are significant in their contexts as summarizing the mood of the two songs: the one a despairing nostalgia for the past, the first awakening of love in an orchard on a summer morning; the second a resolute look to the future, in which, however, the pitiless surface of jealousy is momentarily broken by a glimpse of vulnerable wistfulness. Out of the contrasting themes taken from adjacent Idylls Vergil has formed a new and original pastoral poem, in which the contrasting outcomes thus juxtaposed seem to demonstrate that in the face of love's disappointments as in other crises (cf. 1 fin. n.) success comes not to the gentle and plaintive but to the bold and resourceful.

ECLOGUE IX

1–2 Moeri…Lycida: for *Lycidas* see 7.67n., for *Moeris* 8.96n. For the piquant combination of Greek names, complete with Greek vocatives, and vivid Latin colloquialism see 3.2n.

quo te, Moeri, pedes: in 1.1–4 the dispossessed Meliboeus described Tityrus' security in idyllic terms; here the secure herdsman speaks first, setting a scene of bustling realism. The question recalls Th. *Id.* 7.21 'Simichidas, just where are you plodding along to (πόδας ἕλκεις) in the middle of the day?' For the colloquial ellipse, probably of *ducunt* (Serv., cf. Plin. *Ep.* 7.5), cf. Hor. *S.* 2.4.1 *unde et quo Catius?*

an quo uia ducit in urbem: the particle as usual (3.1n.) introduces an excited question; *in urbem* is antecedent to the relative *quo* 'is it to where the road leads, into town?' The implication is that Moeris' journey is surprising. Whether or not the city here is Mantua

(27 but 7–8n.), it represents something alien and hostile to the rustic way of life. The socio-legal realism of 2–4 is far removed from the pastoral myth.

2–3   uiui peruenimus 'we have lived to see ourselves come to this'; cf. the proverbial *uiuo uidentique* in Cic. *Quinct.* 50. Though clear enough, the personal construction *peruenio* [sc. *eo*] *ut* is uncommon; cf. Hor. *Ep.* 2.1.226–8 *speramus eo rem uenturam ut...* | *...arcessas.* Like Tityrus in 1.19ff. Moeris does not answer the question directly but explains the background to his journey, the subject which preoccupies his mind. His agitation is reflected by the disturbed word order of the two lines.

    aduena...possessor: the nouns are in apposition: 'the immigrant who is in possession'. *aduena* is contemptuous, as in *A.* 4.591. In Cic. *de Or.* 1.249 *aduenae* is coupled with *peregrini* in contrast to *patria.* The immigrant here is one of the barbarous soldiers of 1.70–1. The word-play in *peruenimus, aduena* is presumably deliberate. *possessio* did not in itself confer a legal title to ownership (*dominium*) but it could not be disturbed by a challenger (*petitor*) except through litigation. *possessor* often has connotations of violent usurpation; e.g. Cic. *Agr.* 2.98, *Quinct.* 30. It may imply that the veteran, unwilling to await the outcome of an appeal to the land-commissioners against the dispossession (see Dio 48.8 for the contesting of decisions in 42–41 B.C.), had simply taken the law into his own hands. It certainly raises doubts about the legality of his ownership. *mittimus haedos* (6) indicates that he was content to be an absentee land-lord.

    agelli: the diminutive form may be objective (cf. Var. *R.* 3.16.10 *agellus non sane naior iugero uno*) or emotive, reflecting Moeris' attachment to it; cf. 1.46ff.

4   haec mea sunt may allude to an *actio in rem*, in which the *possessor* as part of his *uindicatio rei* pronounced the formula *ex iure Quiritium meum esse aio* (Gaius. *Inst.* 4.16). But the tone of the line suggests a confrontation on the spot, perhaps after an unsuccessful *petitio* by the former occupants; cf. *uicti* (5). There is a significant contrast with 1.46.

    migrate recalls Meliboeus' plight in 1.64–6.

    coloni 'cultivators' belong not to the pastoral but to the agricultural world; cf. *G.* 1.125 *ante Iouem nulli subigebant arua coloni.* The word also had specialized legal connotations. It was regularly used of the members of a Roman *color.ia* (e.g. Caes. *Civ.* 1.14.4), who in the eyes of the indigenous population would clearly be *cultores aduenae* (cf. Serv. *ad A.* 1.12). Hence for an *aduena* to address the locals as *coloni* would be a bitter reversal of roles. Still more important here is the meaning 'tenant farmers', *alienum agrum locatum colentes* (cf. Cic. *Caec.* 94, *Dig.* 19.2.14 and 25). There are three possible reconstructions of the situation referred to here. (i) The land described in 7–9 comprised the properties of both Menalcas and Moeris. Both have been evicted. The use of *coloni* by the alien possessor is either a deliberate insult or the result of his ignorance. Menalcas has gone, but Moeris, with nowhere to go, has stayed to become ironically a *colonus* of the new owner, just as in Hor. *S.* 2.2.115 the dispossessed Ofellus became Umbrenus' tenant. (ii) Menalcas had owned the land, with Moeris as his tenant. *coloni* is used ineptly, as in (i), for both owner and tenant. After Menalcas' departure Moeris has stayed as tenant or hired man under the new owner, to whom the kids (6) are due, as in (i).(iii) Menalcas was the owner, Moeris the tenant, as in (ii). After Menalcas' eviction and departure Moeris and other tenants (*ueteres...coloni*) had hoped to renew their contract for *rerum usus fructus* (the right to enjoy and take the fruits of another's property) with the new owner. But he had sent them packing too (*migrate*) and the kids are a conciliatory offering.

5 fors omnia uersat: events can no longer be ascribed to a just providential order. For *uersat* cf. *turbatur* in 1.12. The heavy spondaic rhythms of the line are expressive.

6 hos...haedos: carried in a crate (65), the *spem gregis* which like Meliboeus (1.15) he is to be deprived of.

illi: the dative in contrast to *ad illum* (5.6n.) perhaps has its full force here: 'for him', 'to placate him'.

nec here is not the apocopated form of *neque* but the archaic negative particle *nĕ+c* to prevent hiatus, as in *necopinans, negotium*; cf.Greek *ouk* and *ou*. It is attested in archaic formulae, both legal, e.g. *nec escit* in the Twelve Tables and *res nec mancipi*, and religious, e.g. *illud enim nec di sinant* (Plin. *Ep.* 2.2.3); cf. 10.46. Although both orderings of the conventional imprecation are attested, *male res uortunt* (Pl. *Per.* 453) and *quae res tibi uortat male* (Ter. *Ad.* 191), it is perhaps better to read *nec bene* (= *male*) rather than *nec uertat* here. The spondee before the bucolic diaeresis is relatively rare (e.g. 3.40, 7.27) but accords with the jerky and abrupt rhythms of 3–4.

7 certe equidem audieram: 'Certainly what *I* heard was that...'
The force of *equidem* here is somewhat apologetic. For the colloquial combination of the two particles cf. Pl. *Mil.* 433, *Per.* 209.

qua introduces a long clause, summarized by *omnia* (10), in which the topography of Menalcas' and Moeris' former land is briefly sketched. Although ancient and modern commentators have seen in this a description of Vergil's own ancestral farm, *colles* and *fagos* cannot be reconciled with the terrain of Mantua. For the identification of Menalcas with Vergil however see fin. n.

se subducere viz. *se sursum ducere* 'to slope upwards', cf. D. Servius: *alii medium cliuum accipiunt, ex quo superior pars subducitur in collem surgentem, inferior in subiectam planitiem molliter deprimitur.* For the general contrast between *subducere* 'to raise' and *demittere* 'to lower' cf. Hor. *S.* 1.2.25–6. The couplet fixes the upper boundary of the property at the line where the steep slope upwards to the ridge meets the gentler gradient (*molli...cliuo*) which flattens out towards the river. The alternative meaning *ex alto in campos dissolui* (Serv.) would make the following line somewhat redundant.

9 ueteres...fagos: either marking the boundaries on either side between the hill-slope and the river (cf. Hor. *Ep.* 2.2.170–1 *populus adsita certis* | *limitibus*) or less likely lining the river bank. The reading *ueteris...fagi* is more prosaic and blurs the effective echo of *densas umbrosa cacumina fagos* (2.3). *ueteres* suggests a familiar feature of the landscape (cf. 3.12), which means far more to the *ueteres...coloni* than to the *aduena*. For the unprepossessing realism of *iam fracta* cf. 1.47–8, which is however counteracted by the idealized description that follows it.

10 uestrum indicates an association with Menalcas more intimate than Lycidas', yet one that Moeris shared with others, e.g. the other *coloni* (cf. 4). Lycidas, whatever his status, was not one of Menalcas' tenants. There is a contrast with *nostra* (12) 'the songs we countrymen enjoy' and *tuus* (16) 'your friend', both of which associate the two speakers closely.

12 tela inter Martia is emphatically isolated by the rhythmic pauses on either side. The normal peace of the countryside has been rudely disrupted by external events (cf. 1.11–12). But the protest here is more specifically against the impotence of poetry and the civilized arts in time of war.

13 Chaonias...columbas: the threat to poetry is figured in the helplessness of the dove when attacked by a bird of prey; cf. the contrast between *imbellem...columbam* and *feroces...aquilae* in Hor. *C.* 4.4.31–2. Chaonia was the district of Epirus in north-west Greece where the ancient town of Dodona was situated. There was an oracle at Dodona connected with the leaves of an old oak tree (Strabo 7.327f., cf. *G.* 1.8). Its patrons were Zeus and Dione. The priestesses, πέλειαι, πελειάδες, may have been originally Dione's; for Hom. *Il.* 16.233–5 mentions only Zeus and male priests, *Selloi*. Although the priestesses' name probably meant not 'doves' but 'old women' (Strabo 7 fr. 1a), doves seem to have been associated with the origins of the oracle, as they were with the cult of Dione's daughter Aphrodite; cf. Hdt. 2.55–7. The importance of Dodona declined with the rise of Delphi and the oracle never recovered from the sack of the town and its shrines first by the Aetolians in 219 B.C. (Strabo *loc. cit.*, cf. Polyb. 4.67.4 for condemnation of the sacrilege) and then by Aemilius Paullus' brutal devastation of central Epirus in 167 B.C. (Liv. 45.34, Strabo 7.322).

aquilae: in *A.* 11.721–4, Hor. *C.* 1.37.17–18 and by implication Lucr. 3.752 it is the hawk not the eagle that preys on the dove; and although Ovid follows Vergil (*M.* 1.506), the choice of *aquila* here is surely meant to recall the standards of the Roman legions. The *impii milites* who assaulted the sacred places of prophecy were not after all *barbari* but Greeks and Romans. The antithesis of doves and eagles would also be relevant to the lover's hatred of war (e.g. Tib. 1.10.11–13). Doves were particularly associated with Venus (Prop. 3.3.31; cf. 1.9.5), the daughter of Dione (47). The *carmina* of poets and prophets the doves of prophecy and Venus, are all threatened like the peace of the countryside by the eagles of war.

14 quod, as in *quod si*, is acc. of reference: 'as to which'.

quacumque sc. *ratione* (Serv.): 'somehow or other'. For *quicumque* used not as a relative but as an indefinite pronoun cf. 10.38, Liv. 22.58.5.

incidere 'to cut short': cf. Liv. 32.37.5, Hor. *Ep.* 1.14.36.

me: the warning was given only to Moeris. The appearance of a raven on the left seems to have been a guarantee of the omen concerned (Cic. *Div.* 1.85), whether it was good (Pl. *As.* 260–1) or bad (Pl. *Aul.* 624). Auspices on the left seem in general to have been favourable (Var. *L.* 7.97); so Servius may be right in maintaining that it was the hollow oak rather than the raven that portended danger if litigation were reopened (*nouas...lites*).

16   hic is probably the pronoun, not the adverb. Although Greek ὅδε is frequently used thus to refer to the speaker, the Latin usage seems to have been distinctly colloquial, e.g. Ter. *Ad.* 906, Hor. *S.* 1.9.47.

17   cadit...scelus: either of the wickedness that has come upon the usurper or of the evil action resulting from it, which has affected Menalcas. The juxtaposition of *tua* and *nobis* enhances the expression of intense personal loss. For the blurred cadences produced by the fifth-foot pyrrhic (2.26n.) cf. 51, 60. In 33 and 53 the effect is somewhat diminished by the enclitic character of *quoque*.

18   solacia 'the consolations that your music could have given us'. The solaces of Arcady are evoked in 19–20, with the attendant nymphs, carpets of flowers and cool shade.

20   spargeret...induceret: the echo of 5.40 *spargite humum foliis, inducite fontibus umbras* appropriately recalls the power of Arcadian song to soothe the herdsmen's grief (cf. 5.45–7). Like Silenus in 6.62 Menalcas is represented as actually doing what through the power of his creative imagination he depicts as having been done. For the poetic transformation of ordinary nature into Arcady cf. 1.51n., 2.54n.

21   uel: sc. *quis caneret ea.*
   sublegi 'I caught by stealth', 'secretly overheard'. The verb seems to be colloquial; cf. Pl. *Mil.* 1090.
   tibi is addressed like *tua* (17) to the absent Menalcas rather than to Moeris.

22   nostras following *te* need not imply any rivalry. Amaryllis is everyone's favourite. Although her name recurs often in the Eclogues (see p. 25), there may be a particular cross-reference with 1.4, 30, since Tityrus appears in the next two lines.

te...ferres could imply that Menalcas (or Moeris) was embarking on a *kômos*, like the unwelcome serenader of Amaryllis in Th. *Id.* 3.3–5 'Tityrus, my good friend, feed the goats; and take them to the spring, Tityrus, and be careful that the tawny Libyan he-goat doesn't butt you.' For a typically pedantic discussion of Vergil's adaptation of these lines see Gell. 9.9.7. The significant change is the more marked colloquial tone in the syntax of the Latin.

23 dum redeo 'until I return'. Though found at all periods (e.g. Ter. *Eun.* 206, Cic. *Att.* 10.3), this use of the pres. indicative seems colloquial; so certainly are the parenthetic *breuis est uia* and *cornu ferit ille* and, as already in Theocritus, the repeated *Tityre*.

24 potum: cf. 7.12. The supine in -*um* is simply the accusative of the -*tu*- verbal noun used to indicate goal or direction. Widespread in Plautus and still found in late republican prose, it declined rapidly in the literary registers of the language, except as a component of the fut. pass. inf. and in certain technical and stereotyped phrases, e.g. *nuptum dare, cubitum ire*, and was generally replaced by more 'rational' constructions like *ut* + subj., *ad* + gerund. Its use here, prosaic and slightly archaic, could be intended to suggest the character of rural dialect.

inter agendum: cf. Enn. *inc.* 2V, cited by D. Servius here, Pl. *Cis.* 721. The construction like other preposition + gerund phrases belonged predominantly to prose at this period. The repetitions *pasce, pastas* and *age, inter agendum* are colloquial.

25 occursare...caueto 'beware of running against'. For the inf. as direct complement to *cauere* cf. Cat. 50.21, Prop. 2.17.17.

26 immo haec: cf. 5.13, where Mopsus dismisses conventional pastoral themes in favour of the lament for Daphnis. So here Moeris prefers a topical piece by Menalcas on the dispossessions.

necdum may stand for *sed nondum*; since there is no preceding epithet, *necdum perfecta* sc. *sunt* would then be parenthetic: 'but it's not yet finished'. Alternatively *nec*- here may be the archaic negative (6n.), though the compound with -*dum* is not certainly attested before Tac. *H.* 1.31 *incipiens adhuc et necdum adulta*. Whether the phrase implies that Menalcas was at fault in not producing the flattering verses in time or that these were left unfinished when it became clear that Varus was not going to fulfil earlier hopes is impossible to say.

27 Vare: for the land-commissioner P. Alfenus Varus see 6.7n.

superet = *supersit* cf. Cic. *Ver.* 2.3.195, Liv. 22.40.8. The parataxis with *modo* instead of subordinating *dummodo* is archaic and suits the grand style of the address.

28 nimium uicina: about sixty kilometres in fact. For the confiscations see 1. fin.n. D. Servius (7) says that the boundary commissioner Octavius Musa, having used up the land around Cremona, extended the confiscations into Mantuan territory in pursuit of a personal grievance; also (10) that Varus carried this so far as to leave the Mantuans only a tract of marsh-land, for which he was attacked in a speech of Cornelius. He does not identify the latter as Cornelius Gallus, though this is perhaps implied in Donatus' briefer account (*Vita* 67ff.). It is clear that whatever hopes Vergil himself may have entertained of influencing Varus by any such Menalcan verses were thwarted and the dispossessions carried through remorselessly; cf. *G.* 2.198–9 *et qualem infelix amisit Mantua campum | pascentem niueos herboso flumine cycnos.*

29 sublime ferent ad sidera: cf. 5.51, *A.* 7.99. *sublime* is either a predicative adjective in agreement with *nomen* (27) or the adverb, formed from the internal use of the neut. acc.

cantantes...cycni: the singing swans, emphatically placed, enclose the line. Mantua was famous for them (*G.* 2.199). Swans were traditionally associated with Apollo and the Muses (Ar. *Av.* 870, Eur. *I.T.* 1104) and they are common metaphors for epic and high lyric poets, e.g. Leonidas *A.P.* 7.19.2, Hor. *C.* 2.20.1–3, 10–12; cf. line 36. In Hor. *C.* 4.2.25 Pindar is called *Dircaeus cycnus*, and the power of poets to confer immortality on their patrons is a frequent Pindaric theme, e.g. *O.* 10.91ff., *P.* 3.112ff., which recurs also in the non-pastoral *Idd.* 16.29ff. and 17.5–8 of Theocritus. Both the swans and the poets of Mantua will extol their benefactor. But Menalcas' confidence in his powers had been misplaced and Moeris' citation here has a bitter irony after 11–13.

30 sic 'on this condition' is found in both protases (like *si* from which it is derived) and apodoses of conditional sentences; e.g. Hor. *C.* 1.3.1ff., 1.28.23ff. respectively. Here it is usually taken as apodotic and 30–1 as a wish to be fulfilled if the condition implied by *incipe* (32) is met; cf. 10.4–6. However it would be very tactless to wish a friend who has lost his land prosperity for his bees and heifers. So it is possible that the couplet is a continuation of the preceding fragment, with *tua* referring like *tuum* (27) to Varus and the hopes for his prosperity presented in appropriately rustic metaphors; cf. the Golden Age images of the tribute to Pollio in 3.89. With a full stop at *uaccae* the following half-line would still be an invitation to Moeris to resume his own reminiscences from Menalcas.

Cyrneas...taxos: Corsica (Greek *Kúrnos*) was like Sardinia (7.41) notorious for the bitterness of its honey, attributed either to its many box trees (Diod. 5.14.3) or to wild hemlock (Ov. *A.* 1.12.9–10). The yew, which is found on the higher ground in Italy and along the Ligurian coast, seems to be rare in Corsica. However Vergil refers to yews as *nocentes* (*G.* 2.257) and warns against putting beehives near them (*G.* 4.47); so the local epithet may here characterize not the trees but their produce: 'yews that cause honey to have a Corsican flavour'. Cf. *Hyblaeis* (5.54n.).

examina: for this technical term for 'swarms of bees' see 7.13n.

31 cutiso: see 1.78n.

uaccae could belong to Moeris, since *haedos* (6, 62) does not prove that he was exclusively a goatherd. However, the image of heifers with swollen udders may be merely a figure for prosperity (cf. the goats in 4.21, 7.3), and *uaccae* chosen as appropriate to Varus' social status, being more expensive to maintain than goats in the real world (p. 24).

32 si quid habes is colloquial; cf. 3.52, 5.10–11.

et me fecere poetam comes awkwardly after the invitation to Moeris, especially with the insistent references to himself that follow: *et mihi, me quoque* etc. Perhaps we are to imagine as on a stage a long pause after *habes* with Lycidas at last eagerly breaking the silence. Alternatively what follows *habes* may be an attempt to stimulate Moeris by quoting another excerpt from Menalcas. 31–5 like 23–5 is clearly based on Theocritus; cf. *Id.* 7.37–41 'For I too am a clear-voiced mouthpiece of the Muses and everyone calls me the best of singers. But I hesitate to believe them, by Mother Earth I do; for to my mind I don't yet surpass the good Sicelidas from Samos or Philetas in singing but vie with them as a frog against cicadas.' Again (cf. 22n.)

the tone of the adaptation is more prosaic with its bald colloquial phrases marked off by abrupt pauses after *Pierides, pastores* (caesural) and *carmina* (diaeretic).

34 uatem: for the contrast with *poetam* (32) see 7.28n.

35 Vario: L. Varius Rufus, Vergil and Horace were all subsequently members of Maecenas' circle. Varius wrote elegiac poetry (Porph. *ad* Hor. *C.* 1.6.1) and short epic pieces on contemporary themes (cf. 8.88n.), which were highly regarded (Hor. *C.* 1.6.1–4, *A.P.* 53–5). His most famous work was the tragedy *Thyestes*, published early in the Augustan period. With Plotius Tucca he was entrusted by Augustus with the editing of *Aeneid* after Vergil's death.

Cinna: C. Helvius Cinna like Vergil and Catullus, who was a close friend (Cat. 10.29f.), came from Gallia Cisalpina. Prominent among the neoteric poets, he also wrote lyrics and epigrams (Isid. *Orig.* 6.12.2), an occasional hexameter piece *Propempticon Pollionis* (Charis. 158B) and a monumentally learned 'epyllion' *Zmyrna*, which took nine years to complete (Cat. 95). He was murdered in 44 B.C., some years before this Eclogue was published.

adhuc implies that the author of the lines, whether Lycidas or Menalcas, still has aspirations to match the achievements of Varius and Cinna. Only a few fragments survive of either poet, but the tone of the present lines and the image of *olores* (cf. 29n.) suggest that it is their work in the higher, more public, genres that is referred to.

36 anser may or may not be a punning reference to the poet Anser, an associate of Cinna *Cinnaque procacior* (Ov. *T.* 2.435). A similar pun has been suggested in the comparison of geese to swans at Prop. 2.34.83–4. Servius' identification of Anser as *Antonii poetam, qui eius laudes scribebat* may be based on nothing more than Cicero's reference to certain *Anseres* who supported Antony (*Phil.* 13.11).

37 id quidem ago refers to the invitation in 32, ignoring the intervening lines of self-appraisal. The succession of plosive consonants beginning with the harsh *id quid-*, the absence of caesural pauses in the predominantly dactylic rhythms, the heterodynes produced by the sequence of short words and the impeded effect of the three elisions all combine to express Moeris' agitation.

38   si ualeam 'in case I may be able'; cf. the more familiar *si forte...* (6.57).

39   huc ades, O Galatea: cf. 2.45n. The passage is adapted from Th. *Id.* 11.42–7 'But come to me... and leave the grey sea to pound away against the land. It will be more pleasant for you to spend the night in the cave beside me. There are bay trees there and slender cypresses, there's dark ivy, there's the vine with its sweet fruit, there's cold water...' The descriptive detail, however, is Vergil's own.

quis...nam 'What indeed?' The archaic separation of particle from pronoun (e.g. Pl. *Rud.* 945) serves to emphasize the particle, as in *nam quis* (*G.* 4.445). For the question cf. *Id.* 11.49 'Who would rather have the sea and the waves than all this?'

ludus: *uoluptas* (D. Serv.); cf. *Id.* 11.62 'I'll learn to swim... so I'll know why in the world it pleases you to make your home in the deep.'

40   hic...hic...hic (41) is more insistent than Theocritus' deliberately jejune repetitions of the verb 'to be' (39n.). Moreover each successive member of the tricolon is more elaborate than the preceding one.

purpureum 'richly coloured'. Th. *Id.* 18.27 has λευκὸν ἔαρ 'white spring', Vergil himself at *G.* 2.319 *uere rubenti*, but the epithet here as in Lygd. [= Tib. 3] 5.4 is probably not colour-specific. See 5.38n.

uarios, emphatically placed, marks the contrast with the monotonous aspect of the sea, while the phrase *uarios...flores* expressively encloses the whole scene.

flumina circum implies that here the waters are fresh and bring fertility and beauty to the land. The onomatopoeia of the repeated *f*, *o* and *u* sounds in the clause contributes to the effect. For the anastrophe of *circum* cf. 8.59.

41   candida like *albus* in Hor. *C.* 2.3.9 indicates the white poplar (7.61n.). But in contrast to *albus* it suggests luminosity and radiance, an antidote to the darkness of the cave; hence the oxymoron *imminet* 'overshadows', which is emphasized by its position in enjambement.

42   umbracula is defended by Macrobius (*Sat.* 6.4.8) against the charge of neologism with citations from Cicero, where the noun is used of the shade provided by a group of alders, and Varro, where it seems to mean awnings or parasols. It may be significant, however, that no verse precedents are given.

lentae...uites again enclose the scene. For the metaphor of the woven shade cf. Th. *Id.* 7.7-8: 'poplars and elms wove a shady grove, forming an arch with their luxuriant green foliage' (reading ὕφαινον Heinsius' correction of ἔφαινον). The presence of both cave and vines recalls not only Polyphemus' serenade in *Id.* 11 (39n.) but also Mopsus' choice of setting in 5.6-7.

43 huc ades: the address to Galatea ends as it began (39) with an appeal to the nymph in her watery element.

insani...fluctus enclose her world. The contrast of land and sea is emphasized by the parallel word order in 42 and 43. Besides the wildness of the elements (cf. *insanis...uentis* in Tib. 2.4.9) the epithet perhaps alludes to the madness of anyone who would prefer the sea to the land. It thus controls the emotive direction of the image (cf. 5.83).

feriant sine: for the archaic parataxis cf. *A.* 2.669-70, Liv. 2.40.5 *sine, priusquam complexum accipio, sciam.*

44 For the distribution of lines 44-50 between the speakers see 51n.

quid quae 'What about the lines which?' As in *G.* 1.111 *quid qui* 'What of those who?', Cic. *Off.* 3.94 *quid quod* 'What of the fact that?' the elliptical combination introduces a new topic or illustration.

pura...sub nocte: cf. Arat. *Ph.* 323 καθαρῇ ἐνὶ νυκτί 'on a clear night' and *per purum* 'through the clear sky' in *G.* 2.364. For the image of the lonely vigil cf. *noctes uigilare serenas* (Lucr. 1.142). The fact that the verses were sung alone (*solum*) and at night (cf. 10.75-6) indicates their un-pastoral character. See 49n.

45 numeros 'the rhythms' of the hexameter verses.

si uerba tenerem 'if only I had hold of the words'. After *numeros memini* something like *et carmen ipsum reuocarem* is understood.

46 antiquos signorum...ortus is probably by hypallage for *antiquorum signorum ortus*: the stars were ancient but he was witnessing a new rising, though one that had been long rehearsed.

47 Dionaei...Caesaris: Dione, daughter of Tethys and Oceanus (Hes. *Th.* 353), shared the cult of Dodona with Zeus (13n.), to whom she bore Aphrodite (Hom. *Il.* 5.370-1), whose son Aeneas was the mythical founder of the *gens Iulia*; cf. *Dionaeae matri* in *A.* 3.19. The

COMMENTARY: 9.47–49 267

unusual epithet for *Caesar* thus obliquely recalls that the Julians numbered Jove as well as Venus among their ancestors. However Dodona's prophetic doves were impotent in the face of armed force (13) and the peace and prosperity heralded by the comet may be endangered likewise.

processit: of a rising star; cf. 6.86.

astrum, repeated emphatically in the next line, is the *sidus Iulium*. The comet appeared in the northern skies for several nights in July 44 B.C. (Plin. *Nat.* 2.93–4, Suet. *Iul.* 88, Dio. 45.7.1) when Octavian was celebrating the *ludi uictoriae Caesaris* (*ludi Veneri Genetrici*) which Julius Caesar had instituted two years before (*CIL* 1.1.225, 244). Coming within four months of Caesar's death it was regarded as a sign of his deification as well as an apocalyptic portent (see 4.4n., 5. fin. n.). It is represented on coins as an eight-pointed star with a tail and frequently referred to in Augustan literature; e.g. *A.* 8.681, Hor. *C.* 1.12.46–7, Ov. *M.* 15.845–50.

48 quo...frugibus: both ablatives are instrumental, the first (= *ut eo*) signifying cause, the second reference.

segetes 'crop-land', cf. *G.* 1.47, Cato *Agr.* 37.2, Var. *R.* 1.29.1 *seges dicitur quod aratum satum est, aruom quod aratum necdum satum est.*

gauderent: cf. *duceret* (49). The subjunctives express the purpose of the star's appearance, as opposed to the actuality that indicatives would convey.

et quo: the blurred rhythm of the cadence produced by the monosyllables ($\angle \cup \cup - \angle$) is tempered, as in 5.83, 6.9 etc., by the swift enjambement.

49 duceret: from the similar use of *trahere* in *A.* 4.701 and Plin. *Nat.* 19.134 *cum coeperint colorem trahere* and the use of *bibere* to describe the process of dyeing (Plin. *Nat.* 8.193) we may infer that *ducere* here, as in Ov. *M.* 3.485, Sen. *Ep.* 71. 31, means 'to draw in', 'absorb', from the sunlight in this instance.

apricis 'sunny'. The word is contrasted with *opacus* in Cic. *Part.* 36 and may be derived from *aperire*; cf. P. Fest. 2M *apricum locum a sole apertum.* What was exposed to sunshine was equally exposed to bad weather. Comets were normally supposed to precede bad weather (Sen. *N.Q.* 7.28), as in the lore of prophecy they often portended national disaster (4.4n.). Hence the beneficial effects are specified here as in *Ecl.* 4 and 5. Rural prosperity came from nature's rejoicing at the deification of Daphnis in *Ecl.* 5.56ff., and the choice of Daphnis as observer here is clearly an oblique allusion to that poem. *apricis* placed thus in the line contributes to a slow sequence of five heavy syllables: *-tap-rī-cī-sin-col-* as opposed to *-ta-prī-*($\cup$ –), the alternative treatment of mute + liquid clusters.

50 insere, Daphni, piros: cf. 1.73 *insere nunc, Meliboee, piros.* The bitterness of Meliboeus' preceding words *his nos conseuimus agros* like Moeris' plight here contrasts sharply with the confident optimism of *carpent tua poma nepotes.* Daphnis' expectations have not been universally fulfilled.

51 omnia fert aetas: cf. Plato *A.P.* 9.51 αἰὼν πάντα φέρει..., 'Time carries everything away; length of days can change names, shapes and natures, fortunes.' 51–3 is the only indication that Moeris, like Tityrus in *Ecl.* 1, is no longer a young man.

animum quoque: *etiam memoriam* (Serv.), a sense attested in Cic. *de Or.* 2.300 *nihil ex illius animo...umquam effluere potuisse* and Liv. 28.28.8. Equally appropriate is the meaning 'will, desire (sc. to sing)', for which cf. Cic. *Man.* 66 *ab auro gazaque regia manus, oculos, animum cohibere.* The abruptness of the following pause at the bucolic diaeresis is very expressive.

The continuity of the preceding passage can now be summarized. Moeris after some effort (37–8) managed to recollect the Galatea fragment (39–43). He then broke off and invited Lycidas to recite another excerpt, of which he himself could remember only the rhythm (44–5). Lycidas has complied and given the Daphnis fragment (46–50). Moeris now confesses that he is unable to go on with the game (51–5). This analysis depends on a distribution of lines (37–45 Moeris, 46–50 Lycidas, 51–5 Moeris) not found in any of the manuscripts; M and P¹ have 37–43 Moeris, 44–50 Lycidas, 51–5 Moeris; P² has 37–43 Moeris, 44–5 Lycidas, 46–55 Moeris. However it retains the most attractive features of MP¹: (i) Moeris does not plead amnesia immediately after quoting the Daphnis fragment, as he does in P²; (ii) Lycidas has the optimistic *Daphnis* as Moeris had the wistful *Varus* (27–9); (iii) both singers have two Menalcan excerpts, Lycidas 23–5, 46–50, Moeris 27–9, 39–43 (though this balance would be upset if

Lycidas' 32–6 were also a Menalcan quotation, cf. 32n.). At the same time it avoids the inconsistency in MP[1] between Lycidas' admission in 45 and his immediate recall of both *numeros* and *uerba* in the next line.

52 condere 'to lay to rest'; cf. Hor. *C.* 4.5.29. There is perhaps an echo of Callim. *A.P.* 7.80.2–3 'I recalled how often we both had sent the sun down with our talk' (ἥλιον ⟨ἐν λέσχῃ κατεδύσαμεν). For *meminisse* with pres. infinitive see 1.17n.

53 oblita mihi: the dative connotes agency. For the participle of *obliuiscor* used in a passive sense cf. Prop. 1.19.6 *ut meus oblito puluis amore uacet* and the passive use of e.g. *detestatus, meditatus.* Some of these uses, e.g. *comitatus, ueneratus,* are derived from active doublets of deponent verbs, but there is no evidence of **obliuisco.*

54 lupi: for this superstition cf. Pl. *Rep.* 336D, Th. *Id.* 14.22 'Won't you speak? Have you seen a wolf?' Plin. *Nat.* 8.80 *sed in Italia quoque creditur luporum uisus esse noxius uocemque homini quem priores contemplentur adimere ad praesens.* The proverbial phrase *lupus in fabula* (e.g. Ter. *Ad.* 537, Cic. *Att.* 13.33.4) may also refer to this belief. There is a sad contrast between Moeris' words here and the powers attributed to Moeris in 8.98–9. The pauses at the bucolic diaeresis in 53 and after the third-foot trochee in 54 divide the couplet into three abrupt statements whose starkness is intensified by the absence of any grammatical connections beyond the *quoque* of 53.

55 ista 'those verses you want to hear'; the second-person demonstrative.

satis...saepe: the temporal adverb seems almost an afterthought: 'All the same he'll recall what you want well enough...and often too...will Menalcas.' Servius' interpretation, *ordo est 'satis saepe',* is less likely. The tone is again colloquial; the sentiment pathetic, for the truth is that Moeris like Meliboeus in 1.77 has lost the will to sing.

56 caussando 'by your excuses'; cf. Lucr. 1.398. The word seems, no doubt unintentionally on Lycidas' part, to mock *cantando* (52).

amores viz. the desire to hear Menalcas' songs. For *amor = studium* cf. *A.* 2.10, Cic. *Fin.* 4.18.

in longum ducis: cf. Liv. 5.16.4 *nec in longum dilata res est.* A hint to Moeris perhaps that his expectations are hopeless.

57   tibi i.e. 'for you to sing'. Either -*i* is long, an archaism for which see 4.23n., or the syllable division is *ti-bis-tra-*; see 5.68n.

stratum...aequor: the noun could be used of any flat surface. Specification was originally by means of a dependent genitive, e.g. *aequora caeli* (Acc. *trag.* 224R), *a. ponti* (Lucr. 1.8; cf. *A.* 2.780), *a. campi* (Enn. *Ann.* 137V). *stratum* here (cf. *strataque aequaliter unda* in Ov. *H.* 7.49) and the probable reminiscence of Th. *Id.* 2.38 'Look, the sea is silent and the winds are silent' support the interpretation of the word in something closer to its commonest sense 'sea' (e.g. *A.*1.381, 511). (*aequor*) *mare appellatum quod aequatum cum commotum uento non est* (Var. *L.* 7.23). If the setting were specifically Mantuan (and in spite of *Mantua* in 27, *colles* (7) and *fagos* (9) are against this), the word could refer to the lakes formed by the Mincio around the town (Liv. 24.10.7) or to the slow-moving surface of the river itself; cf. *aequora* in Ov. *M.* 13.955, *aequora Danuuii* in *CIL* 3.3676. D. Servius takes the noun as referring to flat land (cf. *G.* 2.541, *A.* 11.599), but the participle is then hard to account for.

58   uentosi...murmuris aurae: the genitive is either descriptive ('the breezes with their blustery roar') or possessive, with the terms of the unmetrical *uenti murmurantis* ('belonging to the roaring wind') transposed. Either way the aural noun is placed in a syntactically more emphatic position. The Greek loanword *aura* is normally used of something milder than *uentus*; cf. Sen. *N.Q.* 3.25.8. But this breeze had a note of violence in it. The aural image is comparable to 5.82 rather than the pastoral rustle of spring (7.1n.). Now the wind has dropped and it looks like rain (63).

ceciderunt: for this use of the verb cf. *G.* 1.354.

59   adeo as in 4.11 stresses the preceding word: 'just from here on'.

namque sepulcrum and *hic, ubi densas* (60) complete the list of verse cadences marked off by a pause at the bucolic diaeresis, which is a remarkable feature of this poem; cf. 17, 23, 33, 51, 53. Most of them occur in excited dialogue and like the present pair are accompanied by rapid enjambement with the following line.

60   Bianoris: memorials and votive shrines were in ancient as in modern times a feature of the Greek and Italian landscape. For the context of this one cf. Th. *Id.* 7.10–11 'We had not yet reached half way and the tomb of Brasilas was not visible to us.' Servius identifies Bianor with Ocnus, son of the Etruscan river god Tiberis and the prophetess Manto (and hence a half-brother of Mopsus; see 5.1n.), who was the legendary founder of Mantua (*A.* 10.198–200). The identification is suspect. For, while *Ocnus* is a plausible name for the founder of an Etruscan (Plin. *Nat.* 3.130) town, the Greek name *Biánōr* is not; and it is strange that he should be buried away from the town. Bianor of Bithynia the epigrammatist (cf. *A.P.* 7.49 etc.) is irrelevant here and was still alive in A.D. 17 (*A.P.* 9.423). The death of a young man Bianor is lamented by his mother in Diotimus *A.P.* 7.261. If this is where Vergil got the name, then it brings a gloomy note to the scene. But, as with Theocritus' Brasilas, we are too ignorant to assess the detail confidently.

densas, taken with the presence of kids (6, 62), suggests that this is the early summer *frondatio* (see 1.56n.). A detail of the realistic countryside is thus introduced into the idyllic image of the leafy carpet from Th. *Id.* 7.132–3 (1.80–1n.).

62 tamen: for the emphatic position cf. 1.27.

63 colligat: now that the wind has dropped (57–8), rain threatens. For the whole phrase cf. *G.* 3.327 *ubi quarta sitim caeli collegerit hora.*

64 cantantes, emphatically repeated in 65, reveals Lycidas' tactless determination to extract another song from the dejected old man, whether they go on their way or pause to rest. The eager invitation to Lycidas in Th. *Id.* 7.35–6 'Come on then, since we have the road and the day to share together, let us make pastoral music' has a quite different emotional context.

usque...eamus 'let's go straight on' is colloquial, like the parenthetic *minus uia laedet*, the insistent repetition of *hic* (60–2) and the sequence of brief statements and exhortations from 59 onwards, which produce pauses at unusual points in the line – the bucolic diaereses in 59, 60, the third-foot trochaic caesura in 62, 64, 65, and the fifth-foot caesura in 64.

laedet, which has equally good manuscript authority, is preferable in sense to *laedit*. Moeris is unwilling to rest (66), so Lycidas hopes to persuade him to sing by the prospect of lightening the journey by song and the offer to relieve him of his burden.

65   fasce leuabo: *fascis* is used of any bundle that is loosely tied; e.g. straw and twigs for burning (Hirt. *B.G.* 8.15.5), a soldier's baggage (*G.* 3.347), the rods carried by the lictors (Pl. *Epid.* 27–8). Here it is a wicker basket or crate of the kind still used by Italian farmers to bring lambs and chickens to market. The ablative with *leuare*, for which cf. *leua me...hoc onere* (Cic. *Fam.* 3.12.3), is separative, rather than instrumental denoting reference. An alternative construction with acc. + dat. of the person (cf. 7.6n.) is probably exemplified in *A.* 2.146–7 *uiro...manicas...leuari | ...iubet.*

66–7   desine plura, puer, the colloquial phrase with which Mopsus declared the start of singing in 5.19, now marks its conclusion. Nightfall (63) is not the hour for pastoral song (10.75–7), and this time it symbolizes the end of singing altogether for Moeris as it did for Meliboeus in *Ecl.* 1, even though at the very end he pathetically reiterates the hopes of 55. Like Tityrus in *Ecl.* 1 Lycidas reveals little sympathy for his friend's plight. His offers of help in 65 had only a selfish motivation and the poem ends abruptly with the picture of Moeris disconsolate and intent on the painful task in hand, *quod nunc instat.*

puer et: the scansion ($\cup$ – –) is unusual; cf. *adloquitur ac* (*A.* 4.222). There are three possible analyses, in descending order of probability: (i) *pu-er-et-* with a marked pause after *-er*, cf. 7.23n.; (ii) *pu-er-ret-* with the resonant consonant prolonged, as in *procul ac* (*A.* 8.98); the earlier form of the word would in fact have been **puerr < *puer(o)s*; (iii) *pu-ē-ret-* with pseudo-archaic *ē* on analogy with genuine archaisms like *amōr* (10.69), *patēr* (*A.* 11.469); cf. 3.97n.

The basic situation is the same as in *Ecl.* 1. Like Meliboeus, the poet Menalcas has been evicted and old Moeris has lost either his land or his tenancy (4n.). Lycidas, though his status and circumstances are left vague, has clearly not been molested. He thus corresponds dramatically to Tityrus, the ageing slave who in *Ecl.* 1 had gained security of tenure over the land that he farmed. But attention is focused in the present poem not so much upon the contrasting fortunes of those affected by the dispossessions as on the disruption of valued personal relationships between those who have been forced to leave and those who, in whatever capacity, remain behind; and the blight that has affected the artistic life of the country. The herdsmen have lost their local poet. Music like farming has become one of the casualties of war; no one here sings *lentus in umbra*.

The Menalcan fragments recall the range of Vergilian pastoral without explicitly paraphrasing particular passages. (i) Two Theocritean adaptations: in 23–5 the rustic dialogue, based on *Id.* 3 but with touches of colloquialism, is reminiscent of *Ecl.* 3; the Galatea piece in 39–43 with its evocations of the idyllic landscape in *Id.* 11 recalls the reworking of the Polyphemus theme in *Ecl.* 7 and more freely in *Ecl.* 2 (ii) Two non-Theocritean fragments: in 46–50 Daphnis contemplating the *sidus Iulium* recalls the optimism of *Ecl.* 4 and of Menalcas' song in *Ecl.* 5; the non-pastoral lines addressed to Varus in 26–9, *necdum perfecta*, remind us of the themes of *Ecl.* 1 and 9 itself. Each of the herdsmen is assigned one fragment of each kind; in the arrangement adopted in the text Lycidas has the optimistic Daphnis-fragment, Moeris, for whom neither the omen of the comet nor the hopes placed in Varus have borne fruit, the rueful Varus-piece. If 32–6 with its powerful echo of *Id.* 7 is also taken as a Menalcan excerpt, then Lycidas will have an extra quotation; but this would not be inappropriate, since he is throughout the pace-maker, Moeris the more reluctant singer.

There is much that recalls *Id.* 7, the one Theocritean pastoral that has links with the poet's own life and times: the presence of Lycidas, the encounter on a journey and numerous echoes in detail (at 1, 32–6, 42, 59–61, 64) which keep the Greek poem constantly in our minds. Yet the contrast between the two is striking. The meeting of Simichidas and Lycidas in the Idyll leads to the outpouring of creative song in a competition which embodies a literary programme, and when that is over Simichidas goes on his way with his friends to the harvest festival. Here the meeting leads to the report of gloomy news and the wistful recollection of fragments of songs past; there is no inspiration to new creativity and the poem ends with the two figures trudging on their silent way, sharing only the vain hope that their absent friend, the master-poet, may yet return.

There is much too – besides the general similarity of situation – that recalls *Ecl.* 1. The more fortunate of the herdsmen is once more por-

trayed as somewhat insensitive to his companion's distress. Realistic
details are introduced to relate the Arcadian world of Menalcas'
poetry, as they related the Arcadian character of Tityrus' security, to
life outside the pastoral. Some of these details are of course essential
to the situation, e.g. *possessor* (3), *lites* (14), others provide connections
with a particular historical context, e.g. *Varo* and *Mantua* (25–6)
Vario, Cinna (35), *Caesaris* (47), others again add picturesque verisimilitude, e.g. Bianor's tomb and the *frondatio* (59–61). On the other
hand, the dialogue is often enlivened by colloquialisms, and this is a
feature of *Ecl.* 3, 5 and 7, not of *Ecl.* 1. An explicit connection with
Ecl. 1 is provided by the cross-reference of 1.73 and 9.50. It is not
impossible that both poems were published as a pair, though
in its present form *Ecl.* 1 gives an impression of much greater
maturity.

The scenery of the poem is too generalized to be identifiable with
any particular region and some of the details are in fact irreconcilable
with Mantua or its neighbourhood. Nevertheless the explicit mention
of Mantua in 28, the similarity in setting to Theocritus' autobiographical *Id.* 7, the choice of the name Menalcas, explicitly identified
as Vergil himself in 5.86–7, for the departed poet-landlord, and the
'Vergilian' character of the songs attributed to him put the identification beyond reasonable doubt. It was already accepted by Quintilian
(8.6.46) and is assumed by Donatus and Servius. The very similar
accounts of the relevant biographical events in Don. *Vit.* 262–80,
Serv. *ad* 9.1 etc., *Buc. prooem.* 2.25–3.13 may be based on little more
than inference from the poems themselves. Like Tityrus in *Ecl.* 1
Vergil was evicted by Varus, but *potentium fauore* (Serv.) he managed
to regain his property, only to be forcibly ejected like Menalcas – by a
centurion called Arrius. The land was finally restored to him by
Octavian's intervention, *missis tribus uiris* (Serv.). Donatus mentions
the good offices of Maecenas and the *triumuiros agris diuidendis Varum,
Pollionem et Cornelium Gallum*; but this blurs the very distinct roles
played by the latter three, who were not all members of the land commission together either in 41 B.C. when the Cisalpine evictions seem to
have begun, or in the following years during which they continued.
There is nothing impossible in all this, though Servius' explicit
identifications of Tityrus with Vergil in *Ecl.* 1 and of the land described in 9.7–10 with Vergil's farm are both untenable. Clearly Ver-

gil's own experience provided much of the inspiration in both poems; but his chief concern is once again a more general one: to depict the way in which war disrupts human relationships and the power of poets to bring comfort, recreation and hope to their community. His own personal fortunes are but a symptom.

ECLOGUE X

1 Extremum indicates that this was the latest Eclogue to be published; see 8.11n.

Arethusa: one of the Nereids (*G.* 4.344). She was bathing in the river Alpheus near its source in Arcadia when the river-god tried to seduce her. She fled and Artemis turned her also into a river, which flowed under the sea to emerge as a spring on the island of Ortygia off Syracuse (Ov. *M.* 5.572–641; cf. the variant in Paus. 5.7.2–3). Vergil in *A.* 3.694–6 has the version (cf. Pi. *N.* 1.1–4) in which Alpheus follows Arethusa and is united with her in the Ortygian spring. This would be a happier precedent for Gallus and Lycoris (5n.) but the explicit antithesis of *Doris* and *tibi* alone (4–5) suggests the former version. The fountain itself was impressive (Cic. *Ver.* 2.4.118) and Arethusa was represented often on Syracusan coins. She is invoked by the dying Daphnis in Th. *Id.* 1.117 and is the source of the Dorian poet's inspiration in *Epit. Bion.* 77. The *uirgo Arcadia* (Ov. *A.* 3.6.30) thus provides a mythological link between the Sicily of Greek pastoral and Vergil's Arcadia.

laborem: not *ludum* (7.17, cf. 1.10, 6.1). This suggests either (i) a reluctance to write any more pastoral, which has been overcome only by the fact (if this is the implication of 3 and 72) that his friend has requested him, or (ii) a recognition that the theme chosen, though superficially pastoral, is novel or even alien to the genre. For another possibility see 64n., 72–3n. Certainly this appeal for divine aid must be significant; cf. 4.1, 8.64.

2 Gallo: on Cornelius Gallus see 6.64n.

Lycoris is named as Gallus' mistress in Prop. 2.34.91–2, Ov. *A.* 1.15.30. Servius says that his love for her was the subject of his elegies (6n.) and identifies her with the actress Cytheris, alias Volumnia, a freed-woman of Volumnius Eutrapelus, an intimate friend of Antony.

She was at different times the mistress of both men and no doubt of others as well; see Cic. *Att.* 10.10.5, *Fam.* 9.26.2. If the identification is correct, then it is no wonder that Gallus found her fickle, nor could Vergil have seriously believed that his poem might influence her. See further 23n.

4 sic 'on this condition' (9.30n.). There is a slightly hectoring tone, perhaps even the hint of a threat, viz. *nisi incipies, orabo ut...intermisceat.* But then Arethusa was hardly likely to be very sympathetic to the plight of lovers in pursuit of reluctant girls.

fluctus...Sicanos i.e. *mare Siculum*, the sea between Sicily and the Peloponnese. This seems to be the earliest Latin occurrence of the epithet.

subterlabere like *intermisceat* (5) adds to the solemnity of the address by its cluster of heavy syllables.

5 Doris was sister and wife of Nereus (Hes. *Th.* 240) and so mother of Arethusa; hence the use of the name here is more than just metonymy for *mare*; cf. *Thetin* (4.32).

amara is both 'harsh', 'cruel' (cf. 3.110), as violating maternal affection, and 'salty', 'bitter to taste' (cf. *G.* 2.238), since the sea would pollute the fresh water of Arethusa's spring. For a similar exploitation of the ambiguity of the word see 7.41. For the situation itself cf. Mosch. fr. 3.1–6: 'Whenever Alpheus leaves Pisa and makes his way under the ocean, he comes to Arethusa, bringing water that bears wild olives...He goes deep into the waves and runs his course beneath the sea; water does not mix with water and the sea knows nothing of the river's journey through.' The moral of this little fragment is that 'The knavish boy who is always plotting mischief and teaching terrible lessons, the boy Love, thus by a spell taught even a river to dive' (*ibid.* 7–8). It is not irrelevant to Gallus, who might have done better to pursue her, instead of moping like Damon's goatherd in *Ecl.* 8.

6 incipe is emphatically isolated by the following diaeretic pause.

sollicitos...amores is more specific than the vague τὰ Δάφνιδος ἄλγε' ἀείδες 'you sing of Daphnis' sufferings' in Th. *Id.* 1.19. The noun *amor* occurs ten times in the poem (including the proper name *Amor*). The plural is often used specifically (cf. 1.6n.), of a single love

affair or loved one; e.g. Prop. 4.4.37, Cat. 45.1. Moreover there may
be an allusion to the title of Gallus' elegiac collection; cf. Servius' note
on 1, *amorum suorum de Cytheride libros scripsit quattuor*, and the *Amores* of
Ovid.

7 simae was a Greek loan-word, rare enough to require a gloss from
Servius, though it occurs as early as Liv. Andron. *sc.* 5R. It is used of
bees in Th. *Id.* 7.80, and of kids, as here, in *Id.* 8.50, Menalcas' contest
with Daphnis.

capellae: there is no social hierarchy in Arcady (see p. 24); so
keeping goats, which in real life would rank very low among herdsmen,
has no particular stigma, nor is it incompatible with musical prowess;
cf. the goatherds Meliboeus, Mopsus and Corydon (1.12, 77; 5.12;
7.3). In Theocritus too it was Lycidas the goatherd who proclaimed
Callimachean doctrine (*Id.* 7.45–8) and sang the *Ageanax*-song (ib.
52–88), and a goatherd who in *Id.* 1 exhorted Thyrsis to sing the
Daphnis-dirge, on which lines 9–30 are based. Vergil's adoption of the
goatherd's role here and in 77 therefore indicates merely the acceptance of Arcadian values.

8 surdis: for the proverbial notion of singing to deaf ears cf. Ter.
H.T. 222, Prop. 4.8.47, Liv. 40.8.10. Even if Lycoris is impervious, the
woods at least respond in sympathy to the pastoral singer.

respondent: for the echoes of the song interpreted as a sympathetic
response by the woods see 1.5.

9–10 quae... qui: interrogative not exclamatory, as the intervening
aut clearly shows.

puellae Naides: the pause after the fifth-foot trochee, coming at
the end of the breathless enquiry, marks off the phrase emphatically in
enjambement. The Greek colour of *Naïdes* is continued in the geographical names of 11–12. For the identification of the Muses with the
water nymphs, patrons of herdsmen and their music, see 7.21n.

10 indigno associates Gallus' plight with that of the jilted goatherd
in 8.18.

peribat: the conventional metaphor of the lover's condition, e.g.
Pl. *Poen.* 1095, Cat. 45–3, Prop. 2.12.14, is here revitalized by the
identification of Gallus with the dying Daphnis of Th. *Id.* 1.66–75.
Lines 9–12 obviously correspond to 66–9 in the Idyll, 'Where were

you, Nymphs, where were you when Daphnis was wasting away? In the fair vales of Peneus or Pindus? For you certainly were not occupying the great stream of the river Anapus or the watch-tower of Etna or the sacred water of Acis.' The question here, as there, is an indignant reproach to the Muses for neglecting their favourite, in contrast to the surrounding trees and hills (13–14n.) which mourned him. An alternative interpretation is based on the fact that 11–12 also recall Callim. *Aet.* fr. 75.23–6Pf., 'For my sister Artemis was not at that time troubling Lygdamis or weaving rushes in Amyclae's shrine or washing away the stains after the hunt in the river Parthenius; she was at home in Delos...' Unlike Callimachus Vergil has no need to follow his series of negatives by an affirmation, since the question (9–10) is purely rhetorical and the answer obvious: *nemora saltusque Arcadiae uos habuere.* This is improbable. For Gallus' whereabouts unlike Daphnis' are not given by tradition and are not actually revealed till 15. Moreover, if the Muses really were in Arcadia with Gallus, it would be hard to explain why their presence is ignored both in the divine consolations (21ff.) and in Gallus' own picture of Arcadian life (35ff.).

11–12   neque...moram fecere: a prosaic phrase; cf. Cic. *Sul.* 58. It could imply either that the Muses were not in any of their usual haunts – but if not, where then had they gone? – or more likely that whichever one they were in at the time did not stand in the way of their coming to Gallus' aid. For the metaphorical significance of the passage see the final note.

11   iuga: the Parnassian mountain-complex has several distinct peaks but the reference here is most likely to the ridges on the north-west side of the sacred enclosure of Delphi, between which the spring Castalia rises. This site was especially sacred to the Muses (cf. Th. *Id.* 7.148 'Castalian Nymphs who inhabit the steep slope of Parnassus') and there was a shrine to them beside the spring (Plut. *Pyth. Orac.* 402c–D).

  nam neque Pindi: although the principal cults of the Muses were around Olympus in Pieria, Parnassus in Phocis and Helicon in Boeotia, their worship was widespread and may well have included shrines in the Pindus range between Thessaly and Epirus (cf. Hor. *C.* 1.12.6). Moreover the river Peneus rises in the Pindus mountains, so there is clearly an allusion to *Id.* 1.67–8 (10n.), which is emphasized by the rhythmic echoes of the couplet: the pause at the bucolic diaeresis in ἢ κατὰ Πηνειῶ καλὰ τέμπεα : ἢ κατὰ Πίνδω, and the trochaic caesura after *fecere* in οὐ γὰρ δὴ ποταμοῖο : μέγαν ῥόον εἶχετ' Ἀνάπω.

12 Aonie Aganippe: Greek nominatives, as Servius noted. *Aoniae* (= *Boeotiae*, cf. 6.65) would imply an improbable personification (1.65n.), and *Aoniae Aganippae* (sc. *iuga*) would be very odd of a spring, especially after *Parnasi* and *Pindi*. For the spring itself see Paus. 9.29.5; for its mythical origin Cat. 61.28-30. The choice of Aganippe rather than the more celebrated Hippocrene, with which it is coupled in Ov. *M.* 5.312, is perhaps due to its association with the Permessus, the river of elegiac inspiration, mentioned in the context of Gallus' initiation (6.64). D. Serv.: *Callimachus Aganippen fontem esse dicit Permessi fluminis*, cf. Callim. fr. 2a.20-4 (*add.* 103) Pf. The Aganippe may therefore connote the elegiac and personal lyric genres, Parnassus and Pindus the loftier impersonal ones. The hiatus in this phrase and in *lauri etiam* add to the Greek colour (2.24n.).

13-14 etiam...etiam...etiam: the repetition is emphatic: 'even', not 'also'.

lauri...myricae: for the poet's bays and the specifically pastoral tamarisks see 8.13n., 4.2n. The former is connected with Apollo's ill-fated love (3.63n.), the latter with his patronage of prophecy (Nic. *Ther.* 612-14).

14-15 pinifer...Maenalus: cf. 8.22.

14 sola sub rupe: hypallage for *solum sub rupe*: cf. Cat. 64.154 *sola sub rupe leaena*.

15 Lycaei: Lycaeus was after Maenalus one of the highest mountains in Arcadia and a centre for the worship of both Zeus and Pan; cf. Th. *Id.* 1.123-4 'O Pan, Pan, whether you are on the high hills of Lycaeus or ranging over mighty Maenalus...' In that Idyll the animals mourn the dying Daphnis (71-5) but the flowers and trees are merely exhorted to do so (132-3). However, in *Id.* 7.73-7 Tityrus is to sing 'how Daphnis the cattleherd once fell in love with Xenea and how the mountain was troubled about him and the oaks that grow along Himera's banks sang laments for him, while he wasted away like snow under high Haemus or Athos or Rhodope or furthest Caucasus';

cf. *Epit. Bion.* 1–7, where the whole landscape mourns for the dead poet. The progression from shrubs to forests to brute rocks is precisely a progression from the poet's bays to the pastoral tamarisks to the specifically Arcadian landscape. But the latter is depicted not in its idyllic but in its harsh and desolate aspects. For *sola sub rupe, gelidi... saxa Lycaei* here cf. *G.* 4.508–9, of Orpheus, *rupe sub aeria deserti ad Strymonis undam | flesse sibi et gelidis haec euoluisse sub antris.* If Prop. 1.20.13–14 *ne tibi sit duros montes et frigida saxa, | Galle, neque expertos semper adire lacus* alludes to the present passage, it confirms the bleak connotations of the imagery here.

16 oues: the Arcadian shepherd's flock replaces Daphnis' herd in *Id.* 1.74–5 'Many cows at his feet and many bulls and many heifers and calves bewailed him.'

17 nec te paeniteat: as the urban Alexis was urged in 2.34 not to be discontented with the humble country Muse, so the urban Gallus is urged not to object to tending the sheep when they do not object to the presence of the shepherd. Thus is a *poeta urbanus* figuratively exhorted to follow the *Musa agrestis* and write pastoral.

    diuine poeta 'inspired poet'; cf. θεῖε Κομᾶτα 'divine Comatas' (Th. *Id.* 7.89). The same phrase is used of Mopsus who sang the Daphnis-lament (5.45) and of Linus who attended Gallus' initiation (6.67).

18 formonsus...Adonis, though a mere shepherd 'pasturing sheep in the mountains' (Th. *Id.* 3.46), inspired the love of Aphrodite (cf. *Id.* 1.109–10). Not a very happy precedent, however, for he was gored to death by a boar during the hunt, and the goddess' grief is movingly portrayed in Bion 1 (*Epit. Adon.*) with its recurrent ἀπώλετο καλὸς Ἄδωνις 'He has perished, the fair Adonis.' In 2.60 the shepherd Paris is cited as an exemplar for *formonsus Alexis.*

19 upilio...subulci: cf. *Id.* 1.80–1 'There came the cattleherds and shepherds, the goatherds came; they all asked what ailed him.' But Vergil's choice of vocabulary is deliberately prosaic. *upilio* for *pastor* is found in agricultural writings, e.g. Var. *R.* 1.18; *subulci* are distinctly unpastoral. Boars are referred to in 2.59, but pig-breeding seems to have been too down-to-earth for the idyllic illusion. The couplet 19–20 forms a tricolon composed in the metrical proportions

2½:3½:6, with the pattern of the second member repeated more elaborately in the golden-line structure of the third and *Menalcas* effectively held back till the very end of the sentence.

20 uuidus...de glande Menalcas: acorns, regularly employed as winter fodder for the animals (Cato *Agr.* 54), had been a staple food of pre-agricultural societies (Cic. *Or.* 30) and are associated both with the hard primitivism of Lucr. 5.965 and the soft primitivism of the Golden Age (*G.* 1.148) and the Pastoral Myth ([Th.] *Id.* 9.19–20), as well as with the historical Arcadia (7.4n.). But the realistic image of Menalcas 'wet from the winter acorns', in itself consonant with the realism of the preceding line and the colloquial tone of the following question to Gallus, reminds us that in Vergil's own day acorns were still part of the human diet in more backward pastoral economies (Plin. *Nat.* 16.15). Menalcas is *uuidus* either from gathering the acorns on the wet ground or from steeping them in water. Cato prescribes (*loc. cit.*) *ubi sementim patraueris, glandem parari legique oportet et in aquam conici*; which means that, as the sowing itself did not normally begin before the equinox (Var. *R.* 1.34), the operation belongs to late autumn or early winter. Either way the description of Menalcas suggests an inclement season and so intensifies the grimness of the landscape-details in 14–15. Menalcas is certainly to be identified with Vergil in *Ecl.* 5 and 9. The fact that he is referred to in the third person *uenit* in contrast to the first persons *canimus* (8), *surgamus* (75) does not rule out the identification here. It would not be impossible for the first-person narrator to include himself in a third person walk-on part in the narrative and Vergil does refer to himself unequivocally in the third person at 71. However, the emphatic *uidimus ipsi* (26) coming so soon after *Menalcas*, if it is not an outright hint to us not to identify him with Vergil, would represent an abrupt switch of the poet's two *personae*.

21 unde amor iste: cf. Hermes' question to Daphnis in *Id.* 1.78: 'My dear chap, who is it that you're so much in love with?'
    uenit Apollo: the preceding diaeretic pause as in *Id.* 1.81 before ἦνθ' ὁ Πρίηπος 'Priapus came' marks the suddenness of the god's arrival. The three gods that visit Daphnis are Hermes, patron of poets and guide to souls after death, lusty Priapus and finally Aphrodite herself, who comes to enjoy her moment of triumph (*Id.* 1.77, 81, 95). In *Epit. Bion.* 26–8 Apollo and Pan both mourn the dead poet. Vergil

has taken these two and added Silvanus. All three gods are associated with rustic life and familiar with the sorrows of love; *notandum sane quod ea numina plerumque quae amauerunt dicit ad amatorem uenire* (Serv.). The metamorphoses of their loved ones, Apollo's *laurus* and *hyacinthus* (3.63n.), Pan's *syrinx* and *pinus* (2.32n., 7.24n.) and Silvanus' *cupressus* (24n.) supplied features of the idyllic landscape and instruments and emblems of the musician's art. The gods are thus appropriate both to Gallus' plight and to its Arcadian setting.

22 insanis has connotations of erotic elegy; cf. Corydon's *dementia* (2.69). Apollo's question corresponds to Priapus' in *Id.* 1.82 'Wretched Daphnis, why are you now wasting away?' But whereas Priapus went on to point a mocking contrast between Daphnis' suffering and the carefree sexuality of the goats, Apollo's advice here recalls rather Cat. 8.2 *quod uides perisse perditum ducas.*

tua cura: cf. 1.57n. The noun is often used of the loved one, e.g. Prop. 1.1.35–6, Ov. *A.* 1.3.16. In contrast to the human inhabitants of Arcady (21) Apollo of course knows the source of his madness.

23 niues confirms the intimations of winter in 15, 20–1.

horrida castra: the epithet means either 'harsh', 'rugged' (Liv. 28.17.12 *Spartana...horrida disciplina*) or 'dread', 'inspiring horror' (*A.* 6.86 *horrida bella*). Unless *sola* (48) is to be taken literally, the *diues amator* of *Ecl.* 2 is now replaced by that other familiar rival of the elegist in love, the military officer. The two are sometimes indistinguishable, e.g. Prop. 1.8, 2.16.1. The suggestion of remoteness in *Alpinas* and *Rheni* (47) is more effective if Lycoris' defection belongs to the period after 41–39 B.C., when Gallus was no longer involved in the administration of Cisalpina. Indeed 38 B.C., when he was probably on Antony's staff in the East and Agrippa was campaigning on the northern frontier (6.7n.), would be an appropriate notional date for the poem. The actual date of publication would of course be somewhat later.

24 Siluanus 'Woodland One'; the *deus siluestris* was, unlike Apollo and Pan, specifically Italian. Like Faunus (6.27) he was often pluralized; e.g. Plin. *Nat.* 12.3, where *Siluani*, *Fauni* and *genera dearum* (viz. *dryades*) are all associated in the patronage of forests. Silvanus' connection with Faunus and Pan (*G.* 2.494) led to iconographic assimilation with them and with the Greek satyrs and Sileni. He is the protector of flocks (*A.* 8.600–1, cf. Cato *Agr.* 83). In a Latinized version of the tale of Apollo's unhappy love for Cyparissus (Serv. ad *A.* 3.680) Silvanus was the lover (Ov. *M.* 10.106–59), and he is commonly represented bearing a cypress (e.g. *G.* 1.20). Unlike the other gods he remains silent here; so his presence is purely symbolic.

agresti...honore: abl. of description: 'with the rural decoration of his head'. Silvanus is often represented wearing a large floral chaplet.

25 ferulas et grandia lilia: both fennel and Madonna lilies are in fact tall plants. The lily was especially prized as *rosae nobilitate proximum* but fennel too was commonly used in garlands (Plin. *Nat.* 21.22, 55). They are summer plants, in flower from May onwards, so their appearance here *florentis* in the winter season is miraculous. Whether there is some further significance in the combination of plants cannot now be ascertained.

quassans: cf. *Pan | pinea semiferi capitis uelamina quassans* in Lucr. 4.586, a context often recalled in the Eclogues; cf. 1.2, 2.34, 6.27.

26 Pan deus Arcadiae: like the sequence from *lauri* to *myricae* to *Maenalus* (13–15) the procession of gods from Apollo to Silvanus to Pan becomes more and more Arcadian. Pan's absence from the scene of Daphnis' last moments is indicated in *Id.* 1.123–30.

quem uidimus ipsi: although the god's appearance could strike terror ('panic') into mortals (Eur. *Rhes.* 36–7), it did not always do so; e.g. the story of Philippides in Hdt. 6.105. The painting of his face would anyway have had an apotropaic effect; cf. 6.22n.

27 ebuli: the berries of the dwarf-elder, Sambucus Ebulus, are reddish black but the dye from them is blue.

minio: cinnabar or red mercuric sulphide was imported from Spain (Prop. 2.3.11), a product of the quicksilver mines around Sisapo in Baetica (Plin. *Nat.* 33.118), though the name is perhaps connected with the river Minius in Galaecia (Isid. *Or.* 13.21.32). It was *minium* that was used for painting the statues of Jupiter at festival times and the bodies of generals celebrating triumphs (Plin. *ibid.* 111–12).

28 ecquis erit modus? Pan's words unlike those of Priapus and Aphrodite in *Id.* 1.82–91, 97–8 are distinctly consolatory. For the phrase cf. 2.68n.

29-30 crudelis: cf. 8.49-50 and for Cupid's delight in human suffering generally Mosch. 1.11, Meleager *A.P.* 5.176, Prop. 1.12.16. The rustic analogies (2.63n.) implicit in *gramina riuis* etc. underline that it is Love's nature to be cruel.

riuis: either 'streams' or 'irrigation channels' (cf. 3.111). The imagery coheres into a typical pastoral scene – streams, meadows, shrubs, and trees, bees and goats – which is appropriate from the lips of Pan, the patron of herdsmen and their music (2.33). Pan is also μελισσοσόος 'protector of bees' (Zonas *A.P.* 9.226.6). Bees provided not only honey, which was the chief source of sugar in Greco-Roman diet (hence the offering of both milk and honey to Pan in Th. *Id.* 5.58-9), but also the wax with which the Pan-pipes were joined together; cf. *Pap. Rainer* (*Buc. Gr.* 168-70) B 54-64. For the bee as a poetic symbol see 1.54n.

cutiso: shrub trefoil (1.78n.) is food for goats also in 2.64 and for cattle in 9.31.

31 tamen: *licet ego duro amore consumar, tamen erit solacium, quia meus amor erit uestra cantilena quandoque* (Serv.). Although Gallus' address is not specifically to the gods, the particle implies the recognition that what they have said to him is true. Nevertheless his suffering like Daphnis' will be commemorated in Arcadian song as an *exemplum* of the bitterness of love. For *Arcades* see 7.4n.

32 montibus is local ablative rather than dative; cf. 2.5n.

soli cantare periti: cf. 5.1-2 of Menalcas and Mopsus, 7.5 of Corydon and Thyrsis, [Th.] *Id.* 8.4 (8.3-4n.) of Daphnis and Menalcas.

33 molliter: the adjective, used in its objective sense 'soft' at 2.72, often has emotive overtones 'gentle', 'tender', 'luxurious'; see 42n. For the adverb, which occurs only here in Vergil, cf. *delicate et molliter uiuere* (Cic. *Off.* 1.106), *molliter impresso conor adire toro* (Prop. 1.3.12) and especially *ut mea defunctae molliter ossa cubent* (Ov. *A.* 1.8.108). For the preoccupation of the elegiac lover with death see Tib. 1.3, Prop. 1.19, 2.13b.

ossa quiescant is a sepulchral commonplace in literature (e.g. *A.* 6.328) and inscriptions (e.g. *CE* 773.1, 1192.9).

34 olim 'at that time' (cf. *olle*) may refer like Eng. *one day* to either past or, as here, future time. Vergil has it in both senses (*A.* 1.653, 203) but unlike other classical authors seems to prefer the future.

35 fuissem: hopes for the future give way to regrets for what might have been in the past or even the present – *esset* (37). Gallus longs to have been an Arcadian himself, as Lycidas in Th. *Id.* 7.86–9 longed to have shared the goatherd's life with Comatas, 'so that I could have herded your pretty goats on the hills and listened to your voice, while you, divine Comatas, lay under the oaks or pine trees making sweet music'.

36 maturae uinitor uuae: viticulture was not an Arcadian occupation, though vines were an ingredient of the idyllic landscape, e.g. 5.7, 7.58. So this may be another of the realistic details by which Vergil enlivens the pastoral myth; cf. 19–20. But it is also the first hint that Gallus' idea of Arcady is more the life of a country gentleman, that *custodia gregis* interest him less than the vintage. The reference to *matura uua* must be pointed, being otherwise redundant with *uinitor*.

37 Phyllis...Amyntas: country life suggests country love. *Phyllis* is the name given to the girl whose charms were extolled in 3.76, 78, 7.59; cf. 5.10. *Amyntas* was a rival poet in 2.35, 5.8 and Menalcas' beloved in 3.66. Gallus accepts the bisexuality of Arcady (2.15n.); it may have come naturally to him in real life, even if he is not the addressee of Prop. 1.20.

38 quicumque furor: probably to be construed together as the third subject of *mihi...esset*: 'whether I had with me Phyllis or Amyntas or some other person I was mad about'. Alternatively *quicumque* alone is the third subject and *furor* to be taken predicatively with *esset*: 'whether Phyllis or Amyntas or someone else was my madness'; but this is less likely. For *quicumque* thus used cf. 9.14n. For the metonymy by which the emotion is put for that which inspires it cf. *cura* (22). The noun is ironic in view of Gallus' present condition – cf. *insanis* (22), *furoris* (60) – and his professed desire to escape from it. Even in Arcady love is still a madness that disrupts the idyllic *securitas*; cf. Corydon's *dementia* in 2.69 and the goatherd's *error* in 8.41, and see pp. 10–11.

si fuscus Amyntas? sc. *est*.

39 uiolae: here in contrast to 2.47 the flower is the sweet violet,

Viola Odorata, which was valued by apiarists (*G.* 4.275) and as a source of the purple dye ianthine (Plin. *Nat.* 21.27).

uaccinia 'bilberries': see 2.50n. For the analogy in praise of a dark complexion cf. Th. *Id.* 10.26-9 (2.18n.), Asclep. *A.P.* 5.210.3-4 'If she is dark, what of that? So are coals; but when we light them, they shine like roses in bloom.'

40   salices: willows were less suitable than elms for training vines, since they provided too much shade and moisture for the grapes to ripen properly. Columella (5.7.1) however notes that willows were so used in the *Gallicum arbustum*, so this may be a reminiscence of a practice that Vergil had observed around Mantua.

42   mollia prata: the adjective connotes luxury and ease as well as lushness (33n.); cf. *G.* 2.383-4 *inter pocula laeti | mollibus in pratis unctos saluere per utres.* In 40-2 the pastoral *locus amoenus* is briefly sketched: willows and vines, meadows and springs, garlands, love and music; cf. Th. *Id.* 5.31-4 (7.45n.). But instead of seeking a refuge from his present woes Gallus longs to share it all with Lycoris. For the inadequacy of idyllic surroundings to compensate for the absence of the beloved see Prop. 1.18, Ov. *A.* 2.16; for the dream of reconciliation in a rustic setting Tib. 1.5.21ff. Both these themes may have been treated by Gallus too in his elegies; see 46n.

43   consumerer aeuo: the variation on the familiar phrase *consumere aeuum, aetatem* (e.g. Lucr. 5.1431, Cic. *Off.* 1.2) is significant. For at present he could only say *dolore consumor* (cf. *amore peribat* in 10). In Arcady with Lycoris he would be consumed by nothing but (*ipso*) the passage of time.

44-5   nunc marks a return from wistful reverie to his present plight. Of the couplet itself there are a number of possible interpretations, none of them entirely satisfactory. (i) Gallus' enthusiasm for campaigning, *amor Martis* (cf. *insani Martis amore* at *A.* 7.550) has prompted him to go off on active service, presumably with Antony in the East; and in his absence Lycoris has run away with another soldier serving on the northern frontier. However the insistence throughout the poem is on the relentless power of Love and the pain and madness that it causes (6, 22, 28, 69), and this favours the reading *Amor*, with *Martis* dependent on *armis*. (ii) Gallus is on active military service. Whether or not he has gone off to the wars like Thyonides in Th. *Id.* 14 to forget his mistress, he is still in the grip of *insanus Amor* even there. Against both (i) and (ii) is the fact that if he really was on active service, *in armis*, Lycoris' preference for *horrida castra* (23) loses most of its point. More important, while it is a plausible figure to have Gallus languishing like Daphnis in a mythical Arcady and longing to have escaped there earlier from the sufferings of love in the real world, it would be most inept to present him explicitly as being in Arcady and on military service at the same time. (iii) *ex affectu amantis ibi se esse putat ubi amica est, ut 'me' sit 'meum animum'* (Serv.). Gallus' attempts to escape in imagination into Arcady are thwarted by his continuing obsession with Lycoris' present whereabouts, the *horrida castra*. Against this is the perhaps not very strong objection that an officer's mistress could hardly be described as being *Martis in armis*, let alone *tela inter media* etc. But the hyperbole may be deliberate, a reflection of Gallus' anxiety for her. (iv) *Mars* and *arma* etc. are purely metaphoric. *Amor* instead of bestowing peace and happiness on lovers only brings the bitterness of constant warfare. The reference is however not to the *militia amoris* which the lover and his mistress engaged in continually (Tib. 1.10.53–66, Prop. 2.5.19–26, Ov. *A.* 1.9); for although this may have characterized Gallus' affair with Lycoris, it is hardly relevant now that she has deserted him. His battle now is the hopeless one (69) against *crudelis Amor*. The reluctant lover at war with Venus or Cupid is a commonplace in the elegiac genres, e.g. Meleager *A.P.* 5.180, 12. 48, Tib. 2.1.81–2, 6.15–18, Prop. 1.1.4, 33–4, 2.12, Ov. *A.* 1.2.19–22, and no doubt appeared also in Gallus' elegies (46n.). Parallels occur in Th. *Idd.* 7.118, 11.15–16, but Vergilian pastoral, with its antithesis of *otium–securitas* and *bellum–discordia* (1.6n., 9.12–13n.), provides a particularly apt context for the figure. Against (iv) is the awkwardness of a metaphorical use of *Mars* etc. after the literal reference in *horrida castra*. On the whole (iii) and (iv) seem the most satisfactory, in that order of preference; but the lines remain obscure. That is however no reason for suspecting textual corruption. The change of *me* to *te*, proposed by Heumann and Heyne, is open to the same objection as (iii) above. Moreover after the mention of both Gallus and Lycoris in 43 the emphatic *tu* (46) surely implies a contrast with the person referred to in the intervening lines. In any case, while Gallus might blame *insanus Amor* for causing Lycoris to desert him (as Corydon in

2.60 accuses Alexis of *dementia* in rejecting him), it is his own madness
that is emphasized in the rest of the poem.

46   patria as in 1.3 evokes the real world beyond the pastoral myth.

nec sit mihi credere: although *est animaduertere* is cited from
Varro by Gellius (18.12.9), this and Hor. *S.* 1.2.101 *tibi paene uidere est*
are the earliest certain instances of the construction with a dative
added. The influence of Greek *ésti* 'it is possible, permitted' + dat. and
inf. seems likely.

tantum is the object of *credere*. To take it with *procul* would entail an
awkward pause at diaeresis within the final cadence, in contrast to
A. 1.231 *quid meus Aeneas in te committere tantum*, where the construction
of *quid* with *tantum* is reinforced by the grammatical concord. For the
sense of the whole phrase cf. Lygd. [= Tib. 3] 4.82 *a ego ne possim
tanta uidere mala*.

46ff Servius remarks *hi autem omnes uersus Galli sunt de ipsius translati
carminibus*. It is not clear how many lines are involved, but the observation must apply at least to 46–9, which form a thematic unit. The
concern for the welfare of the unfaithful mistress – itself an illustration
of *insania amoris* – is an elegiac theme; cf. Prop. 1.8.7ff. (49n.). Together with the preceding and following themes (see 42n., 44–5n.), it
could well have occurred in Gallus' own poetry. The agitated style of
46–9 with the repeated exclamations is certainly appropriate to love
elegy, and a phrase like *me sine sola uides*, which closely resembles the
cadence of a pentameter, could even be an actual quotation. However,
Servius' notion of *translatio* is somewhat imprecise (7 fin. n.) and it may
be only the themes of Gallan elegy that are alluded to in the monologue.

47   dura 'cruel' because she spurns him, and 'hardy' because she is
prepared to suffer the rigours of a northern winter.

frigora 'cold weather': for the plural see 2.14n.

48   me sine: for the inversion cf. 8.59 and the regular *mecum*.

sola: probably a naive projection on to her of his own feeling of
loneliness, *solus sine illa*. However, it could be literal, implying that there
is no specific rival and Lycoris has gone off as a 'freelance', *castra
secuta*.

49 Cf. Prop. 1.8.7–8 *tu pedibus teneris positas fulcire pruinas, | tu potes insolitas, Cynthia, ferre niues?*

50 ibo: his mood has shifted from longing for Arcadian escape (*fuissem* (35), *esset* (37), *iaceret* (40)) to thoughts of Arcadian delights shared with Lycoris (*consumerer* (43)), to realization of his present plight (*detinet* (45)) and anxiety over her welfare (*ne...laedant, ne...secet* (48–9)), finally to positive determination, marked by the future tense and *certum est* (52). These shifts of mood recall Corydon in *Ecl.* 2.

Chalcidico...uersu was taken by Quintilian (10.1.56) to refer to Euphorion of Chalcis, the third-century poet and librarian to Antiochus the Great. Probus here cites Diomedes' opinion that Euphorion was an elegist *cuius in scribendo secutus colorem uidetur Cornelius Gallus.* But although the Greek poet certainly wrote epigrams (e.g. *A.P.* 6.279, 7.651), he was known chiefly for his hexameter poems on mythological subjects, the obscure style of which (Crates *A.P.* 11.218, Cic. *Div.* 2.132) is exemplified in *Select Papyri* 3 (Page) 492–500. Gallus was certainly one of the *noui poetae* whom Cicero characterized as *cantores Euphorionis* (*Tusc.* 3.45), but while the influence of the Greek poet on Gallus' poem about the *Grynei nemoris origo* (6.72) may be taken for granted, the relevance of the Greek poet to his elegies is less obvious. The invention of the elegiac verse-form was at least in one tradition (*Suda* s.v. ἐλεγείνειν) ascribed to a certain Theocles who came from Naxos or Eretria, a city close to Chalcis. So it is just possible that *Chalcidicus uersus* means simply 'elegiac verse'. However, a reference to Euphorion seems more likely.

condita: the verb is often used of literary composition, e.g. Lucr. 5.2, Livy 27.37.7. See 6.7n.

51 pastoris Siculi: Gallus intends forsaking the manner of Euphorion and adapting his earlier elegiac themes to the Theocritean genre.

modulabor auena: cf. 5.14, 1.2.

52 spelaea: *graece ait pro speluncis* (Serv.). Macrobius (*Sat.* 5.17.15) cites the phrase, which is the earliest recorded occurrence of the Greek loan-word *spélaion*, as an instance of Vergil's addiction to Grecisms. Maybe the word was intended to give exotic colour to the line; but *spelunca* itself, though already attested in Lucretius and Cicero, is also a loan-word, from Greek *spélunx*, cf. 1.75n. The haunts of wild beasts belong not to the idyllic landscape of Arcady but to the wilder regions of nature evoked in 14–15.

53 pati is better taken as intransitive than with *amores* as its object; the implication is clearly that Amor is still the cause of his suffering. The carving of erotic inscriptions on trees is an elegiac motif; see Callim. *Aet.* fr. 73Pf., Glaucus *A.P.* 9.341.3–4, Prop. 1.18.22. It is probably another indication of Gallus' imperfect conversion to Arcady. For a different motive for departing from the convention that the herdsmen of Arcady were illiterate see 5. fin. n.

teneris 'young'. The conceit of the following line is elaborated in Ov. *H.* 5.21–6.

55–6 lustrabo may be used in its extended sense 'travel around, traverse' (cf. 2.12, *A.* 3.385) but probably retains as in Hor. *C.* 3.25.12 something of its earlier religious connotations 'travel around ritually, in an act of ritual purification' (cf. *A.* 7.391). It is unlikely that the nymphs of the forest (*Hamadryades* 62) accompanied anyone but their mistress Artemis in the hunt (Hom. *Od.* 6.105) and *aut* is therefore strictly disjunctive: after the gaiety of the rustic festival and wandering dances come the delights of the boar-hunt.

Maenala: the mountain is usually neut. sg. *Maínalon* in Greek, masc. sg. or neut. pl. in Latin; cf. 8.22.

uenabor apros: hunting is peripheral to Arcadian life (2.29n.).

57 Parthenios . . . saltus 'the upland glades of Mount Parthenium'. For the noun see 6.56n. The mountain, lying between the historical Arcadia and the Argolid, was the site of Philippides' encounter with Pan (Hdt. 6.105). Gallus' Arcady is very much dominated by the geography of the real Arcadia, with the mountains – Maenalus (15, 55), Lycaeus (15) and Parthenium – especially prominent in the scenery. Nor do the activities that interest him most at this point, the mountain revels and wild-boar hunts, belong to the normal pattern of life in Arcady so much as to an urban visitor's vacations in the country. In Prop. 2.19.17ff. hunting provides temporary solace to the deserted lover.

58 uideor: the futures of 50–6 give place to the present tense, as Gallus is carried away by the vivid picture of escape that he has created for himself. The chilly mountains and lonely cliffs, which are to provide a refuge from his desolation, are again alien to the idyllic landscape of the pastoral; cf. 14–15.

lucosque sonantis may refer either as in *G.* 4.364 to the roar of the mountain rivers or to the noise of the hunt. Here and in 59 the enjambement with a pause early in the following line, after *ire* and *spicula* respectively, suggests urgent excitement.

59 torquere: an extension from its normal use of brandishing a spear (e.g. *A* 5.497).

Partho... cornu: the bow of heroic times was made of ibex-horn; cf. Hom. *Il.* 4.105–6. The adjective may be evocative rather than objective (cf. 1.54n.): 'such as the Parthians use', 'as supplied to the Parthians'. For the Parthians' reputation in archery see *G.* 4.313–14, Hor. *C.* 2.13.17–18.

Cydonea 'from Cydonea', the ancient town in north-west Crete (probably modern Canea) whose bowmen had long been famous; cf. *A.* 12.858. For the quality of Cretan archery equipment cf. *Cnosia spicula* (*A.* 5.306), *Cydonio...arcu* (Hor. *C.* 4.9.17–18). Nothing but the best gear will satisfy Gallus even in Arcady.

60–1 Like Corydon in 2.69 he breaks off from his reverie with the realization of the futility of it all. The *medicina* of Arcady like the 'medicine of the Muses' in Th. *Id.* 11.1–3 is ultimately ineffectual; resignedly he repeats the substance of Pan's words (28–29).

62–3 Hamadryades...carmina...siluae: the delights that these might afford (cf. 55, 51, 52) are now dismissed.

placent: after 60–1 the return to the present tense of 59 (*libet*) now expresses disillusionment.

concedite siluae: cf. *uiuite siluae* the goatherd's farewell in 8.58.

64 labores could refer specifically to the battle with Amor that was perhaps alluded to in 44–5. But it is not clear whether the labours would be undertaken in the hope of driving Love away altogether, of placating him by acts of penance, or of converting him into an ally and thereby winning back Lycoris, as Milanion in Prop. 1.1.8–10 *nullos fugiendo...labores* overcame *aduersos...deos* and so *saeuitiam durae contudit Iasidos*. At all events he realizes that the effort would be ineffectual. The connotation of *labor* here may illuminate its meaning in line 1; cf. 72–3n. The succession of spondees in the line is expressive of his despondent resignation.

65 frigoribus echoes *frigora* in 48, 57.

Hebrum: the principal river of Thrace, now the Maritza, conventionally associated with hard winters (Hor. *Ep.* 1.3.3). The icy Hyperborean region of Thrace was the site of Orpheus' lament for Eurydice and it was the Hebrus into which the Ciconian Bacchants cast the head of the dismembered poet; see *G.* 4.516–17, 524.

bibamus like *nostri* (64) may be plur. for sg., but is more likely after *hominum* (61) to be a generalization from his own plight.

66 Sithoniasque: *Sithōniē* was the middle one of the three peninsulas of coastal Chalcidice (Hdt. 7.122). The name is often used by synecdoche for the whole of Thrace, between Mount Haemus and the Danube. For its wintry character cf. Hor. *C.* 3.26.10. The Latin poets regularly follow Lycophron (*Alex.* 1357) in shortening the *o* of the second syllable.

aquosae, though strictly inconsistent with *niues*, is a conventional epithet for Mediterranean winters, e.g. *A.* 4.52 (North Africa), 9.671 (Italy).

67 moriens. . .liber contrasts with the moist bark of the young trees which Gallus had dreamt of inscribing in Arcady (53–4).

in ulmo: it was an elm that shaded Tityrus in the *locus amoenus* of 1.59. The parched condition of the tree is a symptom of the intense heat.

68 Aethiopum, coming after *Hebrum* (65), suggests an echo of Th. *Id.* 7.111–13, Simichidas' threat to Pan, if he refuses to restore Aristis to his lover Aratus: 'I wish you in the mountains of the Edonians at mid-winter, turning your steps towards the river Hebrus...and in summer among the Ethiopians with your flocks...'

uersemus: the verb usually implies vigorous activity, e.g. *A.* 12. 664 *tu currum deserto in gramine uersas*, and is probably intended to suggest the desperation of the shepherd, driving his flocks hither and thither in search of pasture. Alternatively it could be by analogy with the intransitive *uersari* (originally middle in sense) 'to be busy, occupied with' or even influenced by Theocritus' τετραμμένος 'turning your steps' (*loc. cit.*). The usage is strange, but not sufficiently so to justify emendation, e.g. to *seruemus* (Christianus Florens).

sub sidere Cancri: the constellation of the Crab, which the sun enters at midsummer in the northern hemisphere (cf. Lucr. 5.617), marks the northernmost point of the ecliptic, and the circle through it parallel to the equator, the Tropic of Cancer, defines one boundary of the Tropical zone.

69 Gallus' final capitulation recalls Corydon's in 2.68; cf. also Th. *Id.* 30.25ff. It is announced in clearly etched homodyne rhythms.

omnia uincit Amor could be a quotation from the cadence of one of Gallus' elegiac pentameters.

Amor et: either the noun has archaic -*ŏr* or a pause must be assumed after it to justify an abnormal syllable division: -*ta-mor-et* ($\cup - -$) instead of the normal *ta-mo-ret-* ($\cup \cup -$); cf. *agitatus amor et conscia uirtus* (*A.* 12.668) and 1.38n.

70 **diuae** at first seems addressed both to Arethusa (1) and the Muses, *puellae Naides* (9–10). It is only given specification in 72, *Pierides*, which thus excludes the divine addressee of the poem and indicates that the passage is a coda not so much to the present Eclogue but to the whole collection.

71 **fiscellam**: like *fiscina* and more rarely *fiscus*, the diminutive denotes a small basket, made e.g. of rushes (cf. 2.72) or as here of marsh-mallows. It could be used for gathering small fruit or olives, pressing cheeses (Tib. 2.3.15–16, Colum. 7.8.3), muzzling cattle (Cato *Agr.* 54.5) and even preventing ewes from mating (Var. *R.* 2.2.14). The word brings us back to the homely world of the countryside that we last saw early in Gallus' monologue (36). Although Gallus has suffered the affliction of Corydon, it is not he but Vergil who in the *persona* of a goatherd (77) returns as a true Arcadian to the humble tasks of Corydon.

gracili: Servius' allegorical interpretation is for once attractive: *significat se composuisse hunc libellum tenuissimo stilo*.

72 **haec facietis maxima**: cf. Bucaeus in Th. *Id.* 10.24–5, about to sing of his mistress in measures above his humble station, 'Pierian Muses, sing with me of the slender girl; for everything you touch, goddesses, you make beautiful.'

72–3 Gallo, Gallo: the repetition, more immediate than in 2–3, suggests an urgent intensity of emotion, which is sustained throughout the following couplet. This goes beyond the requirements of loyal sympathy to a fellow poet, and, coming after the allusion to *Id.* 10, suggests an intense affection for Gallus, which would add a note of poignancy to his treatment of Gallus' *sollicitos...amores* for Lycoris and so explain *laborem* (1). See also 64n.

73 crescit echoes *crescent, crescentis* in 54.

74 se subicit refers to the rapid growth of the alder shoots pushing themselves up from below. The pronunciation *subjicit* is guaranteed by Gell. 4.17.

75 surgamus: the languor of the three heavy syllables is emphasized by the following caesural pause.

umbra: not the cool shade appropriate for music-making in the midday heat but the evening shadows, which are burdensome to singers.

76 iuniperi: *arboribus primum certis grauis umbra tributa | usque adeo capitis faciant ut saepe dolores, | si quis eas subter iacuit prostratus in herbis* (Lucr. 6.783–5). Pliny describes the shade of walnut-trees *(iuglandes)* as *grauis et noxia etiam capiti humano omnibusque iuxta satis (Nat.* 17.89). Why the juniper should be thought to have similar properties is unclear. Perhaps the two trees were connected in folklore or popular etymology.

nocent et frugibus umbrae (cf. *G.* 1.121) recalls the Arcadian bond of sympathy between man and nature. What affects the fruits of the farm affects the music-making of the farmer. Night may be the time for love-making (7.43) but it is also a rehearsal of death; cf. Cat. 5.4–6, *A.* 10.746.

77 Hesperos recalls the end of the other Gallus poem, 6.85–6.

ite capellae echoes Meliboeus' farewell to *his* Arcady in 1.74. In taking leave of the pastoral Vergil retains (cf. 7) the guise of the humble herdsman.

The structure and pessimistic tone of the Eclogue recall Thyrsis' Daphnis-dirge in Th. *Id.* 1.65–136, with the introductory setting (9–30) followed by the dying poet's monologue (31–69). In the introduction the addition of the down-to-earth human mourners (19–20) has given a realistic touch to the mythical pastoral setting; the motif of the three gods is adapted in detail to the theme of the poet in love (21n.), and the allusions to the rugged topography of the real Arcadia (14–15, 55, 57; cf. 7.26n.) create a much more precise and harsh location for the monologue.

Gallus' monologue is even further removed from Daphnis' speech, has none of the defiance of Daphnis, and contains scarcely any echoes of *Id.* 1. His wistful evocation of an Arcadian escape-world, becoming more intense with each shift of verbal mood and tense (50n., 58n.), is interrupted by moments of self-awareness when the illusion is broken and he realizes that Arcady will not save him: thus 44–9, prepared by 42–3 within the first escape passage, and 60–9, following the second. His shifts of mood recall Corydon in *Ecl.* 2, but his predicament is closer to Damon's goatherd in *Ecl.* 8. There are indeed echoes of both poems at 17, 28, 39, 71 and 10, 14–15, 29, 63 respectively. The hopelessness of Gallus' plight and his continual longing for the absent mistress are reinforced by echoes from Simichidas' highly erotic piece on Aratus and the boy Aristis in Th. *Id.* 7 (39n., 68n.).

In presenting to Lycoris (2) the spectacle of Gallus in Arcady Vergil was clearly alluding to a crisis in Gallus' life both as a lover and as a poet. Possibly at a time when Gallus was preoccupied with Lycoris' infidelity and so out of humour for poetry Vergil had urged him to escape from himself and his troubles by writing pastoral. This could be the meaning, figuratively expressed, of 9–12: no other poetic genres – narrative or elegiac – were engaging his attention (*moram fecere*), since none could provide the consolation or escape that pastoral might afford him. But Gallus' efforts had been unsuccessful: whatever he wrote came back to his obsession. This poem would then be Vergil's pastoral exposition of Gallus' predicament, the choice offered to him and his reason for rejecting it.

Alternatively Gallus may have attempted to introduce pastoral themes into his elegies. Traditional pastoral motifs occur in Hellenistic love epigrams, e.g. Mnasalcas *A.P.* 9.324, Meleager *A.P.* 12.128, and in later Latin elegy, e.g. Prop. 1.18, where the situation between lover and mistress is very similar to the Eclogue but the Arcadian landscape is significant merely as the backdrop for protestations of love by the poet. It is quite possible that Gallus himself used some of these motifs.

He may also have used in the context of personal poetry – just as
Tibullus and Horace did later – the antithesis between simple
country life, idealized but not strictly idyllic, and the evils of war,
luxury and avarice, which are implicit themes of Vergilian pastoral
though more explicitly developed in the Georgics (cf. Tib. 1.1.1–50,
5.19–34, 2.5.25–38). But this antithesis is not Arcadian escape from
reality but direct confrontation with it. Moreover the homely rusticity
of Tib. 1.2.71–5 like that of Menalcas and his associates in the present
poem, while appropriate to this moral antithesis, has little to do with
Gallus' image of himself as a country gentleman in Arcady. Ovid's
coupling of Gallus and Tibullus (A. 1.15.27–30, 3.9.59–66) is probably
irrelevant to this topic. Vergil's elegiac pastoral is a tribute to the
elegist but it does not justify attributing to him pastoral elegy in any
form, any more than the tribute to Gallus the narrative poet in Ecl. 6
entitles us to assume that he wrote on all the themes there exhibited.
Clearly if we had some of Gallus' elegiac poetry or more knowledge of
Gallus and his circle in general, Ecl. 10 like Ecl. 6 would yield more of
its meaning than it does now.

It is striking that Vergil should close the collection with what seems
an explicit rejection of Arcadian escapism. It is as if he had excluded
the one area of traditional pastoral that remained untouched by his
earlier efforts to relate the pastoral myth to contemporary moral and
political realities – that of the suffering lover and the medicine of the
Muses that consoles him. Yet Arcady is not quite rejected. For Vergil
places Gallus in a scene of wintry desolation (14–15) that owes more
to the real Arcadia than to any mythical idyll – a reminder that
Arcady is not a place to be travelled to but a state of mind to be sought
here and now in ourselves, and a warning that, as the pastoral
sympathy-figure constantly reasserts, nature can cruelly reflect human
emotions as well as gently transforming them. Moreover Gallus is
throughout a very half-hearted convert. He barely notices (36) the
humbler aspects of Arcady, which Vergil himself portrays with vivid
realism (16–20, 70–2). His thoughts pass quickly to wine and dalliance
in a *locus amoenus* (36–41) and later to revels with the nymphs and the
pleasures of the hunt (55–60), with the single 'rustic' detail (53–4)
taken not from the pastoral but from the elegiac tradition. The
longing for Lycoris to which his Arcadian reverie leads (42–3) is underlined by the intrusion of themes from his own erotic poetry (46ff.). So

perhaps after all Vergil is not conceding the bankruptcy of Arcadian consolation so much as hinting that Gallus is incapable of committing himself fully to the Arcadian ideal and so of participating fully in its benefits: he is like Alexis rather than Corydon. Yet Arcady and the medicine of the Muses was not able to cure the ills of Corydon, or of Damon's goatherd either. If moreover Vergil was himself in love with Gallus (72–3n.), then the portrayal of Gallus' disillusionment with Arcadian consolation has an ironic edge to it. Whatever view we take of this, it is a despondent note that Vergil chooses to sound his farewell to the genre.

BIBLIOGRAPHICAL NOTE

For serious study of the text Otto Ribbeck's monumental edition is indispensable, *P. Vergili Maronis opera: prolegomena critica* (Leipzig 1866), *Bucolica et Georgica* (Leipzig 1894). The best text of the Eclogues however is that of R. Sabbadini, *P. Vergili Maronis opera* vol. 1 (Rome 1930), who also reported in full the readings of the early MSS. Of the two most recent editors of the poet's works R. A. B. Mynors (Oxford 1969), collated a number of the later MSS., M. Geymonat, whose edition (Turin etc. 1973) was unfortunately not accessible when the present text was being prepared, has collated afresh the MSS. of both groups. C. Hosius' *P. Vergili Maronis Bucolica* (Berlin 1915) contains useful indices and lists of parallel locutions in earlier and later classical literature.

There is nothing on the Eclogues comparable to A. S. F. Gow's vast commentary on Theocritus (Cambridge 1952²).[1] The most useful English commentary, that of J. Conington, H. Nettleship and F. Haverfield in *The works of Virgil* vol. 1 (London 1898), has the advantage of being able to treat the Eclogues in close association with the rest of the poet's work. The high quality of E. Stampini's notes on *Ecl.* 1–5 in *Le bucoliche di Virgilio, parte prima* (Turin 1912³) gives cause for regret that what would have been by far the best commentary on the poems was never completed. J. Perret's notes in *Virgile, Les Bucoliques* (Paris 1961) are brief and impressionistic, but stimulating. E. de Saint-Denis' Budé edition (Paris 1967²) in addition to its good translation has long and valuable introductory essays. More popular but still useful is the bilingual English edition, with essays on each poem, by E. V. Rieu, *Virgil, The pastoral poems* (London 1954). No serious student of Vergil should neglect Servius' commentary, edited by G. Thilo in *Seruii grammatici qui feruntur in Vergilii Bucolica et Georgica* (Leipzig 1887). We may now and then smile at the ancient

---

[1] The best text of *Bucolici Graeci* is by the same editor (Oxford 1958²). For Greekless readers these poets are most accessible in Andrew Lang's *Theocritus, Bion and Moschus* (London 1889²) and Ph.-E. Legrand's Budé edition in two volumes (Paris 1925, 1927).

commentator's more naive or fanciful observations, but he represents a philological tradition continuous with Vergil's own day and had the great advantage over us of knowing Latin as a living language. For readers of the Eclogues the most useful edition of the ancient *Vitae Vergilii* is that of J. Brummer (Leipzig 1912).

The volume of modern scholarly and critical writings relevant to the Eclogues is immense. To have recorded only those items with which the present editor is acquainted – a mere fraction of the total – would have exceeded the requirements of this edition. The following is intended to be a representative selection:[1]

Boyle, A. J. (ed.) *Ancient pastoral*. Ramus Essays on Greek and Roman pastoral poetry (Melbourne 1975)

Büchner, K. *P. Vergilius Maro. Der Dichter der Römer* (Stuttgart 1959, repr. from Pauly–Wissowa)

Clausen, W. V. 'Callimachus and Latin poetry', *G.R.B.S.* 5 (1964) 181–90

Coleman, R. 'Tityrus and Meliboeus', *G. &. R.* 13 (1966) 79–97 'Pastoral poetry' in *Greek and Latin literature. A comparative study*, ed. J. Higginbotham (London 1969) 100–23

Curtius, E. R. 'The ideal landscape' ch. 10 of *European literature and the Latin Middle Ages* (= *Europäische Literatur und lateinisches Mittelalter*, Eng. tr. London 1953)

Dick, B. F. 'Ancient pastoral and the pathetic fallacy', *Comparative Literature* 20 (1968) 27–44

Empson, W. *Some versions of pastoral* (London 1935)

Galinsky, G. K. 'Vergil's Second Eclogue: its theme and relation to the Eclogue book', *C. & M.* 26 (1965) 161–91

Garson, R. W. 'Theocritean elements in Virgil's *Eclogues*', *C.Q.* 21 (1971) 188–203

Gransden, K. W. 'The pastoral alternative', *Arethusa* 3 (1970) 103–21, 177–96

Griffiths, C. 'Myricae', *P.V.S.* 9 (1969–70) 1–19a

Johnson, Samuel *The Rambler* 36 (21 July) and 37 (24 July 1750) *The Adventurer* 92 (22 Sept. 1753)

Kidd, D. A. 'Imitation in the Tenth Eclogue', *B.I.C.S.* 11 (1964) 54–64

[1] Abbreviations of titles of journals follow the conventions of Marouzeau's *L'Année philologique*.

Leach, E. W. 'The unity of Eclogue 6', *Latomus* 27 (1968) 13–32

Lovejoy, A. O. and Boas, G. *Primitivism and related ideas in antiquity* (Baltimore 1935)

Otis, B. *Vergil: a study in civilized poetry* (Oxford 1964)

Parry, A. M. 'Landscape in Greek literature', *Y.C.S.* 15 (1957) 3–29

Perret, J. *Virgile, l'homme et l'oeuvre* (Paris 1952)

Poggioli, R. 'The oaten flute', *Harvard Library Bulletin* 11 (1957) 147–84

Pope, Alexander 'A discourse on pastoral poetry' in *Works* (London 1717)

Putnam, M. C. J. *Virgil's pastoral art: studies in the Eclogues* (Princeton 1970)

Rose, H. J. *The Eclogues of Vergil* (Berkeley and Los Angeles 1942)

Rosenmeyer, T. G. *The green cabinet. Theocritus and the European pastoral lyric* (Berkeley 1969)

Schmidt, E. A. *Poetische Reflexion. Vergils Bukolik* (Munich 1972)

Segal, C. P. 'Vergil's Caelatum Opus: an interpretation of the Third Eclogue', *A.J.P.* 88 (1967) 279–308

  'Vergil's sixth Eclogue and the problem of Evil', *T.A.P.A.* 100 (1969) 407–35

Sellar, W. Y. *The Roman poets of the Augustan Age: Virgil* (Oxford 1883[2])

Sickle, J. B. van 'The unity of the Eclogues: Arcadian forest, Theocritan trees', *T.A.P.A.* 98 (1967) 491–508

Snell, B. 'Arcadia: the discovery of a spiritual landscape' in *The discovery of the mind* (= *Die Entdeckung des Geistes* Eng. tr. 1953) 281–309

Wilkinson, L. P. 'Virgil and the evictions', *Hermes* 94 (1966) 320–4

Williams, G. *Tradition and originality in Roman poetry* (Oxford 1968) 274–85, 303–29

Wormell, D. E. W. 'The originality of the Eclogues' in *Virgil* ed. D. R. Dudley (London 1969) 1–26

Many of the above books and essays contain extensive bibliographies, which provide access to earlier work on the poet and the poems.

INDEX

Numbers prefixed 'p.' refer to pages of the Introduction; other references are to line numbers in the Commentary.

pastoral names (*cont.*)
  cas p. 30; 2.15; 5 fin.; 10.20;
  Micon 3.10; *Phyllis* 3.76; *Tityrus*
  1.1; Vergilian, *Alexis* 2.1; *Alphesi-*
  boeus 5.73; *Codrus* 5.11; *Damon*
  3.17; *Iollas* 2.57; *Meliboeus* 1.6;
  Moeris 8.96; *Mopsus* 5.1
perfect: morphology of *clamassent*
  6.44; *noram* 1.23; *risere* 3.9;
  tulĕrunt 4.61
Plato 4.36; 6.14
Pollio pp. 15, 17; 3.84; 4.12; 8.6
proverbs 2.59; 3.91; 9.51

-que...-que, metrical treatment of
  4.51
qui and *quis* 1.18

religion: Italian cults and rites 1.43,
  52; 3.77; 5.75, 80; 6.22; 10.27;
  cf. 5.30; magic and folk-lore
  3.103; 8.64–106, esp. 75, 80,
  97–8; 9.54; prophecy and portent
  1.17; 4.4–10, fin.; 5.37–9; 8.27–8,
  52–5; 9.13, 15, 47–9

satyrs and fauns 5.73; 6.27; cf. 6.14
sexual attitudes p. 10; 2.15; 3.7–8;
  7.67; 10.37
Sibylline oracles 4.4, 7, 17, 22, 29,
  30, 50–1

Sicilia etc. 2.21; 4.1; 10.4
socio-political and legal terms p. 24;
  1.3–4, 27, 32, 53, 71; 2.2; 8.29,
  92–3; 9. 3–4
structural symmetry 5 fin.; 8 fin.
syllable division 4.5; 5.68; 6.53;
  9.49, 66–7; cf. 1.38; 3.97; 7.23;
  8.11; 9.57; 10.69

Theocritus 1.1, 7–8, 51, 79; 2.4, 18,
  23, 25–7, 33, 40, 43–4, 46, 56, 60,
  63, 64, 65, 68, 69, 73; 3.1, 3, 25,
  30, 32–4, 36, 37, 43, 50, 58, 60,
  62, 64, 69, 70–1, 80, 88, 89, 97,
  100; 5.1, 12, 26, 27–8, 32, 36,
  43–4, 46, 47, 60, 67, 69, 83, 85,
  88; 7.2, 5, 6, 7, 18, 43, 45, 49, 53,
  54, 70; 8.21, 34, 37, 41, 52, 53,
  55, 59, 61, 68, 80, 82, 85–7, 91,
  97; 9.1, 22, 32, 39, 42, 60, 64;
  10.10, 15, 16, 21, 22, 35, 39, 42, 68

umbra 1.1; 10.75

Varius 8.88; 9.35

war p. 30, 1.70–1; 4.17, 35; 6.3, 7;
  9.12; 10.23
writing 5.13, 42; 10.53

CPSIA information can be obtained
at www.ICGtesting.com
Printed in the USA
LVHW031952020921
696793LV00003B/316

CAUGHT PREPARED

25
SIMPLE STEPS TO PROTECT YOUR FAMILY
IN AN EMERGENCY

SAM SPENCER

PLAIN SIGHT PUBLISHING
AN IMPRINT OF CEDAR FORT, INC.
SPRINGVILLE, UTAH

ISBN 13: 978-1-4621-1613-3

Published by Hobble Creek Press, an imprint of Cedar Fort, Inc.
2373 W. 700 S., Springville, UT 84663
Distributed by Cedar Fort, Inc., www.cedarfort.com

LIBRARY OF CONGRESS CATALOGING-IN-PUBLICATION DATA
Spencer, Sam, 1949- author.
Caught prepared / Sam Spencer.
pages cm
ISBN 978-1-4621-1613-3 (alk. paper)
1. Survival—Handbooks, manuals, etc. 2. Emergencies—Handbooks, manuals, etc. 3. Emergency management—Handbooks, manuals, etc. I. Title.

GF86.S64 2014
613.6'9—dc23

2014037747

Cover design by Rebecca J. Greenwood
Cover design © 2015 by Lyle Mortimer
Edited and typeset by Eileen Leavitt

Printed in the United States of America

10 9 8 7 6 5 4 3 2 1

This book is dedicated to those individuals who are not sure how to prepare for disaster, to those are looking for real answers, and to those who need just a little help to fine-tune their disaster planning.
Find yourself *caught prepared!*

CONTENTS

INTRODUCTION

In **August 2005, Hurricane Katrina, one of the costliest natu-**ral disasters in US history, battered the Gulf Coast. A news reporter, curious about how survivors were doing, began to canvass a high-rise building to check on survivors.

He and his cameraman climbed twenty flights of stairs and then paused. The reporter faced the camera and detailed his hike up the stairway and the lack of services in the building. There was no electricity, heat, or water. He remarked that many of the tenants were elderly and could not negotiate the stairs. They had been sequestered for three days.

"Let me knock on this door," the reporter said, "and see what we find."

He knocked on the apartment door, and in a moment there appeared an elderly couple. The reporter asked if there was anything that they needed. At first, I thought it was a hollow question. But as I watched the response, I was greatly educated.

"We could sure use some water," the elderly couple replied.

The reporter promptly handed them a bottle of water. My thoughts were of disbelief. The people don't have enough water stored to last even three days?

How about you? How long could you survive if water stopped coming out of your tap today?

Over the years, I have studied many disasters and asked myself, "What do I need to do to prepare myself for such an occurrence?" I have seen

1

the unfortunate victims' glaring deficiencies in each disaster. My process isn't intended to be judgmental. I study emergencies as a way of preparing myself. Using my observations from eyewitness accounts of what people *wished* they had done, I have been able to formulate some concrete, useful disaster preparedness plans.

Using these observations, I continually tweak my emergency preparedness supplies to be able to satisfy the different scenarios that my family might encounter. The only way to truly understand these sequences of events is to study each disaster. The people's needs must be specified in order to implement a solution that works for them. A person must decide which scenarios fit their needs and take appropriate actions.

If you are unprepared but willing to start, you are on the right track. This book will help you navigate twenty-five doable, user-friendly emergency preparedness tips and will give you peace of mind.

You can prepare your family with a good supply of water without spending a lot of time or money. It seems so simple and basic, yet lack of water is probably the biggest survival mistake people make. They just don't have enough on hand to survive. Once we've tackled your water situation, we'll work our way through several other important emergency preparedness tips.

We often expect the government or another agency to step in and help in a disaster. But it takes time for agencies to respond. As self-sufficient families, we have a responsibility to prepare for ourselves rather than leaving it up to someone else.

During Hurricane Katrina, the government's planning was shortsighted. But it also seemed as if the community as a whole expected the government to save them. And ultimately, the communities were disappointed!

Preparedness Basics

Another news report that alarmed me was an obscure story of an overwhelming problem. A consequence of having no water is that toilets will not flush. Not good! Imagine your life without toilet facilities. If only the victims of these disasters had access to this book's section on sanitation, life would have been much easier. Reading reports of people defecating in the halls of their tenements and on lawns and open spaces led me to realize that people become base and unconcerned when faced with few choices. At that point, their decisions start to endanger the lives of others.

Start preparing for emergency services today before the need is critical.

In 2008, there was an earthquake in Wells, Nevada. There was snow on the ground. It was cold. There were no services for a full week. No natural gas for heat. No electricity to run the heaters or lights. Plus, there was no water, and consequently the flush toilets would not work.

As I studied this earthquake, which was basically in my backyard, I imagined that this scenario could very easily have happened to me because I live in the Salt Lake Valley with the Wasatch fault right below me. I paid particular attention to the hardships that the Wells citizens had to endure. What would I do without power? How would I heat my home if we had no natural gas? Did I have enough water? As I pondered these questions, I reviewed my own disaster preparedness planning. What were the things I needed to do to make sure I was not caught so unprepared like my neighbors in Wells, Nevada?

Since I already have my house set up with emergency power, I checked and ran my generator to make sure that my power backup system was in excellent operating condition. I then began to examine my preparedness plan for an alternate heat source. I inventoried and increased my water storage. The Wells earthquake came during the coldest days of winter, with temperatures below freezing even throughout the day.

After several weeks of analyzing the earthquake, plus pondering and planning solutions, I made additional major changes in my preparedness plan. It is very important that with each disaster, no matter where it is in the world, you analyze the event. Pay specific attention to the needs of the individuals, particularly those needs that are hard to meet. Picture your family as the people in crisis, and see yourself acting in each situation. Armed with new information, improve your plan to become better prepared. You will then be able to better save yourself and your loved ones!

From the earthquakes in Chile, I observed that many of the buildings did not totally collapse. Some slid off their foundations and stayed together. What stuck out the most to me was that many of the structures resembled parallelograms, slightly leaning but not totally collapsed. They were still uninhabitable, looking like wooden boxes that had fallen off the back of a truck.

The building codes in Utah (where I live), like Chile, are strict when it comes to earthquake guidelines. With so many internal walls, sheer walls, and metal strapping, we would probably experience similar results during an earthquake. I now have stored at my house some 4"×4" 10' posts that

could be used to support my home or to shore up the structure from further damage. It also became obvious to me that if I had a partial collapse, it might be difficult for me to get to my preparedness items. After some review, I've also made changes to ensure better access to my supplies.

The unprepared people in Hurricane Sandy could have made life more comfortable if only they had prepared in reserve just one week's supply of food and water. That simple preparedness step could have helped many. People were caught off guard with no working appliances and no backup emergency cooking facilities. If they had implemented one of the emergency cooking tips from this book, it would have made a great difference. Preparing today will save a lot of trouble later!

My goal with this book is to share several ideas that would have saved the disaster victims, and to help you create your own plan to alleviate discomfort, and to possibly save lives. However, the information in this book will do you no good unless you make a plan that is designed for you, by you, and then implemented by you. So begin to plan even if your plan allows only for a few days of survival. With time, you can extend it to a weeklong survival plan and eventually expand your plan so that you will be able to survive for an extended period. Your emergency program should be sacred to you. Maintain it and keep it current so that when you need it, everything will be in order.

Do not count on FEMA or any other government agency to satisfy your needs. My father used to always say, "If you want the job done right, do it yourself." That is particularly good advice, especially when it comes to emergency preparedness and survival planning. If, by chance, they do help, then be sure to tell them thank you.

As you read this book, you will find numerous ideas that might interest you. Study them! Analyze your situation, and put in place a plan designed by you and for you. You will find a shopping list at the end of each tip to make it easy to implement, along with some "Do it NOW" tips to get you up off the couch and moving. Sometimes the first step is the most difficult to take, so most of the "Do it NOW" steps can be accomplished in minutes.

A little knowledge and a few precautionary measures can enormously increase your chances of surviving any disaster. The keys are education, planning, and preparation. The safety tips that follow will not make you an expert. But knowing these tips can save property and lives in a

disaster situation. Invest in this knowledge and preparation so that you can weather the storm in a safe and prepared manner.

You will notice that with every disaster discussed in this book, there are three basic steps to survival preparedness. Learn the steps and apply them to the types of disasters that are most common to your area. Imagine you and your family experiencing the disaster, and envision your successful survival of each event because you have planned in advance and have executed your plan well.

Three-Step Plan

1. **Get Educated.** Learn what to do before, during, and after a disaster.

2. **Make a plan.** Design a plan for you and your family, keeping in mind individual needs and locations.

3. **Prepare survival kits.** This should include at least a 72-hour kit of food and water for each person in your household to use in an emergency. It should also include long-term survival preparedness items based on your plan.

Prepare today! Be caught prepared tomorrow!

SURVIVAL PREPAREDNESS TIPS

WATER
STORAGE TIPS

Water is absolutely necessary for survival. A person can survive easily for a week without food. I have often heard stories of people surviving for several weeks without food. However, a human being can survive only about three days without water. It is for this reason that your first priority as you begin your disaster preparedness plan is to store emergency water. We are accustomed to abundant domestic water supplies, and we can hardly imagine water not being available. We take it for granted.

An interruption in the water supply does not necessarily come from a natural disaster. It can also come from other sources, such as a contaminated water supply, a broken water main, or even failed equipment at the utility company. It is a good idea to have a minimum of one week's worth of water stored for all occupants of your home or apartment. You will see how simple this can be as you study this section.

One gallon per person per day is the minimum that you should have in storage. This will give you two quarts to drink each day and two quarts for cooking and brushing your teeth. If you would like more water for hygiene, then you will need an additional gallon per person per day. The ideal amount of water to store for an emergency is two gallons per person per day. That would mean fourteen gallons of emergency water per person per week.

Hot weather can increase the amount of water needed. Children may need additional water. People who are ill, pregnant, and nursing will also

need additional drinking water. Limiting your activity particularly in hot weather can decrease your demand for water. It is important, however, that you give your body the water that it needs each day. *Stay hydrated!*

When disaster strikes, your emergency water storage could save your life. Have enough emergency water.

How Much Water Should You Store?

My recommendation: a minimum of seven days' supply of water per person. Store one gallon of water per person per day. Generally, it takes a few days for emergency services to become available, and water is often the first item that is brought in. The *minimum* preparation for emergency water should be one week. That would be seven gallons per person as a minimum to store in your home.

Start by doing this simple calculation based on your own family's needs. Determine how much water you need to store for your family for one week: number of family members _____× 7 (one gallon per day per person) = total water needed.

What Containers Should I Use?

You should store water only in food-grade plastic containers with tight-fitting screw-on caps. You can purchase new containers if you desire. All used storage containers must be thoroughly washed, sanitized, and rinsed before filling with water for storage. Wash containers with dish soap, and rinse thoroughly with clean water. You can sanitize additionally if desired by swishing a solution of one teaspoon of liquid household chlorine bleach to a quart of water on all interior surfaces of the container. Rinse the container thoroughly again with clean water before you fill it with storage water.[1]

My wife buys apple juice and orange juice in large hard plastic containers. When we have finished drinking the juice, she will clean the container as described and fill it with storage water. We have many containers filled with water stored on shelves and in various places in our home. We write the month and year on each bottle with a felt pen. Generally, you can have confidence that if food was stored in a particular container, it is food-grade plastic. Be sure to thoroughly clean each container! PET and PETE containers are food grade and are designed for this use. Inspect the container to find the recycle triangle. These letters will be printed below it.

You should not store your water in glass containers because there is an inherent risk of breakage. You should not use milk containers for water

storage because they are not designed for long-term use. Whatever you choose to store water in, you should place it out of the sunlight, especially if you have clear containers. If you need to store your water outside or in the sunlight, it is a good idea to use the blue water containers that will keep the sunlight from penetrating the containers or to cover them with a tarp.

What Water Should I Use?

Most public water supplies are chlorinated and are safe to store with no additional treatment. In this case, adding extra chlorine for long-term storage will be your choice. If you choose to add chlorine to your stored water, use only non-scented bleach. Do not use bleaches with soaps, scents or colors added. Use the following guidelines for storage of a culinary or public utility source of water:

- Two drops bleach per quart

- Four drops bleach per 2-quart, 2-liter, or ½-gallon container

- Eight drops bleach per gallon or 4-liter container

- 1⅛ teaspoons per 5-gallon container

- 2 tablespoons plus 1 teaspoon for a 55-gallon drum

Once you have added the non-scented bleach to the container, gently agitate or stir. Let it sit for twenty to thirty minutes before capping.

Vended water is also a good option. Vended water is typically water from the municipality with additional treatment beyond that of the municipality. Treat and store this water in the same manner that you would the public utility water.

Where Should I Store My Water?

Store your water in a cool, dry place away from direct sunlight. Heat and light can break down the plastic containers. Also, do not put the water near gasoline or pesticides because the vapors from these products can penetrate the plastic. Your water should be stored on lower shelves that can support the weight. Each gallon of water weighs about eight pounds.

That means that twelve gallons will weigh a hundred pounds. Make sure that your shelves can support the weight. Also, it is best to store the water on bottom shelves, especially in earthquake-prone areas. You can buy one-gallon bottles of water that store easily and well.

Store the water under your bed, in your garage, or behind your sofa. Put it away and leave it alone. It's for an emergency! Once you use it, replace it. Always maintain a manageable and adequate level. Use your imagination to find creative places to store your water. It is recommended by water utilities that you rotate your stored water once a year.[2]

I store several fifty-five-gallon barrels in my garage. You can store four in a row against the wall and put a 2'×8' piece of plywood on top for a shelf for additional storage. It is simple math; one fifty-five-gallon drum per person per month of emergency water. With that, you will have two gallons per person per day, one for eating and drinking and one for hygiene. Another thing to consider is how to get the water out. Invest in a pump.

You will have to determine how often you need to rotate your water. I have friends that have ten-year-old water that is still good! I also have friends that rotate their water annually or even every six months. If your stored water goes flat, it can be aerated prior to consumption by pouring it between two containers five to ten times. My father has had water stored in his basement in liter soda bottles for more than five years. It is still good. This is not my recommendation. However, I certainly believe that in a time of crisis, his water will be valuable even with the faint taste of root beer being present.

Some Additional Thoughts

- Store water in several locations around your home, particularly on lower shelves.

- Purchase a hand-operated water filter and purifier.

- If you do store water in large drums, also store a siphon or pump.

- Depending on the size of your water heater, you will usually find thirty to sixty gallons of water. This is the same water that you drink and cook with and is ready for use.

- Canned fruits and vegetables also contain water for hydrating yourself.

- A good rule of thumb is to count a pet as another person for water.

A pump will help you take water out of large drums.

- After a natural disaster, water-borne illnesses appear when the water supply becomes polluted.

- If you buy bottled water, buy an extra case for emergency use. When replacing the water, put the new case on the bottom. You'll always have fresh water for your kit!

- Two-liter soda bottles are excellent for water storage.

Stop everything! Go find a container that you can store emergency water in. Wash and rinse it out. Then fill it with water and store it away.

A Final Water Tip

A five-gallon water container can be purchased for five to six dollars. Fill one with water for each member of your family. Now you have five days of emergency water for you and your family. Put them in a row behind the sofa or up against the wall and cover them with a tablecloth, towel, or blanket. Be sure not to place your water near a heat register.

Checklist of Items to Consider

☐ 55-gallon drums (one drum per person per month)
☐ 1 gallon of water per person per day for drinking and eating
☐ 1 gallon of water per person per day for personal hygiene
☐ Water pump

NOTES

1. "Water," last modified April 9, 2014, accessed December 5, 2014, http://www.ready.gov/water.
2. Jordan Valley Water Conservancy District, "Emergency Water Storage," accessed December 5, 2014, https://jvwcd.org/water/emergency.

2

BUILD AN EMERGENCY FOOD SUPPLY

I have seen situations and disasters where people have been unable to access their services for several weeks. This could be because of contaminated water or power outages. Because these people are not *caught prepared*, they are forced to use a communal government shelter, assuming, that is, they have the ability to get there. The best solution is to have two to four weeks of food in your pantry just for emergencies. This will allow you to have food until help arrives, and if it doesn't arrive in a timely manner, you will be prepared to care for yourself.

The real questions are, "What do I store?" "How do I store it?" and "Where do I store it?" As you answer and act on these questions, you will be caught prepared! There are several approaches to these questions, and you need to study the options and decide on the best option for you.

The simplest approach to a sustainable short-term food storage plan is each time you purchase packaged or canned goods at the grocery store, you should buy two packages or cans rather than one. You can use one now and one later. Buy two boxes of cereal, one to use now and one for later. In other words, just have twice your regular amount of food in your daily-use pantry. I find that most people have a week's worth of food at best on their shelves. Double it! Have two weeks minimum. You can now survive two weeks if needed. If you have cereal in your pantry, then you will also want to store some shelf-stable UHT or boxed milk. Most have a one-year shelf life. The other option is to store powdered milk.

What to Do Today

Try an experiment. Go to your cupboard and fill a grocery bag with enough food to stave off hunger that day. Could you feed yourself and your entire family for three days? Could you make it for a week on what you have stored?

Start by taking a look at your pantry shelves to see what is already there that has a shelf life of at least one month. This will give you a good plan for the kinds of things that your family is already eating that can be stored.

Fill a box with crackers, canned soups and stews. Have some canned vegetables like beans, peas, and corn. Some tuna fish or other canned meats can be eaten right out of the can. I know that many will say yuck, but that's what you may need to do. Store this box of food under your bed or someplace out of the way. Put it inside a plastic bag, seal it, and put it away for an emergency. Know what it is and where it is. Have enough to feed your family for two, three, or even four weeks in this box. You know how much to store because you already eat this kind of food everyday.

Add some hard candy for extra sugar and a treat. Add a few granola or energy bars. Put them in a heavy-duty, resealable freezer bag to keep them fresher. You will need a manual can opener and utensils, as well as paper plates and napkins. This box, when completed, can be picked up and taken with you if you need to evacuate, and you will be able to eat for at least a week or two. Also consider including some liquid hand sanitizer or a bar of soap to wash hands.

Role-play with your family through an emergency scenario. As you discuss preparedness with your like-minded friends, you will get additional ideas that are specific for your situation. Add them to your emergency food box. This box of less-than-perfect food is insurance that could save your life and the lives of your family members.

When my father passed away, his pantry was filled with canned goods. Most of it was expired. "Should I throw them all away?" I asked myself. That seemed like a waste, so I decided to at least call the local food pantry to get some direction. The lady on the other end of the phone said, "We will accept any canned goods that are within five years of the 'use by' date as long as the cans are not damaged or bulging." Most of the food qualified! They went to good use.

This was an awakening in a way. Maybe the viability of canned goods was longer than I had previously thought. Maybe you should implement a plan to use the goods in the box every year or two. But remember, replace

it as soon as you take it out. Follow these simple steps and you will always have emergency survival food. You will be *caught prepared!*

Checklist of Items to Consider

- ☐ Canned fruit
- ☐ Canned vegetables
- ☐ Canned meat
- ☐ Boxes of milk
- ☐ Crackers
- ☐ Granola bars
- ☐ Hard candy
- ☐ Heavy-duty resealable freezer bags
- ☐ Utensils
- ☐ Manual can opener
- ☐ Paper plates and napkins
- ☐ Hand sanitizer
- ☐ _____
- ☐ _____
- ☐ _____

Find three items that you can eat in an emergency. Place them in a box and label it "Emergency." If you cannot find three items to place in the box, start a shopping list with at least three items listed here.

Do It NOW!

3

LEARN TO TURN OFF GAS, WATER, AND POWER

Everyone should know how to turn off their gas, water, and electricity utilities. You should know how to turn them off at the delivery point, which is typically at the meter. Most follow similar patterns and methods to be turned off. Once you are familiar with them you can easily accomplish this task.

Caution: If you turn off the gas for any reason, a qualified professional must turn it back on. Never attempt to turn the gas back on yourself.

Natural Gas

Let's start with the gas. Almost all gas meters are the same. An adjustable wrench is all you need. The valve is turned 90° to open or close. It takes one quarter turn clockwise to open and one quarter turn counterclockwise to close. When the two holes in the valve are aligned, a lock can be put in them, and the gas is turned off. When the length of the valve is in line with the pipe, the gas is on.

Learning where your gas valve is and how to turn it off is critical. If you are not sure, ask someone who knows, like the landlord. Call your gas company and ask them how it works. Certainly there is someone you know who is knowledgeable in this area. Don't be afraid to ask for help.

If you have propane, you will turn the valve off at the tank. Treat propane just like natural gas because it *is* just like natural gas.

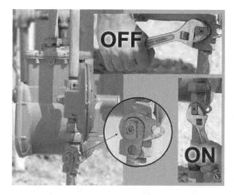

You can turn off your gas at the meter. Contact qualified personnel to turn it back on.

If you have propane, you turn the valve off at the tank.

Use an adjustable wrench or a T wrench to turn off your water at the meter.

Teach your family members what natural gas smells like. If you smell gas, leave immediately and call the authorities.

Caution: If you turn off the gas for any reason, qualified personnel must turn it back on. The pilot lights must be relit. Care must be taken.

Water

Typically the water meter and shutoff are at the street. The property owner should know where the valve is. If you cannot find it, ask your municipality or water provider to locate it and show you how to turn it off. You may need to clean out some dirt and debris to access and turn the valve. Use a stick to remove spider webs and clean around the valve.

An adjustable wrench or a T wrench will do the job. The valve is turned 90° to open or close. It takes one quarter turn clockwise to open and one quarter turn counterclockwise to close. When the two holes in the valve are aligned, it is turned off, and a lock can be put on.

To help stimulate your memory, take photos of the procedure. Print them and keep them available for reference.

Electricity

Electricity can pose a problem. Older homes may not have

a shutoff main breaker at the meter. It is important that you know where and how to turn the power off. It may be necessary to get some help.

My suggestion is that you take enough photos that anyone can easily follow the process. Make a step-by-step card for this process with actual photos of your breaker.

Once you have taken the photos of the process, design a card that you can print and laminate. Have this card available for easy emergency access, and teach others in your family

STEP 1: Locate your main power switch outside west wall of building. Turn main power switch to "off" position.

Here is an example of the card I made for one of my brothers to instruct him on how to turn the power off at his house. Take time to do the same. Give the card to different family members to see if the instructions are easily followed.

to use it. Place it by the breaker box, or hang it on the wall beside the power disconnect.

If your home is newer, it probably has a main switch. Simply turn the breaker to the "off" position. If your house does not have a main breaker to isolate you from the grid or the power company, you will need to turn off all the breakers individually. If you are not sure, then you can always turn all the breakers off at your breaker panel box.

Once again, it may be necessary get help from an electrician and practice beforehand to be sure everyone can do it.

Apartments

If you live in an apartment, ask the landlord or superintendent to show you how to shut off the utilities for your unit. Take several photographs of the procedure. Then make and print out a card with easy-to-follow instructions. Keep this card easily accessible with your emergency preparedness items.

Remember that elevators will not work when the power is out. You will not have heat. Follow some of the tips in this book to ensure that you are warm and can take care of yourself.

 *Identify your gas, water, and electricity shutoff locations. Take photos of each utility's location. Ask your landlord or building superintendent to help you with this information if needed.*

Checklist of Items to Consider

- ☐ T wrench for water
- ☐ Adjustable wrench
- ☐ Photos of procedure
- ☐ Photos of valve and breaker locations

4

LEARN HOW TO USE
A FIRE EXTINGUISHER

One of my friends is a fireman. During a recent conversation, he recounted some stories of personal loss from improper use of fire extinguishers. He told me about some people who had no idea how to even make a fire extinguisher work. Proper operating knowledge could have prevented unnecessary property loss. The day may come when knowing how to act quickly and use a fire extinguisher may save the life of one of your loved ones. The National Fire Protection Association reports that "in 2012, there were 1,375,000 fires reported in the United States. These fires caused 2,855 civilian deaths, 16,500 civilian injuries, and 12.4 billion in property damage."[1] A forty-dollar investment has the potential to prevent thousands of dollars in damage and even preserve lives. If money is tight, ask for one for your next birthday present.

Having the best fire extinguisher without knowing how to use it is only slightly better than not having one at all. Having a fire extinguisher in the wrong location can also be an issue. Having it handy in case of an emergency and knowing how to use it is critical.

It is recommended that you have a minimum of one fire extinguisher on each floor of your home, plus one in the garage. They should be visible and no higher than five feet off the floor. It is not advisable to put extinguishers in closets or hidden behind walls or curtains.

Fire extinguishers are made with different fires in mind. One of the best "around the house" extinguishers is an ABC extinguisher.

Kitchen

The kitchen is where most home fires start. Grease fires can often be contained by a fire extinguisher. Be sure you place the fire extinguisher far enough away from the stove that you can access it without being burned. The best location is by the door.

Garage

The garage is typically a place where a lot of flammable items are stored. It is a good idea to keep a fire extinguisher in your garage. Once again, the best location for your fire extinguisher is by the door.

Fire extinguishers should be checked regularly. Confirm that the pressure gauge indicator is in the operable range; typically, this is the green area. Some extinguishers can be recharged and serviced by licensed professional fire extinguisher maintenance contractors. Others must be thrown out when they lose their charge.

An ABC fire extinguisher is likely your best choice. It can be used on most of the fires you will encounter in the home, including combustible solids like cloth and wood, flammable liquids like grease and gasoline, and electrical appliances.[2] Home centers and hardware stores are a good place to purchase fire extinguishers.

P-A-S-S

PASS is an acronym that stands for *pull*, *aim*, *squeeze*, and *sweep*. This will help you learn and remember how to operate a fire extinguisher.

Fire-Extinguisher101.com gives the following explanation

- *Pull* the pin at the top of the extinguisher. The pin releases a locking mechanism and will allow you to discharge the extinguisher.

- *Aim* at the base of the fire, not the flames. This is important—in order to put out the fire, you must extinguish the fuel.

- *Squeeze* the lever slowly. This will release the extinguishing agent in the extinguisher. If the handle is released, the discharge will stop.

- *Sweep* from side to side. With a sweeping motion, move the fire extinguisher back and forth at the base of the fire until the fire is completely out. Operate the extinguisher from a safe distance, several feet away, and then move toward the fire once it starts to diminish.

A fire extinguisher is only effective on small fires. Plus, a fire extinguisher will only last for ten to thirty seconds, depending on its size. With that in mind, someone should call 911 immediately. Get the professionals there as soon as possible. If the extinguisher fails to extinguish the fire, then get out!

Find a fire extinguisher in the next thirty seconds. Verify that it is still in the green. If you fail this test, create a plan of action to acquire a fire extinguisher.

DO
It
NOW!

NOTES

1. National Fire Protection Association, "Fires in the U.S.," accessed December 5, 2014, http://www.nfpa.org/research/reports-and-statistics/fires-in-the-us.
2. US Fire Administration, "Outreach materials and educational programs," accessed December 5, 2014, http://www.usfa.fema.gov/prevention/outreach/.

5

MINI TOILET PAPER ROLL

Have you ever needed toilet paper and found there was none, or have you been caught out in the wild when Mother Nature came calling? What do you do? It is somewhat awkward to keep a whole roll of toilet paper in the glove compartment. Dragging a large roll of toilet paper with you wherever you go can also be embarrassing.

I offer the perfect solution: Keep an eye on the roll of toilet paper in your bathrooms. When the roll is largely used up, and there is about one-half inch of paper left on the roll, change it out with a new one. Now you have a small roll that is convenient to use.

I take it one step further. I put it in a ziplock plastic bag and press it flat. It will always stay clean in the bag and will not get torn up in the glove compartment or elsewhere. When it is pushed flat, it will work just as well as before; however, it stores much more conveniently. Now it will fit easily into a purse, a glove compartment, or the pocket of your jacket.

Start building your private stash of mini toilet paper rolls. Once you start having them available and see how convenient they are, you will find many additional uses for them. Before long, you will have them stashed in a variety of emergency places.

Put a mini roll in all your 72-hour kits. Put several in your camping supplies. Keep one in your car.

Checklist of Items to Consider

- ☐ Ziplock bags
- ☐ Mini toilet paper rolls

6

SANITATION

Here is an inexpensive and practical answer to emergency toilet needs. This grab-and-go sanitation system is totally self-contained and is always ready for use.

While studying the aftermath of Hurricane Sandy, I read a troubling headline that referred to tenants defecating in the hallways. With no water, toilets will not be working. You will need facilities for sanitation needs. Don't count on the government or relief organizations to take care of you. You will be disappointed. The demand will be overwhelming. Plan ahead, and you will have just what you need to be prepared.

You can easily make a portable potty bucket from items around the house.

The Portable Potty Bucket

Take a five- or six-gallon bucket (six-gallon best for adults because of the extra height). Buckets can be purchased at hardware stores. Also, most large markets have companies that sell containers to manufacturers that should have what you need.

Next, line the bucket with a plastic bag (opaque is best). You want a bag that is large enough to completely fill the bucket, and the bag should be resting on the bottom of the bucket.

Now attach a toilet seat to the top of the bucket, holding the bag in

place. This seat can be purchased online or at most hardware or sporting goods stores for about ten dollars. You can also order one online.

If you do not use a liner in the bucket (not recommended), just dispose of waste as needed, generally by burning it or putting it into a working sewer. However, keep in mind that without a liner you will then need to wash out the bucket each time.

To absorb moisture, sprinkle a small amount of kitty litter into the waste bag after each use. Add more kitty litter as needed. Tie the bag closed and dispose. Kitty litter chemicals will allow you to go longer between disposals.

Other Options . . .

You can use RV treatment chemicals and RV toilet paper for quicker breakdown and odor control. The chemicals will allow you to go longer between cleanups. Without chemicals, you can add wood ashes to the bucket. This will help with the smell and promote decay. Ashes are readily available at any campfire.

I fill my bucket with supplies and have it stored in my preparedness area for quick access in an emergency. Here's what I store inside my bucket:

- Several rolls of toilet paper
- A roll of plastic bags
- Hand sanitizer
- A plastic jar filled with kitty litter

For hygiene, I add a bottle or two of hand sanitizer. You can also use sanitary wipes for your hands. Be sure to have extra to use for cleaning your hands at other times, like when you are preparing food.

For privacy, you can make a tarp enclosure. To do this, you will need a tarp and some rope. You can also purchase a shower tent. These tents are available for less than fifty dollars at sporting goods stores. Be sure to store the tent with your survival toilet for easy access.

In a Pinch

There are other ways to collect and dispose of waste. If you are in your home without services, you can use your commode to simulate the portable potty bucket. Secure a bag to the lid of the toilet to collect the waste. You should then share this tip with other tenants to keep the problem out of the hall.

Before disposing of the waste, seal the bag. If it is completely sealed, there will be no odor. Dispose of the bag in a properly designated area, and be careful not to puncture the bag. If solid waste is not dealt with quickly and properly, serious health issues will develop. Be aware that there is always a great risk of fecal contamination in these situations. Wash your hands after handling any waste.

One More Option

Dig a latrine. Yes, a good old-fashioned outhouse. Dig a hole in which to bury the waste. Cover the waste with a thin layer of dirt to keep the smell and flies away. Always clean your hands with soap and water or a hand cleaner for safety. Constructing a latrine is not complicated, but you will need a shovel and, eventually, some toilet paper.

You may need to be creative and resourceful to provide sanitary toilet services in an emergency. Remove a toilet seat, and build a comfortable latrine area. Make sure that the shovel and pile of dirt are easily available to cover the waste.

This option assumes that you will have a shovel to dig the hole and bury the waste. It is extremely important to bury it. Cleanliness and hygiene are critical to successful survival of any disaster. Health hazards can develop quickly. With a little preplanning, acquiring supplies, storing resources properly, and knowing how to correctly use them, the severity of the disaster will be greatly reduced.

I cannot emphasize enough the dangers of fecal contamination. Sanitation will keep away illness. Make sure that your toilet facilities are a safe distance from your living and eating areas. And always wash your hands when you are finished, especially before preparing food. Maintain a supply of wet wipes and hand sanitizer to enhance personal sanitation.

Checklist of Items to Consider

- ☐ 5- or 6-gallon bucket
- ☐ Toilet lid
- ☐ Toilet paper
- ☐ Hand sanitizer
- ☐ Kitty litter
- ☐ Shovel
- ☐ Shower tent

7

STAYING WARM IN AN EMERGENCY

As previously noted, an emergency during severe weather poses additional risks. You can make it through an emergency reasonably well if the temperature outside is balmy and mild. But if it is below freezing and your home is destroyed or uninhabitable, you have an additional crisis on your hands. Our ancestors survived without electricity and gas furnaces, and so can we. It just takes some planning.

How Many Blankets?

Do you have enough blankets? During Hurricane Sandy, the city of New York passed out twenty-five thousand blankets to those who lost their homes. One blanket will *not* be enough!

It would be a good idea to have one warm sleeping bag per person in your household. Consider buying matching bags that can zip together. Three or four children can keep warm in this double bag. You can line your sleeping bag with additional blankets.

To be sure you have enough blankets to keep warm, I suggest that you sit outside in the cold evening. Wrap up for about fifteen minutes. You will find out quickly if you have enough blankets. You should have three to four warm blankets for each person in your house. Understand that if you have no heat, the temperature inside and outside your home will eventually equalize. The good news is that if you are lucky enough to be indoors, you will be out of the wind and weather. Staying warm is essentially a matter of having enough blankets on hand.

For more detailed survival and preparedness information, see the chapter entitled "How to Survive a Winter Storm."

Space Blankets Are out of This World

Space blankets are compact Mylar sheets intended to help retain body heat. In a severe emergency, they are a great addition to an emergency

Space blankets are a great addition to any emergency kit.

kit. A space blanket has more uses than just keeping you warm. However, keeping warm in a survival situation should be your first priority.

Three Common Uses

- *Blanket*—The space blanket's main purpose is helping you stay warm. Wrap the blanket around you to contain your body heat and to stay out of the wind. You can use it as a sleeping bag liner, or you can make a simple sleeping bag by placing two space blankets on top of each other and sealing the edges closed with duct tape.

- *Shelter*—You can use the space blanket as a tent, tarp, or lean-to. It is waterproof and an excellent windbreaker, so it will protect you from wind, rain, or snow. The shiny side of the blanket can reflect heat from the sun or from a campfire, making you warmer.

- *Signal for help*—Because the surface of the blanket is reflective, it makes a good signal. Use it to signal across the valley or to an aircraft above for help.

Carry two or three in the glove compartment of your vehicle. They are relatively inexpensive.

Checklist of Items to Consider

☐ Sleeping bag for each person
☐ Blankets
☐ Space blankets and bags
☐ Duct tape
☐ Sweatpants, sweatshirt, wool socks

8

HAVE A PERSONAL FIRST AID KIT

The basic personal first aid kit is designed to handle cuts, scrapes, and bruises. These are certainly the most common injuries that you will encounter. In my life, the immediate need for antibacterial ointment and a bandage outnumber all other first aid needs combined. A basic first aid kit should be small, easy to carry, and compact. The real challenge is to have the necessary emergency medical and first aid supplies for one's personal needs.

Probably the main consideration is the scenarios you are most likely to encounter. Since you cannot prepare for every event, you must make your best guess. Leading scenarios will be cuts, bruises, abrasions, and sprains. Yes, you could see lacerations, broken bones, and possibly some other, more serious events, but they will be less likely.

In the many hikes, outdoor adventures, and sporting events that I have been involved in, there have been mostly cuts, puncture wounds, insect bites, and abrasions. In my sixty-five plus years, I have witnessed relatively few sprains and only two broken bones.

Though I grew up in the New Mexico desert and observed many rattlesnakes—even killing a few—I have never known of anyone who was bitten by one. Yes, it happens, but it is quite rare. I have witnessed minor insect bites, and I have heard of a scorpion sting or two. The best treatment for any injury is prevention! My best advice is to keep a safe distance. Stay out of likely habitats, don't take risks, and be smart and attentive.

Prepare your family kit to handle one or two single events. In other words, you are not carrying the whole medicine cabinet. You can always replenish your kit in the evening or the next day. The family kit should be compact and efficient.

A family first aid kit for young children will be different than one for teens. Someone with diabetes, allergies, or other medical conditions will have special needs, so plan accordingly. The youth involved in football or soccer may have different needs than the swimmer or cyclist. Nevertheless, you will find that most of your first aid needs will be common and mundane.

You must realize that you cannot plan for every contingency, but you can plan for the most likely. Build your first aid kit based on what is most likely and practical. Study and learn as much as possible, and creativity will spring from that knowledge.

Let us begin to build the basic family first aid kit. Learn how to use each of the following items. Make a personal decision on what you need and why you need it. As you build this kit, consider your family's unique needs. For a framework to build on, we will use what the American Red Cross recommends that all first aid kits for a family of four include:[1]

- 2 absorbent compress dressings (5×9 in.)
- 25 adhesive bandages (assorted sizes)
- 1 adhesive cloth tape (10 yd.×1 in.)
- 5 antibiotic ointment packets
- 5 antiseptic wipe packets
- 2 packets of aspirin
- 1 blanket (space blanket)
- 1 breathing barrier (with a one-way valve)
- 1 instant cold compress
- 2 pair of non-latex gloves (large)
- 2 hydrocortisone ointment packets
- Scissors
- 1 roller bandage (3 in. wide)
- 1 roller bandage (4 in. wide)

- 5 sterile gauze pads (3×3 in.)

- 5 sterile gauze pads (4×4 in.)

- Oral thermometer (non-mercury/non-glass)

- 2 triangular bandages

- Tweezers

A good first aid booklet can be handy for the novice to have in the kit. You might also decide to use tubes of ointments and creams instead of individual packets. Naturally, there is a lot of flexibility as to the variety in your family kit. There are two things to remember. One, it is your kit; center it around your needs. Two, you very likely will be carrying it with you. Make it complete, but be careful not to overburden it.

Grab a bag and see how many of these items you can organize into one consolidated place. If you already have a first aid kit, check to be sure that it is still complete. Add what is missing. If you don't have a first aid kit, make a plan to build one.

DO It NOW!

NOTES

1. American Red Cross, "Anatomy of a First Aid Kit," accessed December 5, 2014, http://www.redcross.org/prepare/location/home-family/get-kit/anatomy.

9

LEARN CPR AND GET AED TRAINING

My daughter and two of her friends were playing volleyball one afternoon when they heard screams at the pool. They ran to the poolside and saw a mother screaming as her child floated on top of the water. They pulled the child out and immediately began CPR.

Someone yelled, "Call 911!" It was not long until the baby was spitting up and crying. Had it not been for the fast action of someone who knew CPR, the child probably would not have survived.

CPR is not hard to learn. Your local Red Cross will offer training courses that will allow you to certify.

Just think about it for a minute. The person has stopped breathing. His or her heart has stopped beating. If you attempt CPR, you may save a life. There are many stories of people who have done just that and expressed that their only CPR training was from watching TV. Just try! But better yet, take time to learn CPR.

The American Heart Association cites two telling statistics that should inspire you to learn and keep current on CPR: "Seventy percent of Americans may feel helpless to act during a cardiac emergency because they do not know how to administer CPR. . . . Nearly 383,000 out-of-hospital sudden cardiac arrests occur annually, and eighty-eight percent of cardiac arrests occur at home."[1]

There are many places that will teach you CPR. The Red Cross has classes, along with other community resources. There are some good instructional videos on the Internet that will help you acquire some

knowledge. Some communities offer classes through local paramedic or City Hall organizations. I am certain that your city hall or your local paramedics can tell you where you can get CPR training locally. Performing CPR on a child is different than it is on an adult. Set a goal to learn CPR and get trained!

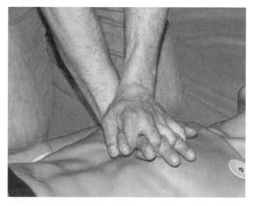

Contact your local Red Cross to learn more about how to administer CPR.

An AED (Automatic External Defibrillator) "is a portable device that checks the heart rhythm." It is easy to use, and the device gives you step-by-step instructions. "If needed, it can send an electric shock to the heart to try to restore a normal heart rhythm."[2] AEDs are used to treat sudden cardiac arrest, that is, when the heart suddenly stops beating.

These devices have become more automated and less expensive. Brief instructional videos are available on the Internet, and you should at least watch to get an idea how they work. You will then have some confidence if the need ever arises.

Go to YouTube, search "LIFEPACK AED," and watch a training video.

NOTES

1. American Heart Association, "CPR Statistics," last modified June, 2011, accessed December 5, 2014, http://www.heart.org/HEARTORG/CPRAndECC/WhatisCPR/CPRFactsandStats/CPR-Statistics_UCM_307542_Article.jsp#.
2. National Heart, Lung, and Blood Institute, "What Is an Automated External Defibrillator?" last modified December 2, 2011, accessed December 5, 2014, http://www.nhlbi.nih.gov/health/health-topics/topics/aed.

KNOW HOW TO CHANGE A TIRE AND BUILD AN EMERGENCY SURVIVAL KIT FOR YOUR CAR

I **was once on a business trip with two associates. One of them,** Jose, was driving and blew a tire while doing a U-turn. We pulled over, and I found out that neither of the men had ever changed, nor did they have any idea how to do it.

I asked if they knew where the spare tire and tools were. Again, neither had any idea. I soon found all that was needed and promptly changed the tire. In ten minutes we were on our way again. Had I not been there, the two young men would have had a great deal of trouble getting the help they needed.

I have taught all of my daughters to change a tire. This training has paid off as they too have educated others who had no idea how to change their tires.

A jack is needed to raise the tire off the ground. The vehicle needs to be raised until the wheel clears the ground and can be turned freely. The jack should be placed securely under the frame of the vehicle.

Next, you need a lug wrench to remove the nuts that hold the tire to the hub. Replace the damaged tire with the spare (most vehicles use the smaller "doughnut" tire), and then you are on your way!

Is there anyone over the age of twelve in your home that has never changed a tire? Have a family activity tonight to learn how. Practicing inside your warm, dry garage will give you confidence and help you make better decisions when you are changing a tire, say, on the freeway on a rainy night.

Checklist of Items to Consider

- ☐ Car jack
- ☐ Lug wrench
- ☐ A pad to kneel on
- ☐ Pair of work gloves to keep your hands clean

Vehicle Emergency Kit

Several years ago, I was visiting my eighty-year-old father and noticed a box in the trunk of his car. This box was filled with survival supplies in the event that he was stranded. A quick look revealed a blanket, a couple of cans of sardines, water, and a few other items. *What a great idea*, I thought. Stake out a claim in your trunk for an emergency survival kit.

You can build your own survival kit for your car by gathering the items listed below. Don't hesitate to add to it based on your personal needs. You might also consider questions like, "How many people generally travel with me?" "What is the average length of my travel?" "Are there any special medical and dietary needs?"

Think each scenario through. Imagine yourself stranded in your car in the various places you frequently travel. Ask yourself what you need to do. This role-play sequence will open your mind to possibilities and help you customize your kit.

Think about eating, keeping warm, and signaling others. A space blanket would be useful here. As you go through the list below, you should consider the uses of each item and determine what you need in your kit and why. This kit makes a great gift for new drivers and is a must for a teen headed off to college.

Checklist of Items to Consider

- ☐ Blanket
- ☐ First aid kit
- ☐ Windshield scraper
- ☐ Booster cables
- ☐ Tool kit
- ☐ Paper towels
- ☐ Work gloves
- ☐ Bag of sand or cat litter for added traction
- ☐ Towrope
- ☐ Tire chains (based on geography)
- ☐ Collapsible shovel
- ☐ Container of water
- ☐ High-calorie canned or dried foods
- ☐ Hard candy
- ☐ Can opener
- ☐ Flashlight and extra batteries
- ☐ Flares or light sticks for nighttime safety
- ☐ Short-handled shovel
- ☐ Whistle (for use as a distress signal)
- ☐ Hand warmers
- ☐ Syphon pump (to get gas out of your tank)
- ☐ Cell phone adapter to plug into a lighter
- ☐ Space blanket (for warmth and a reflector) See tip #7
- ☐ _____
- ☐ _____
- ☐ _____

The most frequently needed auto-emergency tools are a tire jack, a lug wrench and a good pair of booster cables. Check your trunk now to make sure that you have them in there and that they are good working order. If not, formulate a plan to correct it. **DO IT NOW!**

'11'

CREATE A FAMILY COMMUNICATION PLAN

What we have here is a failure to communicate!" This is my favorite line from the movie *Cool Hand Luke*, starring Paul Newman and George Kennedy. Good communication can be critical in a crisis. It will save lives, warn of impending danger, and calm the troubled soul.

In any emergency, there is an inherent desire to know what is going on. You'll want to know what the dangers are as they relate to you. You'll want to know if you can travel and when. You'll want to know when help will arrive. Above all, you'll want to know that your family and loved ones are safe. An emergency presents a heightened need for continued and good communication.

Cell phones have become indispensable. It seems that everyone has one now. If the power goes out, however, the cell towers might not operate. No calling. No texting.

The FCC has several recommendations for communication during an emergency:

- Limit non-emergency phone calls. This will minimize network congestion, free up space on the network for emergency communications, and conserve battery power if you are using a wireless phone.

- Keep all phone calls brief. If you need to use a phone, try to use it only to convey vital information to emergency personnel and family.

- For non-emergency calls, try text messaging, also known as short messaging service (SMS) when using your wireless phone. In many cases, text messages will go through when your call may not. It will also help free up more space for emergency communications on the telephone network.

- If possible, try a variety of communications services if you are unsuccessful in getting through with one. For example, if you are unsuccessful in getting through on your wireless phone, try another messaging capability like text messaging or email. Alternatively, try a landline phone if one is available. This will help spread the communications demand over multiple networks and should reduce overall congestion.

- Wait ten seconds before redialing a call. On many wireless handsets, to redial a number you simply push *send* after you've ended a call to redial the previous number. If you do this too quickly, the data from the handset to the cell sites do not have enough time to clear before you've resent the same data. This contributes to a clogged network.

- Have charged batteries and car-charger adapters available for backup power for your wireless phone.

- Maintain a list of emergency phone numbers in your phone.

- If you are in your vehicle, try to place calls while your vehicle is stationary.

- Have a family communications plan in place. Designate someone out of the area as a central contact, and make certain that all family members know whom to contact if they become separated.

- If you have Call Forwarding set up on your home number, forward your home number to your wireless number in the event of an evacuation. That way you will get incoming calls from your landline phone.

- After the disaster has passed, if you lose power in your home, try using your car to charge cell phones or listen to news alerts on

the car radio. But be careful—don't try to reach your car if it is not safe to do so, and remain vigilant about carbon monoxide emissions from your car if it is a closed space such as a garage.

- Tune-in to broadcast and radio news for important news alerts.

Another option is the two-way radio. You can purchase a couple of radios with chargers and headsets for less than thirty dollars that will allow you to communicate with family members within a short distance. If you step up to the fifty-dollar category, you can get a transmission range of up to thirty-five miles. Range varies based on terrain. Be sure to have extra batteries that fit your units, and practice in advance. You should also make sure that family members know what emergency channel to set a two-way radio to.

I have four households of family members living within four miles of my house. This is the perfect backup system for emergency communication. Have one for each member of your family. Teach them to use them and practice. Keep fresh batteries available for replacement. These radios can also be used for vacations and outings for additional communication and safety.

Emergency Contact Information

List family members' names, phone numbers, and addresses—even those out of town. You can include select friends that you share resources with. Make a list of emergency numbers for services like the police, ambulance, and fire department. The numbers on the list should include whatever numbers are used by the individual's home, cell, or work phone.

It is a good idea to list contact numbers of out-of-town family members. This is especially important in the event that the local communications are unavailable. Designate someone as your out-of-town primary contact and another as your out-of-town secondary contact.

Fill out the "Emergency Phone Numbers" list. Get help from the family. Also include out-of-state contacts, and designate primary and secondary numbers. All that is left now is to make copies, post them, and hand them out.

Emergency Phone Numbers

	Phone	Name	Address
Clergy			
Dad			
Dentist			
Doctor			
Emergency	911		
Family			
Fire			
Grandparents (Maternal)			
Grandparents (Paternal)			
Mom			
Neighbor			
Pediatrician			
Poison Control	800-222-1222		
Police			

Checklist of Items to Consider

- ☐ Two-way radios
- ☐ Chargers
- ☐ Extra batteries

12

WATER PURIFICATION

Your best option is stored emergency water or bottled water. When it's not available, you must know how to treat contaminated water. Review tip #1 on storing water before proceeding. The importance of storing water can't be stressed enough. You never know what kind of an emergency you will be surprised with. However, almost any emergency will require a store of water.

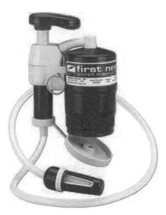

You can puchase water filters in most sporting goods stores.

Water Filters

There are several excellent choices in water filters used for emergencies and camping. You can purchase an inexpensive camping filter that removes giardia for about twenty-five dollars. It is found in most sporting goods departments and stores. Other filters of better quality will cost from fifty to one hundred dollars. Of course, the price continues to climb with better brands, qualities, and features. Remember that this is an emergency item, and it probably will have limited use, but it is essential when in an emergency situation. Practice using your water filter regularly so you won't be faced with learning to use it during a crisis.

Chlorine

Here are some guidelines for adding bleach to your collected or cloudy water. Add sixteen drops (⅛ teaspoon) of unscented liquid chlorine bleach to each gallon of collected water. Stir or gently swirl. Let it stand thirty minutes. If you can smell chlorine, it is okay to use. If there is no chlorine smell, you must add an additional sixteen drops (⅛ teaspoon) of non-scented liquid chlorine bleach to each gallon of collected water. Let it stand another thirty minutes. If, after adding a second treatment of bleach, you still cannot smell chlorine, then throw away the water and find a better water source.[1]

You can use unscented liquid chlorine to clean up water for drinking.

Boiling Water

If the water you are treating needs some filtering to remove solid particulates, you can use coffee filters or a cloth. Fill a jar with the water to be boiled and let it sit so the solids settle to the bottom. Once the solids have settled, gently pour off

Set water at a rolling boil for a full minute to kill bacteria.

the water, being careful not to disturb the sediment at the bottom.

Now you can bring the water to a rolling boil (that means big bubbles) for about one full minute. This should kill the bacteria. Once the water has cooled, you can pour the water back and forth between two clean containers to improve its taste before drinking it.

If your municipality issues a "boil order" for your water, you need to be sure and use boiled water for the following:

- Brushing teeth
- Cooking
- Preparing drinks

- Drinking water

- Washing raw foods or foods in general

- Making ice

- Drinking water for pets

Typically, the water is safe for washing dishes, but hot soapy water should be used. Add one tablespoon of bleach per gallon as a precaution. Dishes should be rinsed in boiled water. There are no restrictions on doing laundry, and regular water should be safe for bathing. If your municipality has lifted the "Boil Order" there are a few precautions to follow after the order is lifted. You will need to flush the lines to remove the contaminated water. Do the following:

- Flush water lines by running all cold water faucets in the home for a couple of minutes.

- Flush automatic icemakers by discarding the next three batches of ice made.

- Run water softeners through a regeneration cycle.

- Run drinking water faucets or fountains for a couple of minutes.

- Run water through all other water connections for five minutes.

Caution: Don't use floodwater, because it may be contaminated with toxic chemicals such as gasoline, pesticides, and other contaminants. Do not even attempt to treat floodwater. Remember, err on the side of caution!

Put unscented chlorine on your "to buy" shopping list. If you can, buy it today and store it safely away.

DO IT NOW!

Checklist of Items to Consider

- ☐ Water purifier
- ☐ Unscented bleach and dropper

NOTES

1. Jordan Valley Water Conservancy District, "Emergency Water Storage," accessed December 5, 2014, https://jvwcd.org/water/emergency.

13

CLOTHING

What should you consider for emergency clothes? Should you have a separate stash just for emergencies? Should clothing always be in your 72-hour kits? Where and how should you store your preparedness clothing? These are just a few of the questions that you need to answer to begin to solve your preparedness clothing issues. Here are a few tips to get you going.

Levi's and sweatpants should be the mainstays in your clothing inventory. Blue jeans are rugged, warm, and can handle a lot of abuse. Sweatpants should be large enough to wear over the jeans. Layering is essential to keeping warm. On camping trips, I will wear sweatpants in my sleeping bag for additional warmth without having to carry a larger sleeping bag.

T-shirt, long-sleeve shirt, sweatshirt, or coat? Once again, your choices should be centered around layering your clothes. Two long-sleeve shirts can be as warm as a sweatshirt. If you wear your sweatshirt over two shirts, you may find that this combination can be equal to a coat. You need to think about having these items in your 72-hour kit. Keep seasonal needs in mind.

Choose what you need and personalize kits for you and your family.

Go to your closet and pick out as many items listed below that you have to spare. There is no doubt that you have many items that you never wear that qualify for this tip. Put them in your 72-hour kit. Add what you are missing to your shopping list.

Checklist of Items to Consider

- ☐ Two pairs of socks plus one pair of wool socks
- ☐ At least one change of underwear
- ☐ Blue jeans
- ☐ Sweatpants
- ☐ Long-sleeve shirts
- ☐ Coat
- ☐ Sweatshirt
- ☐ Gloves
- ☐ Hat
- ☐ Shoes

Bonus Tip

Pack your clothes in a resealable heavy-duty plastic bag. Press out as much air as possible and seal. Your clothes will now stay dry and clean.

TWO MUST-HAVE KITCHEN ITEMS

It doesn't matter how much you plan and prepare, it is still easy to overlook something. Here are two emergency kitchen items you will want to be certain you've included with your emergency supplies:

- **A Manual Can Opener**. Without power, chances are that you are going to have some difficulty opening canned foods you have stored. A manual can opener is a survival must. I have opened many cans with an assortment of knives with great, but dangerous, success. But why bother? I merely need to spend a dollar and have either the old-fashioned-style opener or the squeeze and crank style. Neither one is very expensive.

- **A Manual Eggbeater or a Whisk.** Whipping eggs or mixing pancake batter are just a few reasons to have a manual eggbeater or a whisk. In survival mode without electricity, cooking is easier with these two items. Get good ones because some are quite cheap and will not hold up. You would not be happy if your equipment fails in time of need.

15

SPROUTING: NATURE'S SECRET

Here is an amazing way to have fresh vegetables even if the grocery store is underwater or the shelves are empty. Learn how to grow your own sprouts. Follow this process, and you can have fresh sprouts on a regular basis. When sprouting, you need to remember that it typically takes six or seven days before you can harvest your sprouts.

Choose a handful of seeds that you like. Not all sprouts are created equal. Once again, I urge you to become familiar with this process. Use sprouts from time to time in your menus. This is about as easy as it gets! All you will need is a glass quart jar, some sprouting seeds, a piece of breathable fabric, and a jar lid.

I can recommend alfalfa, clover, radish, broccoli, wheat, and pea seeds. This is a well-rounded selection of seeds you can keep on hand to make a nutritious sprout salad. These seeds are easy to obtain and easy to sprout. In the event of a prolonged food-supply shutdown, you will be grateful for fresh vegetables, and sprouts can be an easy, inexpensive answer.

You can purchase sprouting seeds at most health food or organic grocery stores. They are also available online. Start with a small supply while you are learning.

Be sure you purchase seeds that are for sprouting, because garden seeds may be chemically treated.

Left: Sprouts are an easy and nutritious source of food in an emergency. Right: Dehulling is part of the process of preparing sprouts for eating.

Follow These Three Simple Steps

1. Step 1—Soak overnight

Place a total of two tablespoons of seeds, mixed or individual, in a one-quart mason jar. Cover the jar opening with a piece of nylon stocking, cheesecloth, or other breathable fabric, and secure it in place with a jar ring. Cover the seeds with three times their volume of water. Let the seeds soak 8–12 hours, and then pour water off. For peas, lentils, and wheat, use ½ to ¾ cups of seeds.

2. Step 2—Rinse twice a day

Rinse twice daily by covering the sprouts with water. Gently swirl the water in the jar. Drain off all the water after five to ten minutes. This is just like watering your garden. Repeat this rinse twice each day for four to six days. There is no need to expose the seeds to direct sunlight yet. See sprouting chart for peas, lentils, and wheat.

3. Step 3—Dehull in final rinse

Once you are ready to harvest, place all the sprouts in a bowl of water and gently agitate, separating sprouts and hulls. Let the sprouts sit in sunlight for eight to ten hours to absorb chlorophyll. The leaves will turn a rich green and increase in nutrition.

Enjoy! And keep refrigerated!

Sprouts will last up to two weeks if well drained and stored in the refrigerator. Add peas, lentils, and wheat to stews and soups. Use sprouts to garnish salads and sandwiches or to just eat straight.

Sprouting Chart

Seeds	Seeds in Quart Jar	Soaking Time	Days to Harvest	Notes
Wheat*	1 cup	8–12 hours	2	Harvest when sprout is ½ the length of the seed
Alfalfa	2 tbsp.	8–12 hours	6–7	Exposed to sunlight for the last day
Broccoli	2 tbsp.	8–12 hours	6–7	Exposed to sunlight for the last day
Radish	2 tbsp.	8–12 hours	6–7	Exposed to sunlight for the last day
Clover	2 tbsp.	8–12 hours	6–7	Exposed to sunlight for the last day
Peas*	1 cup	8–12 hours	4	Harvest when ⅓ length of seed
Mung Beans	3 tbsp.	8–12 hours	3–5	Harvest to personal preference 3 to 5 days
Lentil	3 tbsp.	8–12 hours	3–4	Harvest when ¼–½" tail

*Peas and wheat should sprout until sprout is about ⅓ the length of the seed.

The best part about sprouting is that it is easy and can be done without special equipment.

Some Sprouting Hints and Facts

- For best flavor and nutrition, use sprouts within one week.

- Keep harvested sprouts refrigerated.

- Sprouts are an excellent source of vitamin C.

- Green, leafy sprouts full of chlorophyll are full of vitamin A.

- Sprouts are easy to digest.

- Sprouts are low in calories and high in fiber.

- Save and reuse the rinsing water.

- Use fresh water for final rinse and to dehull.

Sprouts can be used in breads, soups, pancakes, omelets, casseroles, meatloaf, salads, or just eaten straight. They can also be used in smoothies and other nutritional drinks. Sprouts are even excellent in place of lettuce on a sandwich.

Sprouting is one of nature's best-kept secrets. A preparedness pantry with sprouts will always have healthy options. There is much written about sprouting, and you may choose to expand your knowledge. This section is intended to give you some basics with a well-rounded inventory of seeds. The most important thing here is to have a working knowledge and enough seed variety that you will be able to add health and nutrition to your emergency and everyday diet. Begin today, and get a head start on preparedness.

Visit your local grocery or health food store and purchase several fully matured sprouts. Try using them in a variety of foods to see which sprout seeds you prefer eating. Purchase seeds for your favorite sprouts and begin growing them today!

Checklist of Items to Consider

- ☐ Large-mouth quart mason jar with ring
- ☐ Screen
- ☐ Rinsing bowl
- ☐ Alfalfa

- ☐ Wheat
- ☐ Radish
- ☐ Broccoli
- ☐ Mung beans
- ☐ Lentils
- ☐ Clover
- ☐ Peas
- ☐ _____
- ☐ _____
- ☐ _____
- ☐ _____
- ☐ _____

FUEL IN A CRISIS

After Hurricane Sandy, it was impossible to obtain gasoline in most of the storm-ravaged areas. The gas pumps didn't work without power. When a gas station *was* able to pump gas, it was because they had backup power or that power had been restored. Long lines formed and gasoline was rationed. This problem persisted for a couple of weeks.

The power was out for several days. In fact, most people did not see power return for more than a week. A few did not get power back for more than a month. Our dependency on oil is not the problem. We will always have interruptions in supply. The problem is preparedness—the ability to successfully handle an interruption. With planning and preparation, you can solve it beforehand.

When I watched the news reports of people standing in long lines with their gas cans, my first question was, "Where did they get the gas cans?" I wondered if they had them stored in their apartments, their garages, or in their cars. I then began to wonder about the many people who did not even have a gas can stored for just such an emergency.

A gas can is a must for survival preparedness. Not only does it make sense to have one on hand for your own use, but you'll also probably have an opportunity to be a Good Samaritan to someone else someday. Just be careful to store it carefully and away from the main house.

Another thing to keep in mind is that five gallons of gasoline will weigh about thirty-five pounds, and that is a lot of weight to carry back to where you have your car parked. An easier solution would be to have

several two-and-a-half gallon containers for gasoline. Each container will weigh approximately eighteen pounds when full. It would be much easier to carry eighteen pounds in each hand a long distance than to drag one thirty-five pound container the same distance.

You can keep these containers in the back of your car, empty and ready to fill. This is an excellent place to store them because the gasoline will most likely go into the car in which they are stored. If you own several cars, consider putting one container in each vehicle.

If your situation allows, it is a good idea to always have at least one five-gallon container full of gasoline that is safely stored. You can rotate the fuel every few months by putting it into your vehicle and filling it up again. There are additives that you can put in the stored fuel to extend its life.

Whether you store two gallons, five gallons, or more, these guidelines should be followed for storing gasoline safely:

- Store only in specially designed and approved plastic or metal containers.

- Do not fill to the top. Leave at least one inch of room for expansion.

- Store at least fifty feet away from any ignition source, such as a gas water heater, gas furnace, boiler, or other open flame.

- Do not store in direct sunlight

- Do not store directly on a cement surface. Place on a wood board or a mat.

- When filling, remove from the vehicle and place on the ground. Be careful not to spill when filling.

- Be sure the cap and spout are on properly.

- Store in the garage, a shed, or another well-ventilated area rather than inside the house.

- If you must store it outside, store it under a small, breathable tarp to keep it out of direct sunlight.

It is also a good idea to keep your gas tank at least half full. When you know that there is an impending emergency, such as a winter storm warning, it is a good idea to periodically top off your tank to be better prepared. If gasoline is being rationed, it is wise to always take what is

yours. In other words, if you are rationed five gallons and you don't need it, I would suggest that you keep your rationed allotment for future use or to barter with.

You can also consider using the buddy system. You and a neighbor can team up to carry the rationed fuel back to your respective vehicles or wherever you will store it. Helping each other with the lugging of the fuel and the sharing of each other's containers will make a hard job easier.

Checklist of Items to Consider

☐ 5-gallon gas can
☐ 2½-gallon gas can

'17

DON'T FORGET THE PETS!

My daughter and her husband often visit us with their over-sized dog. She always brings two stainless steel bowls, one for water and one for food. She also brings a ziplock bag full of dog food. Finally, she brings a chain to restrain the dog in the back of our property if necessary.

Your pet is a member of your family. It deserves to have you consider its needs along with your own. The principle is simple. Have a minimum three- to five-day supply of food stored away where you will not use it except in an emergency and create a plan to rotate it regularly. If you use canned food, make sure you have included a manual can opener. Add to your stash one bowl for water and one bowl for food. Place all of the items in another large ziplock bag, box, or container of some sort. It is that simple.

Store it in a convenient place, rotate your food, and replace what you use immediately. Always be ready to leave quickly. Adjust this plan according to the unique needs of your pets. Keep in mind that most emergency shelters will not accept pets, so have a plan for what you will do to keep your pet safe if your own home becomes uninhabitable. Plan in advance where you will go with your pets. Explore several options today so you have the answer before a problem arises. If you have more than one pet, prepare individual emergency ration bags for each one. Keep in mind that you may have to take them to separate locations.

You will also need to have a plan for dealing with pet sanitation, such as a supply of plastic bags to retrieve pet waste.

Checklist of Items to Consider

- ☐ Food and water bowls
- ☐ Plastic waste bags
- ☐ Leash
- ☐ Chain
- ☐ Sleeping bed or mat
- ☐ Kennel or travel tote

'18

WHAT ABOUT CASH?

Money is an arbitrary means of exchange. You can buy any-thing if you have enough money to sway the seller. Bartering is the purest way of selling goods and services. If you have what somebody wants and they have something you want, it is easy to make an exchange. Both will likely come out with a good deal. In a crisis, don't be afraid to exchange goods and services to obtain what you need. In an emergency, your can of tuna fish may be worth a gallon of water to someone else.

For short-term emergencies, you need to have some cash on hand. There will likely be items that you need, and a little cash can help solve the issue. When the power is out, the ATMs will not work. The banks and many businesses will also be closed. It is said that cash is king. In our ATM society, we need to have an alternative—cash on hand.

Store a total of twenty, fifty, or one hundred dollars. Only you know how much you should have available. Keep it safely put away. Keep reminding yourself why you put it away, and don't spend it! It is for an emergency. It doesn't need to be a large amount, and you might never use any of it. But just like any of the preparedness items that you store for an emergency, it becomes valuable when you need it, but only if you have it.

Storing small bills is best. This is just in case you may not be able to get change. Have some one-, five-, and ten-dollar bills sealed in an enve-lope and stored with your 72-hour kit

A few words of caution. It is not wise to let others know that you have money. If you carry the cash with you, I would recommend that you put it in two or three pockets. If someone were to see you take cash from one pocket and subsequently grab it from you, you would not have lost everything.

Get an envelope and put in ten one-dollar bills, two five-dollar bills, and one ten-dollar bill. This is only a start. You should double or triple these amounts as you can afford it. Put the envelope of money in your 72-hour kit.

Do It NOW!

Checklist of Items to Consider

☐ Small bills in an envelope

'19

EMERGENCY COOKING: INDOORS AND OUT!

I **recommend a butane cookstove as perhaps the best universal** option for emergency cooking. These stoves are easy to use and are totally self-contained. For most models, an igniter eliminates the need for matches, and you can safely store a supply of fuel as well. A butane stove can generally be used both indoors and outdoors. Check the manufacturer's instructions prior to purchase.

Caution: A butane stove is NOT a heater and should only be used for cooking.

A butane cookstove is available at most Asian markets and can be purchased quite economically. You'll find them in sporting goods stores or online as well.

The butane canisters nestle into the side compartment of the stove and are often a bargain at Asian markets. One canister will provide fuel for several meals, depending on cook time.

Each canister contains 220g of butane. The stove has a maximum rating of 7,650 Btu/hour, with a maximum fuel consumption on high of 160 g/hour. The heat output of this stove is roughly equal to the large burner on high of most electric ranges. One canister should then last about 1.25 hours on high, and butane will store indefinitely. The Asian market I go to sells the fuel at four canisters for five dollars. That breaks down to $1.25 per canister.

Butane stoves are easy to use and are totally self-contained resources for cooking food.

You would do well to practice with a few simple meals that you can prepare in a crisis before putting your stove away for an emergency. You should also practice using your butane stove so that you can get an idea of fuel consumption at your altitude. This will help you determine an appropriate amount of fuel to store and keep on hand.

For example, use your stove to make pancakes and scrambled eggs. When I tried this recently, I weighed the canister both before and after cooking the meal to determine my fuel usage. The morning meal consumed fifty grams of fuel. With two hundred and twenty grams per canister, that meant that I used about twenty percent of a canister to cook breakfast. Cooking the same twenty minutes for each meal would mean that I would be able to cook at least five meals with one canister. If you were to just boil water for noodles or heat a can of soup or stew, you would use less fuel, and the canister would last even longer.

I recommend that you store your stove in a box with a few fuel canisters. Add a pot and a few packs of noodles or some easy-to-prepare canned foods. You should also store some plates, bowls, and utensils with your stove. You can pick up some used items at the secondhand store or use some of the odd items that you have at home. Store it somewhere that is easy to find. Be sure that when you use your kit, you always replace the used items so you are always ready for the next event. You are now ready to grab and go or survive at home with no utilities.

Three keys to success in surviving any emergency are

1. **Have what you need.**

2. **Know how to use what you have.**

3. **Keep it easily accessible.**

Be Caught Prepared! Make a plan and follow your plan!

Checklist of Items to Consider

- ☐ Cooking pot
- ☐ Frying pan
- ☐ Plates
- ☐ Bowls
- ☐ Knives, forks, and spoons
- ☐ Canned food
- ☐ Dried soups
- ☐ Ramen noodles
- ☐ Manual can opener
- ☐ _____
- ☐ _____
- ☐ _____
- ☐ _____

20

DUTCH OVEN EMERGENCY COOKING KIT

Here is a grab-and-go idea that will have your Dutch oven always ready to cook at least three meals. It stores easily and is totally self-contained. I recommend that you have at least two alternative methods to cook a meal. You should be familiar with how to use them.

Dutch oven cooking is an old method of cooking. The basic concept is that your Dutch oven acts just like a regular oven. It can produce an even heat basically like your oven at a specific predetermined temperature.

What you will need

- *12" Dutch oven.* This is the most efficient size. I own two. They are always filled and ready to go. The deep oven is the best choice.

- *3 bags of briquettes.* Use a one-gallon ziplock bag for twenty-seven briquettes. This number of briquettes will provide enough steady heat to warm a twelve-inch Dutch oven to 375°. Store three bags of briquettes: two bags of twenty-seven and for the third bag, fill the starter can (see the following section on "How to Make a Charcoal Starter Can") with twenty-seven briquettes. Then bag it, can and all. Now you are prepared to cook three meals.

  The starter can is used to start the briquettes. Place all twenty-seven briquettes into the starter can. Next, pour starter fluid over

the coals, and then stand back and drop a match on the coals. Whoosh! It will take ten to fifteen minutes to get the coals started and ready for cooking.

Assembling a Dutch oven kit long before there is an emergency will mean that you have access to cooked food when you need it.

- *Matches*. You will need a lighter or matches. I have both. The matches should be strike-anywhere matches that should be available at the local grocery store.

- *Lighter fluid* is purchased at any grocery store and most drugstores. Your best choices are the 5- or 8-oz. size. Ask the clerk if they have small containers of lighter fluid. Once you have this unique container, you can pry the top off and refill it as needed.

- *Tongs* are needed to handle the hot coals. Make sure that they are small enough to fit in the Dutch oven.

- *Homemade starter can*. This can is easily made and perfect for starting your briquettes. (See "How to Make a Charcoal Starter Can.")

- *Cleaning sponge* is optional.

- *A copy of the "Baking Temperature Chart for Dutch Oven Cooking"* will assist you in achieving the desired temperature in your oven.

Once you have assembled your emergency Dutch oven kit, you will be ready to go. Keep the kit accessible. Consider preparing a ziplock pouch of dried vegetables and rice for a quick emergency meal. (See "Quick and Easy Emergency Recipes.")

Now that you established an alternative cooking method, practice it so you will become proficient in this skill. Use your Dutch oven every month or two to cook a meal. Part of being prepared is knowing how to use what you have.

These two tables are designed in the book to be photocopied, cut out, and folded in half so that they can be laminated and kept with your Dutch ovens.[1]

Baking Temperature Chart for Dutch Oven Cooking

Oven Top/ Bottom	325°	350°	375°	400°	425°	450°
8"	15 10/5	16 11/5	17 11/6	18 12/6	19 13/6	20 14/6
10"	19 13/6	21 14/7	23 16/7	25 17/8	27 18/9	29 19/10
12"	23 16/7	25 17/8	27 18/9	29 19/10	31 21/10	33 22/11
14"	30 20/10	32 21/11	34 22/12	36 24/12	38 25/13	40 26/14

*To bake, place ⅔ of the briquettes on the top and ⅓ on the bottom
*To simmer, reverse briquettes to ⅔ on bottom ⅓ on top
*Each briquette will produce about 10°–15°F of heat

"Rule-of-Thumb" Dutch Oven Cooking Guidelines

1. One charcoal briquette, or an equally sized hot coal, will equate to approximately 10–15° of heat on a fair camping day (not really cold, rainy, or windy).

2. Generally, to get a 350° inside-oven temperature, the number of coals would be two times the Dutch oven diameter. For example, 12" oven = 24 briquettes. (Use a little judgment here. Sometimes you'll need more briquettes, sometimes less.)

3. For baking, put twice as many coals on top as underneath. For example, if your heat range calls for fifteen briquettes, then put ten on top and five underneath. To simmer, reverse briquettes to ⅔ on bottom and ⅓ on top.

4. For even heat, rotate oven and lid 90° in opposite direction approximately halfway through recipe cooking time.

Hot coal amounts are not a set-and-go thing. To maintain desired temperature, you will need to replenish the coals and briquettes as they burn down.

©2012 Sam Spencer

Make a photocopy of this chart. Fold it over and laminate it. Place the chart with your Dutch oven equipment.

How to Make a Charcoal Starter Can

1. Start with a 52-oz. can. This will hold twenty-seven briquettes and also fit inside of a twelve-inch Dutch oven.

2. Consume the contents of the can. (Soup, tomato or vegetable juice. It should have a diameter of four and one-quarter inches and be seven inches tall.)

3. Wash the can. Peel off the label.

4. Use a step drill for large holes or a half-inch drill bit for smaller holes. Just drill a few more.

5. If the holes are rough, use a round file to deburr them.

Charcoal starter cans make quick work of Dutch oven heating.

A handy friend can help you drill the holes. You do not need large holes. Even one-half inch holes would work. If you have holes only around the bottom of the can, that would also work. The air is drawn through the bottom holes. As the hot air rises, it pulls air up through the can and keeps the coals burning well. This is easy, very cheap, and portable!

Quick and Easy Emergency Recipes

Five-Can Chicken and Rice
Makes 20 (6-oz.) servings

> 1 can green beans
> 1 can peas
> 1 can corn
> 1 can cream of chicken soup
> 1–2 cans chicken
> 2 cups long-grain rice
> 1 quart water
> Seasoning as desired

Pour all ingredients into Dutch oven. Stir occasionally. Cook until rice is done. This recipe makes about four quarts. That's a lot of food!

Mixed Vegetable Stew
Makes 20 (6-oz.) servings

> 3 cups mixed dried vegetables
> 1 can cream of chicken soup
> 1-2 cans chicken
> 3 quarts water
> Seasoning as desired

Pour all ingredients into your Dutch oven and stir. Cook until vegetables are soft. This recipe makes about four quarts of stew.

Practice for Preparedness

Gather all the ingredients for your recipes. Put them into a small box so that you can grab and go with your Dutch oven kit. The ingredients for the two recipes above will easily store for several years. One idea is to prepare the recipe that you have stored ingredients for once or twice a year. This will keep you practiced and you will also rotate your goods. Practice with other recipes to develop the skill of Dutch oven cooking.

Checklist of Items to Consider

- [ ] 12" Dutch oven
- [ ] 3 bags of briquettes
- [ ] Matches
- [ ] Lighter fluid
- [ ] Tongs
- [ ] Homemade starter can
- [ ] Cleaning sponges
- [ ] A copy of the "Baking Temperature Chart for Dutch Oven Cooking"

NOTES

1.   Sam Spencer. *Survival of the Fittest, Survival Preparedness Tips Volume II: Cooking in an Emergency* (Sam Spencer, 2013).

21

LEARN HOW TO SHELTER IN PLACE

To "shelter in place" (SIP) means to take immediate shelter wherever you are, whether you are at home, at work, or anywhere in between. It may also mean, "seal the room." In other words, take steps to prevent outside air from coming in. This is because local authorities may instruct you to "shelter in place" if chemical or radiological contaminants are released into the environment. It is important to listen to the TV or radio to understand whether the authorities wish you to merely remain indoors or take additional steps to protect yourself and your family. For tips on how to shelter in place, watch the video on survivalpreparednesstips.com.[1]

How Do You Prepare?

At Home

- Choose a room in advance for your shelter. The best room is one with as few windows and doors as possible. A large room, preferably with a water supply, is desirable. This might be something like a master bedroom that is connected to a bathroom.

- Shut and lock all windows (this provides a tighter seal) and close all exterior doors.

- Have precut plastic sheets to cover all doors, windows, and vents in your chosen room.

- Have duct tape to seal off the plastic.

- Develop your own family emergency plan so that every family member knows what to do. Practice!

- Bring your 72-hour kit, including emergency water and food supplies, into the chosen room.

- Seal all openings as shown below.

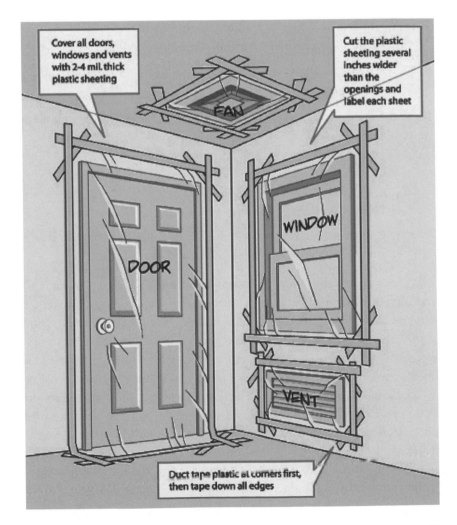

At Work

- Help ensure that the emergency plan and checklist involves all employees. Volunteers or recruits should be assigned specific duties during an emergency. Alternates should be assigned to each duty.

- A shelter kit should be assembled, including duct tape, plastic sheets, and first aid supplies. A battery-operated radio and at least one flashlight with spare batteries should also be in this kit. Periodically, it is a good idea to refresh the kit and replace the batteries.

How Will I Know When I Need to "Shelter in Place"?

Fire or police department warning procedures could include

- "All-call" telephoning—an automated system for sending recorded messages, which is sometimes called "reverse 911."

- Emergency Alert System (EAS) broadcasts on the radio or television.

- Outdoor warning sirens or horns.

- News media sources—radio, television, and cable.

- NOAA Weather Radio alerts.

- Residential route alerting—messages announced to neighborhoods from vehicles equipped with public address systems.

I have chosen the master bathroom as our room to "shelter in place." It has one door, one window, and an exhaust fan. I have in a plastic container one roll of duct tape and plastic cut to size to cover my door, window, and vent. I also have some extra plastic and a utility knife. Heavier plastic is best because if you need to open and then reseal the sealed door again, thin plastic might tear and not be reusable. It is a good idea to have some extra plastic in your kit in case of rips. Also, the kit will then be ready for continued use.

For practice, it would be a good idea to use painter's masking tape to seal off the plastic in the practice. Duct tape will likely damage the painted surfaces.

When you are told to "shelter in place," it will typically be for a short period of time. You should also have a battery-operated radio in your kit

so that you can know when the danger has passed. A flashlight and food and water from your 72-hour kit will add to your comfort.

Watch "Great Shelter In Place Video" at http://survival-prepareddnesstips.com. Identify which room in your house is most suitable for "sheltering in place." Go to that room and imagine how it will work.

Checklist of Items to Consider

- ☐ Plastic cut to fit all openings
- ☐ Duct tape
- ☐ Utility knife
- ☐ Battery-operated radio
- ☐ Water and snacks
- ☐ Masking tape
- ☐ Container for SIP items
- ☐ Flashlight
- ☐ Extra batteries for radio and flashlight

NOTES

1. "Survival Preparedness Tips," accessed December 5, 2014, http://survivalpreparednesstips.com/.

22

PROTECT VALUABLES FROM WATER DAMAGE

I have watched several flooding situations and seen the property of many people get destroyed. Not only did the basements flooded, but the main levels also flooded from flood surges, mountain snow runoff, and even torrential rainstorms. People often have only a short time to prepare and are left to the mercy of Mother Nature. However, in many cases there was some warning. Flood warnings are issued. Storm surges are predicted with great accuracy. How often a river crests is also a good indicator. People frequently have time to prepare. With supplies on hand and an emergency plan in place, losses can be reduced.

One day while walking in my shop, I noticed some contractor trash bags. These heavy-duty bags hold at least forty to fifty gallons per bag. My mind turned to Hurricane Sandy and the great personal losses of precious memories. What if the flood victims had sealed items they wanted to protect in one of these heavy-duty, airtight bags? Thus this tip was developed.

Heavy-duty bags are available in sizes up to sixty-five gallons and even larger. Some are clear and some are black, but the color doesn't matter. You're looking for the thickest heavy-duty bag you can get your hands on. The heavier the bag, the better the chance it has of withstanding the disaster. Two-millimeter thickness is great, but I recommend three-millimeter.

Carefully put into the bags any precious household items that might get damaged in a flood. Be careful not to puncture the bags. Next, carefully press most of the air out of the bag. Seal the bag by twisting the top tightly, and then fold the top over. Finally, put a rubber band around the

neck of the bag to hold it closed. To add strength to the seal, you can put some duct tape over the rubber band.

You can even prepare in advance by storing seldom-used items permanently inside of these heavy-duty bags inside of their storage boxes or containers. Basement storage rooms are a good place to start.

What would you regret losing to a flood? Can you protect your property in advance? After a tsunami in Japan, residents reported that next to loss of life, they most regretted the loss of their family photographs and other historical documents. Photographs, journals, histories, Grandma's heirloom quilts, and any other irreplaceable items are the first you might consider pre-bagging. Consider some watertight storage containers for the long-term storage of precious items.

To be prepared, make sure you have these three things: a box of large heavy-duty bags, large rubber bands, and some duct tape or packaging tape. A box of fifty heavy-duty fifty-gallon bags will cost between twenty and twenty-five dollars and can be purchased at any hardware store or home center. They have both two-millimeter and three-millimeter-thick bags. Don't use twist ties. Use a rubber band and put several loops around your fold to help keep it closed better. Don't be afraid to use several rubber bands for added security. These are your valuables!

Once you have your bags filled, you can put them in the closet. Close the door so they won't be thrown around. If by chance you puncture or tear a bag, there is no need to remove the contents; simply double-bag it!

This is an inexpensive way to protect your valuables.

Checklist of Items to Consider

- ☐ Contractor bags
- ☐ Duct tape
- ☐ Rubber bands

23

A SIMPLE ROLL OF PLASTIC

The storm takes out several of your windows, and the cold night air is filling the house. The rain is falling and entering through the broken windows and falling onto the carpet. You are freezing, and you are getting wet. What do you do?

A simple roll of plastic and duct tape will save the day. Every emergency preparedness program should have at least one roll of plastic sheeting. You can buy a roll at almost any hardware store for less than the cost of a restaurant dinner for two. You can buy six-millimeter thick, heavy-duty plastic. At two hundred and fifty square feet, it will go a long way.

It would also be a good idea to have a utility knife for trimming the sheeting to the size you need. The sheeting is waterproof, of course, and can also be used as a trap, drop cloth, or covering.

Duct tape is the modern-day bailing wire and is universally used to fix things. You should have several full rolls stored away in your emergency preparedness storeroom.

Checklist of Items to Consider

- [ ] Roll of heavy plastic
- [ ] Duct tape
- [ ] Utility knife

24

EMERGENCY "GO SHOES" AND A HEADLAMP

I live within miles of a major earthquake fault line. What would happen if the big earthquake that is predicted as "overdue" were to happen tomorrow? What if it happens in the middle of the night when we are all asleep? I imagine myself in my pajamas running outside, standing next to my wife in her nightgown in the middle of the night. In my imagination it happens on a cold, snowy, and dark winter night, and we are all barefoot!

In your case, it might be a wildfire, a landslide, or a drunken driver ramming his car into the side of your house. Maybe in the middle of the night you hear a loud knock on the door. The knock echoes of panic. You turn on the light and look through the door to see an anxious neighbor. "Get out, get out!" she screams. "My house is in fire, and the flames are blowing over to yours!" You must evacuate immediately. Everyone grabs his or her "go shoes" and safely escapes.

Think ahead about ripping the blankets and sheets from the bed. Drag them with you as you escape. Now you have a blanket for warmth and shelter. Now you have a tarp to lay on the ground or over an injured person.

Here is a must-do idea: Have a pair of slippers or an extra pair of shoes under your bed that can slip on easily. It's okay if they are a little big; in fact, that might even be best. They will be easier to get on quickly. Practice grabbing the shoes and preparing to leave so that in the heat of an emergency, you will remember your preparation. Make it a part of your emergency thinking.

Now let's make this tip even more useful! Stuff inside the shoes three items: a light stick or a flashlight or headlamp with good batteries, a space blanket, and two granola bars in a resealable plastic bag. It is even better if you put everything into one resealable bag, and then when you take the items out to slip on your shoes, they will be in your hands.

An emergency pair of "go shoes" can ideally be kept in one of two places: under your bed (as mentioned above) or by the exit door that you would typically use to leave the house.

Checklist of Items to Consider

- ☐ Shoes that slip on easily
- ☐ Light source, such as a flashlight, headlamp, or light stick
- ☐ Space blanket
- ☐ Two granola bars
- ☐ Resealable plastic bag

25

EARTHQUAKE-PROOF YOUR HOME

Here you will find a few ideas that will help you make your home safer during an earthquake. Once you have read through this section, walk through your house to get an idea of what you need to do. Next, make a list of the specific steps you will take to make it safer.

- Secure large appliances like refrigerators, water heaters, and ovens to a wall stud using bolts and plumber's tape.

- Fasten televisions, stereos, and computer monitors to sturdy surfaces.

- Put heavy objects on lower shelves. In an earthquake, falling objects cause the most injuries.

- Store hazardous and flammable fluids away from potentially explosive appliances such as gas dryers, gas ranges, and gas water heaters.

- Store chemicals in sealed containers on a low shelf.

- Affix decorative items to their locations with poster putty.

- Attach latches to cabinet doors to prevent items from falling out.

- Anchor large fixtures such as bookshelves, cabinets, dressers, and china hutches to the walls. You can use plumber's tape or you can purchase special fastening straps that are specifically designed for anchoring large fixtures to the studs in the wall.

- Position your beds away from potential hazards like windows, pictures hanging on the wall, and ceiling fans.

- Move items that are hanging above couches or chairs, such as mirrors, framed artwork, and other items that can fall on someone sitting there.

- Learn how to turn off the utilities.

- Have a 72-hour kit ready to use if you are ordered to evacuate.

Get a notepad. Walk through your house and list the steps you would like to take to earthquake-proof your home. Next, prioritize these items, listing them from the most important first. Put the list on the refrigerator. Check off items as you complete them.

DO IT NOW!

Checklist of Items to Consider

- ☐ Plumber's tape
- ☐ Poster putty
- ☐ Appliance anchors
- ☐ Cabinet door handles
- ☐ Survey your house for problems

DISASTER PREPAREDNESS INFORMATION

HOW TO SURVIVE AN EARTHQUAKE

It's impossible for any structure to be considered earthquake proof. Earthquakes vary in type, location, and magnitude. Even so, you can take measures to secure a structure before an earthquake and help minimize potentially dangerous complications afterward. Knowledge and preparation take away fear. You cannot eliminate the eventual disaster, but you can minimize its effects on you.

Earthquakes can happen almost anywhere. However, there are some regions that are at greater risk than others. If you live in one of these areas, you should read and ponder these pages. Don't stop with this information. Always be learning and studying. Like a good Boy Scout, "be prepared!"

Observe earthquakes occuring around the world. Learn from victims' challenges and successes. Continually make adjustments to your emergency preparedness plan as you gain more insights and practical knowledge.

Prepare Yourself and Your Family Now[1]

- Have a 72-hour kit on hand.

- Have cash in small bills.

- Plan family emergency procedures, and make plans for reuniting your family afterwards.

- Know emergency telephone numbers.

- Anchor large, heavy objects—such as bookcases, mirrors, cabinets, water heaters, and appliances—to the wall.

- Never place heavy objects over beds or places where people usually sit. A good rule is to keep heavy objects below the head height of the shortest member of the family.

- Educate your family about earthquake safety. Learn what actions you should take when an earthquake occurs.

- Maintain adequate emergency supplies and tools, such as battery-operated radios, flashlights, first aid kits, bottled water, two weeks of food and medical supplies, blankets, and cooking fuel.

- Organize your home for earthquake safety. Store heavy objects on lower shelves. Put your bottled goods on bottom shelves in base cabinets or as low as possible in your pantry. Store breakable objects in cabinets with doors that latch.

- Be sure that any flammable liquids are stored away from potential ignition sources, such as water heaters, stoves, and furnaces.

- Learn where the main turn-offs are for your water, gas, and electricity. Know how to turn them off and the location of needed tools. (See tip #3)

During an Earthquake, Stay Calm and Alert[2]

- If you are indoors, stay inside. Move to a safe location such as under a strong desk, a strong table, or along an interior wall. Stay away from windows and glass. The goal is to protect yourself from falling objects and be located near the structural strong points of the room. Avoid taking cover near windows, large mirrors, hanging objects, heavy furniture or appliances, or fireplaces.

- If you are cooking, turn off the stove, remove the pans from the stove, and take cover.

- If you are outdoors, move to an open area where falling objects are unlikely to strike you. Move away from buildings, power lines, and trees.

- If you are driving, stop on the side of the road. Stay away from underpasses and overpasses. Stop in a safe area. Stay in your vehicle and away from trees, large signs, and power lines.

Drop, Cover, and Hold On!

This is the recommended action in an earthquake. Drop to the ground, get under some cover, and hold on so the cover doesn't shake away. The goal is to protect you from falling objects.

After an Earthquake

- Check for injuries and attend to them as needed. Help ensure the comfort and safety of the people around you.

- Check for gas leaks and water leaks. Also check for sewage line breaks, downed power lines, and electrical shorts. Turn off the appropriate utilities.

- If you smell or hear a gas leak, get everyone outside. Turn off the gas at the meter. Get at least two hundred feet away from the leak. Report it to the gas company and fire department. Do not use any electrical appliances, because even a tiny spark could ignite the gas—even something as simple as a light switch!

- If the power is out, turn off breakers or unplug major appliances to prevent possible damage when the power comes back on. If you see sparks, frayed wires, or smell melting insulation, turn off the electricity at the main breaker. Do not step in any water!

- Check structures for damage. If you see excessive damage, you should leave it and have it inspected by a safety professional.

- Check for additional damage after major aftershocks.

- Look for and clean up dangerous spills.

- Always wear shoes or boots.

- Listen to the radio for public safety instructions.

NOTES

1. Federal Emergency Management Agency, "Earthquake," accessed December 5, 2014, http://m.fema.gov/earthquake.
2. Ibid.

HOW TO SURVIVE A HURRICANE

Much of the following comes from the FEMA safety guide-lines for hurricanes and Ready.gov.[1, 2] I have added a few extra ideas that you can incorporate into your planning, because your needs may vary. If you are in a hurricane-prone area, you'll want to read these guidelines and plan ahead. As I watch disasters around the world, I see a great lack of preparedness. I cannot emphasize enough that as you read this book you must study your situation and become knowledgeable. Then develop a plan that is designed for your particular needs. Finally, implement the plan.

It also is a good idea to share your plans with others. As you do this, you will open discussions that will lead to additional ideas. Keep in mind that the better prepared you are, the better your chances are of surviving any disaster. Take time to become familiar with the next few pages so that you will be well prepared in the event of a hurricane. Hurricanes cause heavy rains and storm surges that can cause extensive flood damage. You should also study the section in this book on flooding.

Before a Hurricane

- To begin preparing, you should build an emergency kit and make a family communications plan.

- Learn the elevation level of your property and whether the land is flood-prone. This will help you know how your property will be affected when storm surges or tidal flooding are forecast.

- Identify levees and dams in your area, and determine whether they pose a hazard to you.
- Learn community hurricane evacuation routes and where to find higher ground. Determine where you would go and how you would get there if you needed to evacuate.
- Reinforce your garage doors. If wind enters a garage, it can cause dangerous and expensive structural damage.
- Plan to bring in all outdoor furniture, decorations, garbage cans, and anything else that is not tied down.
- Install a generator for emergency power.
- If in a high-rise building, be prepared to take shelter on or below the tenth floor.

Make Plans to Secure Your Property[3]
- Permanent storm shutters offer the best protection for your windows. A second option is to board up windows with ⅝" marine plywood that is cut to fit and ready to install. Tape does not prevent windows from breaking.
- Install straps or additional clips to securely fasten your roof to the frame structure. This will reduce roof damage.
- Be sure trees and shrubs around your home are well trimmed.
- Clear loose and clogged rain gutters and downspouts.
- Determine how and where to secure your boat if you have one.
- Consider building a safe room.

During a Hurricane[4]

If a hurricane is likely in your area, you should

- Listen to the radio or TV for information.
- Secure your home, close storm shutters, and secure any outdoor objects or bring them indoors.
- Turn off utilities if instructed to do so. Otherwise, turn the refrigerator thermostat to its coldest setting and keep its doors closed.

- Turn off propane tanks.

- Avoid using the phone, except for serious emergencies.

- Moor your boat if time permits.

- Ensure a supply of water for sanitary purposes, such as cleaning and flushing toilets. Fill the bathtub and other larger containers with water.

- Find out how to keep food safe during and after an emergency.

- Avoid elevators.

You should evacuate under the following conditions

- If you are directed by local authorities to do so. Be sure to follow their instructions.

- If you live in a mobile home or temporary structure. Such shelters are particularly hazardous during hurricanes, no matter how well fastened they are to the ground.

- If you live in a high-rise building. Hurricane winds are stronger at higher elevations.

- If you live on the coast, on a floodplain, near a river, or on an island waterway.

If you are unable to evacuate, go to your wind-safe room. If you do not have one, follow these guidelines

- Stay indoors during the hurricane and away from windows and glass doors.

- Close all interior doors. Secure and brace external doors.

- Keep curtains and blinds closed. Do not be fooled if there is a lull. It could be the eye of the storm. Winds could pick up again.

- Stay in a small interior room, closet, or hallway on the lowest level.

- Lie on the floor under a table or another sturdy object.

After a Hurricane[5]

- Continue listening to a NOAA Weather Radio or the local news for the latest updates.

- Stay alert for extended rainfall and subsequent flooding, even after the hurricane or tropical storm has ended.

- If you have become separated from your family, use your family communications plan or contact the American Red Cross at 1-800-RED-CROSS (1-800-733-2767).

  The American Red Cross also maintains a database to help you find family. Contact the local American Red Cross chapter where you are staying for information. Do not contact the chapter in the disaster area.

- If you are evacuated, return home only when officials say it is safe.

- If you cannot return home and have immediate housing needs, text *SHELTER* + your zip code to 43362 (4FEMA) to find the nearest shelter in your area (example: *shelter 12345*).

- For those who have longer-term housing needs, FEMA offers several types of assistance, including services and grants to help people repair their homes and find replacement housing.

- Drive only if necessary, and avoid flooded roads and washed-out bridges. Stay off the streets. If you must go out, watch for fallen objects, downed electrical wires, and weakened walls, bridges, roads, and sidewalks.

- Keep away from loose or dangling power lines, and report them immediately to the power company.

- Walk carefully around the outside of your home, and check for loose power lines, gas leaks, and structural damage before reentering.

- Stay out of any building if you smell gas, if floodwaters remain around the building, or if your home was damaged by fire and the authorities have not declared it safe.

- Inspect your home for damage. Take pictures of damage, both of the building and its contents, for insurance purposes. If you have any doubts about safety, have your residence inspected by a qualified building inspector or structural engineer before entering.

- Use battery-powered flashlights. Do *not* use candles. (Flashlights should be turned on outside before entering because the battery may produce a spark that could ignite leaking gas.)

- Watch your pets closely, and keep them under your direct control. Watch out for wild animals, especially poisonous snakes. Use a stick to poke through debris.

- Avoid drinking or preparing food with tap water until you are sure it's not contaminated.

- Check refrigerated food for spoilage. If in doubt, throw it out.

- Wear protective clothing and be cautious when cleaning up to avoid injury.

- Use the telephone only for emergency calls.

Some Other Items to Consider before the Emergency

- Turn off the utilities.

- Turn off the propane tanks.

- Contact family members and tell them your plans.

- Have your medications organized and ready to take in case of evacuation.

- Keep your vehicle gassed up and ready to evacuate.

- Have a good raincoat as part of your evacuation supplies.

- Make sure your insurance is both the right type and is adequate for your needs.

- If power flickers off and on, turn off all of the circuit breakers except the ones that you need for emergency lighting.

- Secure all outdoor objects or bring them indoors. Hanging plants, trashcans, toys, and lawn furniture can become projectiles during a storm.

- *Never* use a generator inside homes, garages, crawlspaces, sheds, or similar areas, even when using fans or opening doors and windows for ventilation. Deadly levels of carbon monoxide can quickly build up in these areas and can linger for hours, even after the generator has shut off.[6]

- Discuss preparedness ideas with friends and neighbors to get additional ideas. Incorporate into your plan the ideas that are a good fit for your preparedness plan.

NOTES

1. Federal Emergency Management Agency, "Hurricane," accessed December 5, 2014, http://m.fema.gov/hurricane.
2. Ready: Prepare. Plan. Stay Informed, "Hurricanes," last modified May 27, 2014, accessed December 5, 2014, http://www.ready.gov/hurricanes.
3. Federal Emergency Management Agency, "Before a Hurricane," accessed December 5, 2014, http://m.fema.gov/before-hurricane.
4. Federal Emergency Management Agency, "During a Hurricane," accessed December 5, 2014, http://m.fema.gov/during-hurricane.
5. Federal Emergency Management Agency, "After a Hurricane," accessed December 5, 2014, http://m/fema.gov/after-hurricane.
6. CPSC Safety Alert, "Portable Generator Hazards," accessed December 5, 2014, http://www.cpsc.gov/PageFiles/121944/port-gen.pdf.

HOW TO SURVIVE A TORNADO

It is said that tornadoes are nature's most violent storms. Tornadoes can carry winds up to three hundred miles per hour. These winds can level buildings. They can throw a car hundreds of feet as if it were weightless. I remember seeing a video of a semitrailer rig being thrown into the air more than one hundred feet as it flipped over and over. That is a lot of power! Lightning and heavy rains often accompany tornadoes. Hail and flash floods are also often accompany them, which only adds to their terror.

You seldom have much time to prepare when a tornado actually strikes. Planning ahead is the most important survival process you can do to improve your chances of surviving a tornado. If you live in a tornado-prone area, take time to study the following pages and increase your knowledge. Add to your personal preparedness program and teach others around you this information. Help raise the awareness and preparation of your family and friends.

Contrary to popular belief, opening the windows of a house will not reduce tornado damage. In fact, it likely will increase damage by drawing more debris inside the house. Remain calm, and try to keep your family together during and after the tornado. Provide first aid as needed. Have 72-hour kits available for each member of your family.

The weather signs below could mean that a tornado is approaching
- A dark or green-colored sky.

- A large, dark, low-lying cloud.

- Large hail.

- A loud roar that sounds like a freight train.

If you notice any of these weather conditions, take cover immediately, and stay tuned in to local radio and TV stations or to a NOAA Weather Radio.

The Following Is Adapted from the CDC's Advice[1]

Sighting a Funnel Cloud

If you see a funnel cloud nearby, take shelter immediately. If you spot a tornado that is far away, help alert others to safety and report the hazard to local officials. Use common sense. Exercise caution. If you believe that you might be in danger, seek shelter immediately.

Taking Shelter

Your family could be anywhere when a tornado strikes—at home, at work, at school, or in the car. Discuss with your family where the best tornado shelters are and how family members can protect themselves from flying and falling debris.

The key to surviving a tornado and reducing the risk of injury lies in planning, preparing, and practicing what you and your family will do if a tornado strikes. Flying debris causes the most deaths and injuries during a tornado. Although there is no *completely* safe place during a tornado, some locations are much safer than others.

At Home

Pick a place in the home where family members can gather if a tornado is headed your way. One basic rule is to avoid windows. An exploding window can injure or kill.

The safest place in the home is the interior part of a basement. If there is no basement, go to an inside room without windows on the lowest floor. This could be a center hallway, bathroom, or closet.

For added protection, get under something sturdy, such as a heavy table or workbench. If possible, cover your body with a blanket, sleeping bag, or mattress, and protect your head with anything available—even your hands. Avoid taking shelter where there are heavy objects, such as

pianos or refrigerators, on the area of the floor that is directly above you. They could fall though the floor above you if the tornado strikes your house.

In a Mobile Home

Do not stay in a mobile home during a tornado! Mobile homes can turn over during strong winds. Even mobile homes with a tie-down likely will not withstand the force of tornado winds.

Plan ahead. If you live in a mobile home, go to a nearby building, preferably one with a basement. If there is no shelter nearby, lie flat in the nearest ditch, ravine, or culvert, and shield your head with your hands.

If you live in a tornado-prone area, encourage your mobile home community to build a tornado shelter.

On the Road

The least desirable place to be during a tornado is in a vehicle. Cars, buses, and trucks are easily tossed by tornado winds. *Do not try to outrun a tornado in your car!* If you see a tornado, stop your vehicle and get out. Do not get under your vehicle.

Outdoors

If you are outside and a tornado is approaching and there is no adequate shelter immediately available, get into a ditch or gully. If possible, lie flat and cover your head with your arms. Avoid areas with many trees.

Long-Span Buildings

A long-span building, such as a shopping mall, theater, or gymnasium, is especially dangerous because the outside walls are often the only ones supporting the roof structure. Most such buildings hit by tornados cannot withstand the enormous pressure. They simply collapse. If you are in a long-span building during a tornado, stay away from windows. Get to the lowest level of the building—the basement if possible—and away from the windows.

If there is no time to get to a tornado shelter or to a lower level, try to get under a doorframe or get up against something that will support or deflect falling debris. For instance, in a department store, get up against heavy shelving that is secured to the walls or against counters. In a theater, get under the seats. Remember to protect your head.

Office Buildings, Schools, Hospitals, Churches, and Other Public Buildings

Extra care is required in offices, schools, hospitals, or any building where a large group of people is concentrated in a small area. The exterior walls of such buildings often have large windows. If you are in any of these buildings, move away from windows and glass doorways. Go to the innermost part of the building on the lowest possible floor. Do not use elevators because the power may fail, leaving you trapped. Protect your head, and make yourself as small a target as possible by crouching down.

After a Tornado

Injury may result from the direct impact of a tornado, or it may occur afterward when people walk among debris and enter damaged buildings. A study of injuries after a tornado in Marion, Illinois, showed that fifty percent of the tornado-related injuries were suffered during rescue attempts, cleanup, and other post-tornado activities. Nearly a third of the injuries resulted from stepping on nails.

Because tornadoes often damage power lines, gas lines, or electrical systems, there is always the risk of incurring injuries from fire, electrocution, or explosions. Protecting yourself and your family requires promptly treating any injuries suffered during the storm and using extreme care to avoid further hazards.

Injuries

Check for injuries. Do not attempt to move seriously injured people unless they are in immediate danger of further injury. Get medical assistance immediately. If someone has stopped breathing, begin CPR if you are trained to do so. Stop a bleeding injury by applying direct pressure to the wound. Have any puncture wound evaluated by a physician. If you are trapped, try to attract attention to your location.

General Safety Precautions[2]

Here are some safety precautions that could help you avoid injury after a tornado:

- Continue to monitor your battery-powered radio or TV for emergency information.

- Be careful when entering any structure that has been damaged.

- Wear sturdy shoes or boots, long sleeves, and gloves when handling or walking on or near debris.

- Be aware of hazards from exposed nails and broken glass.

- Do not touch downed power lines or objects in contact with downed lines. Report electrical hazards to the police and the utility company.

- Use flashlights or battery-powered lanterns, if possible, rather than candles to light homes without electrical power. If you use candles, make sure they are in safe holders away from curtains, paper, wood, or other flammable items. Never leave a candle burning when you are out of the room.

- Never use generators, pressure washers, grills, camp stoves, or other gasoline, propane, natural gas, or charcoal-burning devices inside your home, basement, garage, or camper—or even outside near an open window, door, or vent. Carbon monoxide—an odorless, colorless gas that can cause sudden illness and death if you breathe it—from these sources can build up in your home, garage, or camper and poison the people and animals inside. Seek prompt medical attention if you suspect carbon monoxide poisoning and are feeling dizzy, light-headed, or nauseated.

- Hang up displaced telephone receivers that may have been knocked off by the tornado, but stay off the telephone except to report an emergency.

- Cooperate fully with public safety officials.

- Respond to requests for volunteer assistance by police, firefighters, emergency management, and relief organizations, but do not go into damaged areas unless assistance has been requested. Your presence could hamper relief efforts and you could endanger yourself.

Inspecting the damage[3]

- After a tornado, be aware of possible structural, electrical or gas-leak hazards in your home. Contact your local city or county building inspectors for information on structural safety codes and standards. They may also offer suggestions on finding a qualified contractor to do work for you.

- In general, if you suspect any damage to your home, shut off electrical power, natural gas, and propane tanks to avoid fires, electrocution, or explosions.

- If it is dark when you are inspecting your home, use a flashlight rather than a candle or torch to avoid the risk of fire or explosion in a damaged home.

- If you see frayed wiring or sparks, or if there is an odor of something burning, you should immediately shut off the electrical system at the main circuit breaker if you have not done so already.

- If you smell gas or suspect a leak, turn off the main gas valve, open all windows and leave the house immediately. Notify the gas company, the police or fire departments, or state fire marshal's office, and do not turn on the lights, light matches, smoke, or do anything that could cause a spark. Do not return to your house until you are told it is safe to do so.

Safety During Cleanup

- Wear sturdy shoes or boots, long sleeves, and gloves.

- Learn proper safety procedures and operating instructions before operating any gas-powered or electric-powered saws or tools.

- Clean up spilled medicines, drugs, flammable liquids, and other potentially hazardous materials.

NOTES

1. Centers for Disease Control and Prevention, "During a Tornado," last modified February 13, 2014, accessed December 5, 2014, http://www.bt.cdc.gov/disasters/tornadoes/during.asp.
2. Federal Emergency Management Agency, "After a Tornado," accessed December 5, 2014, http://m/fema.gov/after-tornado.
3. Ibid.

HOW TO SURVIVE A WINTER STORM

A n ounce of prevention is worth a pound of cure!" This adage certainly applies when it comes to surviving any disaster, and winter storms are no exception. Extreme cold spells hit our nation every winter. They can happen anywhere. Even Florida, Texas, and Arizona can see extreme cold, and many unprepared people suffer because of their lack of preparation. Take some time to prepare today to ensure that you are *caught prepared* tomorrow!

Here are some suggestions that will help you to prepare. Remember that in a winter storm, you will likely be stranded in your home for several days. Water pipes may freeze, power may be out, and as a result, staying warm will be an issue. Prepare for a week of survival at the minimum.

Taking preventive action is your best defense against having to deal with extreme cold-weather conditions. By preparing yourself, your home, and your car in advance of any winter emergency, and then by observing safety precautions during times of extremely cold weather, you can reduce the risk of weather-related health problems.

Extreme cold-weather events can usually be predicted in advance, but not always. Most weather forecasts will provide you with several days' notice of an extreme cold event. Stay aware and listen to weather forecasts on a regular basis. Check and maintain your emergency supplies regularly.

If you have a fireplace or wood stove and plan to use it as backup heat source in an emergency, have your chimney or flue inspected each year. Be sure you have adequate dry fuel ready for use. Have a place to safely

dispose of coals, and it may be a good idea to have a fire extinguisher available. (See tip #10.)

Regardless of the heat source you use—fireplace, wood stove, or kerosene heater—install a smoke detector and a battery-operated carbon monoxide detector near the area to be heated. Each detector should have battery backup in case the power goes out. Test them regularly, and replace batteries at least once a year. Remember that all fuel-burning heating equipment should be vented to the outside.

Prepare Your House

Keeping the warm air in your home and the cold air out is paramount. Limit the number of times you enter and leave to keep the warmth in and the cold out. As you study the following checklist, prioritize and set some goals.

Your Home's "Get Ready for a Winter Storm Checklist"

- ☐ Insulate the walls and attic. *Keep the heat in.*
- ☐ Caulk and weather-strip doors and windows. *Keep the cold out.*
- ☐ Insulate any water lines that run along exterior walls. *Keep them from freezing.*
- ☐ If you have lines that are prone to freezing, open the faucet to allow a small stream of water to keep flowing. *Flowing water is less likely to freeze.*
- ☐ Install storm windows or cover the windows with plastic from the inside. *Keep the cold out.*
- ☐ Service your snow-removal equipment. *Be caught prepared.*
- ☐ Purchase at least one snow shovel, even if you live in an area where snow is rare.
- ☐ Keep the doors and windows closed as much as possible.
- ☐ Keep the window coverings closed to retain heat.
- ☐ Have an adequate supply of products available to melt the ice.
- ☐ Have your chimney and flue inspected regularly.
- ☐ Install an easy-to-read outdoor thermometer.
- ☐ Repair roof leaks.
- ☐ Trim tree branches that could fall on your home or other structures during a storm.
- ☐ If you use heating oil, have sufficient amounts in reserve in case you cannot get service quickly. *Be caught prepared.*

- ☐ If you have pets, bring them indoors if possible. If you cannot, provide adequate shelter to keep them warm, and make sure they have access to unfrozen water.
- ☐ Make sure your outdoor winter clothing (coat, boots, hat, gloves) is good quality. Make sure every family member owns a pair of properly sized boots, even if they don't use them often.

Prepare Yourself

Food, water, and clothing need to be addressed. You may have everything you need already. What you need to do here is organize and double-check your preparations. Refer to tips #1, #2, and #17 for more detailed information.

You should have enough food and water to survive a minimum of five to seven days. I personally recommend that you have two to four weeks of food that can be eaten with little to no cooking. As you review tips #1 and #2, ask yourself, "How can I make this work for me?"

In a winter cold event, extra warm clothes, blankets (see tip #4), gloves, and hats can help you stay warm. Make sure that you have enough of these items and that they fit properly. If you are going to layer clothing, consider having a few warm items of clothing that are the next size up.

Prepare Your Car

You will avoid many dangerous winter travel problems by planning ahead. Have your vehicle's winter maintenance service performed per the manufacturer's recommends. You can check the antifreeze level yourself with an antifreeze tester. Add antifreeze as needed. Replace windshield wipers if needed. Add washer fluid with a wintertime mixture. Be sure that your tires are properly inflated and that they have sufficient tread. Make it a habit to keep the gas tank near full. This strategy will help avoid ice from forming in the tank and fuel lines.

Your Car's "Get Ready for a Winter Storm Checklist"

- ☐ Check the antifreeze. *Easily done.*
- ☐ Washer fluid. *Wintertime mixture.*
- ☐ Heater. *Is it working properly?*
- ☐ Defroster. *Is it working properly?*
- ☐ Brakes. *Many companies offer free brake checks.*

- [ ] Emergency flashers. *Are they working properly?*
- [ ] Tires. *Check both air pressure and wear.*
- [ ] Fuel. *Keep tank mostly full.*
- [ ] Battery. *Many companies offer a free battery check.*
- [ ] Radiator. *No leaks?*
- [ ] Car Emergency kit stored inside the car. (See tip #10.)

During the Crisis[1]

Once you are in the middle of the crisis, observe the following:

- Stay indoors during the storm whenever possible.

- Walk carefully on icy sidewalks and driveways.

- Take your time and avoid overexertion when shoveling snow. Always stretch before attempting to shovel snow. Pace yourself to avoid possible injury.

- Drive only when it is absolutely necessary. The following is good travel advice:

  ‣ Travel only in the day.

  ‣ When possible, do not travel alone.

  ‣ Keep others informed of your schedule and your route.

  ‣ Stay on the main roads and stick to the route that you told others you would be taking.

  ‣ Notify those at your destination of your estimated time of arrival.

- If your water pipes freeze, completely open all faucets and pour hot water over the pipes, starting where they were most exposed to the cold. If pipes are covered and cannot be accessed, you may need to call an experienced professional or just wait until they thaw. You should know where to turn the main water off to the house. Be ready in the event that you end up with a broken pipe.

- When using portable heaters, be sure that they can be used indoors. Maintain ventilation to avoid buildup of carbon monoxide fumes. Refuel heaters outside, and keep them at least three feet from flammable objects. Use a battery-operated carbon monoxide detector in good working condition for safety.

- It may be a good idea to conserve fuel. This, of course, can be done by keeping your residence a little cooler than normal. Strategically shut off the heat to unused rooms. Seal cracks that allow cold infiltration. Keep window coverings closed to retain heat.

- Keep dry! Wet clothing loses its insulating properties; therefore, frostbite and hypothermia are more likely to become a problem.

- Watch for signs of hypothermia. These include uncontrollable shivering, memory loss, disorientation, incoherence, slurred speech, drowsiness, and apparent exhaustion. If symptoms of hypothermia are detected, get the victim to a warm location, remove wet clothing, warm the center of the body first and give warm, non-alcoholic beverages if the victim is conscious. Get medical help as soon as possible.

- Watch for signs of frostbite. These include loss of feeling and white or pale appearance in extremities such as fingers, toes, ear lobes, and the tip of the nose. If symptoms are detected, get medical help immediately.

What about Hypothermia and Frostbite?

It doesn't take long to get into trouble in extreme weather conditions. On the next page, you will see a wind chill factor chart, which has been adapted from the National Weather Service Windchill Chart. You will notice that it may be 40º, but when you add twenty mile per hour winds, the results will yield sub-freezing windchill factor. Notice that if the temperature is 0º with the same twenty mile per hour winds, the wind chill factor drops to -22º, and frostbite can set in in thirty minutes.[2]

Wind Speed (mph)	Air Temperature (ºF)								
	40	30	20	10	0	-10	-20	-30	-40
10	34	21	9	-4	-16	-28	-41	-53	-66
20	30	17	4	-9	-22	-35	-48	-61	-74
30	28	15	1	-12	-26	-39	-53	-67	-80
40	27	13	-1	-17	-29	-43	-57	-71	-84
50	26	12	-3	-17	-31	-45	-60	-74	-88
60	25	10	-4	-19	-33	-48	-62	-76	-91

Frostbite Times

30 minutes	10 minutes	5 minutes

Being prepared for the cold is your best choice. Have the proper clothing, blankets, hats, and gloves. Follow good practices to avoid serious complications.

Hypothermia[3]

When exposed to cold temperatures, your body begins to lose heat faster than warmth can be produced. Prolonged exposure to cold will eventually use up your body's stored energy. The result is hypothermia. When the body's temperature gets too low, it affects the brain, making the victim unable to think clearly or move well. This makes hypothermia particularly dangerous because a person will be unable to recognize what is happening and unable to respond as quickly.

Hypothermia usually comes on at very cold temperatures, but it can occur even at cool temperatures if a person becomes chilled from rain, sweat, or submersion in cold water.

If medical care is not available, begin warming the person as follows:

- Get the victim into a warm room or shelter.

- If the victim has on any wet clothing, remove it.

- Warm the center of the body first—chest, neck, head, and groin.

You can use an electric blanket if one is available. You can also use skin-to-skin contact under loose, dry layers of blankets, clothing, towels, or sheets.

- Warm beverages can help increase the body temperature, but do not give alcoholic beverages. Also, warm does not mean hot! Do not try to give beverages to an unconscious person.

- After body temperature has increased, keep the person dry and wrapped in a warm blanket.

- Get medical attention as soon as possible.

- A person with severe hypothermia may be unconscious and may not seem to have a pulse or may not seem to be breathing. In this case, get emergency assistance immediately. CPR should be provided immediately and should continue while the victim is being warmed, until the victim responds or until medical aid becomes available.

Frostbite[4]

Frostbite is an injury to the body that is caused by freezing. Frostbite causes a loss of feeling and color in affected areas. It most often affects the nose, ears, cheeks, chin, fingers, and toes. Frostbite can permanently damage the body, and in severe cases, amputation is necessary. The risk of frostbite is increased in people who are not dressed properly for extremely cold temperatures or as a result of overexposure.

Avoid the risk of frostbite by getting out of the cold or protecting any exposed skin. At the first signs of redness or pain in any skin area, take precautions against frostbite.

Any of the following signs may indicate frostbite:

- White or grayish-yellow skin area

- Skin that feels unusually firm or waxy

- Numbness

A frostbite victim is often unaware of the change until someone points it out because the frozen area is numb.

What should you do if you see symptoms of frostbite? First, seek medical care. Because frostbite and hypothermia both are caused from exposure to cold, determine whether the victim also shows signs of

hypothermia, as previously described. Hypothermia typically requires immediate emergency medical assistance.

How to Treat Frostbite

- Get into a warm room as soon as possible.

- Immerse the affected area in warm, *not hot*, water.

- Do not walk on frostbitten feet or toes if at all possible. Doing this may increase the damage.

- Do not rub the frostbitten area with snow or massage it at all. This can cause more damage.

- Don't use a heating pad, heat lamp, or the heat of a stove, fireplace, or radiator for warming because the affected areas are numb and can be easily burned.

Three Rules to Follow

1. Be wise and respect the elements.

2. Dress properly.

3. Seek proper medical help when needed.

NOTES

1. Federal Emergency Management Agency, "During Winter Storms & Extreme Cold," accessed December 5, 2014, http://m.fema.gov/during-winter-storms-extreme-cold.
2. National Weather Service, "NWS Windchill Chart," accessed December 5, 2014, http://www.nws.noaa.gov/om/windchill/.
3. Centers for Disease Control and Prevention, "Cold Stress," last modified December 4, 2014, accessed December 5, 2014, http://www.cdc.gov/niosh/topics/coldstress/.
4. Ibid.

HOW TO SURVIVE A FLOOD

One of the most costly and frequent natural disasters in the world is flooding. Every year, millions of dollars of property and as many lives are lost because of floods. Most people in the world are going to experience the aftereffects of a flood at least once in their lifetime, and those who life in flood-prone areas may experience regular flooding. Floods happen in many ways and tend to accompany other disasters such as hurricanes, heavy rainstorms, and snowpack with heavy spring runoff. It doesn't matter how a flood may be caused; they are extremely destructive, very costly, potentially deadly, and can cause major health issues.

Heavy rains can change the landscape, cause mudslides, and fill properties with both mud and water. They can disrupt transportation, take lives, and destroy crops. Owners of properties located in flood plains should take extra precautions and planning to mitigate damages from the sure-to-come floods. Flood insurance is a must. If you live in a flood plain, get it!

If You Live in a Flood Plain, Here Are a Few Suggestions

- Basement walls should be sealed with waterproofing compounds.
- Consider installing check valves in building sewer traps.
- Consider installing a sump pump in your house.
- Build your home in an elevated manner.

- Confer with contractors and officials for new ideas.

- Put your furnace, water heater, and electric panel on a higher floor.

The most important thing you can do is pay attention to the National Weather Service. They will let you know about floods in advance with their warnings and watches. If emergency personnel tell you that you should evacuate to higher ground, do it! A good rule of thumb is when it is comes to flooding . . . move to higher ground!

Remember that as little as six inches of moving water can knock you off your feet. Twenty-four inches can float most cars. If you are caught in a flood, staying put and waiting for rescue is your best option. Seek safety on the roof of a house. Remember that there are other dangers besides running water, including poisonous snakes, submerged objects, debris piles, and strong currents.

A flash flood comes with little to no warning. It is often caused by very intense rainfall. A thunderstorm many miles away will likely be the culprit. Often, there are no dark clouds in your immediate location. The storm that generates a flash flood can be many miles up the canyon.

Be Prepared[1]

- Listen to the radio or TV for information.

- Be aware that flash flooding can occur. If there is any possibility of a flash flood, move immediately to higher ground. Do not wait for instructions to move.

- Be aware of streams, drainage channels, canyons, and other areas known to flood suddenly. Flash floods can occur in these areas with or without typical warnings like rain clouds or heavy rain.

Planning and Preparing for a Flood

You should also have a plan for protecting your valuables when you know a flood is coming. Often, you will know a flood is coming and have ample time to protect your important items. However, you should only execute your plan to protect your valuables if you have enough time and are not given the order to evacuate by emergency personnel.

A 72-hour evacuation kit is useful for any emergency, particularly if you have to evacuate. You'll find more detailed instructions in this book.

It is also important that you personalize your 72-hour kit for your needs and the types of disasters you are likely to experience. (See the section on 72-hour kits.)

Be informed. Heed the watches and warnings that are issued in your area. Stay tuned in to local weather reports, and check in with the National Weather Service.

Be Aware of What Causes Flooding So You Can Recognize the Signs and Be Better Prepared

- Steady rainfall that lasts for an extensive period of time.

- Heavy rainfall.

- Approaching heavy rains, tsunamis, or hurricanes.

- Weakening dams or levees.

- Rising rivers and streams.

Plan Ahead

There are also steps you can take when a flood is imminent:

- Move all your furniture and valuable items to the highest area of your home, whether it's the second floor or an attic.

- Fill sinks and bathtubs with fresh water in case contamination to the water supply occurs during flooding.

- Move your outdoor belongings inside.

- Pack valuables in heavy-duty bags, seal, and secure.

- Have a full tank of gas.

FEMA Flood Safety Guidelines

Evacuation

- Secure your home. If you have time, bring in outdoor furniture. Move essential items to an upper floor.

- Turn off utilities at the main switches or valves if instructed to do so. Disconnect electrical appliances. Do not touch electrical equipment if you are wet or standing in water.

- Do not walk through moving water. Six inches of moving water can make you fall. If you have to walk in water, walk where the water is not moving. Use a stick to check the firmness of the ground in front of you.

Driving in Floods

- Do not drive into flooded areas. If floodwaters rise around your car, abandon the car and move to higher ground if you can do so safely. You and the vehicle can be quickly swept away.
- Six inches of water will reach the bottom of most passenger cars, causing loss of control and possible stalling.
- A foot of water will float many vehicles.
- Two feet of rushing water can carry away most vehicles, including sport utility vehicles (SUVs) and pickup trucks.

After a Flood

- Listen for news reports to learn whether the community's water supply is safe to drink.
- Avoid floodwaters; water may be contaminated by oil, gasoline, or sewage. Water may also be electrically charged from underground or downed power lines.
- Avoid moving water.
- Be aware of areas where floodwaters have receded. Roads may have weakened and could collapse under the weight of a car.
- Stay away from downed power lines, and report them to the power company.
- Return home only when authorities indicate it is safe.
- Stay out of any building if it is surrounded by floodwaters.
- Use extreme caution when entering buildings. There may be hidden damage, particularly in foundations.
- Service damaged septic tanks, cesspools, pits, and leaching systems as soon as possible. Damaged sewage systems are serious health hazards.

- Clean and disinfect everything that got wet. Mud left from floodwater can contain sewage and chemicals.

After-Disaster Strategies

After any disaster, well-planned steps should be taken as the recovery process begins. If you count on the government to assist you, you may be waiting a long time. You must be proactive and take the initiative. However, it is important to be cautious; there are many dangers that lurk in the aftermath. Keep your eyes open for dangerous situations. Be aware of your environment. Help those you can, and notify the authorities when it is necessary.

The following information, at times, is redundant and a repeat of information aforementioned. However, I have expanded and organized this information under a general heading to give you consolidated information that can be used in all situations.

Injuries[2]

Check for injuries. Do not attempt to move seriously injured people unless they are in immediate danger of further injury. Get medical assistance immediately. If someone has stopped breathing, begin CPR. Stop any bleeding injury by applying direct pressure to the wound. Clean out all open wounds and cuts with soap and clean water. Apply an antibiotic ointment and dress the wound. Contact a doctor to find out whether more treatment is needed, such as a tetanus shot. If a wound gets red, swells, or drains, seek immediate medical attention. Have any puncture wound evaluated by a physician. If you are trapped, try to attract attention to your location.

General Safety Precautions after Disasters

Here are some safety precautions that could help you avoid injury:

- Continue to monitor your radio or TV for emergency information.

- Be careful when entering any structure that has been damaged. Use the buddy system and keep someone on the outside until safety is determined.

- Wear sturdy shoes or boots, long sleeves, and gloves when you are handling or walking on or near debris.

- Be aware of hazards like nails, broken glass, and unstable objects.

- Do not touch downed power lines or objects in contact with downed lines. Report electrical hazards to the local authorities and the utility company.

- Use battery-powered lanterns, if possible, rather than candles to light homes without electrical power. If you use candles, make sure they are in safe holders away from curtains, paper, wood, or other flammable items. Never leave a candle burning when you are out of the room.

- Never use generators, pressure washers, grills, camp stoves, or other gasoline, propane, natural gas, or charcoal-burning devices inside your home, basement, garage, or camper—or even outside near an open window, door, or vent. Carbon monoxide—an odorless, colorless gas that can cause sudden illness and death if you breathe it—from these sources can build up in your home, garage, or camper and poison the people and animals inside. Seek prompt medical attention if you suspect carbon monoxide poisoning and are feeling dizzy, light-headed, or nauseated.

- Hang up displaced landline telephone receivers that may have been knocked off the hook. Stay off the telephone except to report an emergency.

- Cooperate fully with public safety officials.

- Respond to requests for volunteer assistance by police, firefighters, emergency management, and relief organizations, but do not go into damaged areas unless assistance has been requested. Your presence could hamper relief efforts, and you could endanger yourself.

Inspect for Damages

- After any disaster, be aware of possible structural damage. Inspect the walls, roof, and foundation first from the outside to determine if it is safe to enter.

- If you suspect any damage to your home, shut off electrical power, natural gas, and propane tanks to avoid fire, electrocution, or explosions.

- If it is dark when you are inspecting your home, use a flashlight rather than a candle or lighter to avoid the risk of fire or explosion in a damaged home.

- If you see frayed wiring or sparks, or if there is an odor of something burning, you should immediately shut off the electrical system at the main circuit breaker.

- If you smell gas or suspect a leak, turn off the main gas valve, open all windows, and leave the house immediately. Notify the gas company, the police or fire departments, and do not turn on the lights, light matches, smoke, or do anything that could cause a spark. Do not return to your house until you are told it is safe to do so.

- Never use a torch unless you are absolutely sure that you are safe from the dangers of fire and explosion.

Safety During Cleanup

- Wear sturdy shoes or boots, long sleeves, and gloves.

- Learn proper safety procedures and operating instructions before operating any gas-powered or electric-powered saws or tools.

- Clean up spilled medicines, drugs, flammable liquids, and other potentially hazardous materials.

- Watch for hazards when traveling both on and off the road.

Children's Needs

After a natural disaster, children may be afraid that the earthquake, fire, or tornado will come back again and they will be injured or left alone. Children may even interpret disasters as punishment for real or imagined misdeeds. Reassure your children by explaining that natural disasters do not occur because someone was "bad."

Children will be less likely to experience prolonged fear or anxiety if they know what to expect after a disaster. Here are some suggestions:

- Talk about your own experiences with severe storms, tornadoes, fires, or hurricanes. Read books about natural events.

- Encourage your child to express feelings of fear. Listen carefully and show understanding.

- Offer reassurance. Tell your child that the situation is not permanent, and provide physical reassurance through time spent together and displays of affection.

- Include your child in cleanup activities. It is comforting to children to watch the household begin to return to normal and to have a job to do.

Your emergency supplies should be adequate for at least 72 hours (three days). A ten-day supply of water, food, and medicine is good thing to have. Always prepare as if you will be the last to receive assistance.

See the following section on 72-hour kits for ideas and suggestions for your kits.

NOTES

1. Federal Emergency Management Agency, "During a Flood," accessed December 5, 2014, http://m.fema.gov/during-flood.
2. Centers for Disease Control and Prevention, "After a Tornado," last modified January 16, 2014, accessed December 5, 2014.

Make Your Custom Emergency 72-Hour Kit

MAKE YOUR CUSTOM EMERGENCY 72-HOUR KIT

Three-day survival kits are becoming increasingly common, with many styles available commercially. But you can easily make your own kit, customized to your personal situation. Be sure to update your kit with additional items as your needs and situations change. We will use the next few pages to cover suggestions and ideas you should consider. Make a list of what you need personally, and then prepare your 72-hour kit. As you choose the items that you want in your kit, keep in mind that each person's needs vary and that you may need to carry the kit when you evacuate. You don't require everything, so focus on the basics. The list is intended to give you ideas to consider.

The basics should include enough food and water for at least three days, an extra change of clothes, and a sleeping bag or space blanket. If you do not have a sleeping bag or a blanket, a space blanket is a good emergency choice. If your kit includes canned food, you will also want a manual can opener.

You should also consider the unique circumstances and needs of infants, the elderly, people with disabilities, and others who require special attention. Place all the collected items in a large plastic bag, a backpack, or anything that can easily be carried. Remember, this is an emergency situation. A designer-hip look is just not that important.

The best part of this planning is that you probably already have most of the items in your home. So once again, start with a plan, and then work the plan. Choose from the following lists what you will put in your

evacuation kits. Only pick the items that you *need*. Remember, the weight of the kit is important because you may need to carry it.

Keep in mind that a 72-hour kit will quickly be used up. Many emergencies could last much longer. There are people who have waited three to five weeks to get services restored after a major disaster. With this in mind, it is a good idea to have a minimum thirty-days supply of food, medications, and clothing. These items should be securely stored in your home. Even if you have government help, after 72 hours there will be holes in what you need and what they have to give.

Essentials

- ☐ Battery-powered or hand-crank radio and extra batteries
- ☐ Large kitchen garbage bags (to keep clothing and blankets dry)
- ☐ Blanket (fleece or wool works great)
- ☐ Flashlight and extra batteries
- ☐ Ready-to-eat food (see food section)
- ☐ Shirt
- ☐ Socks
- ☐ Pants
- ☐ Underwear
- ☐ Sweater
- ☐ Shoes
- ☐ Manual can opener for food
- ☐ Matches and lighter
- ☐ Emergency cash in small bills
- ☐ Change for phone calls
- ☐ Sleeping bag for each person
- ☐ Additional bedding if you live in a cold climate.
- ☐ One gallon of water per person per day for three days
- ☐ _____
- ☐ _____
- ☐ _____
- ☐ _____
- ☐ _____

Food

- ☐ Peanut butter (protein)
- ☐ Dried fruit and fruit snacks (drink extra water)
- ☐ Ramen noodles
- ☐ Fruit cocktail
- ☐ Instant oatmeal
- ☐ Raisins, prunes, fruit leather
- ☐ Hot cocoa mix
- ☐ Canned fish or chicken
- ☐ Chips (best in tube)
- ☐ Crackers
- ☐ Nuts, nut rolls, pudding (other high-protein snacks)
- ☐ Granola bars
- ☐ Soup
- ☐ Powdered milk
- ☐ Sugar cookies
- ☐ Candies that don't melt
- ☐ Candy corns
- ☐ Taffy
- ☐ Hard candy
- ☐ Sweetened cereals
- ☐ Table salt
- ☐ _____
- ☐ _____
- ☐ _____
- ☐ _____
- ☐ _____

Personal

- ☐ A copy of important documents (will or trust information)
- ☐ Additional warm clothing if you live in a cold climate
- ☐ Copy of health insurance and identification cards
- ☐ A go-bag for your pets
- ☐ Extra keys to your house and vehicle
- ☐ Money
- ☐ Extra glasses
- ☐ Hearing aids

- [ ] Cane
- [ ] Crutches
- [ ] Photographs family members and pets for identification purposes
- [ ] List of allergies to any drug (especially antibiotics) or food
- [ ] List of emergency contact phone numbers
- [ ] Local map
- [ ] Permanent marker, paper, and tape
- [ ] Rain gear (poncho)
- [ ] Any special-needs items
- [ ] Cell phone with chargers (solar charger are available)

Adults

- [ ] Books
- [ ] Needle work
- [ ] _____
- [ ] _____

Children

- [ ] Coloring books
- [ ] Crayons
- [ ] Books
- [ ] Games
- [ ] Puzzles
- [ ] _____
- [ ] _____
- [ ] _____
- [ ] _____
- [ ] _____
- [ ] _____

First Aid

- [ ] Adhesive or paper tape
- [ ] Baking soda
- [ ] Bandages
- [ ] Disinfectant
- [ ] Dust mask to help filter contaminated air and dust

- ☐ Elastic bandage
- ☐ Eye drops
- ☐ First aid kit
- ☐ Hand lotion
- ☐ Lip balm
- ☐ Roll of gauze
- ☐ Scissors
- ☐ Spirits of ammonia
- ☐ Splints
- ☐ Sunscreen
- ☐ Cough drops
- ☐ Triangle bandage (37"×37"×37")
- ☐ Tweezers
- ☐ _____
- ☐ _____
- ☐ _____
- ☐ _____

Sanitation

- ☐ Bottle of hand sanitizer
- ☐ Comb or brush
- ☐ Deodorant
- ☐ Feminine hygiene supplies
- ☐ Improvised toilet seat (for bucket)
- ☐ Moist towelettes, garbage bags, and plastic ties for personal sanitation
- ☐ Unscented liquid household bleach (Dilute: nine parts water to one part bleach as a disinfectant. Use sixteen drops of unscented bleach per gallon of water)
- ☐ Shampoo
- ☐ Shaver
- ☐ Soap
- ☐ Toilet paper
- ☐ Toothbrush and toothpaste
- ☐ Washcloth and towel
- ☐ _____
- ☐ _____

Other

- ☐ Backpack or duffle bag (to store and carry all these items)
- ☐ Disposable camera
- ☐ Heavy string
- ☐ Fire extinguisher, A-B-C type
- ☐ Work gloves
- ☐ Paper and pencil
- ☐ Pet food and extra water
- ☐ Plastic bags and ties
- ☐ Plastic bucket with tight-fitting lid
- ☐ Plastic sheeting, duct tape, and utility knife for covering broken windows
- ☐ Pocket knife
- ☐ Reflectors and flares
- ☐ Safety pins
- ☐ Sewing kit
- ☐ Tent
- ☐ Ground cloth

Tools

- ☐ Crowbar
- ☐ Hammer and nails
- ☐ Staple gun
- ☐ Adjustable wrench
- ☐ Bungee cords
- ☐ Rope
- ☐ Pliers
- ☐ Saw
- ☐ Screwdriver
- ☐ Shovel
- ☐ Utility knife
- ☐ Whistle to signal for help
- ☐ _____
- ☐ _____
- ☐ _____

Special Needs

- ☐ Individual medicines
- ☐ Baby needs
- ☐ Contact lens supplies
- ☐ Infant formula
- ☐ Diapers
- ☐ _____
- ☐ _____

Cooking Equipment

- ☐ Mess kits
- ☐ Paper cups
- ☐ Paper plates
- ☐ Paper towels
- ☐ Plastic utensils
- ☐ Pack stove
- ☐ Fuel bottles
- ☐ Frying pan
- ☐ Cooking pot
- ☐ Spatula
- ☐ Scouring pad
- ☐ Dish towel
- ☐ Dish soap
- ☐ _____
- ☐ _____
- ☐ _____

BONUS TIP: PUT YOUR 72-HOUR KITS IN ROLLING BAGS

As you gather the items for your 72-hour kits, the contents seem to build, and so does the weight and bulk. Therein lies the problem. A rolling suitcase makes an excellent alternative to a backpack. Consider the terrain that you will traverse as you make your decision. Sidewalks and paved roads are easily navigated while a trail in the woods may be a challenge.

In a recent business event that I participated in, I had to get about seventy-five pounds of material to my booth. The trek started in the parking lot and wound through the convention center where I was presenting. The complete trip included at least a half-mile of walking. I used a steamer-size rolling suitcase, and the long haul was quite easy. In an emergency, I am for anything to make life easier.

You have a variety of choices in design and size. There are hard exteriors and soft exteriors. You can purchase one that is a soft duffel bag or even a backpack with back straps, a handle, and wheels. There are small youth-size bags up to large steamer bags that can hold enough survival supplies for several people. This size may be a good choice for a young family or for someone who needs to care for another such as a senior or person with special needs.

As you prepare kits for each member of your family, you should keep in mind the physical abilities of each, and a roller board may be the best answer. If you store your kits in your garage, you might consider placing them in a sealed heavy-duty plastic bag to keep spiders, dust, and moisture out of them.

You can get used rolling suitcases rather economically at secondhand stores and garage sales. In my area, we have a local classified ad section on the Internet that is excellent for finding good used items that I use all the time. Use your community's classified ads website to locate great deals on used luggage. I personally own a couple of backpacks that have an extendable handle and wheels—the best of both worlds.

Over time, you can upgrade, add, and improve. Build as you can, but start getting organized today! Don't try to build your entire kit overnight, but develop and work on your plan a little each week. Set goals, write them down, and place them where you see them each day. Be realistic, and hold yourself accountable to your goals.

Checklist of Items to Consider

- ☐ Rolling suitcase for each family member
- ☐ Rolling backpack for each family member
- ☐ Emergency kit for each family member

ABOUT THE AUTHOR

Sam Spencer has been actively involved in personal preparedness for over forty years. He has studied many disasters, both natural and man-made. His research has helped him develop and improve numerous ideas for survival preparedness. Sam's streamlined and simplified disaster and survival techniques are organized for reliable results.

Year after year, he produces a backyard garden that provides a year's worth of food for him and his wife. These practical backyard gardening techniques have developed from a lifetime of preparedness thinking. Much of his garden produce is shared with others as he encourages them to develop their own personal preparedness programs. He encourages others to garden even a little to learn now and be ahead of the learning curve if the need to live on their own garden arises.

He has taught various preparedness classes and tutored many individuals as they developed practical personal preparedness programs. Now in book form, Sam's experiences and ideas can be shared with all who wish to become better prepared. Additional titles he has written include *Food Storage Made Easy: A Practical Approach*; *Drying Fruits and Vegetables Made Easy: An Instructional Handbook*; and *Survival of the Fittest, Survival Preparedness Tips Volume II: Cooking in an Emergency*.

Sam has said, "Preparation eliminates fear. It will give you confidence in crisis. You don't have to spend much money to be caught prepared!"

Sam and his wife, Patrice, live in Utah and are the parents of six children and the grandparents of nine.